THE WILDEST PROVINCE

Born in 1974, Roderick Bailey is a graduate of Cambridge and Edinburgh universities and a former Alistair Horne Fellow at St Antony's College, Oxford. In 2003 he was appointed to run a major project to acquire new material for the Imperial War Museum's SOE collections

RODERICK BAILEY

The Wildest Province

SOE in the Land of the Eagle

VINTAGE BOOKS
London

FOR MY PARENTS

Published by Vintage 2009

2 4 6 8 10 9 7 5 3 1

First published in Great Britain in 2008 by Jonathan Cape

Vintage
Random House, 20 Vauxhall Bridge Road,
London SW1V 2SA

www.vintage-books.co.uk

Addresses for companies within the Random House Group Limited
can be found at:
www.randomhouse.co.uk/offices.htm

The Random House Group Limited Reg. No. 954009

A CIP catalogue record for this book
is available from the British Library

ISBN 9781845950712

CONTENTS

LIST OF ILLUSTRATIONS

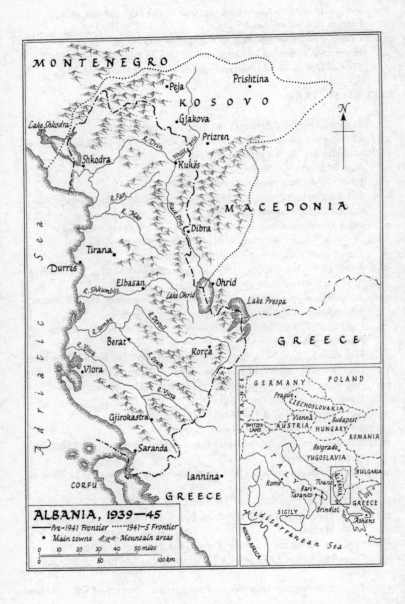

MONTENEGRO

KOSOVO

Prishtina

Peja

Gjakova

Prizren

Lake Shkodra

R. Drin

White Drin

Shkodra

Kukës

R. Fan

MACEDONIA

R. Mat

Black Drin

Dibra

Tirana

Durrës

Elbasan

Ohrid

R. Shkumbin

Lake Ohrid

Lake Prespa

R. Seman

R. Devoll

Berat

R. Viosa

R. Osum

Korça

GREECE

Vlora

R. Vjosa

Gjirokastra

Saranda

CORFU

Iannina

GREECE

Adriatic Sea

N

ALBANIA, 1939—45

——— Pre-1941 Frontier   ········· 1941–5 Frontier

• Main towns   Mountain areas

0 10 20 30 40 50 miles

0   50   100 km

GERMANY

POLAND

Prague

CZECHOSLOVAKIA

Vienna

Budapest

SWITZER-
LAND

AUSTRIA

HUNGARY

ROMANIA

FRANCE

Belgrade

YUGOSLAVIA

ITALY

Rome

Tirana

ALBANIA

BULGARIA

Bari

Taranto

GREECE

SICILY

Brindisi

Athens

NORTH AFRICA

Mediterranean Sea

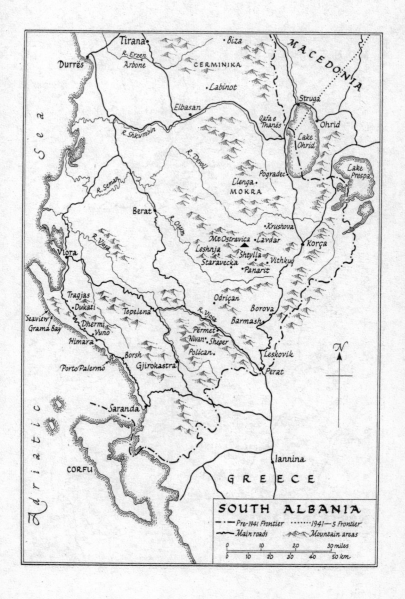

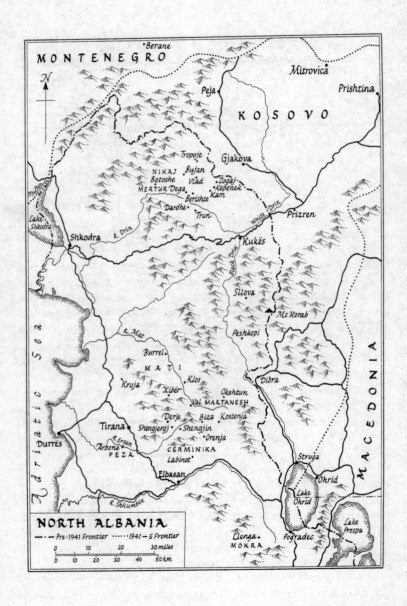

MONTENEGRO

•Berane

Mitrovica

Prishtina

Peja

K O S O V O

N

Tropoje

Gjakova

NIKAJ   Bujan
Betoshe   Vlad   Zogaj
MERTUR Dega   Kepenek
               Berishte Kam
        Dardhe
               •Trun   White Drin   Prizren

Lake
Shkodra

Shkodra   R. Drin   Kukës

                                Black Drin

                        Sllova

                                        Mt Korab

                        Peshkopi

        R. Mat

        Burrel
                M A T I
                        •Klos
•Kruja   Dibra
        •Xibër
        Val MARTANESH
                        Okshtun

                Derje •Biza Kostenja
Tirana   Shengjergj •Shengjin
        •Erzen   Orenja
Durrës Arbon   Struga
        PEZA   CERMINIKA
               Labinot   Ohrid

        Elbasan   Lake
                                   Ohrid

        R. Shkumbin   Lake
                                         Prespa

NORTH ALBANIA

——— Pre-1941 Frontier   ········ 1941–5 Frontier

0   10   20   30 miles

0   10   20   30   40   50 km

                Llenga•
                MOKRA   Pogradec

Adriatic Sea

MACEDONIA

PROLOGUE

THE *General of the Dead Army*, the first novel of the Albanian writer
Ismaïl Kadare, tells of an Italian officer searching for the remains of
Italian soldiers killed in Albania in the Second World War. It is a bleak,
desolate tale, set years after the conflict in a rain-swept landscape of
mountains and mud. The general is hardly welcome. The Italians had
invaded in 1939 and, though harassed by guerrillas and badly mauled
by the neighbouring Greeks, stayed for more than four years. The
general, in turn, loathes the locals, both the peasants who stare at him
as he hunts and digs and the surly band of labourers in his pay. On
one damp mountainside he crosses paths with a one-armed German
officer looking for his own countrymen. Germany had taken over the
occupation after Italy's collapse in 1943.

Away from the hills a café owner remembers the severed hand and
burnt shirt, displayed in the square, of a downed English pilot. But
while Kadare makes no other mention of British dead, the war had left
a number in Albanian soil and there does exist a story of a post-war
search for them. That tale is found in the files of the British Army's
Graves Registration Units. Unenvied and unsung, the role of these tiny
teams of dedicated officers and men was to comb old battlefields for
the makeshift graves of British servicemen, remove the remains to military cemeteries and, in the process, try to identify each casualty found.
As the records of these units show, it was a grim and exacting task,
too harrowing for some, which began before the war was over and
continued for long months afterwards.

'A hard working officer of a Graves Unit is entitled to the sympathy
and respect of all those whose duty is different,' reads one report, from

the headquarters files of Graves Registrations, Central Mediterranean Forces, on the mental strength required properly to do the job. The best officers were volunteers, 'because it was found in practice that certain people are simply incapable of doing a thorough search of a body which has been buried for some time'. Recent postings had not volunteered 'and the first of them to arrive has said that he simply cannot face exhumations. He is, therefore, completely useless to us.' In this line of work, the report explains, 'we are not so concerned with the officers' feelings as we are with the fact that if the search is not efficiently done an identity may be lost'. Even a volunteer could find it too much for him. 'Unless he can arrive at a mental state in which he can pull a blanket over his mind as soon as he has finished his day's work, he never becomes any good. Those who cannot do this have to be let go.'[1]

When that study was written, in late 1945, HQ Graves Registrations, CMF, with its office in Florence, still directed a spread of twenty teams from the southern tip of Italy up to Austria and across to the Balkans. Months had passed since Germany's surrender but there remained much work to do, particularly in territory held by the enemy until the end. Although the British and Americans had landed on Italy's toe in September 1943, the push north had been slow: Rome fell in June 1944, Florence in August, Ravenna in December. The advance had been held up again and again and, in the spring of 1945, Austria and much of northern Italy remained in German hands. As for the Balkans, never invaded by the western Allies, the German withdrawal was barely complete by the end of the war. But even with the fighting over and the Germans gone, searching for the dead in some of these places could still prove problematic. One such spot was Albania.

Forty miles east of the Italian heel, thickly forested and heavily mountainous, Albania had been controlled by the Axis for nearly six years and more than fifty British and Dominion soldiers, commandos and airmen were thought to have died out there. And at first the graves office in Florence seemed to have just the man to find them: an officer on its books, who, very unusually for an Englishman, had been to Albania before; he had even known some of the men Florence wanted him to find. The Brixton-born son of a train driver, twenty-six-year-old Ian Merrett was then digging up Florence's battlegrounds and reinterring remains in the city's new military cemetery. An ex-commando, he was also a former officer in Britain's Special Operations Executive, a secret organisation set up in 1940 to encourage subversion and carry out sabotage behind enemy lines. It was SOE that had sent him to Albania, after it was given the task in 1943 of intensifying resistance throughout the occupied Balkans. Looking to go on the offensive and return to the Continent, Churchill and his senior strategists had viewed guerrilla activity there as a useful means of diverting enemy troops from other fronts, hastening Italy's collapse and preparing the way for any future thrusts through Europe's 'soft underbelly'. The region became a major SOE theatre, with dozens of small missions of specially trained troops, almost all of them British, dispatched to find and encourage resisters, blow up bridges, ambush convoys and call in supplies of weapons and ammunition.

By the end of the war, SOE had sent into the Balkans several hundred men. Of the hundred destined for Albania, most had expected to get to grips quickly with the enemy and many, including Merrett, had rather hoped to find themselves fighting a romantic and worthwhile war of liberation. Waiting for them, in a striking setting, were indeed enough chiefs and tribes and rifle-wielding guerrillas to conjure lively images of Lawrence and the Arabs. But here, too, were squalid villages and burning homes, terrible privations and a hazardous existence plagued by lice, malaria and the constant threat of capture and death. Winter, when missions were chased high into the snowbound peaks, was horrific. 'At dusk the road is safely recrossed and a forced march made up the mountain,' reads the diary, recently discovered, of one hunted mission.

> This is as steep as the side of a house, very rocky and slippery and in our weakened state a terrible trial . . . The effort required to maintain and recover one's balance is truly appalling – none of us has ever experienced so severe a trial of physical and moral strength and endurance. At 2100hrs having nearly reached the summit, the guides, after much questioning, have to admit that they have lost the way! The decision is taken to make camp but if we are to survive the night fires must be lit. Our clothes are already standing out stiffly round us like boards and every twig and branch is heavily covered in gel frost. To stand still for a moment is to court frostbite and death.[2]

SOE personnel in Albania performed feats of great enterprise and stamina, but the dangers took their toll. Of the first fifty men sent in, sixteen died or were captured and seventeen were subsequently decorated. Tasked with dropping men and stores, the Royal Air Force also suffered, losing several crews as they wove through the mountains at heights of a few hundred feet.

Merrett had parachuted into Albania in December 1943. He was brought out by boat ten months later. In September 1945, however, when the Florence office tried to send him back, the Albanian Government refused to have him. As a note in the files explains, 'he had been employed in Special Operations in that country and the present Administration regard him as an "undesirable character"'.³ Merrett's offence would seem to have been that he had worked during the war with the wrong Albanians. When he and other SOE men had gone out there to fight, they had found themselves dealing with a variety of rival bands, many of whose leaders, their eyes on post-war power, were happier killing each other than fighting Italians or Germans. Merrett himself had lived and worked for months with supporters of King Zog, the rakish chief who had crowned himself monarch in the 1920s and fled the country at the time of the Italian invasion. Other SOE officers had been attached to Albania's communist-led 'Partisan' movement. And at the end of 1944, when the Germans pulled out and a brief civil war was coming to a close, that movement had seized control. Headed by Enver Hoxha, the former schoolteacher who had led the Partisans for most of the war, a ruthless communist government was swiftly in place, anti-Western sentiment embedded in its outlook. Particular hostility was reserved for the British, who, the communists felt, had worked against them by trying to prop up the hated old order.

So Florence tried again, this time with a staff major called McIntosh who had no prior experience of the place. This was more successful. McIntosh crossed the Adriatic with his jeep, maps and notes and the Albanians let him in. But it was soon quite clear that the new regime was hardly keen on any graves officer's presence. Four months later, so the Florence files record, McIntosh, his job unfinished, was back, 'filled with disgust with the treatment accorded him in his effort to collect British dead who had given their lives to liberate Albania'.⁴ McIntosh had assumed the Albanian Government would help him, but from the start, he reported later, 'they had little interest and were not in the least willing to co-operate'.⁵

First, the government had refused to let him leave the capital, Tirana, where he 'lived and fed' in the Dajti Hotel as Kadare's general would do, until he had submitted full particulars of where each grave was thought to be. 'This collecting of information was no mean job, considering the channels of communication . . . which were sometimes literally by courier on horseback to isolated villages.' Weeks passed before enough evidence was found for him to be allowed to start work. Even then, the government demanded that he visit the country's ten prefectures individually, then return to Tirana after each one to seek permission to visit the next: 'one had to count on at least a week between each journey'. Then, when finally at work, McIntosh found himself escorted everywhere by a Partisan lieutenant, 'ostensibly to protect me but in fact his job was to see that I did not talk politics or do spying or photograph the quite non-existent military objectives'.[6] Early on this man was 'an absolute nuisance', taking notes on everyone McIntosh met.[7] In time he impressed McIntosh as 'an agreeable fellow' and worked well and willingly as his assistant. In the end he became so 'pro-British' that he was suspended from duty. 'He was told by his chief that he had been too kind to the "English Major" and had failed in his counterespionage duties.'[8] Less impressive was a two-man bodyguard once detailed to accompany them. 'The only good they were was to pull me out of a river when I fell off a horse's back into water waist deep. The river was in flood and we had either to cross it or do a three day march round about.'[9]

The terrain caused serious problems. Of one 'very successful' journey, a five-day round trip through mountains behind Korça, a market town close to the border with Greece, when he recovered eleven sets of remains, McIntosh reported:

> There was approx 6 hours walking each day and at night sleeping accommodation was found in isolated villages. The going was difficult: up to 7,000 feet and down again to about 1,000 feet several times a day. For about half the time there was snow on the ground. Result – bad cold, covered with lice bites, sore feet from walking and sore bottom from riding a mule with a crude wooden saddle . . .
>
> In this country the weather is severe and for 4 months much of the interior is completely cut off. During these 4 months, the people there – who all work on the land – do absolutely nothing and if they have no animals to look after,

they seldom ever leave their houses. They have no newspapers – and of course radio is unheard of.[10]

Later he estimated that three-quarters of all graves lay in 'difficult loca-
tions' which meant 'going on mules or in the very difficult parts on
foot over mountains with mules carrying the bedding and food'.
Everywhere locals had gone to 'endless trouble' to help him. 'On every
occasion their hospitality was outstanding, to the extent of giving up
part of their own meals rather than allow us to eat our own food.'
Village guides and working parties were always obtainable, seldom
accepted payment and proved themselves invaluable. 'Only in isolated
instances were the graves marked, and without the help of these local
people location would have been quite impossible.'[11]

   Still, by February 1946, in spite of the government's obstruction
and the harshness of the terrain, McIntosh had achieved a great deal.
He had gathered the remains of fifty-two personnel and reinterred
them in Tirana, carefully laying out a small British cemetery and
erecting new wooden crosses, and thought only two 'definite' graves
were left to find. It was then that the communists expelled him. Their
reasons, he felt, were simple. Partly it was their general 'anti-British
policy'; partly it was 'feebly to get their own back' after the United
Nations deferred discussion of their membership; and partly it was
because 'they decided I was a spy and a political reactionary'.[12]
Protests were made. Hoxha's government shrugged them off.
McIntosh, it pretended, had had 'more than sufficient time' and 'all
the necessary facilities and exceptional help'.[13] The British colonel
in charge at Florence appealed for someone, anyone, to force these
'barbarians' to give his men better treatment.[14] Little could be done;
the Albanians were unmoved and the last two graves were never
collected.

   Worse was to come. In October 1946 two Royal Navy warships
struck mines in the narrow stretch of water between Albania and Corfu.
Lives were lost, Britain accused Albania of deliberately mining the
channel and diplomatic links, already bad, were effectively severed.
With no Britons now on hand to watch over McIntosh's cemetery, the
British Government asked French diplomats to check on the site and
make arrangements to keep it tidy.[15] But when a French military attaché
visited Tirana in 1950 he could find no trace of the cemetery and feared,
in fact, that the Albanians had dug it up.[16] Only in the 1990s, with

the collapse of the communist regime and the opening of Albania's borders, was that fate confirmed.[17]

High among Albania's southern ranges sits Sheper, a leafy little settlement of hanging vines and stone-built homes. Not much has changed up there for years: goatherds tend flocks in the scrub; the road to neighbouring villages is a potholed track; rusting containers, dropped by parachute sixty years ago, now empty and hammered flat, patch outhouse roofs and walls. And on bare ground on the edge of the village, unmarked and untended, lies one of the graves that McIntosh ran out of time to collect. It belongs to Major Philip Leake, killed outside Sheper in June 1944. A wooden cross once marked the spot but soon after his death, so locals recall, German soldiers entered the village and blew up the church, after finding arms and explosives hidden inside, and the rubble collapsed over the grave. It also covered the graves of a Dakota crew buried a few yards away. Today the slates and stones have long been removed and reused for building. Leake and the airmen remain, though village memory is the only guide to where the old churchyard had been.

Oxford-educated and a former headmaster of Dulwich College Prep, Leake was thirty-eight when he died. He was also the highly regarded head of SOE's Albanian country section. A month earlier he had been safely behind a desk in Bari, the port in liberated southern Italy where the section had its office, and he died the day he was due to make for the coast and return. Drawing on a range of sources, from declassified records and diaries kept against orders to unpublished memoirs and personal memories, what follows traces the tortuous and costly course of what Leake and his men had been sent there to do. It is not a history of the resistance in Albania. Nor, indeed, is it primarily about that country. Rather it is an attempt to open a window into one small corner of SOE history and the experiences of a few young Britons trying to do a difficult job in a strange and dangerous place. By shedding light, too, on life and work at SOE headquarters, it also seeks to resolve one of the most enduring and disturbing conspiracy theories to surround SOE's wartime record.

Of the men who survived, many emerged with fine memories of camaraderie, and of an exhausting but exhilarating and defining time lived with a rare intensity. Some emerged with long-term scars, physical and mental. Yet a vocal few, appalled at Hoxha's success, came away convinced that the British themselves had condemned Albania to communism. No other power had been more deeply involved in working with Balkan guerrillas, but Britain's policy, these men felt, had erred terribly, arming the Albanian Partisans excessively and to the unfair exclusion of rival bands. Some suggested that communist sympathisers at SOE headquarters, perhaps even Soviet agents, had worked deviously and deliberately to lead policy-makers astray. Such subterfuge was thought to have occurred during the summer of 1944 when German withdrawal and communist victory were still several months away. Leake's death is seen by some as the turning point: had he lived, the British and particularly the SOE office might not have become so biased towards the Partisans and other guerrillas might have been accorded more support.[18]

But the story of SOE's work in Albania begins earlier than that. The British, that summer, had had missions there for more than a year, while desk-bound plotting outside the country had started as early as 1940. And to understand why, from the outset, SOE and its predecessors had to rely so heavily on so many young men with no prior knowledge of the place, it is instructive to glance first at how little, before the war, Albania had ever really interested the British.

I

'TIP AND RUN THUGGERY'

FROM the island of Corfu, the stony and scrub-covered slopes of southern Albania can be seen quite clearly across the sea. Looking north, to where they run straight down to the shore, it is sometimes possible to make out on one mountainside a small white zigzag. That is Albania's coastal road, rising to cut through the peaks at a spot called the Llogora Pass. It was through those peaks that Edward Lear, the English land-scape painter and poet, had picked his way in the autumn of 1848. Lear, then in his thirties, had gone to Albania to draw and paint and he believed himself the first Englishman to have 'penetrated' the coastal 'fastnesses' visible from Corfu.[1] He was wrong, but not many of his countrymen had been there before him. Nor have many been there since: Albania has never been a land much visited by the British. Given the unsettling images presented by men like Lear, perhaps that is not surprising.

Lear's published letters and journals brim with descriptions of the stir-ring terrain and anguished reports of how hard had been the travelling. For every passage praising the mountains, forests, rivers and gorges there is another about the oddness of the locals or the fatigue he was feeling or the squalor of his lodgings. By the walls of the 'unclean & horrible' town of Elbasan, trying to sketch, he had been surrounded by a crowd shouting *'Shaitán scroo!'* ('The Devil draws!') and chased away in a shower of stones.[2] Tirana was 'as wretched and disgusting' as Elbasan.[3] Impressed by the mosques and market squares, he found his night-time billet revolting. 'How people can live in such places I can't imagine,' Lear wrote to his sister. 'A mad Dervish was my next neighbour – but he did me no harm. As for the mice and spiders – I kept them off by a mosquito net.'[4]

More unpleasantness followed. Done with Tirana, Lear left for the coast and, near the top of the Llogora Pass, looked down on the village of Dukhádhes. 'Shut out as it stood by iron walls of mountain, surrounded by sternest features of savage scenery, rock and chasm, precipice and torrent, a more fearful prospect and more chilling to the very blood I never beheld.' To 'this strange place, perhaps one of the most secluded in Europe', Lear descended to spend the night. A bed was found. Before dawn he was woken by 'the most piercing screams . . . nearer – nearer – close to the house'. Lighting a candle, he illuminated 'all the Albanians in the room, sitting bolt upright, and listening with ugly countenances to the terrible cries below . . . I do not remember ever to have heard so horrid and deadly a sound as that long shriek, perpetually repeated with a force and sharpness not to be recalled without pain; and what made it more horrible, was the distant echo to each cry from the lonely rocks around.'[5]

The cries were those of a woman who had just been told of her husband's death in a local feud. She had also been presented with his head, which dogs had found lying near the river. The screaming, Lear learnt, usually continued for nine days, 'commonly in the house of mourning, or when the performers are engaged in domestic affairs'. In this instance, however, 'the distressed woman, unable to control her feelings to the regular routine of grief, is walking all over the town, tearing her hair, and abandoning herself to the most frantic wretchedness'. For Lear, since it also appeared that the weather would delay his departure, this was 'no cheerful beginning for the morning'.[6]

Byron, whose own travels there had helped inspire Lear's, may well have been among the first of his countrymen to see other parts of Albania, and tales of his adventures were to prove especially resonant. In 1809, aged twenty-two, he had sailed to Greece and, riding north, in thunderous rain, past a severed human arm hanging from a tree, ventured as far as the fortress at Tepelena, seat of Ali Pasha, a notorious despot. In letters home Byron wrote excitedly of 'a country of the most picturesque beauty', of 'the savage character of the natives' and of 'the wildest province of Europe, where very few Englishmen have ever been'. Ali, with whom he stayed, he described to his mother as 'a remorseless tyrant, guilty of the most horrible cruelties . . . He has been a mighty warrior, but is as barbarous as he is successful, roasting rebels &c &c.'[7]

In his notes to *Childe Harold's Pilgrimage*, his epic poem of a young man looking for distraction in foreign lands, Byron wrote later that he believed he had been further into Albania than any other Englishman 'with the exception of Major Leake'.[8] This was William Leake, a lone British officer resident at Ali Pasha's court during Britain's wars with Napoleon. Albania was then a province of the Ottoman Empire, as it had been for four hundred years and would remain for another hundred, and Leake, sent to make military surveys, would be tasked with assessing and improving the potential of local pashas to resist any French incursion. Years later, Leake, too, published his journals.[9] Topography, antiquity, customs and local character were his principal themes. Pained tales of physical hardship were not, perhaps, to be expected of a cultured man who came to Albania after fifteen years of soldiering and had survived the shipwreck of the Parthenon marbles. Nor did Leake write much about his dealings with Ali, although his despatches, found in Foreign Office files, reveal how dramatic some of that work had been. Once, Leake made a hazardous landing on a storm-blown beach, sheltered with Ali in the lee of the cliffs and held secret discussions to improve relations with Constantinople. On another occasion, Ali asked Leake to poison the local French consul.[10]

The extent to which Leake engaged with the Albanians and travelled about was exceptional. Most Britons who set foot there in the nineteenth century were seafaring passers-by or, more commonly, soldiers of the Corfu garrison who crossed the channel with packs of spaniels to hunt on the plains round the ruined ancient city of Butrint. Few stayed very long or wandered very far. 'English officers,' wrote Captain J. J. Best, in *Excursions in Albania: Comprising a Description of the Wild Boar, Deer and Woodcock Shooting in that Country*, 'always contrived to keep clear of hostile collisions with the half-savage people that are found near the coast.'[11]

Best did describe how, in 1838, he and three other officers, more adventurous than most but all well armed in case of attack, had ridden a few miles inland. The locals, he recorded, were 'little better than semi-barbarians', capable of the 'most outrageous acts of murder and piracy'. Every man, 'even from five years old, is obliged to be armed up to the teeth'. Women were spotted bearing 'tremendous' loads 'which I should have scarcely expected a strong man to lift'. Local dogs were fierce and feared but it was 'unwise' to shoot one 'because an Albanian's dog is his companion and friend, and a sly shot at the offending person from behind a rock would inevitably follow'. And there was a sudden moment of alarm when, shouting and shooting, a couple of dozen Albanians appeared, heading in their direction. The four Britons 'waited patiently for the bullets, which we expected any minute to whiz past our ears', and prepared to shoot back. 'The numbers were on the side of the Albanians but our guns were double-barrelled and not so likely to miss as theirs.' But the 'belligerent host' turned out to be a marriage party merely 'testifying to their glee and delight'.[12]

By the early 1900s a few more Britons had been to the country. Among those inclined to write about it, one or two, like the formidable English spinster Edith Durham, did their best to look beyond the prevailing picture of a primitive and lawless land. They took care to distinguish the population as racially and historically different from its Slav and Greek neighbours. They remarked on divisions within the race: Ghegs in the north and Tosks in the south, separated roughly by physique, dialect, custom and the fast-flowing River Shkumbin that bisected the country from east to west. Minorities were mentioned, like Slavs, Greeks and Vlachs. Distinctions were drawn between the untamed, tribal and feud-ridden north and the marginally more advanced south, and attention was given to the complex, diverse systems of customary law. The country's religious mix was noted: most of the population was Muslim; there were some Catholics in the north and the Greek Orthodox Church was strong in the south. And sometimes sympathy was expressed for Albanian calls – albeit confined mostly to a few educated exiles – for greater autonomy.[13]

One Briton who took up the cause was the much travelled MP Aubrey Herbert, John Buchan's model for Sandy Arbuthnot, a character described in *Greenmantle* as 'blood-brother to every kind of Albanian bandit'.[14] Herbert's efforts played their part in 1913 when, meeting in London, the Great Powers finally recognised Albania's sovereignty and drew its borders when settling the First Balkan War. Herbert was even in the frame when the Albanians, eager to cement their new status, wanted a suitably respectable king; legend has it that C. B. Fry, the cricketer, was also considered. In the end a German prince took the job, though he was in it only six months before the First World War swept him home. That war saw six foreign armies occupy the country and Herbert tasked in 1918 with running agents there behind the Austrian lines. Afterwards he campaigned again in Albania's interest and was instrumental in securing its entry to the League of Nations in 1920. He died three years later at the age of forty-three.

It is notable that such burning British commitment to Albania was confined to a few private individuals. The British Government's interest in Albania's status in 1913 and 1920 stemmed more from a desire to maintain the stability of the region than from any compassion for the rights and plight of the Albanian people. Albania's independence, indeed, remained unsteady for years and Britain did not go out of its way to preserve it. In 1921, with British assent, Albania was placed effectively under Italian protection, paving the way for Italy greatly to increase its influence there. In fact, improving Albania's condition had never figured highly among Britain's priorities in the Balkans: there were more important concerns. Chief among them was a pragmatic desire to get on with Albania's larger, richer and more powerful overlords, occupiers or neighbours, a reality spelt out by William Leake when buttonholed in 1805 by an agitated Greek in Delvinō, a town today in southern Albania. 'My host complains to me, in the usual style, of the hardships which his nation suffers from the Turks, and asks me why the great powers of Europe, but particularly the English, will not assist in liberating their fellow-Christians. It is not a very agreeable task to explain, that nations seldom act but from self-interest, that we have a cruel war on our hands, and that our present policy is to support the Turkish empire.'[15]

More sympathy might have been forthcoming, of course, had the British public been more engaged by the place. As it was, down to the outbreak of the Second World War, little occurred to alter the image – if Britons had any image of Albania at all – of a wild and mountainous country far away and best avoided. At the beginning of Buchan's thriller *The Thirty-Nine Steps*, before he becomes the object of a breathless manhunt, the intrepid Richard Hannay muses on being 'the best bored man in the United Kingdom' before striking on the idea 'that Albania was the sort of place that might keep a man from yawning'.[16] In the 1920s and thirties, though a few more visitors wrote about their experiences, and one young Briton, Joseph Swire, published two pioneering histories, most continued to dwell on its dangers, discomforts and oddity. The rise to power of Ahmed Zogu, a chief from the highlands north of Tirana, did attract some press attention, especially when he crowned himself King Zog I in 1927. British newspapers made the most of the name and the Ruritanian image and did so again when he married eleven years later. Otherwise Albania rarely merited much of a mention save for the occasional feature. 'British General Beats the

Balkan Brigands' declared one *Sphere* photo-story, in 1933, about a retired army officer, Sir Jocelyn Percy, hired to organise Zog's gendarmerie.[17]

Touring Albania for the *Daily Telegraph* in 1928, the war correspondent Ellis Ashmead-Bartlett produced an article more incisive than most. Certainly, like other visiting Britons, he was struck by the country's apparent backwardness:

> Half-a-mile outside the towns you are back in the primitive Albania of two thousand years ago. The herds of cattle, sheep, and goats are being tended by the womenfolk; the two-wheeled carts, with the oxen 'neath the yoke date from Celtic times, and the men slouch around in the same dress; only modern rifles have replaced the spear and the club . . .
>
> The poverty of sections of the population is terrible, more especially in the mountains. Maize is the staple diet, and when the crop fails there is starvation throughout the land . . . In winter conditions in the mountains are horrible. In the remoter districts, which can only be reached by mountainous paths, if the patches of maize have failed, whole families have literally nothing to eat . . . It is incredible how the women and children survive. Only a people brought up under iron conditions could outlive the privations they endure.

But Ashmead-Bartlett also noted how rapidly was Zog's financial reliance on Italy bringing Albania under Mussolini's control: 'colonisation' was well under way. Already the Italians were organising the army, running the national bank and beginning to lease vast chunks of land. 'No reasonable person can blame the King for throwing in his lot with the Italians,' Ashmead-Bartlett felt. 'As he himself has explained, Albania had to find assistance in some quarter, and Italy was the only country prepared to come to her aid. But the terms have been hard, and both country and throne are now mortgaged to Mussolini for many years to come.'[18]

Albania's fledgling independence was finally eclipsed on Good Friday, 7 April 1939 when Italian soldiers went ashore at the country's four principal ports. Outright occupation, Mussolini hoped, would enable the Italians to better harness Albania's resources, strengthen Italy's strategic position and allow him to emulate Hitler's own recent record of territorial gain. Still, preparations for the invasion were hasty and poor and the planners relieved indeed when opposition turned out to be slight. In the sheltered bay at Saranda, not far from Corfu, as the Italians stepped on to the port's tiny cobbled quay, a few surprised townsfolk shot one or two but did not keep firing for long. Even while the cobbles were still being washed clean of blood, Italian soldiers, one local remembers, queued to buy Easter sweets from his family's shop on the front.[19]

Only at Durrës, the country's largest port, did the Albanians put up much of a fight. On the morning of 8 April, when the British naval attaché in Rome sailed in to see for himself what had happened, 'shell holes in the walls of houses and empty cartridge cases' were much in evidence. People told him that the Albanians, mostly gendarmes, had killed 'a good many' as the Italians tried to land. 'An eye-witness said "they fell in two heaps" which suggests that the defenders had at least two machine guns – and the "empties" I saw confirm this.' Then the Italians had gone back to their boats, shelled the port and landed 'fifteen direct hits on walls and quays' before a larger force went ashore with flanking parties and tanks. After an hour or two of street fighting – 'walls are peppered with bullets' – the last Albanians fled. They had, it seemed, acquitted themselves well. Locals estimated Italian dead at four hundred. 'Half that number is probably not far wrong, and the Albanians have lost more.'[20] Sir Andrew Ryan, minister at the British Legation in Durrës, met the same day an Albanian gendarmerie officer 'who had lost, dead or wounded, all his body of 52 men'.[21]

Whatever the real figures – the official total for Italians killed during the entire invasion was twelve – the resistance seen at Durrës was not repeated elsewhere. Two decades of growing Italian control aided by Zog's increasing unpopularity – recent years had seen him accused of corruption and abuse of power – saw the conquest quickly complete. As the Italian columns snaked inland few locals tried to stop them. Tirana, lying unprotected twenty miles from the coast, was occupied on the morning of 8 April with barely a shot fired. Zog fled to Greece with his wife and baby son.

No country went to Albania's aid. Some governments expressed dismay but none wanted war over a place so remote. In Britain, though the invasion made headlines, there was little serious call for Italy to be confronted. Mussolini had behaved 'like a sneak and a cad', Neville Chamberlain, the Prime Minister, wrote privately, for the Italians had pledged the previous year that they would respect the Mediterranean status quo.[22] Winston Churchill heard of the invasion while he was lunching at Chartwell with Harold Macmillan. 'Maps were brought out; secretaries were marshalled; telephones began to ring,' Macmillan would recall. 'I shall always have a picture of that spring day and the sense of power and energy, the great flow of action. He alone seemed in command, when everyone else was dazed and hesitating.'[23] But although Churchill held no office at that moment and could bring little influence to bear, the muted response of the British Government was in keeping, as ever, with more pressing concerns, not least the threat of imminent war with Nazi Germany.

A desire not to provoke the Italians also explains why, after Britain went to war with Germany that September, the British Cabinet and Chiefs of Staff sought to maintain a strict ban on Britain's military and intelligence services from even preparing any kind of anti-Italian activity. Italy had proclaimed itself neutral but Mussolini's potential as an enemy was obvious: if such activity was discovered it might prompt him to enter the conflict on Hitler's side, compromising Britain's ability to protect its interests, especially use of the Mediterranean and the Suez Canal. An additional concern was to keep the war out of the Balkans for as long as possible. That, too, reflected the weakness of Britain's position. 'All the countries in the Balkans, except Turkey, are liable to be over-run by the Germans . . . before we could do anything to help,' was the Chiefs' conclusion days after war with Germany broke out. 'It would be preferable to have the whole of the Balkans and Italy neutral.'[24] In December they were reminded that policy was still 'that we should not irritate Italy' and 'should, if possible, prevent the war spreading to the Balkans'.[25]

Four months later, in the spring of 1940, Albania became the target of Britain's first serious attempt of the Second World War to foster guerrilla resistance in occupied Europe. British diplomats and intelligence officers began to lay plans for an anti-Italian revolt and the climax of a year's covert preparation came on an April night in 1941. From the safety of neutral Yugoslavia, a party of several dozen Albanians, one British officer and a baggage train of mules crossed the border and picked its way south from the Kosovo plain into the northern Albanian mountains. 'It was April 7th, the second anniversary of Mussolini's invasion of Albania, so at least we were doing our little bit to celebrate the day,' the lone Briton wrote later. 'Soon some firing started ahead of us . . . and some bullets smacked past.'[26] Within days the party dispersed. No revolt took place. Two years were to pass before British officers reappeared in the mountains.

Britons who had taken part in the planning, however, were to maintain in post-war memoirs that its ignominious end was unworthy of the project's grand design. Their efforts were frustrated and foiled, they claimed, by obstacles imposed unnecessarily by others. Had more support been forthcoming that winter from British military commanders, or had the Germans not overrun Yugoslavia that spring, greater success, they said, would have been had. Today, looking at the episode in the light of declassified records, it is clear that the plans received limited backing. But it also appears that those who complained later speculated rather too freely about why that support was so limited, while overlooking the full range of dangers and difficulties that planners had identified at the time as standing in the way of success.

That serious plotting for an Albanian revolt began only in April 1940 was deliberate: prompted by intelligence reports and intercepted signals that suggested that Italy was about to turn hostile, the Chiefs of Staff lifted the ban on subversive planning. On 6 April the Chiefs approved a policy paper spelling out an intention, in the event of conflict, to target Italy's overseas possessions. And on 8 April, a year to the day after the Italians marched into Tirana, Captain Tommy Davies of the War Office in London asked Foreign Office colleagues for the whereabouts of a Dr Malcolm Burr, 'last heard of working under the auspices of the FO'. Burr, Davies explained, was wanted to put together an 'up-to-date appreciation on Albania' as the War Office was currently 'investigating projects' for 'irregular activities in Italy or her colonies'.[27]

While Davies' search for Malcolm Burr marks the moment that the British began to think seriously about causing trouble in Albania, it also illustrates the paucity of knowledge that secret planners had to hand. Davies worked for Military Intelligence (Research), or MI(R), a small, secret department of the War Office set up in 1938 to undertake sabotage and promote guerrilla warfare in enemy and enemy-occupied countries. Other of its tasks included advising senior commands about that kind of work and drafting research papers like the one now wanted from Burr. The sixty-two-year-old Burr was a man of many parts, widely published as a travel writer, a translator of Russian and an expert on earwigs and grasshoppers. He had also worked before for MI(R), briefly studying, the previous year, the possibilities of encouraging Albanians to revolt. He was no Albanian expert, however, and his first-hand experience of the country appears to have been thin. In 1900 he had followed up his first book, *British Orthoptera*, with a short book on Montenegro after two brief trips while on holiday from Oxford. In 1935 he published a memoir of his wartime service in Macedonia and Montenegro which included a chapter on three fleeting visits to the northern Albanian town of Shkodra. Aside from that, Burr's last three books prior to 1940 had been *A Fossicker in Angola*, a translation of V. K. Arseniev's *Dersu the Trapper* and *British Grasshoppers and their Allies: A Stimulus to their Study*.

Burr, in the end, was not re-engaged and MI(R) had better luck with Sir Jocelyn Percy, the former Inspector General of Zog's gendarmerie. Quiet, modest, tall and thin, Percy had left the British Army in 1920 after a distinguished career that culminated in the command of the British military mission to the Whites in southern Russia. Civilian life had not been easy. For a time he had tried to farm in Canada; by 1926 he was back in Britain selling central heating. So, to an adventurous spirit in need of an income, the offer that year of a responsible if unconventional job in Albania, a place of which he knew nothing, had been rather welcome and he was to prove well suited to the task. When he arrived, banditry and blood feud were rife and the gendarmerie was riddled with corruption. Under his guidance a new structure was set up, training schools were established, the gendarmes were better paid, uniformed and armed, crime and feuding became less intense and trust in the gendarmes grew. Helping him was an inspectorate, about a dozen strong, of more retired British officers, most of whom he recruited in person on quick trips back to London. They thought a lot of him. One described Percy's service to Albania as 'magnificent'.[28] By 1938, when he and his men had their contracts terminated under Italian pressure, he had spent twelve years out there.

Percy's diaries show that he had been in touch with MI(R) since July 1939 when he was asked to update its Albanian dossier. He was then nearly seventy and, though enthusiastic, not best suited to work in the field. 'Nothing should I like better than to go out to Albania,' he told the planners in 1940, 'but I fear that my old carcass would not stand the strain these days. It fails me at times even in England.'[29] He also had other commitments: the command of a Home Guard battalion and a directorship of Charrington's brewery. But he remained happy enough to offer advice when he could, which included providing details of younger men with experience of Albania, and in the spring of 1940 MI(R) recruited two ex-officers who had served there as inspectors. Bill Barbrook had worked under Percy in the late 1920s, Robert Cripps from 1930 until 1938 after two years in Albania with Anglo-Persian Oil. Commissions reinstated, they were soon on their way to Greece with a view to preparing action in Albania in the event of Britain going to war with Italy. In Athens they were given embassy cover. Major Barbrook was assigned to plotting sabotage and liaising with the Greeks. Captain Cripps began to shuttle around the region doing courier and contact work.

MI(R) also got hold of Nicholas Hammond, a young Cambridge academic. He had been on their books since 1938 when the War Office had asked all dons whether they had any knowledge of possible use. Hammond had replied that he knew something of southern Albania from fieldwork there in the 1930s. When the call came, in May 1940, he was duly earmarked for MI(R) work in Albania, given a crash course in explosives and flown to Athens. But the Greeks refused to let him in, Hammond was diverted to Palestine and that was the end of that.

As plans for Albania began to evolve, however, their form became dictated less by MI(R) than by Section D, a small, secret department of MI6, the Secret Intelligence Service, which MI(R) approached to do its preliminary work. Section D's job was to investigate irregular methods of causing problems for potential enemies. In April, in London, Jo Holland, head of MI(R), and George Taylor, head of Section D's Balkan Section, duly hammered out a plan to cooperate in encouraging Albanians, inside and outside Albania, to resist the Italian occupation. And, with that, the centre of planning on Albania shifted from London to neutral Belgrade, the Yugoslav capital, where Taylor, an Australian businessman, believed there was a community of Albanian exiles and émigrés. He also had faith in the abilities of Section D's main Belgrade representative, a South African arms dealer called Julius Hanau who had lived in the Balkans since the end of the First World War.

At the end of April, in a letter that acted as Hanau's directive, Taylor outlined the new approach to Italy and stressed the 'most urgent' need for 'immediate' action 'before the balloon goes up'. Section D, he explained, would act 'as a sort of Advance Guard' for MI(R) by establishing and exploiting anti-Italian contacts with a view to starting guerrilla warfare inside Albania. It would seek out Albanians willing to cooperate, send in warlike supplies across the Greek and Yugoslav borders, extract intelligence and generally prepare the ground 'for military action proper' if and when Italy entered the war.[30] The specifics were left to Hanau.

Although well acquainted with the murky worlds of Balkan business and politics, Hanau had little knowledge of Albania or Albanians and fewer contacts and assets than Taylor had hoped. He was also busy and too well known in Belgrade to be able to participate very fully in the venture. As a result, some junior members of the British Embassy in Belgrade found themselves charged with fomenting a revolt in a country about which they, too, knew next to nothing.

The first was the embassy's assistant naval attaché, Lieutenant Commander Sandy Glen. He was in his late twenties and almost bald and doubled as a member of Section D. Hanau asked him to draw up a note on Albania. 'I know nothing about the beastly place and wondered if you could help me,' Glen said, palming the job off on the assistant press attaché, twenty-one-year-old Julian Amery.[31]

Dark, slight and sharp-featured, Amery was the son of Leo, the wartime Secretary of State for India, and younger brother of the disreputable John Amery, a philandering fascist who brought great shame on the family and was later hanged for treason. Julian was energetic and ambitious, combative and well connected, with an air of self-belief that could grate and make him enemies. In breaks from Oxford in 1938 he had visited the Nationalist side in Spain and written articles for newspapers at home. And when Germany's invasion of Poland had found him revising on the Dalmatian coast, he had abandoned his studies, rushed to Belgrade and, armed with a letter from his father, successfully asked the British Ambassador for a job. Since then he had kept mostly to press matters. Now he took up Glen's brief with enthusiasm, ringing Ralph Parker, Belgrade correspondent of *The Times*, to ask if he knew any Albanians. Parker said he did know one or two. They fixed a meeting for that evening.

At six o'clock, Amery went round to Parker's flat where he was introduced to Gani Kryeziu and his brother, Said. Gani was in his forties, stocky and short, 'with a frank expression and distinctly military bearing', Amery would recall. 'He was a man of few words.' Said was younger, slimmer and taller, 'and, if Gani was the soldier, Said was the diplomat'. He had studied in France and 'was at heart a passionate believer in social-democracy'.[32] The pair spoke with Amery for an hour and a half. Afterwards Amery wrote eagerly to Hanau that 'a war of liberation' might be possible in Albania and that here, in Gani, was a candidate to lead it.[33] These were the first Albanians Amery had met. At a stroke, however, the British were in touch with a prominent Albanian family apparently well placed for causing the Italians problems. The Kryezius' home was in Gjakova, a red-roofed market town in Kosovo, the southern Yugoslav province bordering the mountains of northern Albania, but they had considerable influence and interests over the frontier: ideal, Section D thought, for running in arms and agents. Gani, the family's head, was also a former officer in the Yugoslav Army and well regarded as a leader: the British heard later that the Yugoslav Foreign Ministry, which had little affection for Zog, had even earmarked him as a future Albanian king.[34] In fact the rare esteem in which the Yugoslav authorities held him meant some support in Belgrade for what Section D was trying to do. Impressed by Gani, his willingness to help and his 'strongly anti-Italian' attitude, the British quickly placed the Kryezius at the centre of their plans.[35]

The next few weeks, according to Section D records, were spent mostly 'sifting through names of various exiles with a view to finding potential leaders and points of resistance'.[36] Hanau wrote to London asking that 'all available information regarding Albania be fished out from the FO and WO records, and sent to us as soon as possible'. He also wanted lire, gold and some accurate maps and, if one existed, an expert on Albania.[37] In Belgrade several more Britons had been brought in, including Glen, Parker, who had resigned from *The Times* to join Section D, John Bennett, a young lawyer in the embassy, and Fred Lawrence, a young Royal Tank Regiment captain. Lawrence, Amery would recall, had once been to Albania on holiday.

Nevertheless, progress was made. A list of 'potential leaders' drawn up in mid-May contained several names besides those of the Kryezius. One man mentioned was Mustafa Gjinishi, a young, English-speaking communist living in exile in Yugoslavia, who, in due course, was brought on board the project on the advice of Said Kryeziu. Another was Abas Kupi, heard to be in Istanbul and believed to be loyal to King Zog. 'We are informed that he would do much if given ammunition.'[38] Kupi came from Kruja, in the highlands of Mati, Zog's own region. After years as an outlaw and occasional opponent of the king, his local standing had become such that Zog had made him a major in the gendarmerie. It was in that role that Kupi had apparently led the defence of Durrës in April 1939. He, too, would soon be working with the British. Amery was to remember a small man, aged about fifty, charming, warm and illiterate, who looked a bit like Napoleon: 'a likeness accentuated by a lock of hair brushed forward on his forehead to hide the deep scar of a bullet wound'.[39]

By the summer, three groups, including Gani's, were being funded to work into Albania from Yugoslavia. Gunrunning might start once they proved satisfactory. And by July Belgrade was confident that 'an Albanian revolt, at any rate in certain frontier areas, can be produced'. Gani wanted £3,000 in gold to distribute among northern chiefs and a further £40,000 once the 'revolution' was on. An offer had also been made by 'the highest military authorities in Yugoslavia' to supply five thousand rifles 'complete with slings and bayonets', ten million rounds and twenty-five light machine-guns 'with drums and ammunition'. The supplier would receive payment once his wares were over the border.[40]

Given events elsewhere it might seem to have been a good time to strike. The war was not going well for the British. In May, after attacking Denmark and Norway, the Germans had thrust into France and the Low Countries and the retreat and withdrawal of the British Expeditionary Force began. On 10 June Italy finally entered the war on Germany's side. Two weeks later the French signed an armistice, leaving Britain to fight on alone. But although Italy was now an enemy, Britain's Mediterranean strategy remained focused, at that moment, on keeping the fight out of the Balkans for as long as possible. And so, when word of the planned Albanian revolt reached Cairo and General Sir Archibald Wavell, Commander-in-Chief at GHQ Middle East, whose responsibilities included operations in the Balkans, he quickly ruled against it. Instructions were issued 'that no immediate action should be taken to foment revolt'.[41]

Wavell's objections were apparently precipitated by news of a single but unfortunate incident on the Greek–Albanian border. While Section D's men in Belgrade had been busily working up contacts, other Section D and MI(R) men in Athens had been trying to establish secret dumps of explosives for use in hindering any Italian attack on Greece. And in June, a Greek doctor, who had already smuggled into Albania a hundred kilograms of dynamite, had run into trouble. Dr Karvounis, a later report explains, had found his car out of order and, to get from his home in Athens to the Albanian frontier, decided to take a taxi. In this he had loaded four suitcases of dynamite. 'All went well till they stopped for a drink at some point between Yannina and the frontier, where the taxi-driver, his curiosity aroused by the weight of the suitcases, succeeded in the absence of the Doctor in opening one. Alarmed by the treatment he might expect if the Italian customs discovered the nature of the luggage, the taxi-driver denounced the Doctor to the Greek military authorities of the frontier-zone.' Karvounis was arrested. His defence, 'that he had been indulging in a speculation in dynamite as a side-line', was not believed and he was 'sent into exile for a year'.[42] And when word of all this reached Cairo, a threat to British strategy was spotted at once. Section D was duly instructed 'not to do anything which would stir up trouble on the Albanian border, and thus give the Italians an excuse for an Italian invasion of Greece'.[43]

The Karvounis episode also highlights one of the principal reasons why, in July 1940, Section D and MI(R) were wound up and the Special Operations Executive created in their place. The potential importance of sabotage and subversion had been recognised at the highest levels; so had the need for a fresh organisation harnessed more closely to strategy and policy. Section D, to quote from SOE's War Diary, was 'essentially a weapon of offence'. In aim it was 'largely short term and opportunist'. Action was taken 'when and where possible' and 'the policy of H.M. Government and the wishes of H.M. Representatives were not always taken into full consideration'.[44] The Foreign Office was partly responsible for that, given its insistence that Section D's work should be kept entirely separate from that of diplomatic missions. But eventually, as Section D's own War Diary explains, the resultant mix of mistakes, errors, quarrels and successes had convinced 'even the most conservative of diplomats' that there were certain necessary activities which embassies and official missions could not undertake.[45]

SOE, by contrast, came under the control of the Minister of Economic Warfare, the Labour MP Hugh Dalton. He would have to approve its plans and obtain the agreement of the Foreign Office and any other interested ministry. He would have to maintain particularly close contact with the Chiefs of Staff and they, in turn, were told to keep him informed of relevant matters of strategy. But SOE also had considerable autonomy and power. Its existence was highly secret, its name was unknown outside a small Whitehall circle, and it would operate outside parliamentary control and be financed from secret funds. And sometimes, particularly when SOE officers were Britain's only eyes and ears in enemy territory, its opinions were to carry great weight at the highest level.

SOE also absorbed much of MI(R) and Section D and many of their plans and personnel, which ensured that the groundwork and contacts made previously with Albanian exiles survived. As a result, the British remained in touch with the Kryezius and others and at work on preparing resistance in Albania, albeit in line with Cairo's instruction to do nothing that could lead to 'incidents' or threaten revolt.

What blew fresh life into the Albanian project was the arrival on the scene of Colonel W. F. Stirling. A man of action, forceful in his views and with a wide circle of important contacts and friends, 'Mike' Stirling brought to the project influence and determination and personal experience of both Albania and guerrilla war. He had won his first DSO against the Boers at the age of twenty. During the First World War he became 'Stirling the suave', T. E. Lawrence's 'skilled staff officer, tactful and wise'; the pair drove into Damascus together in 1918.[46] After three years as governor of southern Palestine he had spent eight more, from 1923, as an adviser to Albania's government and eventually to its king. In May 1940 Section D found him working, to his frustration, in telephone censorship and only too keen to help. In August, after flying out to Athens and touring SOE's various Balkan outposts, he drew up and tabled a new plan.

SOE, Stirling thought, was the 'ideal tool' for encouraging resistance in Albania: 'not being a military body, it has no scruples, few morals and is without shame. Its operations can, if necessary, be denied with an oath.' But he found its present potboiling role unimpressive and proposed three new stages by which, he felt, work should now proceed. First, forward dumps of arms and munitions should be hidden for use by rebels when the time came to fight; at the same time an Albanian committee ought to be set up to coordinate the émigrés' and exiles' efforts. Next, in the event of Italy attacking Yugoslavia or Greece, acts of sabotage inside Albania should begin. The final stage was 'the main revolution' timed to break out when it suited British policy and could be assured of adequate support.[47]

Wavell approved the plan and agreed that Stirling, an old friend, should be in the commanding role. A chat with Hugh Dalton during a lightning visit to London seems to have helped boost Wavell's confidence. 'Everything was stuck – and nothing was allowed – owing to General Wavell's distrust of the old "D" Organisation,' Dalton explained later to the new Prime Minister, Winston Churchill. 'On the understanding that he was kept fully informed and that everything was done under his authority, I said I hoped that he would now allow preparations. He responded by putting Colonel Stirling in charge and telling him to go ahead.'[48]

Although Stirling was soon on his way to Turkey to try to put together a committee of exiles, it was not long before his project reached its second stage. Mussolini had long been looking to invade something new and, for a while, Yugoslavia was a likely target. But on 28 October 1940, along a 150-mile front, eight Italian divisions began instead to pour from their Albanian bases into Greece. The Greeks held the advance and a major battlefront, high among the mountains along the Greek–Albanian border, soon developed. And within hours of the invasion, in line with the agreed plan and command arrangement, GHQ Middle East had authorised Stirling to start small-scale guerrilla operations behind the Italian lines.

Only a handful of men, mostly Greek-speakers from southern Albania, would actually be involved and their operations would never achieve very much. Over the next few weeks the odd report trickled back of a road being mined or a small bridge blown. The most impressive agent, records suggest, was a certain Spiro Milio, who passed back to Bill Barbrook much 'useful information' and, with twenty-five men, operated in front of the Greek Army as it began to push the Italians back into southern Albania. Milio's family, apparently, had been established in the region for six hundred years 'and his grandfather was the general under whom Byron fought'.[49] But such minor successes were never intended to be more than that and Stirling remained focused on a major revolt as the best way of causing the Italians problems.

Stirling's idea for a revolt was similar to Section D's in that the 'actual fighting' would be done, he envisaged, by the 'mountaineers of the north-east and centre' organised around Gani Kryeziu. 'The men of the south have no clans, but are divided into towns and villages. They are excellent fighters provided men of repute can be found to lead them.'[50] Where his idea chiefly differed was in its greater focus on achieving unity among the guerrillas and on the importance of holding out substantial rewards to encourage them to take part. Section D had not been oblivious to the conflicting politics of the Albanians with whom it had been in touch. As Julius Hanau had noted in May, they divided themselves into three rival groups: Zogist (that is, pro-Zog), anti-Zogist and communist. Beyond throwing money at them, however, Section D had suggested few ways of coaxing the maximum number of Albanians out to fight. But the mountaineers, Stirling stressed, were 'divided into distinct clans who will only fight under their own chieftains' and the only way of uniting them, he believed, was by securing Zog's 'approval and general blessing'. The king was not universally liked, Stirling conceded, but he would be a significant figurehead. 'In spite of the blood feuds with which King Zog is entrammelled, in spite of the unpopularity of his later administration, he is the only pivot around which all classes and creeds can centre.'[51]

Other Britons with Albanian experience and now working for SOE held similar views. Dayrell Oakley-Hill was one. A short, wiry, vital man, another of Percy's ex-inspectors, he had re-enlisted in 1939 and arrived in Belgrade in November 1940 after SOE secured his release from a post on Malta. Belgrade needed him. The little band engaged on the earlier Albanian plans had shrunk considerably by then. Hanau had gone, forced to leave in June when three Gestapo agents were heard to have arrived in the city to kill him. Ralph Parker had left in August when it transpired that he, too, was a marked man: his wife was a Czech and her mother and a friend had both been arrested in Prague. Julian Amery had also gone. Ronald Campbell, the British Ambassador, had not been pleased to discover that Amery had been working for Section D against what he thought had been 'my express and formal instructions'.[52] Nor had Campbell been happy to hear of Amery's alleged indiscretions: paying Albanians on the embassy premises and, without authority, meeting Bulgarian politicians during a recent trip to Sofia and suggesting their king's removal. In London, Philip Broad, a Foreign Office official attached to SOE, agreed that he was a worry. 'I rather feel that Mr Amery, who is certainly young and enthusiastic, is liable to get us into trouble, however much we try to keep him on the rails at this end, and it might be in our best interests to withdraw him.'[53] Amery's removal was arranged.

Oakley-Hill, like Stirling, was adamant that a revolt had to be properly supported and not launched prematurely, and that Britain had to provide substantial moral, material and political support to convince Albanians, both inside and outside the country, that it was worth their while taking part. 'The Northern Albanian does not take readily to mere brigandage for pay. He is very attached to his own home and his own part of the country and requires a sufficient stimulus to make him leave it and take up arms.' Also, 'owing to his feudal background and clan system he is dependent on the chiefs of his clan and obedient to them. To convince the chiefs is to obtain the support of the people, but the chiefs are similarly dependent on higher leaders in whom they have confidence.' Thus the essential 'pre-requisites' for success, Oakley-Hill proposed in late 1940, were arms and ammunition, a trusted leader or leaders, evidence of 'the friendly intentions of Greece' and British support for Albanian claims to 'just treatment'. That meant British support for the restoration of Albanian independence. Only 'the big stakes, which are their only real interest', would induce important leaders outside the country to return and lead the revolt. 'Such a stimulus could best be provided by the prospect of a successful struggle for the independence of Albania.'[54]

Looking on from London, Percy agreed. 'With all their faults those old mountaineers were a grand and very loveable lot,' he wrote in December. 'I only wish we could rope them in on our side where I am sure they would pull their weight.' And after 'thinking things out late last night in the air raid shelter', he felt that promising the Albanians their independence could be 'a most powerful incentive for them to throw in their weight against Italy'. Certainly, he believed, they were entitled to some sort of assurance over their future:

> We have proclaimed time after time that we are fighting against the Axis Powers for the purpose of liberating the states which have come under their domination. We have named these states but nothing has ever been said about Albania. Why should not the Albanians enjoy their freedom like any other people?
> ... The main thing is to bring about the defeat of the Italians in Albania, and if we are more likely to ensure that with the help of the Albanians, surely the promise of their independence is a very small price to pay.

And if a promise of independence was made, he added, 'the news will have to be conveyed to them in such a manner that they will believe that the decision of the British Government is bona fide ... It must come from someone they know and trust ... Zog ... whatever his faults may have been, is still the only man who could hold sway over the whole of Albania.'[55]

Colonel Edmund de Renzy Martin, who had also worked with Percy in Albania before the war and was now working in London for SOE's

Spanish section, felt the same. Incentive was all-important and had to be clear-cut. 'Smooth words are no use with an Albanian. He must be told to "d—d well do something" and that he will be shot if he doesn't!'[56] Zog, he agreed, was 'the only man who can unite all classes and tribes of Albanians, in spite of his previous misrule', but the issue of Albania's future was crucial. 'I doubt whether a general revolt can be brought about unless the Albanian, who is no fool, is promised that Great Britain will see to it that as a consequence he will some day regain his independence,' he concluded. 'Albanians do not care for the Greeks any more than for the Italians, and they argue that to remain quiet they are fairly safe whoever wins, whereas to revolt means certain death to those caught and to many others also.'[57]

SOE had no authority to harness Zog to its plans or guarantee Albania's independence. But when it appealed to the Foreign Office for help, SOE learnt very quickly that British diplomats were not at all keen on permitting Zog's involvement or pronouncing on Albania's status. Zog, after much wandering, was then living in Britain, and the Foreign Office had never been entirely comfortable with that. The king's ostentatious occupation of an entire floor of the Ritz, paid for, it was rumoured, by gold he had brought with him from Albania's national bank, seemed a little inappropriate. Scotland Yard was not happy either with the sawn-off shotguns carried by his bodyguard. Although, for a time, the Foreign Office considered moving him along to the United States, in the end he was allowed to stay. When SOE requested Zog's involvement in its plans, however, objections were made on more serious grounds. Keen to maintain good relations with Greece and aware of Greek territorial claims to southern Albania, diplomats saw that British interests were much better served by refraining from anything that smacked of a British commitment to Albania's future.

Thus the Foreign Office confined a statement to SOE's Albanians to saying simply: 'HMG have the cause of Albania very much at heart.'[58] And when SOE proposed to send Zog out to the Balkans to rally his subjects, the Foreign Office refused to allow it. Zog, who had proposed a similar plan, did not endear himself when he subsequently refused to be flown to Cairo. But after bouncing the proposal off the British Embassy in Greece, the Foreign Office soon appreciated how opposed were the Greeks to anything that might lead to the restoration of Albania's pre-war borders. When asked for his views, Metaxas, the Greek Prime Minister, claimed that Zog was so unpopular that his presence in the

Balkans would only help the Italians. Undoubtedly Greek objections were reinforced by the fact that the Greek Army had pushed the Italians back into southern Albania and was now occupying territory that Greece felt should be its own. Yet British diplomats across the Balkans and the Middle East also urged against the plan and the final word came from Wavell, who shared concerns that Zog's arrival on the scene would upset the Greeks.

Years later, Stirling would write in his memoirs of the lamentable level of support his plans had received from the British general then liaising with the Greeks. There had been a good chance of fashioning a successful revolt, Stirling claimed, since SOE's Albanians had been eager for action, Wavell had promised a few thousand rifles and the Greeks, at that moment, had the Italians on the rack. Unfortunately, so Stirling wrote with regret, the British general in charge in Greece had been 'insufficiently tough' and failed to give the venture the necessary push. 'I was practically forbidden to carry out the plan and every obstacle was put in my way.'[59] Certainly, in the weeks after the invasion, the Greeks had made good progress. Yet in his memoirs Stirling did not acknowledge that responsibility for authorising a full-scale revolt still lay in Cairo, with Wavell, and that Wavell never directed SOE or General Heywood, the British officer in Greece whom Stirling believed had been so obstructive, to proceed with it. The subsequent release of five thousand Italian rifles captured in North Africa, after all Yugoslav offers had fallen through, was as far as Wavell was ever willing to go. In London the Chiefs of Staff did agree in principle to a plan, drawn up by Oakley-Hill in December, for Gani Kryeziu to enter north-east Albania, occupy the town of Kukës, close to the border, and declare an Albanian government in Zog's name.[60] When the Chiefs referred the plan to Wavell, however, he dismissed it.[61] The 'gist' of Wavell's views, SOE's man in Cairo observed, was that a 'general revolt' would demand substantial assistance 'which he cannot afford to give' since 'priority must be given to the Greeks'.[62] But the 'governing factor' was that 'nothing should be done to prejudice the Greek will to win'.[63]

Stirling was not to mention in his memoirs how serious were the physical difficulties that stood in the way of getting enough supplies to the guerrillas. Nor would he acknowledge, as men familiar with the region did at the time, quite how substantial were the guerrillas' needs for outside supplies and logistical help. 'The poverty of the people is unbelievable,' de Renzy Martin remarked in December. 'The majority exist on the border of starvation. Infant mortality is high.'[64] And a key obstacle to success, de Renzy Martin felt, was the problem of maintaining and moving large numbers of men in that environment:

> In spite of the Italian training of the Albanian army for 12 to 15 years, there is not nearly enough knowledge or discipline to enable large masses of men to be moved about with precision. Food and munition supplies for large numbers would provide almost insuperable difficulties. The good targets provided by ill-disciplined masses would be a heaven-sent opportunity for the Italian Air Force ... For the Albanians to unite in large bodies incapable of living on the country or of hiding by day would be to court disaster.

Securing a 'food supply' for the guerrillas was of particular importance. 'It might be possible,' he suggested, 'to arrange for maize (the mountaineers' staple diet is maize bread and cheese) to be sent in from Jugoslavia.'[65]

A former colonel in Yugoslav military intelligence, an Albanian specialist, sharing his thoughts with Section D in May, also drew attention to those barren conditions. Large bands of men trying to survive in northern Albania, he warned, would face serious problems. Movement would be hazardous and 'along what are little more than goat tracks, which could be used only for small bodies of mountain troops. Even these could not advance at any speed, since the troops could obtain no food supplies on the way.' The terrible experiences of the Serb Army, as it tried to reach the coast through that very area in 1912, provided ample historical proof of the difficulties: 'the troops had to cover the entire distance practically without food, and their losses on account of starvation were very great'. Serbs retreating through the same region in 1915 faced similar conditions. Albania, the colonel stressed, was 'very poor' and 'besides small livestock there is no food to be got there'.[66]

Oakley-Hill's plans did envisage a rapid march on Kukës, where Gani and his men would need to receive 'essential' supplies dropped by the Royal Air Force: £40,000 in gold, plus 'rifles, sub machine guns, pistols, ammunition, grenades ... greatcoats and battle dress trousers ... maize and wheatflour'. It was assumed, in fact, that the Italians would close the Albanian–Yugoslav border once they realised what Gani was doing, so the force would 'depend entirely on British support from the air'.[67] But as an SOE officer in Athens pointed out to London, the token RAF contingent sent to help the Greeks was wholly incapable of delivering that kind of extra assistance to the Albanians. When the plan had come up for consideration there, the RAF liaison officer in Athens had told him that it was 'not his wish to be uncooperative' but 'under present circumstances it was quite impossible for the RAF to fall in with the proposals made by Belgrade'. There were not enough aircraft, there was no spare food or clothing and the equipment for dropping arms and stores by parachute was in England. Also, the 'unreliability of the weather, and particularly the sudden and unpredictable formation of cloud over the Albanian mountains makes it impossible to arrange a rendezvous with the object of dropping supplies with any certainty of being able to keep it'.[68]

Stalemate on the Greek–Italian front, meanwhile, led to further doubts among British military commanders that an Albanian revolt would succeed. By January 1941 trenches trailed across the mountains and horrendous winter conditions removed any remaining likelihood of a sudden advance by either side. To SOE officers in Athens that month Heywood explained that 'higher authorities' believed a revolt 'should not be attempted without an at least 80% chance of success' and were not convinced at present that there was that chance. While Greek reluctance to fall in with the plan remained part of the problem, GHQ Middle East also felt 'that the only time for such a revolt to take place is simultaneously with a major Greek advance'. Of such an advance, however, there was 'no indication whatsoever'. In fact the Greeks seemed 'completely bogged'. Without such an advance, and because the RAF was patently unable to provide support, GHQ Middle East, 'with their professional confidence in the superiority of regular over irregular troops, feel that the revolt would be crushed'. On top of that, the 'deterrent effect of a crushed revolt upon the spirits of the people in occupied territory is exactly what higher authorities even than Mideast [GHQ Middle East] are supremely anxious to avoid'.[69]

'I hope you do not feel that Heywood is being obstructive,' SOE in Athens told their colleagues in Belgrade. 'It is quite clear . . . that his instructions are very definite. As an example of his anxiety to help us he tried to get us 30 squirts [sub-machine-guns] out of the thousand delivered here for the Greeks, and tell the Greeks that these had been short delivered.' Heywood was really 'very keen' on intensifying small-scale guerrilla activity and Athens was 'quite sure that he will do everything in his power to assist you in anything short of a full scale revolt'. As it was, Heywood felt that Belgrade should explain to its Albanians that no support for anything other than 'tip and run thuggery' could be expected for months.[70]

Nothing changed to allow SOE's plans for Albania to receive greater support before Hitler's armies swept into the Balkans in April 1941, conquered Yugoslavia and Greece and pushed the British from their last footholds on the Continent. In March Churchill had authorised Wavell to reinforce the Greeks with British troops, but no authorisation was ever forthcoming from Wavell to allow SOE to go ahead with its Albanian revolt. Nor was there any alteration to the British Government's refusal to support Zog or pronounce on Albania's independence or future frontiers. The RAF, meanwhile, with the resources it had to hand in 1941, never solved the problem of how to deliver substantial material to guerrillas in northern Albania. And all of that helps explain why the most that was ever approved was a limited plan for a few 'irregulars' to enter northern Albania from Kosovo and carry out minor acts of sabotage: cutting telephone lines, attacking police posts and so on.[71]

Julian Amery, who heard later of the party that crossed the border on 7 April, would write grandly in his memoirs of a gallant 'United Front' of three hundred men, led by Gani Kryeziu, accompanied by Oakley-Hill and including Said Kryeziu, Abas Kupi and Mustafa Gjinishi. Once over the frontier, according to Amery, they met and defeated two strong Italian patrols, won much local support and pressed on through the mountains with more than a thousand men and the aim of attacking Shkodra. When Catholic tribes in the hills above the town refused to back them, the party withdrew to Muslim territory to establish a base, regain contact with Yugoslavia and prepare to harass the roads. Then news came through that Germany had invaded Yugoslavia on the morning of 6 April, whereupon the United Front 'ceased to be the vanguard of a powerful army and were transformed into a band of fugitives, trapped in the mountains'.[72]

Oakley-Hill, however, in a little-known account unpublished for years, painted a different picture. While he did recall that some border guards fired a few shots and then ran away, he wrote nothing of meeting and defeating two strong enemy patrols. Nor did he echo Amery's tone of a valiant body, a thousand-strong, marching on hopefully through the snow towards Shkodra. Instead he described the disappointments of a small, cold and hungry party whose leader seemed to have doubted their chances of success even before they left Kosovo. Arriving from Belgrade at the Kryezius' Gjakova townhouse, Oakley-Hill had found Gani 'subdued and not very forthcoming and gave me the impression of being worried'. Once across the border they attracted less support than expected and, though some locals did rally and join him, the sparseness of the region, which had been of such concern to the SOE planners, soon forced Gani to 'cut the numbers down to about a hundred'. The 'commissariat problem', as Oakley-Hill put it, 'began to stick out a mile. If several hundred men moved from place to place they could not be fed by the villagers, who had only just enough [food] of their own. There was only one answer – to reduce the numbers of our moving body to a minimum.'[73]

Also, for Oakley-Hill, what brought the enterprise to ruin was not so much Germany's invasion of Yugoslavia but the moral effect of large numbers of Yugoslav soldiers advancing into Albania alongside Gani's men. Amery made no mention of these. Oakley-Hill considered their presence critical:

> We had planned to enter Albania as a small group and find shelter with the highland chiefs. We would then sound the local feelings and try to initiate sabotage and local minor actions. If the situation was ripe and circumstances were suitable we would work towards a general rising which, with a neutral Yugoslavia at our backs, was far from impossible . . . But now we were to be involved with Yugoslav troops, who would never be welcome in Albania owing to the many centuries of hostility between Albanian and Slav. So what would be our role now?

News of the German invasion did create, he felt, a 'general feeling of panic or paralysis' that 'undermined all chance we had of staying in the mountains and secretly working against the Fascists'. But 'the fatal blow' was the Yugoslav entry into Albania, short-lived though it was. 'Without that we might still have crawled quietly into the hills and found shelter with no publicity, the local highlanders dispersing to their homes. As it was, the whole of the north knew of our presence and some might think of us as tools of the Yugoslavs.'[74] Days later, Gani, with all hope gone, dispersed his men. He and Said returned to Gjakova. In time the brothers were arrested, taken to Italy and interned on an island prison off the coast. Oakley-Hill, disguised as a peasant, made it as far as German-occupied Belgrade, where, after vainly seeking help from the United States Embassy, he turned himself in. The Germans put him in prison. Two and a half years later he was repatriated owing to illness, whereupon he rejoined SOE and went to work in London in its Baker Street headquarters.

To claim that events in April 1941 had wrecked hopes of a major rising, however, is to ignore the range of preconditions that planners had felt at the time were vital for success. Certainly Yugoslavia's collapse and the presence beside Gani of hated Yugoslav troops may have discouraged many Albanians from helping him. But while SOE had also favoured a revolt rather than minor acts of resistance, it had felt, too, that British-delivered arms, food and incentives were essential if a revolt was not to fail. Due to reasons of logistics and wider diplomacy and strategy, not one of those essentials was in place when Gani and Oakley-Hill left for the mountains.

'A FEW VOLUNTEERS'

WITH the Axis dominant on the European mainland, SOE chose Cairo, with its established British presence, as the place to begin rebuilding its Balkan projects. There was much work to do. The triumphant German thrust through the Balkans in the spring of 1941 had carried away all of SOE's plans and severed most of its links. And though interest was quickly fired once again as reports filtered out of small pockets of resistance, SOE's ability even to contact those resisting was to remain for months extremely limited.

With Yugoslavia and Greece overrun, Britain and its Dominions stood defiant but alone. The prospects of rapid recovery were remote; priority was placed on survival. June 1941 suddenly brought Britain an ally when Germany invaded the Soviet Union, but the Red Army was coping badly under the onslaught. German U-boats were winning in the Atlantic, Rommel was gaining the upper hand in the desert and in December the Japanese burdened the British with another war in the East. Although the Americans, too, came in that month, their armies were a long way from making a decisive impact. Demands on British forces in North Africa and elsewhere meant few resources left over for SOE, while there was much scepticism at the highest levels as to whether SOE, this new and largely unproven body, should be given anything at all. Manpower, aircraft, communications, finance, arms, equipment: all proved hard to come by.

Still, as SOE and its Cairo office tried to work with what little they had, some progress was made. By 1942, narrow lines had been re-established back into Greece, the first British officer had returned to Yugoslavia and a little attention was turning once again to Albania.

That January SOE in London noted 'a long story of unrest and rising'
in Albania reported recently by a Jerusalem-based journalist. London
cabled Cairo, asking officers there to do what they could to verify the
report and explore the possibility of encouraging any unrest.[1] Cairo's first
step was to dispatch to neutral Turkey one of SOE's more unusual recruits.

She arrived in Istanbul in March 'under an assumed name with
disguised appearance and dyed hair'.[2] Her real name was Margaret
Hasluck. She was fifty-six, a farmer's daughter, born at Drumblade in
Aberdeenshire, and brought up in Moray, and the widow of an eminent
archaeologist and classical scholar. Today she is best known in her own
right as an ethnographer. Her *Unwritten Law in Albania* drew on years
of fieldwork and remains the authoritative tract on the phenomenon
of the Albanian blood feud in the early twentieth century. But from
February 1942, when SOE found her in Cairo, to where she had fled
Athens and the advancing German Army the previous spring, she was
to spend two years in a different field. Hasluck's initial instructions
were to contact Turkey's Albanian community, largely a relic of Ottoman
days, collect intelligence and find volunteers prepared to work for the
British. For over a year, first in Istanbul, then at Rustem Buildings, the
block of flats in Garden City where SOE had its Cairo headquarters,
she was the only person in SOE focused full-time on the country. From
the spring of 1943, when SOE sent out its first mission to Albania, she
then took on the tasks of briefing and teaching the language to British
officers earmarked for the field.

Some of those men have written since, and fondly, of a kindly woman
who applied herself to the tasks at hand with industry and devotion.
One recalls how, with her 'greying hair swept back into a bun and a
pink complexion with bright blue eyes', she reminded him 'of an old-
fashioned English nanny. Full of energy and enthusiasm, she was totally
dedicated to her beloved Albania.'[3] Different impressions were left on
staff officers with whom Hasluck spent more time and worked more
closely. One who knew her in Cairo compares her to characters played
by the film actress Margaret Rutherford: 'that kind of school mistress
type, both physically and mentally'.[4] He and others at headquarters
found her brisk personality and total dedication to Albania hard to
deal with and came to view her passionate opinions, particularly on
which guerrillas to support, as more of a hindrance to their work than
a help. But in 1942 SOE in Cairo knew little enough about Albania.
In any case there were no other experts about. Oakley-Hill was still in

a German prison. Stirling, Barbrook and Cripps had all moved on to different work. Percy and de Renzy Martin remained at home but there was little for them to do; Percy was to be called upon to make the odd BBC broadcast and sign letters of introduction for British officers going into the field. In 1940 SOE had found another Briton who had been there before the war: a young Scot, David Maitland-MacGill-Crichton, who had started work on a biography of Zog. SOE found him 'intelligent and certainly keen' and possibly suitable as 'an unofficial contact with Zog'.[5] Sent out to the Mediterannean to join Oakley-Hill and the others, he never arrived: his ship was torpedoed in February 1941. Nevertheless, when the need arose twelve months later for someone to study Albania and work up contacts afresh, the credentials of this accomplished and studious woman must also have seemed strong.

Born Margaret Masson Hardie in June 1885, she had been schooled at Elgin Academy and taken first-class degrees in classics from Aberdeen University and Newnham College, Cambridge. In 1911 she arrived in Anatolia on a studentship from the British School at Athens and in Greece met Frederick Hasluck, Fellow of King's College, Cambridge, and leading light at the British School. They married in 1912. During the early years of the First World War they worked together in Athens for British Intelligence. Although her own role was a minor one, the author Compton Mackenzie wrote of her doing similar work in London in 1915 and she herself was to tell of smuggling messages between Athens and London in her garters. In 1916, Frederick's ailing health then took the couple to Switzerland, where they lived in a series of sanatoria until he died in 1920 at the age of forty-two. His widow would apparently blame herself for his early death, believing that the tuberculosis that slowly killed him had been contracted on a trip to Konia in 1913, his wedding present to her: the destination had been her choice. Returning to Britain, she devoted herself to assembling his notes for posthumous publication.

Only when that work was done had Hasluck developed the specialist knowledge for which SOE recruited her. In 1921, with a travelling fellowship from Aberdeen University, she threw herself into ethnographic fieldwork in Macedonia and Albania, where her husband had studied the Bektashi, an Islamic sect. From 1923 she lived in Albania, travelling all over the country, alone and in all weathers, spending full seasons in the mountains. Collecting folk tales and songs was a constant passion but her interests ranged from dialects, coinage and customs to witches,

blood feuds and botany. She sent dozens of artefacts to Aberdeen's
Marischal Museum. In methodology and commitment she far surpassed
Edith Durham, who, though better known, never learnt the language
and spent just a fraction of Hasluck's sixteen years in the country. In
1939, on the eve of the Italian invasion, Hasluck found herself accused
of espionage and expelled. Later she would say that the Italians had
demanded it. The charge, though difficult to prove, has stuck. Sixty
years later, standing in the street outside Hasluck's old home in Elbasan,
a ninety-year-old neighbour confided that he was sure 'the tall
Englishwoman with the fruit garden' had been 'some sort of spy'.[6]

From Albania she moved back to Athens, where she returned to the
arms of the British School and lived for the next two years. It was
there, apparently, that she crossed paths with Olivia Manning and
became the inspiration for the bustling Mrs Brett in *Friends and Heroes*,
the final novel of Manning's Balkan Trilogy, set in Athens in 1940–41.
Almost certainly in Athens Hasluck worked again for British Intelligence.
Her SOE personal file states simply that she had worked in the British
Legation's press office throughout her Athens stay and does not confirm
Julian Amery's later claim that Section D recruited her in 1940. However,
other records indicate that MI6's 'principal contact for Albania' that
May was 'a lady' in Athens whom Section D had considered approaching
for 'expert advice'.[7] Later she herself would write that she had 'briefed'
Albanians in Athens as early as August 1939.[8] That MI6 knew of
Hasluck is confirmed by the fact that it 'advised' SOE against her
employment.[9]

Although MI6's reasons for urging caution are unclear, it was not
long after bringing Hasluck on board that SOE officers doubted her
aptitude for the jobs she was given to do. Memoranda and progress
reports reveal that, though she threw herself into it with spirit, much
of her first year's work met with mixed success and soon drew criticism from officers in London. By June 1942 Hasluck had found four
young Albanians prepared to go through parachute and sabotage
training and return to their country to fight. Two others were brought
on board before the party left that summer for SOE's training schools
in Palestine. Yet two more volunteers had backed out at the first
mention of parachuting, while even those who wanted to go were
under pressure to stay behind from exiles less keen to work with the
British. Trustworthy couriers, prepared to carry messages between
Turkey and Albania, were as hard to obtain. The first sent out was

'an old man of Dibra, one-way only', in April.[10] A few more couriers
followed in later months. Some went to contact three guerrilla leaders
heard vaguely to be active: Abas Kupi, who had worked with the
British in 1941, Myslim Peza, who was believed busy around Tirana,
and Muharrem Bajraktar, a northern chief reputed to be in touch with
guerrillas in Serbia. Six hundred gold sovereigns were also sent. It was
a slow, imperfect business. By November 'only two couriers' had
managed to make the return journey; at least one other had been
caught and imprisoned.[11] It was also largely reliant on the goodwill
and patronage of prominent exiled and émigré Albanians. Only in
February 1943 did SOE send out a man with 'cypher and secret ink'
who was prepared to do only SOE's work.[12]

Circulated letters and memos show that SOE in London held Hasluck
at least partly responsible for this apparent lack of progress. Peter
Boughey, of London's Balkan desk, was the chief recipient of her correspondence for more than a year. By the summer of 1942 he already
feared she was 'not the right person for contacting agents and recruiting
men to return to Albania'; in fact he felt she was 'incapable of the job'.
He had not been happy to hear from MI6 that Italy knew of SOE's
work with Albanians in Istanbul. Nor was he pleased by the sound of
the Istanbul moneychangers to whom Hasluck had paid a substantial
commission to help send money to Albania: a third of the first four
hundred sovereigns had gone straight to them. Nor was Boughey
impressed by the methods by which she claimed to have secured volunteers for special training. 'According to her own correspondence, these
recruits were in an almost starving condition, with a large number of
debts,' he told Jimmy Pearson, head of the Balkan desk. 'She approached
them with a gift of money, new clothes and promised that their debts
would be paid and that they should go and have a happy time in
Palestine. It would appear almost unreasonable for these people to
refuse such a glowing vista in front of them, even though in the end it
would lead them to the mountainous hills of Albania! This form of
recruiting does not enhance my confidence, either in the recruiting
officer or in the recruits themselves.'[13]

Boughey was thirty and had joined SOE in Yugoslavia in 1940 while
convalescing from tuberculosis; he had no great knowledge of Albania
and few of his criticisms are fair. For one thing Hasluck's contact and
intelligence work was hampered by significant factors out of her control.
She could do little about the poor availability of accurate and up-to-date

information and quickly observed that Turkey was unlikely to provide the torrent of intelligence that SOE had hoped it would:

> The sources are scanty and not always reliable. Trade between Albania and Turkey has completely ceased so that Albanian merchants no longer come through, bringing solid news. A few sick people come with their attendant relatives, who bring scraps of information, but these make erratic couriers. 'Tomori', the Fascist paper published at Tirana, half in Albanian and half in Italian, has not arrived lately and is unlikely to arrive any more. Letters come through fairly quickly.

Most news stories necessarily came from 'the Balkan Press Translation Bureau, AP, United Press and Reuters'.[14] Not until the middle of 1943, when SOE officers newly arrived in Albania began transmitting information out of the country, were the British to see a significant improvement in the quality of intelligence available.

Most of Hasluck's contacts in Istanbul were also of poor quality. As she explained, three types of Albanian lived in the city: those that had emigrated for good and become Turkish subjects, those that were living as members of the Albanian colony, and those that had fled Albania after the Italian invasion. Even those who were now Turks had difficulty visiting Albania due to Italy's control of visas, while the 'poverty and humble position' of those who made up the colony ruled them out of any useful employment by SOE. Among the refugees were a good number of army officers and men of political standing, but when dealing with these Hasluck was hindered by the fact that, since their arrival in Istanbul, 'the exiles have all lost their tempers and quarrelled among themselves. They have separated into little groups, the members of one group not being on speaking terms with any other.'[15] Two or three did their best to help 'the folk-tale lady' as they called her.[16] But most Albanians she approached either refused or proved too busy squabbling to help, or tried to make their assistance conditional on British compliance with their own demands. Others informed the Italians of her activities. By the autumn she had returned to Cairo.

Hasluck's efforts were handicapped further by having little to offer, other than money, to prospective informers, intermediaries and recruits. When starting her work she had been told that while she 'must aim at getting in touch with people who in the interests of Albania's future would work against the Axis', she 'must not give any political undertaking'.[17] But as men like Percy, Stirling and Oakley-Hill had warned in 1940, persuading Albanians to help the Allies win the war was difficult when little could be offered in return. Hasluck herself appreciated the problem and did try to address it. In June SOE forwarded to the Foreign Office her appeal for a declaration on Albania's independence that might encourage its population to resist. The Foreign Office barely gave it a thought: 'the SOE angle is not in itself sufficiently weighty to justify us in making such a declaration now'.[18]

The need perceived by the Foreign Office for a noncommittal policy on Albania's frontiers in 1940 had, if anything, been reinforced in 1941 when the Axis incorporated most of Kosovo into Albania. So, in 1942, conscious of Yugoslav desires to reclaim Kosovo as well as of Greek designs on southern Albania, British diplomats, judging the Yugoslavs and the Greeks and their exiled kings and governments the more vital allies, had little hesitation in turning down SOE's fresh appeal. '[I]f we make a declaration of policy we are likely to stir up a small hornet's nest, for the Greeks and the Jugoslavs will, whatever reservations we may make, feel that they must not miss the opportunity for staking out their claims,' Sir Orme Sargent, Deputy Under-Secretary of State, advised. 'The most it could do would be to enable SOE to enlist a few more agents . . . On the whole therefore I should be inclined to leave the declaration alone for the moment.' Anthony Eden, the Foreign Secretary, agreed.[19] When, after further SOE pleading, a statement was finally made in the Commons that December, it carefully avoided reference to the state of Albania's post-war borders. While Britain wished to see Albania 'freed from the Italian yoke and restored to her independence,' Eden told the House, 'His Majesty's Government regard the question of the frontiers of the Albanian State after the war as a question which will have to be settled at the peace settlement'.[20]

The problems this caused for SOE may well explain stories of Hasluck's 'ruthlessness' told months later to a young American, Dale McAdoo, of the Office of Strategic Services. OSS was an American organisation, created six months after the United States' entry into the war and whose duties equated roughly to those of SOE and MI6; McAdoo had arrived in Cairo to set up an Albanian desk. It was not long before he contacted several Albanians with whom Hasluck had been in touch. 'She has apparently approached every important Albanian in the Middle East with various half-baked schemes,' he told Washington. '[Qemal] Butka, who seems to have been her chief victim, claims that she is crazy and takes a truly sadistic pleasure in pointing out that Albania is finished, that the Greeks are going to be given new territory because they are more adroit at dealing with the all-powerful British, and that the will of Great Britain is not to be questioned by mere Albanians.'[21]

Hasluck was not always tactful or patient, while it is quite possible that she sought to exert leverage by warning Albanians in the strongest terms of the consequences should they refuse to help her. Butka, meanwhile, was an 'ex-Mayor of Tirana, politician and intellectual' and an awkward customer.[22] Hasluck wrote of her dealings with him: 'after an eight hours' day I just have not got the physical strength to see somebody who is so touchy that you have to watch, not merely every word you say, but even every breath you draw, in case he takes offence'.[23] But Foreign Office reluctance to associate itself with Albanian nationalist aspirations meant SOE could offer little encouragement to Butka and his idea for a committee-in-exile. The stories told to McAdoo may say more about Butka and his friends and their grudges against the British than they do about Hasluck. McAdoo himself would later regret having spent so long 'courting the Nostalgic Exile Faction in a sterile campaign for recruits'.[24]

Given these problems, Hasluck's achievement in finding six volunteers may be commendable; and not all of them were in rags or had to be swayed by offers of cash. Thirty-one-year-old Faik Elmas, a lieutenant in Zog's Royal Guard, was the outstanding recruit. Of the six he was the only one who would be considered suitable for operations and Hasluck thought much of him. 'Elmas is doing very well,' she wrote to Cairo after finding him in Istanbul. 'He states quite simply that he is only a peasant from King Zog's own village and he stands exactly 5 foot 0.'[25] But he had been educated since early childhood at European boarding schools, had attended and lectured at military academies in Modena and Tirana, spoke Italian and some French and 'looks as strong as a horse'.[26] His fellow volunteers, who shared few of his qualities and little of his background, 'are ashamed of him for being so small . . . I find him wise and helpful.'[27] She was particularly impressed when he and two others 'ruined their futures' when their pro-Italian CO, 'calling them traitors to their country and a few even more opprobrious epithets', tried to stop them going to Palestine. 'Elmas rounded on him and finally bade him strike him off the list of his officers. "We have decided to go, we have given our word, and we're going" was all he would say.'[28]

That summer, when the six began their Palestine training, Hasluck sat in on one occasion and watched Elmas translate for the others. 'I noticed how he amplified the instructor's remarks and twisted and turned the information till it took a form the others could understand.' In fact, she felt, his 'European outlook' set him apart from the others, 'who lived all their lives in Albanian surroundings till their exile began, and it makes a difference. They show up as the stupider type of British officer, who has never been out of England, would do if suddenly transplanted to France and put through a course of instruction by a Frenchman with only a halting interpreter to transmit his ideas to them in, say, Italian.'[29] A final measure of the man may be the fact that he acted as Hasluck's go-between with the Istanbul moneychangers through whom she sent sovereigns to Albania. 'He was fully aware of the penalty his widowed mother, who remains in Albania, might be made to pay if it was discovered that he had sent money to men considered to be their worst enemies by the Italians.'[30]

Perhaps the style and content of Hasluck's reporting, which could be discursive, opinionated and heavy with conjecture and anecdote, were enough for SOE officers in London to lose confidence in her abilities. One fairly typical report from Istanbul merely told 'a queer story' of an Albanian who had recently arrived in Vienna from Turkey to be confronted by the Austrian authorities with the fragments of a letter he thought he had torn up on the train. 'At first sight this seems a traveller's tale,' Hasluck warned. 'On reflection one notes that any one who wished to destroy a compromising letter in a train would go to the lavatory to do so unseen and would most probably drop the pieces down the pan. It may be, then, that . . . the Germans have arrangements slung under the lavatory pans for catching incriminating papers.'[31]

Her audience, however, expected fact that was hard, fast and to the point, with an indication that her work on establishing lines into Albania was secure, making progress and professionally done. Hearsay, musings and lists of the problems she faced were not so welcome. Nor, for that matter, was Hasluck's unsettling response in June 1942 to news that the Turkish authorities knew of SOE's recruitment of 'Albanians to be parachuted back into Albania'. When informing London, Hasluck evidently hit the wrong note by making light of the leak. 'Childish,' scribbled Boughey next to one passage of her letter that struck him as particularly flippant. 'Besides,' she had written, 'who spoke of para-chuting? There is no documentary evidence of it. Several of us have started making fun of the idea, saying that the Palestine party were only asked about it to test their courage.' 'I give up,' noted Pearson at the top of the page.[32] Eighteen months later reactions in London to Hasluck's correspondence remained much the same. 'The usual waffle,' Boughey wrote across a letter of Hasluck's of November 1943.[33]

Despite Boughey's belief that 'anyone with a rudimentary knowledge of the Balkans, and of our work, could undertake the preliminary stages of our work back into Albania far better', Hasluck was not replaced.[34] He had identified something of her irregular nature but underestimated the difficulties facing her and the value perceived by SOE in Cairo of having recourse to specialist experience and knowledge. And by the spring of 1943, as the 'preliminary stages' gave way to serious opera-tional planning, staff in Cairo viewed Hasluck as indispensable. 'She is the only person in the Middle East with a knowledge of the Albanian language, Albania and Albanians,' they wrote in her defence. 'Without that intimate knowledge . . . it is quite impossible for us to obtain either the information necessary to plan operations or to be able to direct the operations of parties inside the country.'[35]

The decision in 1943 to dispatch SOE's first mission to Albania owed something to rumours and reports of unrest collected and passed back by Hasluck. It owed more, however, to the turning tide of the war and to the desire of Allied planners for increased guerrilla activity every-where in the Balkans. By 1943 the Allies had started at last to inflict telling blows on enemy forces. On the Eastern Front the Germans were in the throes of their shattering defeat at Stalingrad. The recent British victory at El Alamein had been the catalyst for a rapid and unstop-pable advance through the Western Desert, while British and American landings further west made total success in North Africa likely. And as control grew over the southern shores of the Mediterranean, moves began to be planned against Axis possessions in southern Europe.

At the Casablanca Conference in January 1943, looking to maintain the offensive and make further gains, the British and Americans agreed to invade Sicily: a major step, it was hoped, towards removing Italy from the war. They also identified increased resistance in the Balkans as a means of hastening Italy's collapse, easing pressure on other fronts and preparing the way for limited Allied landings. In March SOE duly received instructions to step up its Balkan efforts. 'An intensified campaign of sabotage and guerrilla activities in the Balkans during the spring and summer is of the first strategic importance,' the British Chiefs of Staff stressed in their directive. The key aim was 'to impede the concentration and consolidation of German forces on the Eastern Front'. Efforts should also be made to disrupt Axis supplies from the region of oil, chrome and copper.[36] Already there were indications that such a strategy might be effective. Particularly eye-catching had been the sabotage, in November 1942, by an SOE demolition team aided by local guerrillas, of the Gorgopotamos railway viaduct in northern Greece, cutting an important German supply line during Rommel's retreat from El Alamein. In Yugoslavia, meanwhile, where SOE was already working with General Draža Mihailović's royalist 'Chetniks', reports were growing of another guerrilla movement: Tito's communist-led Partisans.

To meet this demand for action, SOE required various resources essential for greater activity. This meant finding more men, munitions and equipment to send behind enemy lines and addressing the problem of how to deliver them. With priority placed by senior commanders on building in Britain a vast force for the invasion of Europe, only limited resources were left over for other ventures. As far as warlike stores were concerned, SOE received a boost to its arsenal in May 1943 when Eisenhower, Allied commander in the Mediterranean, permitted the dispatch to guerrillas in southern Europe of Axis weapons and munitions captured in North Africa. Slowly the means of supply, too, was addressed. At that time air drops were the only realistic way of getting missions and material quickly into the Balkans, yet only long-range bombers, flying from North Africa, were capable of the trip. Strategic bombing had priority and, for nearly a year, four B-24 Liberators were all SOE had to cover the Balkans. In the spring of 1943 the situation improved when 148 Squadron, RAF, was equipped with fourteen four-engined Halifax bombers, specially modified for dropping men and stores, and installed at Derna in Cyrenaica. RAF reluctance to divert aircraft from bombing duties proved a formidable obstacle but, in time, more were made available. By the end of 1943, another RAF squadron, 624, had been allocated to Mediterranean special duties, while 1944 was to see Poles, Americans and even Russians, all based in southern Italy, flying supplies to the Balkans.

Finding personnel suitable for work in enemy territory posed its own problems. Unlike SOE agents working in France, for example, officers and other ranks sent out to the Balkans were to live a largely guerrilla existence that rarely required them to look, speak or behave like locals in order to survive: it was not for nothing that officers there called themselves BLOs, British Liaison Officers, not agents. Often, however, they had little choice but to operate in that way. When trying to find individuals willing to work in the Balkans and fluent in local languages, the pool of potential recruits could be small indeed. Nor were enthusiasm and languages the only qualities desired. The pool could dry up entirely when SOE demanded fitness and fighting ability and a range of technical and personal skills. Those most skilled in the relevant tongue, of course, were nationals of the country concerned; but their loyalty, especially to Britain and British war aims, was not always guaranteed.

These demands and difficulties explain why, for operations in the Balkans, SOE drew so heavily on British and Dominion-born volunteers, mostly from the armed forces, recruited not for any specific country knowledge but for their potential to operate anywhere as liaison officers, w/t (wireless telegraphy) operators or skilled saboteurs. Very early recruits were frequently friends or even family of men and women already in it. But as the war wore on and SOE's global commitment grew, greater numbers were required than personal contacts could provide. Notices began to circulate and appear on unit bulletin boards calling, in couched and mysterious terms, for suitable volunteers for hazardous operations. Names came in. Interviews followed. Gradually SOE's strength increased.

An image sometimes gathered from the memoirs of officers who worked in the Balkans is of young establishment types engaged in swashbuckling adventures. Certainly SOE was officer-heavy and friends from school and university could find themselves sharing the same flea-ridden mountain hut, while the exciting sound of this kind of work inevitably enticed the energetic, the daring and those bored with regular service. But hundreds of SOE personnel were sent out to the Balkans and their backgrounds and experiences were more diverse than the memoirs might suggest. Of the men dispatched to Albania, most were indeed young: two in their forties, a few in their thirties, most in their twenties and one or two in their teens. But half were not officers at all but Other Ranks recruited as paramilitary experts or to work the w/t sets that kept missions in touch with the outside world. And plenty of officers were not from privileged stock. Nor was every man British. One officer was South African, another was Rhodesian, two at least were Irish-born and one was a Pole. And of all these men, only one had been to Albania before: Aircraftsman Cutchie, a twenty-five-year-old Albanian-born RAF flight mechanic, who went in as an interpreter in 1944. But though fluent in the language, he had little knowledge of the country itself, as he had left when he was ten to live in Rhodesia.

One volunteer was Tony Neel, a thirty-year-old RAF equipment officer. He had joined the air force in 1935, qualified as a pilot and been promptly grounded owing to a slight loss of sight in one eye. Anxious to avoid a desk job, for a time he had seen unusual service in Palestine with a company of RAF armoured cars. Staff work proved hard to avoid, however, and the outbreak of war found him at the Air Ministry in London. Sent out to South Africa as a senior equipment officer, he wangled hard to get nearer the action and eventually secured a posting to Cairo. By early 1943 he was in Benghazi but still restless:

> And then one day . . . [in] Middle East Routine Orders . . . there was a little note saying: 'A few volunteers are required for individual and special duties. Please have active service experience and recommendations.' I liked the sound of that, so I put in my application . . . and the next thing I heard was [when] the AOC of the headquarters staff on which I was working said, 'They want you in Cairo for an interview.'
>
> . . . So off I went, next day, through to Cairo . . . and I was interviewed by various people, starting with an elderly lady, Mrs Hasluck . . . and we chatted and she said, 'Do you know anything about the Balkans?'
>
> 'No.'

Neel went back to Benghazi. A few weeks later another summons came. He returned to Cairo, 'flown up again, in another Dakota, got there, put up in Shepheard's Hotel and reported to Rustem Buildings' where he was told that a Major Leake would meet him next morning at Cairo's Gezira Club.

> It was a beautiful day . . . blue sky . . . and the Gezira Club had these huge grounds, so we walked up the grounds and we came to a big tree . . . Well, we sat there and he didn't

say much, he was very reserved and he wanted me to talk, you see.

He asked me a little about my background and I told him I'd had this experience in Palestine with the RAF armoured cars in 1938 and thereafter I'd carried on in the RAF in the equipment branch, and I'd got a bit fed up with sitting on my backside doing nothing. And so, when I saw this chance of doing something more active, I volunteered to go along.

He said, 'Well, you know what it means?'

And I said, 'No, not really.'

'Well, it means parachuting.'

And I said, 'Yes, that's alright.' I said I'd never parachuted but I'd flown a lot.

'And it would mean going to a country which is a bit primitive and, if you do go in there, you'll either stay there for the rest of the war or, if you're lucky, you'll be taken out, one way or another. Or you'll never come back at all.'

And I said, 'Well, that sounds fine.'

Neel was accepted and joined SOE in June.[37]

The net for prospective recruits for the Balkans was cast wider than the Middle East. As Neel was reporting for duty at Rustem Buildings, the second battalion of the Gordon Highlanders was stationed on Orkney, off the north coast of Scotland, when a note arrived from the War Office asking for men to parachute behind enemy lines. 'I'm proposing to put in a nil report,' Hugh Munro's company commander announced after breakfast. 'Is that alright?' Munro, a thirty-year-old subaltern commissioned two months before, put his name down. Not long afterwards he was ordered to a secluded private house outside Oxford, where he joined more than a hundred other officers all wondering what they had volunteered for:

Going into the house we were taken into a room, doors were closed and we were sworn to secrecy. We were told that, after the lecture we were to receive, we should feel free to disengage ourselves with no hard feelings.

We were told that we would do our training in the Middle East after which we would go into the field. Tito was mentioned but it was admitted that they did not know what

Tito stood for – they thought it was an acronym! Details were given on what working with Partisans would entail. No one backed out.

After individual interviews everyone returned to their units and waited for news of the outcome. In due course Munro was accepted. He was shipped out to Cairo that autumn.[38]

Jack Dumoulin, a twenty-four-year-old doctor in the Royal Army Medical Corps, was one officer who volunteered as much from despair with his present lot as from a desire to do something exciting. From Malvern College he had gone straight to St Thomas' Hospital, qualifying in October 1942. Six months followed as a house officer at Botley Park War Hospital in Chertsey before he was called up, commissioned and dispatched to work with a field ambulance unit under an alcoholic CO. When a call went round for medical officers for operations that demanded parachuting, Dumoulin, restless and unhappy, volunteered. Ordered to London, he was ushered into a waiting room, where he spotted several friends among the other MOs sat there, then in for the interview. Was he prepared, he was asked, to do work so dangerous that there was a chance of him losing his life? Dumoulin replied that he was prepared to do such work if there was at least a chance of his keeping it; and what work, exactly, did they have in mind? 'To be honest, old chap,' the interviewer said, 'I don't actually know what I'm recruiting for.' Once accepted, Dumoulin spent a month learning coding, ciphering and other skills, before being flown out to Cairo that August.[39]

Eighteen-year-old John Davis, born and bred on the East Sussex coast, was another who responded, like Munro and Dumoulin, to SOE's recruitment drive among British-based units in 1943. Davis' unassuming nature belied an impatient desire for action that had seen him try hard to join the RAF when he was barely in his teens. Poor eyesight saw him turned down when he tried to enlist as an aircraft apprentice, then age saw him turned down by the army and poor eyesight again saw the RAF decline him when he reapplied to join as aircrew. Finally, in April 1942, after service in the Home Guard and in view of the Morse he had learnt in the air cadets, he joined the Royal Corps of Signals. 'After a period of training and exercises I was painting aerials and feeling rather bored,' Davis recalled. 'A team came to the HQ, asking for volunteers for "a job which may involve one parachute descent".

Along with two mates I volunteered and we went to Oxford for an interview where we were told we would be going to Albania, Greece or Yugoslavia.' All three were accepted and given two stripes 'which we immediately put up' before returning briefly to their old unit 'where we were told to take the stripes off'. Then some leave, then to the Middle East by boat. 'I didn't know what to expect . . . It was all a bit of an adventure.'[40]

For some Other Ranks, volunteering for SOE was not always such a matter of personal choice. Twenty-six-year-old Bob Melrose was a tough, no-nonsense, hard-to-impress sergeant, also in the Royal Corps of Signals. Before the war he had been a cinema projectionist in Penicuik, outside Edinburgh. In 1943 he was training with his unit in Tenterden in Kent when, to his surprise, he was ordered suddenly and alone to Oxford. Met at the station by a car and a driver, he was swept through the town, as he recalled after the war, 'and on into the outskirts where we eventually drove into a driveway and around to the rear of a big house'. There was a patio, a couple of chairs and 'an air of easy-going, tomorrow-will-do about the place and the men I saw followed suit'. Melrose was introduced 'to no one in particular, just everybody in one go' and, asked why, as a trained w/t operator and senior NCO, he had volunteered for this type of work, had to reply: 'What type of work and who volunteered?' But he was intrigued by the set-up, keen to learn more and, though the conversation 'was of no great interest . . . I did feel I was being assessed'. He had his Morse skills given a 'pretty tough test' but the results 'apparently pleased them'. So they should have, he reflected, 'because I was at that time doing around twenty words a minute'. They seemed 'more than pleased' when he said he knew the civilian Q code system of standard message from his days as a ham operator before the war. Melrose returned to Tenterden with a sealed letter for his commanding officer. He traced him to the local cinema, then looked out the manager.

> I told him I had to see my CO who was in the first house and it was urgent. 'I'm sure you can sort something out with my projectionist,' was his reply and I went up to the projection room where we made a slide to superimpose on the film. 'Will Col so-and-so please go to the manager's office ASAP'. This was displayed until a movement was seen and the CO appeared . . . livid! He was beside himself when the manager

pointed me out as the culprit . . . Before he could muster up
enough invective . . . [I] presented him with the buff envelope with the red inscription uppermost: 'Immediate action'.

The envelope held orders to equip Melrose at once for overseas service.
When finished, 'the CO had a few words with me saying he had put
me through for this type of work as it required people who were independent and liked to work on their own . . . With that he said, "Best
of luck, sergeant" and shook my hand.' The next morning, Melrose,
alone, left for the Middle East. 'I felt a bit lost; after all, I was leaving
a unit I had been part of for about four years.' Weeks later, in Cairo,
he reported to Rustem Buildings. 'I gave my particulars to the recep-
tionist who informed me there was a bit of a panic on at the moment
but if I went upstairs someone would see to me.' Upstairs 'no one paid
the slightest attention . . . I eventually got talking to a civvy who said,
"So you're Sergeant Melrose, pleased to meet you".'[41]

One man who never learnt how he came to SOE's notice was Paul
Gray, a regular soldier in his early twenties who had joined the Royal
Artillery underage before the war. He had since joined the commandos
and fought in North Africa. When he was summoned one day from the
desert not even his CO knew what was afoot. The mystery deepened
when Gray was told to look out at Cairo railway station for an officer
wearing a particular colour of beret, was duly greeted by the officer
with some grandeur – 'Gunner Gray? I've a car here for you' – and had
his kit carried by the officer's batman. Gray was interviewed, volunteered and was accepted. After several months in Turkey, hiding weapons
for use in the event of a German invasion, he returned to Egypt and
was assigned to Balkan operations as a paramilitary specialist.[42]

Almost all SOE personnel destined for the Balkans had to receive
special training to allow them to be sent safely into the field and operate
effectively once they were there. A few received this at schools in Britain,
like Ringway, Arisaig and Beaulieu, where most agents destined for
places like France and Norway were trained. The majority of men bound
for the Balkans, however, attended courses in the Middle East and
Mediterranean. To learn to parachute, for instance, most went to Palestine
and the busy school at Ramat David, not far from Nazareth. Other
parachute schools existed at different times at Kabrit, on the Red Sea,
Algiers and Brindisi, but the basics, wherever they were taught, remained
much the same. Every day started with intensive PT to make the students

supple; every course began with simulations, groundwork and theory. Then came the jumps. Ordinarily, five or six had to be made, including one at night, beginning at 1,000 feet and working down to 500. Parachuting was still an evolving art, accidents did happen and many students found the course unnerving and painful. Jumping at Ramat David, Paul Gray's static line caught around his thigh and held him fast, for a moment, to the outside of the aircraft. Seconds later he found himself free, with his parachute open, floating to the ground, but he had come close to losing a leg and was soon in a Bethlehem hospital.

Paramilitary skills were taught mostly at another school in Palestine, this one on the slopes of Mount Carmel, overlooking Haifa. Here again the training was tiring and tough. Each day began with PT at dawn before students were put to work handling, stripping and firing various Allied and Axis weapons, studying enemy battle orders and insignia, learning field craft and intelligence-gathering or brushing up their map-reading. Instruction was given in military demolition and industrial sabotage, with students introduced to a range of explosives, fuses and detonators and taught to blow anything from roads and bridges to pylons and power stations. Lock-picking, telephone-tapping and safe-blowing were all taught; so were unarmed combat and silent killing. At Haifa station students learnt to drive trains. At Athlit, on the coast, they paddled around in canoes and trained with limpet mines. Other courses were available in the Middle East for those with orders or the time and desire to go on them. Skiing and climbing were taught at a mountain warfare school in Lebanon, where a mule management course was also run. Hugh Munro looked back on the last one as 'just about the most useful course of the lot'.[43]

As departure dates neared, specialist equipment and weapons were issued. Compasses, gold coins and silk escape maps were sewn into clothes for emergency use. Concealment training could also include a lesson in Cairo from Jasper Maskelyne, a well-known music-hall conjuror. At one point, Jack Dumoulin would recall, Maskelyne 'would hide all sorts of items on his person' and, after challenging his students to search him, 'produce about twenty things we'd failed to find'.[44]

With personal arms, some choice was allowed. Often men were led to the armoury and told to pick what they wanted. 'It was like Christmas Day,' one officer recalled. 'We were shown this storeroom which had every sort of armament you could think of: German pistols, Japanese fighting knives, every sort of weapon. And I thought, "I'll have one of those, one of those, one of those".'[45] In the end he took a Marlin-Hyde

M2, an American weapon of very limited make; others chose Schmeissers, Thompsons and Welguns, the latter an SOE-developed sub-machine-gun. 'After careful consideration I chose a Smith & Wesson revolver and a dagger,' Bob Melrose remembered. 'I was given a box of 50 rounds of .38 ammo for the revolver with the instruction that this would be all I would get and advised to obtain an enemy weapon and ammo locally.'[46] Other equipment, like w/t sets, was standard. The B2 was the set used most commonly in the Balkans and consisted of a transmitter, receiver and power pack plus headphones, Morse keypad and spares, all packed together in a suitcase. When full it weighed nearly thirty pounds.

Standard, too, was the wearing of uniform. Most missions earmarked for Balkan countries were to live lives very different from those of SOE agents in France, Denmark or the Netherlands, for example, where the need to blend in with the local population made civilian clothing essential. Once in the Balkans men might add native flourishes, from cloaks and cummerbunds to fez-type hats and curly-ended slippers, while local clothes were sometimes necessary to avoid detection in enemy-held towns. But in the mountains battledress and boots formed the basis of most outfits and not only for reasons of prestige: regulation kit was functional and tough.

Once assigned a destination, missions were briefed. If time allowed, officers received crash courses in the relevant language. It was then that most of those bound for Albania came into contact with Margaret Hasluck. Few were then even half her age and those who survived the war would recall her with fondness, albeit mixed with a certain benevolent amusement. They came to know her as 'Fanny' after the much younger women, known by the initials of the First Aid Nursing Yeomanry, who worked at SOE headquarters. Some of the FANYs themselves found Hasluck rather intimidating. Even Hugh Munro, a fellow Scot who 'got on famously with her' in the office while he waited to leave for Albania, also 'got one hell of a bollocking off her once for barging into her room without knocking'.[47]

But if Margaret Hasluck lacked warmth, the interest she took in her officers and the fuss she made of them seems clear. One wrote later of 'a grey, birdlike woman who made up in energy and determination what she lacked in patience . . . Because of her love for Albania she regarded us B.L.O.s with special affection; we were "her boys", and when we were in the field we would often receive signals from her, directing our attention to some beauty spot nearby where we could enjoy a picnic.'[48] Another recalled Hasluck sending him and his mission out of the room while she held back Jack Dumoulin, the medical officer. When they walked in again she was saying earnestly, 'You must keep them away from the women. Syphilis, you know.'[49]

Although missions were assembled and sent off with such haste that there was never enough time for Hasluck to prepare them very much, her efforts at teaching officers the Albanian language could have been more efficient. One found Hasluck 'enchanting' and 'a great authority on the ancient laws and language of the Albanians' but she 'gave us little instruction in the kinds of questions we were most likely to need – questions such as: How deep is the river? Can the mules get across? Where are the enemy? How many of them are there?'[50] In fact, in 1944, Hasluck did publish a military phrasebook containing a useful range of translated phrases, from 'Do you speak English?' and 'Do you like the English?' to 'You have charged me too much', 'Are there bugs in the house?' and 'Does the dog bite?'[51] But when sitting before her in Cairo in the hour-long language lessons they just had time to attend, her bemused pupils found themselves translating texts from a small *Albanian–English Reader* that Hasluck had had published in 1932. The texts consisted entirely of nursery rhymes and folk tales she had collected from adults and children in Elbasan. For Hasluck, as she argued in the *Reader*, folk-tales justified their selection as texts because 'folk-tales are accepted as one of the best mediums for learning to speak a language with a scanty literature'.[52] For one young officer 'it was a bit like having Enid Blyton in charge'.[53]

There was one tale she had officers learn by heart. 'Kocamici' told of an elderly, childless couple who adopted a mouse as their son, called him Kocamici, then found one day he had fallen into a pot on the stove. Several lines of the story are then repeated:

> *Kocamici ra në vorbet,*
> *Plaka shkuli flokët,*
> *Plaku shkuli mjrekrën*

Which mean:

> Kocamici fell in the pot,
> The old woman tore out her hair,
> The old man tore out his beard.[54]

The exercise was to have bizarre consequences when, at a later moment of crisis, memories seized on what little of Hasluck's Albanian had managed to sink in. 'Albania was approaching fast,' one officer would remember of his wintry arrival by parachute, which ended 'with a crash into a high bush' and the sound of someone running towards him in the snow. 'A bearded character covered with bandoliers and wearing a goatskin coat came towards me . . . I tried to remember some Albanian but the only thing I could think of was "Kocamici ra në vorbet" – the nursery rhyme Fanny Hasluck had taught us in our one Albanian lesson.'[55] Another defused a heated meeting between rival guerrillas when, just as a revolver was being loosened in its holster, he broke in suddenly to recite the same line.[56]

Despite Hasluck's efforts, most missions were likely to have felt much as one officer wrote, 'that it was into an utterly unknown country that we were about to launch ourselves'.[57] And no mission bound for Albania knew less about where it was going than the first sent out. In fact, a final factor in the decision to dispatch a team to Albania was the enthusiasm of the man in command, twenty-four-year-old Major Neil McLean, for embracing the idea of exploring a country that seemed so undiscovered.

'Billy' McLean was a product of Eton and Sandhurst and had been commissioned into the Royal Scots Greys in 1938. Frustrated by long months of dull service in Palestine, especially after news of his younger brother's death from wounds at Dunkirk, he had volunteered for SOE in 1941. For several months he had fought in Abyssinia against the Italians, leading a force of local irregulars known unofficially as 'McLean's Foot'; a fellow officer remembered him looking 'twice his age, with a great yellow beard . . . the reincarnation in the wet Amhara hills of some Gaelic chieftain'.[58] In late 1942, after a series of staff jobs in the Middle East for SOE and MI9, the escape and evasion specialists, he was finally earmarked for SOE work in the Balkans. 'He was tall, slim, with long, straight hair that he had a habit of sweeping back as it fell over his eyes,' wrote David Smiley, who was to go in as McLean's second-in-command. 'His charming character seemed languid and nonchalant to the point of idleness but underneath this façade he was brave, physically tough and extremely intelligent.'[59]

Two years older, stocky and fair, Smiley, like McLean, was a cavalry officer with a keen appetite for action and had seen earlier service with irregular troops. Commissioned into the Royal Horse Guards in 1936, he had served in the Middle East and North Africa since 1940 and for a time with commandos in Abyssinia. In late 1942, depressed to hear that his regiment was to be posted to the Turkish–Syrian border which sounded too quiet for his tastes, he sought out McLean, who he had met before and knew was working for SOE. Smiley told him he was keen to join. Interviews were arranged. Soon he and McLean were being briefed to drop together into Yugoslavia.

The switch to Albania came, Smiley remembers, when McLean 'worked out a plan, based on sketchy information' and had it approved by the SOE office in Cairo.[60] McLean's very general objectives, noted by him on 29 March, reflected both the Chiefs of Staff's desire for more disorder in the Balkans and the extent to which it was felt he would be starting from scratch:

(a) To transmit regular information on the military and general situation in Albania to Cairo by w/t;

(b) To contact existing local guerrilla organisations and to 'lay on' the disruption of the chrome and Trans-Balkan routes;

(c) To organise an 'area system' with dropping places, and also to recruit mobile guerrilla bands for immediate operations, and later large scale operations;

(d) To work up 'contacts' between Greece, Jugoslavia, and Macedonia, with a view to British liaison in the Balkans;

(e) To arrange a method of getting people out from Albania, and reception committees for further infiltration parties.[61]

Surviving planning papers confirm how little was known of the situation he might find. Though aware of the location of the chrome mines and roads, SOE had still heard the names of just a handful of guerrillas and had only the vaguest idea of where in the country they might be. Brigadier Eddie Myers, the senior SOE officer in Greece, was asked to find out more and had sent one of his officers, Captain John Cook, to the Greek–Albanian border to learn what he could. But the main effort was to be made by McLean and it is clear enough that he was happy to proceed on the basis of such scanty information. Such was his eagerness to get in that he was even prepared to drop blind, to a spot where no friendly contacts were on hand to light fires and receive his party. In the end, Margaret Hasluck managed to persuade him not to parachute in that way into Macedonia, pick his way into eastern Albania and try to contact Muharrem Bajraktar, as he had initially proposed. Instead he would drop into northern Greece, to an SOE mission there, and try to lead his team into southern Albania. Close to the Greek border, other guerrillas, it was rumoured, might be found. Little was known about them but they occupied a region that seemed more accessible.

With the plan approved, McLean expanded his team. A w/t operator was essential for maintaining contact with Cairo, by dispatching reports, receiving messages and calling in supplies, and the man selected was Willie Williamson, a twenty-eight-year-old Scot who had worked before the war in a chemist's in Leith. Called up into the Black Watch and sent out to North Africa, he had come down with dysentery, missed all the fighting his battalion had seen and was stuck in a fly-blown camp when an officer came round looking for volunteers. 'I can offer you a job,' the officer had said. 'I can't tell you what it is.'[62] In Palestine Williamson received full w/t training at the school on Mount Carmel, building on the Morse he had learnt as a sideline to his regular soldiering. Last came parachute training at Kabrit where he completed the requisite jumps despite 'sheer terror' before the second at 800 feet and ripping his tunic and hurting his arm, after catching them in the static line, during the third at 600. 'Handed in jumping kit,' he wrote in his diary after the last. 'Thank God to have finished.'[63] McLean also wanted an Albanian interpreter and this was to be Faik Elmas, Hasluck's Royal Guard lieutenant. And at the last moment he decided to take twenty-three-year-old Gavan Duffy, a Royal Engineers lieutenant experienced in explosives. 'Garry' Duffy came from Leeds, though his forebears were Irish, and had joined SOE locally after service in the desert.

In early April, Smiley, Elmas and Williamson left Cairo for the airfield at Derna, an uncomfortable three-day journey by truck and train with dusty tents and bombed-out buildings at the end of it. At Derna each mission stayed together and Williamson was soon remarking in his diary of the odd experience of messing and sharing his tent with his officers. The airfield was busy. It was tense, too. Missions for Greece and Yugoslavia were backing up and men had little to do but wait for the night a pilot could take them. If there was enough light from the moon and the weather seemed fair, aircraft would fly. Even then, some missions came back. Cloud might have obscured the signal fires on the ground or perhaps the aircraft had malfunctioned or been damaged by flak. 'Get quite a thrill as the Halifaxes fly low over the camp,' Williamson noted on 13 April. 'Suppose it will be my time very soon?' Two days later he added: 'One party have gone five nights and returned. Don't think I could stand the strain.'[64] Next day, when McLean arrived from Cairo with Duffy in tow, the party was complete.

On 17 April, planning to fly that night, all five drew their final kit from the stores. After lunch, as they went to be fitted for parachutes, Elmas declared suddenly that he was not yet ready to go. His reasons remain unclear. According to McLean, Elmas demanded written instructions from Zog; according to Smiley, Elmas wanted to communicate with Albanians in Cairo; the SOE officer who escorted them to the airfield, meanwhile, would report that Elmas had refused 'under provocation' and would have gone 'if he had been more wisely handled'.[65] Whatever that meant and whatever the reason, McLean resolved quickly to leave without him and, to ensure the mission's security, Elmas was put under arrest and locked away. It was not a good start: five were now four and without an interpreter and, that evening, McLean remembered, 'we had a very bad supper in the mess, everyone making rather forced jokes'.[66] Then it was time to go.

As the Halifax thundered through the night, the four men in the fuselage sat mostly in silence. A dim light shone. Smiley read *Horse and Hound*. Williamson remembered reading *Rough Passage*, the pocket novel he had chosen for coding messages.[67] By eleven, nearly four hours into the flight, it was time to put on parachutes. Twenty minutes later one of the crew opened a hole in the floor. 'We sat round the hole with our legs dangling through,' McLean recalled. 'It was all rather unreal and ghostlike. The landscape below us was grey and white and green with the dark shadows thrown up by the clouds from the full moon.' Then, far below, they saw the tiny fires of a dropping ground. 'Suddenly the red light went out and a green light flashed on. I jumped immediately, followed by David, then Williamson and then Duffy.'[68] 'It was a wonderful sensation after the parachute had opened,' Smiley's diary reads. 'First the engine of the Halifax growing fainter and fainter in the distance, then silence; the snow capped mountains on either side; then, on getting near the ground, the noise of the bells on the sheep and goats; then the shouts of the men on the ground; then the bump.'[69]

Smiley came down in a dry riverbed, tearing a leg muscle. The others landed safely. All were soon surrounded by dozens of excited Greek guerrillas. Also waiting for them was John Cook. A good-natured

Yorkshireman, he had been in Greece since going in with Myers in October and was now working with Guy Micklethwait, an SOE friend of McLean's from Abyssinian days. McLean left at once for Micklethwait's headquarters in a nearby mountain monastery, where Smiley, Duffy and Williamson joined him next morning after collecting the stores dropped with them. On 21 April, while Williamson stayed behind to wait for a replacement w/t set, the first having been broken in the drop, McLean, Smiley and Duffy, with Cook, some mules and an escort of Greek guerrillas, left for the Albanian border.

Much of the next week was spent marching through the hills, valleys and villages of northern Greece. 'Often a feeling of unreality came over me,' McLean recalled of these early days.

> Would one wake up and find oneself in Cairo again? Everything was so lovely. The countryside was green, the sun was bright and clear . . .
>
> The fact of being in Europe once again was a thrill. All retreat was cut off and with it the past. The strain of para-chuting was over and finished with. There was only the future to look forward to. In short, one had been parachuted into a different life altogether. One's senses could not adapt them-selves quick enough. One's brain grasped it . . . but a strange feeling of something unreal persisted. Both David and I found this.[70]

Williamson, still in Micklethwait's monastery, also found this new life strange:

> I remember when we were in that monastery, I said very choosily 'Where's the bathroom?' and I was told that you should walk round the outer wall and choose your spot. So I chose a spot and an old lady in black, completely in black, lifted up her skirts and downed her knickers and sat down beside me and blethered twenty to the dozen. And I thought, 'Good Heavens, I've landed in the Middle Ages.'[71]

In one Greek village, so McLean scribbled in a notebook, 'an old boy came up and produced an Xmas card of 1937 from Nick Hammond, who must have been a great success'.[72] Through binoculars the mission also had its first sight of the enemy: an Italian convoy trundling along a mountain road below. On Easter Sunday the British reached Drymades, very close to the frontier, where children gave them presents of red-painted eggs. There they stayed three days before, on 28 April, following the track over the unmanned border. Cook and the escort returned to Greece.

On the last day of April, leaving Duffy to mind the supplies, McLean and Smiley pressed on alone, in the rain, down a remote and fertile valley. A dozen miles in they reached the little village of Nivan. There, on the morning of 1 May, they met Bedri Spahiu, head of a band of Albanian guerrillas.

'EVERYTHING GOING FINE'

ALBANIA is a country little larger than Wales. The Shkumbin, tumbling and winding westwards to the Adriatic, cuts it roughly in half. To the north more rivers spill down from the mountains and a thin strip of coastal plain stretches up to the Yugoslav border. In the very north the terrain is extremely mountainous, with bare, jagged peaks steepling to heights of over 8,000 feet. Gouging its way through these to the sea is the deep and twisting valley of the Drin; beyond are the mountains of Montenegro and the Kosovo plateau. South of the Shkumbin the plain continues and extends a little further inland but the terrain beyond is another mountainous mass, slashed by more rivers, and along most of the coast there is no plain at all and the mountains and hills run into the sea. Main roads curl along a few valley floors, follow the coast and disappear over the border. Scattered about are a dozen or so sizeable towns and ports and hundreds of mountain villages.

McLean had led his mission into the towering southern ranges. Entering that way had certainly proved safer than the route originally proposed. Two nights before the party parachuted into Greece, Major Cliff Morgan, another SOE officer, had dropped to the spot in Macedonia that McLean had first considered. Morgan intended to move north and join Mihailović. Instead he disappeared.[1] But if the switch of destination saved McLean and his men, it also ensured, by chance, that SOE's first contact with Albanian guerrillas was made with a communist-backed movement.

That contact was slow to develop. Spahiu, the man they met in Nivan, was suspicious of the British and told them to return to Greece while he sent for guidance from his superiors. So McLean and Smiley turned round, picked up Duffy and Williamson, the latter having caught up with the new w/t set, and wound their way back to Drymades. For three weeks McLean heard nothing but his reports to Cairo were upbeat, for the meeting in Nivan confirmed that some sort of resistance actually existed. 'Anti-Fascist elements' were apparently united under a central command with branches in 'all main towns', while Spahiu himself claimed to control 'six regular bands minimum 40 men each'.[2] McLean also asked Cairo for stores and, to allow the mission's officers to operate more independently, a second w/t operator. At the end of May, Halifaxes roared low over Poliçan, not far from Drymades, and the mission received its first drops of arms and ammunition. A few days later, Corporal Bell of the Royal Signals was dropped into Greece with a w/t set and orders to push north and join McLean.[3] On 1 June, having at last received word that he could move into the country, McLean set off on a fifty-mile march, round mountains, along valleys, deep into Albania. Eight days later a halt was called in Leshnja, an isolated village on wooded slopes roughly in the centre of Albania's southern half. Smiley, whom McLean, while at Drymades, had sent back into southern Albania to seek out fresh contacts and generally have a bit of a look round, joined him there next day. His own various adventures had included watching a lively and effective guerrilla attack on Leskovik, an Italian-garrisoned border town, and being confined for a time as a suspected Greek spy. Like McLean he was getting by, just about, in French and through local interpreters.

At Leshnja more sorties were received, more reports were keyed back to Cairo and closer contact was established with local guerrillas. To judge from the captured tunics, webbing and boots some wore and the captured weapons some carried, they were clearly an irritation to both the occupying Italians and the odd passing German. It was a picture reinforced by sights and stories of enemy reprisals, including, in early July, the fate of Borova, a village in south-east Albania close to the border with Greece. Smiley, marching through nearby hills at the time, had seen smoke in that direction. Within days the British were aware that something terrible had happened. In time the full story came out. Guerrillas had ambushed a convoy not far away, on the main road to Greece, and a German unit armed with flame-throwers had responded, crossing from Greece to incinerate and machine-gun more than a hundred men, women and children and burn the village to the ground. Borova would be seen as Albania's Lidice; today the ruins have gone but the graves are there, headstones different-sized to depict different ages and arranged in little circles according to each family.

The Albanian 'Partisans', as SOE began to term them, also told the British about a conference held in the wooded hills of Peza, outside Tirana, in 1942, where their organisation had been set up. Although communists had called the meeting, all 'patriots' had been invited and the decision taken to form a national liberation movement, the Levicija Nacional Çlirimtarë, or LNC, open to all without discrimination to class, politics, religion or region. The movement's stated aim was to wage a united war against the invaders and all traitors with the ultimate goal of seeing a free, democratic and independent Albania. 'LNC 80 rpt 80 per cent non communist,' McLean reported. 'But communists most active.'[4]

The British learnt, too, of a second organisation, the republican Balli Kombëtar, literally 'national front', or BK, Ballists, Balkom or Balli as SOE also came to call it. It professed to be anti-Italian but stood principally for safeguarding what it saw as Albania's true borders and pre-war social, economic and political structure. Its supporters and sympathisers were many and mixed, from landowners and merchants to ageing patriots and young professionals. Most were united largely by their extreme suspicion of the Partisans' communist element and aims. Very few were doing any fighting, as the Partisans never ceased to tell the British. Balli Kombëtar policy, McLean told Cairo, was 'not fight Italians now. Let Allies win war. Conserve strength.'[5]

The Partisans' own passionate anti-fascism was brought home to McLean when, in July, with Corporal Bell, who had caught up from Greece, he marched to Labinot, a sprawling village hidden among mountains just north of the Shkumbin where the LNC had called another conference. It was a striking spot. 'There were green woods and green grass, fruit trees and orchards,' McLean recorded. 'There was an abundance of apples, pears, plums, cherries, mulberries, grapes, quinces and figs.' A 'great crowd' had also assembled. 'All were intensely inquisitive at our arrival and rather excited. There were flags and a linen banner saying "You are welcome. Long Live the Great Allies".'[6]

Most members of the LNC's Council were present. One, a big man, tall and intelligent, with a plump, soft face, was Enver Hoxha, destined to become the country's dictator. Then thirty-five, he was well educated, came from Muslim stock in the south and had lived for several years in France from where he had returned, in 1936, a convinced communist.

For a time he had taught at the *lycée* at Korça until his politics compelled the Italians, in 1939, to fire him. Then he went to Tirana where he ran a tobacco shop frequented by left-wing radicals until further pressure forced him underground. In 1941 he had been appointed secretary of the country's communist party; since then, guided by skilled Yugoslav emissaries and with Hoxha at its head, the party had taken the leading role in organising resistance and seen its power and support grow considerably. Many of the British with whom he would deal found Hoxha amiable, even amusing. They could also find him exasperating. 'An actor, he plays his part extremely well and has enough presence to make an impression on the people who see or meet him,' one officer wrote of him. 'He is ambitious, very able and hard working, taking a lot on his own hands, but is apt to get excited and to lose his perspective. He can be gracious and charming or extremely obstinate when it suits his purpose.'[7]

Also at Labinot were three men with whom the British had worked before. One was Haxhi Lleshi, who, in 1940, had tried to drum up support for the British among Albanians in Macedonia. The other two had gone with Gani Kryeziu and Oakley-Hill into the north in 1941. One of these was Mustafa Gjinishi, now on the LNC Council, who struck McLean as 'a very energetic and capable political agitator, speaking good English and easy to work with'.[8] The other was Abas Kupi, who, McLean noted, was at first 'very gloomy and never uttered a word. Then he asked the inevitable question – "Are you here on a short visit and when will you return to Greece or are you going to stay?"' His mood brightened when news reached the conference that the Allies had landed in Sicily: Kupi 'beat his leg and let out a yell of excitement and called for raki.[9] Aside from Kupi, only two other members of the Council were not communist: Baba Faja, a big, bearded, Bektashi priest, and Myslim Peza, an old-school brigand and outlaw. Both men had local influence and were 'middle-aged, rather old-fashioned, good livers, very heavy drinkers and possessed of considerable personal charm and courage,' McLean reported. 'They are at the same time comparatively uneducated, lethargic and somewhat incompetent.'[10]

At Labinot McLean explained his mission. It was purely military, he said. He was there to do what he could to help the Albanians against the common enemy and to coordinate their efforts with those of the Allies. Aid would be given to anyone, regardless of politics, provided he was committed to fighting. In response the Council assured McLean that its members were 'true patriots' fighting for a 'free independent popular Albania' and it strongly denied the 'enemy assertion' that the LNC was 'manipulated by Communists in their own interests'.[11] The Council also agreed to McLean's suggestion that its strength, numbered then at three thousand Partisans but split and widely scattered into many small çetas, the local term for bands of a few dozen men, should be reorganised and a three-unit 'striking force' formed.[12] The Council agreed, too, that McLean could begin training elements at his mission's new headquarters in Shtylla, a little village perched at the top of a valley running down towards Korça.

By August the British were well settled at Shtylla, having moved into an old mud-and-brick-built mosque, and received more drops of supplies and also reinforcements, in the shape of two new missions. Each was led by an RAF officer and the first to arrive was Squadron Leader Arthur 'Andy' Hands who dropped at Shtylla on the night of 13–14 July. Born and schooled in Nuneaton, Hands was thirty-two and had been in the RAF for thirteen years, eight of them as a nursing orderly; commissioned in 1941, he had volunteered for SOE in April 1943 after a series of Middle East staff posts. The other RAF officer was Tony Neel, who was dropped three nights later. McLean recalled 'a tall, thin, quiet man with a scholarly, detached and lackadaisical manner but full of shy charm'. Hands he remembered as 'a short, active and aggressive little fellow' of 'great initiative and courage'.[13] Between them the new officers brought six British NCOs. Three, Sergeant Cooper and Corporals Roberts and Smith, were w/t operators. The others were paramilitary specialists: Sergeant Brandrick and a pair of ex-commandos, Corporals Jenkins and Jones, who, apparently, both lived on the same street in Liverpool.

The arrival of these men fitted in with McLean's plans to open up the country and increase SOE's reach. Hands and Neel were Catholic and Cairo had thought that might prove helpful when dealing with tribes in the north. McLean did send them north, though not, at first, to the Catholic region: Hands, with Smith and Brandrick, left for the hilly Mokra region in eastern Albania to work with Haxhi Lleshi's Partisans, while Neel, taking Cooper and Jones, moved off to join Abas Kupi north of Tirana. Before they left him, however, Hands and Neel had drawn the same conclusion as McLean: that the potential for encouraging resistance in Albania seemed considerable. Cairo was told of their impression 'that situation here 1. More difficult than you realise.

2. But prospects and scale greater'.[14] In another message McLean detailed some of his 'difficulties'. One was that the LNC Council was not in full military control of all its *çetas*. Another was that the Italians had started a 'whispering campaign' that the British were '1. Greeks. 2. If too blond for Greeks then Jugoslavs'. But by August the 'worst period' was over. The LNC Council was in 'full rpt full co-operation with us'. Training was proving a 'tremendous success'. The mission was 'in very good form and everything going fine'.[15]

The difficulties faced by SOE missions in the field did not stop at failing to get the most out of the LNC or the Balli Kombëtar or having to cope with being thought Greek. As McLean and his men were beginning to learn, life in Albania was hard, tiring and dangerous, and took some getting used to.

The terrain alone was formidable. Keeping to the mountains, as most missions had to do, ensured that the pace with which the British moved about and explored the country was painfully slow. Sometimes horses or mules could be ridden; often enough it was all done on foot. McLean's account of his return from Labinot, scribbled in a notebook, records a typical summer journey, enjoyable for the arresting scenery but many days long:

> July 14 . . .
> We left Labinot at about seven o'clock in the evening and travelled all night . . .

> July 15 . . .
> [A]fter a march of about eleven hours . . . stopped at a house at the bottom of a long narrow valley. Here we rested and ate a breakfast of maize and fresh milk which refreshed and restored us . . . The country around was very pleasant, green grass and pastureland with many sheep grazing . . .

> July 16 . . .
> [W]alked for three hours to Sopil where we had lunch . . . [S]tarted again travelling for another five and a half hours until we reached Porocin where we stayed the night . . . [A] very pleasant and talkative evening with plenty of raki and meze, followed by an excellent meal. We had long and incon-

clusive debates with an old Sophist priest into the early hours of the morning. It was anyway very hot and so difficult to sleep.

July 17 . . .
We left Porocin at 9am in the morning escorted by a strong Balli ceta and marched until 12.30pm when it became very hot as the sun was at full strength. Then we rested until about 4.30pm. We were travelling through the great forests of Shpati with their beautiful beech trees. The Balli escort kept firing at every conceivable target to show off their marksmanship. An old peasant woman we met on the track . . . described in vivid and colourful miming terms some ancient battle between Albanian clans – or perhaps, a skirmish with Ottoman Turks. But no one knew any more or cared which it was . . .

We finally stopped (well after dark) at a very poor and dirty peasant house in the village of Keshte where we spent the night in some discomfort.[16]

In the most treacherous, precipitous parts, even when paths and goat tracks were used a journey of a mile could take hours as the route twisted and rose and fell, while stumbling mules, weighed down with kit, did occasionally go over the edge. Once, on Mount Nemerçka, between Korça and Gjirokastra, David Smiley's horse slipped and fell, 'but by the grace of God I had my feet out of the stirrups and slid off just in time. The horse fell down a clear drop of over 100 feet.'[17] Winter, when temperatures plummeted and snow was metres deep, could make conditions far worse. Rivers, too, could be major obstacles, even when not swollen with snowmelt. Bridges were often guarded and wading or finding a raft was not always possible. All of this also impeded the ability of the British to communicate with each other. Missions could not send w/t messages between themselves so letters full of news had to be sent by hand, but the couriers, of course, were often dependent on the same long chain of tracks and paths to get them through.

Although mountains and mountainous weather could also prove a barrier between a mission's w/t set and the SOE home station, the sets themselves were excellent. Those not captured, lost down a mountain or wrecked in other ways were well used. Bell, McLean's second w/t operator, estimated later that over a seven-month period he had worked his set an average of three hours a day; like other operators he found it reliable, easy to move around and pretty durable despite some 'hard knocks'.[18] The equipment that went with it was another matter. Batteries were heavy and needed recharging. This could be done in towns but it was risky sending them, particularly since some were stamped 'British-made'. A few missions were issued with petrol chargers but these could be heavy, bulky and difficult to move: a set complete with chargers usually required three mules. Hand chargers were smaller but noisy and hard work. Aerials were light but necessarily long: at least one mission had to run theirs up the local minaret.

Operators worked to a schedule, or 'sked' as it was called, sending and receiving during hours agreed with headquarters. If they missed one window they had to wait for the next. Messages had to be short and concise, so pronouns were kept to a minimum and standard abbreviations used, like rpt for repeat, pzns for partisans, nats for nationalists, Itis for Italians and Huns for Germans. Even then, when receiving, 'you had to be on your toes', Willie Williamson remembered, 'because by and large it was girls who were transmitting from Cairo and, by Jove, they were good. Oh, the speed they sent out.' Decoding could be done at greater leisure. 'There would be maybe half a dozen messages come in and lots of us sat round the table to decode them . . . Decoding was simple.'[19]

Messages could be marked as urgent but the time taken waiting for a sked and encoding, sending, receiving and decoding meant that information was not passed instantly. Inevitably that meant it might be out of date before it reached its intended recipient. At one level, this could mean, for example, that outside observers in Cairo or London who wished to be kept informed might receive a days-old picture of events that bore no relation to what was happening at that moment. Operationally it could mean that men might stand around all night on a freezing dropping ground, in seemingly perfect conditions, wholly unaware, since it was impossible for them to be informed in time, that poor flying weather or some technical hitch meant no drop was on its way. Similarly, when it was obvious on the ground that the cloud was so thick that the aircraft would never see the fires, missions would find it impossible to warn headquarters and prevent a wasted trip.

Dropping grounds themselves had to be chosen with care and their location often dictated where a mission could be based. Deep in the mountains, where there was less risk of sudden ground attack, was best. Even then there were dangers. Night-time fires left tell-tale burns that enemy spotter planes might see during the day. One extraordinary incident occurred at Shtylla, the night after Tony Neel arrived, when, as another Halifax came in to drop stores, an Italian aircraft appeared and dropped bombs. 'I luckily heard it coming and recognised the engine as that of a Caproni and not one of ours,' David Smiley wrote in his diary.

> I shouted to the partisans on the dropping ground to clear off and take cover which they did. Unfortunately I forgot Garry, who was in the middle of the DZ flashing the recognition letter to the Iti bomber, did not speak French. It made a mess of the dropping ground, but luckily we had no casualties. They dropped 12 fifty kilo bombs in all, very accurately, and blew out over half of the signal fires. I was lying flat on my face in a riverbed which was very wet. Sgt Cooper – one of the new operators – was with me and was very scared. I don't blame him as the nearest bomb was only 20 yards from us and they all sounded as if they were coming straight at us . . . It was really a fantastic sight as the Halifax and the Caproni were taking alternate runs dropping supplies and bombs but they never appeared to see each other.[20]

Sometimes parachutes failed to open and containers thudded or exploded into the earth destroying everything inside: Smiley found that 10 per cent of a drop could be lost that way. A poor drop in the wrong place or from too great a height could mean supplies spread for miles, a long search the next day and much material gone for good. 'As is known, the Albanian is a "jackdaw," and if packages arrived out of guarded areas, parachute and package might completely disappear,' one SOE officer reported.[21] Another advised that containers holding the sovereigns that financed each mission should be marked with a code word, and that changed monthly 'as even the most primitive inhabitants of the Balkans recognise the meaning of the word gold in an amazingly large number of languages'.[22]

Missions relied heavily on this link with the outside world. Until the end of 1943, when SOE opened a precarious sea link to a hidden cove below the Llogora Pass, it was the only way of getting arms,

ammunition and explosives to where they were needed. Nor were
warlike stores and gold the only supplies dispatched. 'Free drops',
heavy bales of boots and battledress pushed out without a parachute,
could be as common as containers of Stens, Brens and grenades, if
more alarming for the men receiving them as they whistled down in
the dark. Sometimes packed in the containers were books, newspapers and letters from home, all of them always welcome. 'Have you
quite forgotten us?' read one mission's pained signal that winter. 'For
God's sake send at least mail . . . Conditions here enough strain
without this addition.'[23] Food, too, was dropped or shipped across,
from rice, porridge, bully beef and tea to American K rations, chocolate and Scotch. In winter, when even local staples like maize bread
could be difficult to find, such supplies could be lifesaving.

For the most part missions had to make the best of their surroundings. In the south this meant sharing the outlaw life of the Partisans.
Further north it meant relying more on traditional hospitality. In both
cases conditions could be far removed from what most British soldiers
had known before. The poverty encountered could be extreme: McLean
was to hear that autumn of 'peasants digging up dead Itis' for clothes.[24]
All missions, seeking shelter in caves and homes and sheepfolds, found
themselves ridden with lice. Inevitably poor diet and hygiene affected
health: boils, infections and stomach trouble were common complaints.

Sometimes in the villages the British found themselves treated to acts
of great kindness and time-honoured custom. Meals could be especially
memorable: shoes were removed, weapons put aside and men sat together
on the floor; coffee was served; a roasted sheep or goat was shared.
Usually there was plenty of raki, the powerful local spirit. 'Raki? Oh
my God. It was ten times worse than whisky,' Willie Williamson recalled.

> I remember the first time I had that, and knocked it back.
> Oh my goodness grief. It was fierce . . . I never remember
> getting anything else and they all had their stills up in their
> villages . . . And you see you had to drink it because the host
> was being very generous by giving you a cup.[25]

Hospitality only went so far. Rent had to be paid for houses and huts
taken as quarters, headquarters, stables and stores. All missions spent
money on guides, servants, porters and guards. Mules and horses had
to be fed and shoed; sometimes they were bought, though hiring was

preferable. 'The idea that mules might be sold to Albanians when a mission is leaving an area is founded on a grave misconception of the Albanian character and commercial instincts,' one SOE officer commented later. 'No one, except perhaps an Englishman, would buy a mule which he knows will in any case be left behind free of charge.'[26] All missions soon grew weary of the haggling and price-hiking as locals tried to chisel as much cash as they could. Williamson wrote in his diary how one 'complete rogue' at Shtylla 'demanded that we pay for the field used as a dropping ground saying our fires had burnt the grass'.[27]

The gold the British carried and were known to carry was a two-edged sword. Elsewhere in the Balkans some were murdered for it; in Albania one or two may have come close: at least three officers were robbed while they slept and all thought the outcome would have been worse had they woken as their pockets were being rifled. Even spending the gold could be difficult. 'Sometimes they wouldn't accept the sovereigns because the sovereigns were of no use to them,' Williamson remembered. Once, desperate to find fodder for two starving mules, he approached an Albanian for two sacks of hay. 'I went up to 10, 20 sovereigns but his answer was that hay could feed his mule but the sovereigns couldn't buy him anything. I ended up by shooting the mules.'[28] At Shtylla, so his diary records, 'we started buying food with parachutes and later when our chutes were finished the people would not accept cash'.[29] Gold could be exchanged for local currency: the napoleon, the franc and the lek. One paper napoleon, called after the French gold coins in circulation that bore Napoleon's head, was equal to twenty francs or 100 lek. In the autumn of 1943 one SOE-issued gold sovereign was equal to about twenty paper napoleons. Depending on a mission's location, that could buy about twenty kilos of meat, six of sugar or six of butter, while four sovereigns bought a mule. As the war progressed, prices rose. Twelve months later one SOE sovereign was found to be worth thirty napoleons and would buy thirty kilos of meat or the same of sugar or fifteen of butter, while a mule cost ten or more sovereigns.

How to avoid paying extortionate prices or being robbed in other ways were problems never fully overcome. Another was the Albanian language. Locally recruited interpreters, as one mission put it, were 'essential' but 'invariably a bloody nuisance. They could not be trusted, they knew we could not get on without them, and therefore demanded colossal pay and privileges.' Consequently it was 'much better to do without', but that was rarely possible.[30] Most of the British found the language impenetrable and very few managed to speak much of it. Occasionally knowledge of other languages offered a way round. Many educated Albanians, including Enver Hoxha, spoke French, which allowed some officers to speak to them direct.

Even when the British found a means of communication, the serious difficulties were often just beginning. 'The Albanians are very suspicious of the motives of all foreigners, even when they know them well,' observed one officer after a year in the field, and the insularity of the locals, he thought, was responsible for that:

> The average Albanian has never travelled outside his small country. It is, therefore, far more difficult for him to understand the British outlook than for us to adapt ourselves to see his. To spend hours trying to make an Albanian see the British point of view is a waste of time; the only possible method is to persuade him that some project desired by you is desirable from his point of view as well.

Still, he continued, 'to get anything done in Albania, one has to be prepared to apparently waste much time, whether it is in making a journey or an operation. Time is of less importance to an Albanian than to us.' In summary, 'no better recommendation can be made than that which was made to me before going into the field, which sounds easy enough to follow, but is in fact extraordinarily difficult always to have uppermost in one's mind: "Remember that Albanians are always Albanians and *NOT* Englishmen"'.[31]

Working with the communist-led Partisans could be especially awkward. 'All Albanians are extremely touchy and on the look-out for apparent slights, as they feel that they and their country are of little account to us as being so small,' the same officer noted. In the case of the Partisans this was worse, for 'they are taught to believe that as representatives of a capitalistic state we must automatically be personally antagonistic to them as the supporters of a revolution'.[32] Another officer, after eight months in Albania, advised 'prospective BLOs':

> It must always be borne in mind that the Partisan is an undisciplined volunteer; he is in fact an individual and he resents

strongly any form of direct order. On the other hand, it is possible to give him an order, using an indirect method, the best way being to 'take him into one's confidence'.

Money must NEVER, on any account, be offered to a Partisan in repayment for services rendered. He will regard it as an insult. If you wish to reward a Partisan write a report to his commandant. Never on any account threaten or strike a Partisan – the code is sudden death to the offender, regardless of nationality or rank . . .

Join in any singing or dancing etc but if there are any Partisan girls present for goodness' sake don't be a Groppi Gallant; the Partisans do not like it. The penalty inflicted on Partisan girls for mispropriety is death.

Never make insulting remarks about the size or importance of Albania. This might seem an obvious remark, but I have actually known cases.[33]

Certainly the men whom SOE sent out were soldiers first and not trained diplomats. Some took it all in their stride. Others could not always hide their annoyance or despair at what they saw as the Albanians' failings. This could be unfortunate. 'An Albanian will tolerate what he may consider highly curious conduct from a foreigner as long as he considers it to be a national characteristic, but not if he considers it due to a personal whim,' one officer warned. 'Loss of temper at delay, or for that matter at anything else, is merely considered as a sign of weakness.'[34]

Nor did the British always cope easily with the strain of trying to survive in these conditions. Separated once from the rest of McLean's mission, Willie Williamson found himself relying on a local guide to lead him, alone, through the mountains. 'Hour after hour we walked and walked during the night, and I distrusted him so far that one time I took out my revolver and pointed it at his back. Thank God I didn't kill him because he was in fact leading me to the group, but I distrusted him so far and I was frightened.'[35] On another occasion, one night in the mosque at Shtylla, David Smiley awoke to the sound of 'odd noises' and the sight of two men fighting. 'I quickly pulled my .45 from my pillow and cocked it, but could not see well enough to fire at anyone so luckily did not,' he wrote in his diary. 'It turned out that Williamson was going out to relieve himself and accidentally stepped on Bill. Bill was having a nightmare at the time and thought we were being murdered in our sleep by [an] Iti deserter, so he leapt up and seized the wretched Williamson by the throat and half strangled him. Williamson was yelling, Bill was making very queer animal-like noises, and I was longing to shoot at somebody. I suppose it is really all the result of a high mental strain. I myself quite often have nightmares.'[36]

Much of this might have been tolerable had more Albanians proved willing and able to resist. Most did not. Many seemed happier to deceive, rob and threaten the missions than help them, and the bitterness this bred among the British could be extreme. One officer, dependent on the most isolated northern villages, confided in his diary:

> How pleased I shall be to return to civilisation again. To be able to have a hot bath and wash whenever I want to, to be among people one can trust, to sit on chairs instead of on the floor, to eat food that is properly cooked and properly served and not to be surrounded by dirt, filth and bad manners . . . Two months in this country are equal to at least two years of normal service overseas.
>
> It is not as if one was doing anything useful here or could do. There is so little charity among these people that they cannot believe anyone would come all this way just to help them and because they cannot at once find any other motive for our presence they are all the more suspicious of us. Lacking any sort of trust in each other they are incapable of fighting as each suspects the others will leave him in the lurch as soon as the battle starts. They are boastful and vain with nothing to be boastful or vain about. They have no courage, no determination, no consistency and no sense of honour. They are like . . . children and giggl[e] . . . and squabble like them. They only laugh at other people's misfortunes, and they'd die of laughter if one of us fell over a cliff. It is a great pity that a beautiful country like this is not peopled by a more enlightened race.[37]

Of those Albanians who did attack the Axis, few did so simply to help the Allies. Killing Italians and Germans, many came to recognise, might also elicit levels of popular support and Allied weapons and recognition to use in other struggles. Caught between rival guerrillas and parties vying bloodily for post-war power, SOE was to find its job far more complex than it had expected.

Despite these problems and obstacles, the summer of 1943 saw progress continue and McLean and his men in positive mood. More supplies were requested and received: by September more than twenty tons of weapons, ammunition, grenades, mines, explosives, uniforms and other stores had been parachuted in, almost all of it being passed to the Partisans. To meet McLean's request for more men to explore the country, four more missions were also dropped.

'Our briefing in Cairo had been, as its name implies, brief and we went in knowing very few facts,' recalled one of the new officers, Major George Seymour. 'We were told shortly that our task was to organise the local populations for purposes of sabotage, subversion and guerrilla operations against the Axis occupying troops. The population was to be armed and organised irrespective of political or religious creed.'[38] McLean did his best to enlighten them on local conditions and assigned them each an area.

Grandson of the 6th Marquess of Hertford, Seymour was thirty-one, tall, thin and good-humoured, had been in the army for ten years and sported a wide handlebar moustache. 'His thirst for speed and hazard was the main influence in most of his activities and led him away from the orthodox,' his regiment wrote of him later.[39] Badly wounded in a North African minefield in 1942, he had joined SOE in June 1943 from an instructor's post at the mountain warfare school in Lebanon. He would now work with Myslim Peza, active in the Peza hills, south of Tirana, where the LNC had been founded. Taking his w/t operator, Bombardier Hill, and paramilitary expert, Corporal Jim Smith, a former RAF air gunner, Seymour was soon on his way.

Another new officer was forty-five-year-old Major Bill Tilman, who, with his w/t operator, Corporal Gerry Dawson, a cheerful Scot from Falkirk, and paramilitary expert, Sergeant Butterworth, once of the SAS, was sent by McLean to work with Partisans in the south. Short and stocky, Tilman was tough, private, quiet and shy and the oldest man dropped into Albania. 'We held him in complete awe,' one SOE staff officer recalled.[40] During the First World War he had won two Military Crosses while still in his teens and been wounded three times, twice severely; but it was his reputation as one of the century's most outstanding mountaineers that impressed most. In 1936 he had made the first ascent of the Himalayan peak of Nanda Devi, the highest mountain then scaled. As expedition leader of the 1938 British attempt on Everest, he had climbed without oxygen to over 27,000 feet. Rejoining the Royal Artillery in 1939, he had seen service since in France, the Middle East and the Western Desert before volunteering for SOE in June 1943. Later, a British airman downed in Albania was to tell his mother how he had heard 'everywhere' of Tilman. 'He was the only man who could outwalk the Albanian mountain men, and in the coldest winter on the highest hills, he always bathed outside in a spring. Apparently his reputation is simply terrific.'[41] Locals in Sheper, where Tilman was based, still remember the bathing.

The other officers were Major Peter Kemp and Major Julius Faure-Field. Tall, slim and fair, Kemp was another adventurer. In 1936, aged twenty-one, he had come down from Cambridge to read for the Bar but instead left for Spain to join Franco's cavalry. Later he claimed that while his conservatism had dictated his choice of sides, it was really the promise of danger and excitement that impelled him to join the conflict. Still, he was a convinced anticommunist and became a fine soldier. Transferring to the elite Spanish Foreign Legion in which he served as an officer, a rare distinction for a non-Spaniard, he was four times decorated and four times wounded, once by a mortar bomb that almost killed him. An early MI(R) recruit, Kemp had served continuously in SOE and taken part in night raids in 1942 on the Channel Islands and French coast.

Faure-Field, known in SOE as Jerry Field, was thirty-five, slim, square-jawed and fit, once a member of a team that broke the army record for the 110 yards relay. A regular officer in the Cheshire Regiment, he had spent the last two years as an officer-training instructor, turning down the command of a school to join SOE. McLean now sent him off to the coast, to watch the main coastal road and explore the possibility of bringing in stores by sea. With him went his paramilitary specialist, Corporal Billy Eden, a hardened and self-reliant Londoner, and his w/t operator, Corporal Austin DeAth, a quiet young man from Croydon. DeAth and his brother, both of the Royal West Kents, had volunteered for SOE while recuperating together from wounds received on the same day in the same North African battle; his brother would be dropped into Greece. 'When all was ready our team of three complete with mule train commenced our journey along mountain paths and unmade roads toward the west,' DeAth remembers. 'We were warned not to stare at the women.'[42] Soon they were settled in hills near the port of Vlora and Field had already had one uncomfortably close encounter worth recording. Dropping down to observe, alone, a strong Italian column heard to be on the coastal road, he had managed to find himself stranded on open ground between the road and the shore just as the column hove in sight. To his horror it halted yards from him. Then the troops disembarked, sat down and started smoking and chatting. Wearing full kit, complete with weapons, beret and binoculars, Field began, so he recalled, 'nonchalantly dumping my arms and clothing' until he was sauntering across the open beach 'clad only in my pants'. Trying to look like a local, he began paddling, 'stooping down with my arms trailing in the water, hoping that the Italians, three yards away, would think that I was looking for shrimps or something'. Finally 'whistles were blown, men jumped to their feet' and the column moved off, whereupon Field picked up his clothes and went home.[43]

As SOE's presence in Albania increased, the training of the first Partisan units at Shtylla reached completion. On 15 August, at Vithkuq, the next village down the valley towards Korça, the first eight hundred men were inaugurated as the 1st Partisan Brigade. In command was Mehmet Shehu, a communist and veteran of the International Brigades in Spain. Shehu was in his early thirties, officer-trained, short, wiry and serious. It was rumoured that he had personally cut the throats of seventy captured Italian carabinieri. '[U]ndoubtedly the best commander in the LNC', one SOE report reads, 'he is respected or feared by everyone with some reason.'[44]

Also in August the British were able to see more guerrillas in action, albeit, as Seymour noted, in operations 'led and mostly carried out by British personnel, the locals appearing more or less in a watching brief with a good deal of trepidation'.[45] One ambush organised by David Smiley and notable for the fact that a Balli Kombëtar çeta was persuaded to help took place on a hillside road at Barmash, not far from Borova. It was a good spot, Smiley felt: with sheer cliffs on one side and a ravine dropping away on the other there was nowhere for the victims to escape. He and the çeta were in position when a German troop carrier, towing an 80mm gun, arrived one morning from the direction of Korça. The carrier blew up on mines laid overnight; Smiley, firing a 20mm machine-gun, also hit it. Twelve Germans were killed in the carrier and another six trying to get out and away. When the guerrillas had picked over the wreckage and finished off the wounded, more transport appeared from the south. Mines and the 20mm accounted for three lorries. 'From uniform on right sleeve, oval-shaped cloth white edelweiss with green stem on dark green background surrounded by white chain,' the mission reported afterwards to Cairo, confirming that the dead were elite mountain troops. 'In cap silvery metal edelweiss with brass centre. In pockets Polish and German money.'[46] But though delighted with the results, Smiley was unimpressed that many of the Balli Kombëtar guerrillas had run off during the action. And ten days later it was the Partisans' turn to disappoint. When a small German post, eighteen-strong, dug itself in at the spot where Smiley had laid his earlier ambush, the 1st Brigade, fearing casualties, refused to attack it.

Another poor Partisan performance was put in at the end of August, when the Italians launched a sudden drive aimed squarely at Shtylla and Vithkuq. It was the first time the Italians had tried to come up there and the first time the British had been attacked, and it came as a surprise. Sitting one morning in Shtylla's mud-brick mosque, McLean and Smiley had been playing snap when the first shell landed on the roof, bringing down the ceiling and blowing in the windows. Shelling continued for the rest of the day while aircraft wheeled overhead, spotting and strafing, and an Italian column from Korça, burning villages as it came, pressed slowly up the valley. McLean, Duffy and Jenkins had narrow escapes when the Italians reached Vithkuq, Jenkins receiving a bullet hole through his breast pocket and paybook. Willie Williamson saw one young Partisan hit. 'There was a lump of lead sticking out of his stomach. And the poor soul, he was saying "ujë, ujë, ujë" which is Albanian for water and nobody gave him water and he just died.'[47] Then the Partisans pulled back into the mountains, compelling the British, too, to withdraw, and afterwards McLean told Cairo that while Italian morale, tactics and marksmanship had been 'quite fantastic' and the accuracy of the shelling and shooting 'first class', the Partisan response had been 'disgraceful'.[48] Though casualties had been light, little effort, the British felt, had been made to resist. 'The artillery fire was neither heavy nor destructive, but the moral effect of it was shattering to the Partisans,' remembered Kemp, who knew a thing or two about being shelled. 'My interpreter, a fierce looking man, with black moustaches, who had previously been very warlike, very proud of himself and the Partisans and very contemptuous of the Italians, spent most of the morning and afternoon of the 27th moaning piteously "Il faut nous éloigner d'ici, Monsieur, c'est très dangereux" whenever a shell burst within 200 yds of us. But as soon as the battle was over, his tail went up and he informed me contemptuously that the Italians could never have taken Shtylle [sic] but for their artillery.'[49]

But these were still early days. The Partisans had their flaws but improvement was expected. Kemp reflected later that McLean had been training the 1st Brigade for a style of stand-and-fight warfare to which the Partisans were not suited: expecting even five hundred untried men to fight a pitched battle against eighteen well-trained, well-armed, dug-in troops had been a mistake. Such an action, Kemp felt, suited smaller units attacking with the benefit of surprise.[50] Reports from other missions, meanwhile, were encouraging. From a remote mountain monastery at Llenga in the Mokra hills, Andy Hands wrote several times to McLean about how pleased he was with the Partisans with him. 'This is a very good battalion here; full out for having a crack.'[51] Bill Tilman, in the south, watched three hundred Partisans make a spirited night assault on the village of Libhova; 'the Iti replied with mortars, killing six'.[52] Tony Neel, on his way to join Abas Kupi, reported that Partisans near Berat 'are at it all the time' even though 'very badly off for arms'.[53] As for the local Balli Kombëtar, Hands was close to despair: 'they still do nothing but talk'.[54] Neel, though, was able to report that Abas Ermenji, a young Balli Kombëtar commander, had attacked Berat with seven hundred men. The assault was a failure: 'he lost 6 dead and 1 wounded. Italian casualties nil'. But they 'did put up quite a good effort'.[55]

Just as SOE was beginning to establish itself, the complexion of the war changed dramatically. In Italy, popular unease at being part of the Axis had been growing for months, fuelled by a stream of disastrous defeats and fears that the fighting would soon reach the mainland. May 1943 had seen the Allies victorious in North Africa and thousands of Italian troops captured; July had seen the Allies invade Sicily. On 25 July patience with Mussolini ran out. He was dismissed, the Fascist Party dissolved and Marshal Pietro Badoglio, the Italian chief of staff, appointed Prime Minister. On 3 September, as British troops began landing on the Italian toe, Badoglio's government signed an armistice with the Allies. It was made public five days later. Everywhere it took Italian forces by surprise.

SOE missions in Albania had had no warning either that an armistice was imminent, but knew what they needed to do to try to make the most of the moment: Italian units were to be told to surrender and, if the Germans appeared and tried to intervene, encouraged to resist. With headquarters at Tirana, the Italian Ninth Army, part of Army Group East, was then responsible for most of Albania and garrisoned the country with more than 100,000 men. The *Firenze* and *Arezzo* divisions had charge of most of the north and east, the *Parma*, *Perugia* and *Brennero* covered most of the centre and south and the *Puglie* was responsible for the northernmost regions and parts of Kosovo. Within hours, British officers everywhere were moving to contact senior commanders.

The Germans, however, also reacted. Aware that Italy's appetite for war was disappearing and anxious to protect Germany's Balkan interests and flank, plans had been laid for this moment. Accordingly, at dawn on 9 September, troops and tanks from three divisions of Field Marshal von Weichs' Army Group F began rolling in from Greece and Yugoslavia, wresting weapons from every Italian they met and taking control of town after town. The first column arrived on the outskirts of Tirana the following afternoon. 'They disarmed Italian officers and soldiers by force in the streets,' remembered a carabinieri colonel there at the time; 'they requisitioned military vehicles, even going so far as to stop them on the road; they occupied warehouses, stores, barracks, etc.' Telephone and telegraph lines were soon in German hands and on the morning of 11 September a 'mob of German troops burst into the premises of Army Group HQ and after having thrown the Italian military personnel out of the offices, smashed up the place'.[56]

George Seymour was then closest to the capital, in the hills outside with Myslim Peza's guerrillas. It was Seymour who took on the task of contacting General Lorenzo Dalmazzo, the Ninth Army commander. On 9 September, after hearing of the armistice over the BBC, Seymour asked Peza to get him into the city, 'but it took me twenty-four hours to convince him that speed was essential'.[57] Finally, on the evening of 10 September, disguised as an Italian, Seymour drove into Tirana in the back of an Italian staff car. German soldiers could be seen but it was still possible, Seymour thought, for the Italians to put up an effective fight. At Ninth Army headquarters, housed in Zog's old palace, he spoke with Dalmazzo's intelligence chief who seemed keen to do what he could and agreed on a plan: all Italian divisions would concentrate on Tirana and, in the event of an Allied landing, seize the city and secure a bridgehead. Seymour returned to the hills, hopes high. He soon realised that the Italian command had little intention of doing anything at all. First the Tirana garrison surrendered: as he had negotiated with Dalmazzo's intelligence chief, Seymour learnt later, Dalmazzo had been in the next room speaking with German officers, while General Rosi, the Army Group commander, had issued orders already that Italian soldiers should surrender their arms. Then the *Brennero*, based nearby, capitulated, and did so, Seymour felt, without much honour. Days later, disarmed by the Germans, the division had its weapons returned when it promised its support. The *Brennero*'s chief of staff told Seymour this was a ruse; the real plan, he said, was to resist. In the end the division left for the coast, found boats and sailed for Italy.

Later Seymour remarked that Myslim Peza's early inaction illustrated 'what incredible obstinacy and stupidity we were up against when dealing with the Partisans'. But he also reflected that 'even if we had got there before the Germans, we should still have failed owing to the cowardice and indecision of the high-ranking Italian officers'.[58] Gino Carrai, the carabinieri colonel, who managed to flee into the mountains and join the Partisans, was convinced that some Italian soldiers in Tirana would have fought had senior commanders shown encouragement. As it was, 'the absence of anyone to stimulate, incite and guide' ensured that 'the morale of the troops, who still had a certain amount of fighting spirit and the will to resist the Germans, was within three days reduced to its lowest ebb'.[59]

Elsewhere other divisions were reluctant to take on the Germans or uncertain what to do. One was General Torriano's *Arezzo*, with its headquarters at Korça and a sizeable garrison at Pogradec, on the shore of Lake Ohrid. David Smiley spent hours trying to win over the Pogradec commander and at one point was disarmed and locked in a room, then released with apologies and rearmed. Though he did get through on the telephone to Torriano at Korça, the general rang off after explaining he could say nothing since the room he was in was full of Germans. In time most of the *Arezzo* was disarmed and taken to Germany.

The *Perugia*, with its headquarters and barracks at Gjirokastra, also tried, like the *Brennero*, to go home. On 14 September Bill Tilman walked down to speak to its commander, General Chiminello. Tilman asked him to attack the Germans or give his weapons to the Partisans. Chiminello refused to do either. Returning two days later, Tilman found the division had left in the night for the coast. Six days later he caught up with it at Saranda, Albania's southernmost port. Two thousand soldiers had already sailed and Chiminello told Tilman the Partisans could have his heavy weapons. His remaining men would keep their rifles to defend themselves, he explained, should the Germans try to stop them leaving: already German aircraft were dive-bombing Italian units on Corfu. Then, on 25 September, Tilman spotted, he reported later, an Italian ship in the bay 'having apparently fouled its anchor'; seen also by a German reconnaissance plane, it eventually sank 'after five separate attacks by six Stukas'. At that point what was left of the *Perugia* 'abandoned everything' and fled north to Porto Palermo, a wide bay twenty miles up the coast. Here these 'unhappy men' waited in the hope that more ships might come to take them off. 'Very few more got away. I was told later, and believed it true, that Chiminello and 150 of his officers were found there by the Huns, shot, and thrown into the sea.'[60]

Only the *Firenze* undertook to resist the Germans from the moment of the armistice. Andy Hands was based near its garrison at Dibra, in eastern Albania, close to the Macedonian border, and immediately contacted one of its commanders, General Piccini. Germans were heard to be advancing on the town, Hands told him, and he and his men should get out quick if they wished to keep their arms and equipment. Thousands of Italian soldiers duly left for the mountains. Days later, when Tony Neel found the division in the forests above Burrel, in Mati, it was already reduced to eating its mules and horses but still had its weapons and pledged itself willing to take part in a major attack on Tirana. On 22 September, fighting alongside Neel, Abas Kupi and some partisans from Dibra, the *Firenze* captured the citadel and road junction at Kruja, outside the capital. Strong opposition soon stalled the advance but Kupi and the Italians held Kruja for three days before German artillery drove them out: one shell crashed into the house Neel was in, killing a woman in the next room. Although most of the division escaped back into the mountains, its cohesion had gone and the *Firenze* never fought again as a unit.

Of all SOE officers in Albania at the time of the armistice, the one whose experiences were the most dramatic was Jerry Field. By then he and his mission had made their base in Tragjas, a hillside village south of Vlora, and were aware that the port was home to the *Parma* division and an established contingent of several hundred German troops. When half-heard radio broadcasts and garbled w/t messages suggested 'that the Wops had had enough', Field took Billy Eden and set off with the aim of demanding the *Parma*'s surrender.

Picking their way down from Tragjas and with Field waving a white handkerchief on a stick, the pair made for an Italian pillbox by the side of the coastal road. They persuaded the men inside to telephone ahead to Vlora, then held up a passing bus. It was 'packed with Albanians like sardines in a tin' but 'after firing a couple of shots over the top, Bill soon got the smelly mob out . . . and, with my revolver, I persuaded the driver to turn the dilapidated old vehicle round. "Valona" I said, and towards Valona we went.' Outside the port they were stopped at a roadblock. An Italian officer, dark and bespectacled, introduced himself in English as Lieutenant Manzitti and took them to a waiting staff car and on, into the town, to divisional headquarters, an imposing government building flying the Italian flag. Sentries flanked the door. 'Bill and I straightened out our equipment and pulled our belts down a little so that our revolvers hung ready.' Two German officers appeared. Field, alarmed, wondered whether he should start shooting, before 'two hands were whipped up with two of the smartest salutes I've ever seen'.

Manzitti led them inside, up a staircase and along a parquet-floored passage to a conference room overlooked by a painting of Mussolini. Then he fetched General Lugli, commander of the *Parma*. Over Martell brandy and with Manzitti translating, Field asked the general to surrender. Lugli replied that he was waiting for instructions from Tirana. The Germans were sure to try to seize control, Field told him, and the general had to act now if his division was not to be captured. Lugli was unmoved. Field decided to leave. 'Having had three more brandies and put two of the General's cigars into my pocket, I got up and said I must be going.' Manzitti took Field and Eden back to the roadblock, where the pair climbed into their bus and drove off.

Back at the pillbox Field found an excited joint force of Partisans and Balli Kombëtar guerrillas, all impatient to disarm an Italian-manned fort at Himara, between Vlora and Saranda. Though not optimistic of their chances of success, since the garrison was thought to be 250-strong, Field agreed to help, took a rifle and set off with seventy-odd men down the road. It was dark when they reached the fort, perched on a stony hill above the shore, and Field went ahead and called on the Italians to surrender: General Lugli, he said, had ordered it. 'I am Fascisti,' came the garrison commander's shouted reply. 'What General Lugli says has nothing to do with me. I will fight the dirty English with the Germans.' When Field returned next morning the Italians invited him in and now explained they could not give in without a fight. Field told them he would attack at nine, shook hands and left. Outside he placed his guerrillas in firing positions and, to halt any Germans arriving from Vlora, laid a roadblock north of the fort. At nine he fired three shots and the battle began. The garrison had heavy mortars and machine-guns and the din and display were impressive, Field remembered, but that was about it. 'I could see nothing worth aiming at and I am sure that neither the besieged Italians nor the attacking partisans could either.' Then he spotted an Italian head moving near one of the mortars. 'I carefully took a bead on it and squeezed the trigger. Two arms were thrown up and the head disappeared.' The Italians waved a white flag. Field went forward. The commander explained that he had lost one man killed, honour was vindicated and the garrison was ready to surrender, whereupon the Italians piled arms, boarded lorries and left.

At that moment Field heard firing from the direction of the road-block, hurried to investigate and found a halted German armoured car, doors open, 'and three Huns sprawled on the road'. Two other cars had fled. Field returned to the fort, where, as the Albanians spirited away all the weapons and material they could carry, he set fire to it. That done, he prepared to drive the armoured car back to Tragjas only to arrive at the roadblock and find his guerrillas pointing at distant dust clouds on the road ahead. He took out his binoculars. 'Eight troop carriers, four armoured cars and a mobile kitchen. This little party was evidently coming to the help of Himara; it was also coming up the road along which I wanted to go.' As the enemy column began to climb towards him, Field, in his own armoured car, set off towards it, weaving his way down a tightly winding road with a sheer drop on one side and a wall of rock on the other.

> I accelerated and between one bend and the next passed two armoured cars and two troop carriers. Through the slit of the driver's aperture I could see the surprise on the Germans' faces as they saw one of their own armoured cars coming down the mountain road. On the next bend I nearly ran into a troop carrier. I pulled right over towards the precipice and was sure I had two wheels over the edge. Just around the bend I found a tank on the wrong side of the road, I swerved over and felt the wings grating against the cliff. I got past.

Nearly half way. Another tank, five troop carriers and a mobile kitchen on the bend. I blew my siren. The kitchen moved over to its correct side and I squeezed past.

I was now sweating as much as if I was in a Turkish Bath. All that now remained were two armoured cars. I expected to meet them in the next straight – but no – nor on the next bend. I was nearly down the pass. I was at the last bend, and after that the road ran fairly straight for five miles. Where were the two cars?

As I came round the last bend I accelerated. I was now doing over 50 miles an hour. There they were at the side of the road. The occupants stood talking in the middle of the road. As they heard the roar of my engine they turned to look. I drove straight at them. I watched the expression on their faces change from surprise to anger, bewilder[ment], horror when I was ten yards away, and then panic. In trying to get out of the way, they pushed and hustled in their terror. Two fell. My armoured car leapt in the air as I went over them. I suppose I touched the road again some 20 feet further on.

Once clear of the column, Field stopped twice: first to light his pipe, then to push the car off a bridge. When at last he returned to Tragjas, Eden and DeAth met him with news that the Germans, as predicted, had put the *Parma* 'in the bag'.[61]

Not all of the Italians in Albania fell into German hands. Perhaps as many as 15,000 took to the mountains after the armistice. Some hundreds, including valuable pack artillery, would attach themselves to the Partisans. A few dozen were taken on by SOE missions as porters, cooks, interpreters and orderlies. The morning after Field had returned to Tragjas, six Italians 'surrounded by infuriated Albanians' turned up in the village and he recognised one as Lieutenant Manzitti, who explained that he was 'so ashamed of the performance' his country had put up that he wanted to work with the British. 'I was glad to have him.'[62] A trained intelligence officer who spoke some Albanian, Giuseppe Manzitti was thirty-three, had been a lawyer in Genoa before the war and was to serve SOE loyally and at great personal risk for months.

Most Italians, however, had little interest in being fashioned into any armed force and tried simply to eke out whatever existence they could.

Soon SOE missions were seeing apocalyptic scenes. In October, in woods
near the coast, Bill Tilman found what he thought were at least five
thousand men, the 'remains' of the *Parma* and *Perugia* divisions, 'living
on roots and berries'.[63] Elsewhere other officers saw ragged Italians
being bought and sold in village marketplaces and, yoked together,
hauling ploughs across fields. It was all much worse in the winter. 'I
remember two Italians lying up on a hillside, on the snow,' Willie
Williamson recalled. 'We weren't interested in them and these two were
just lying, waiting to die.'[64] Sharing a spicy stew prepared by one group
of starving soldiers, David Smiley thought the main ingredient might
have been another Italian.

Another result of the capitulation was greater friction between the Partisans
and Balli Kombëtar. Already, before the armistice, the situation had been
serious. An agreement accorded in August by representatives of both
parties did not last long, rejected first by senior communists, then officially by the LNC Council. Though McLean had made clear at Labinot
that Britain wished to see unity of resistance, he had played no role in
arranging the meeting, at Mukja, where the short-lived agreement was
reached, nor knew, at first, what had taken place. Still, the British did
know that relations were bad. Later that month, George Seymour,
marching with Partisan guides to join Myslim Peza, 'was never permitted
to enter a Balli village nor to speak to a member of the Balli Kombëtar.
At the same time I was subject to intense Partisan and anti-Balli
Kombëtar propaganda'.[65] Kemp and McLean, climbing back into the
hills after ambushing a German staff car, 'encountered extreme hostility' from nearby Balli Kombëtar villages 'and in one of them were
very nearly shot'.[66]

'Tension increasing between two movements,' McLean warned Cairo
in early September. 'As far as can see no hope of agreement.' The LNC,
while 'violently' anti-Axis and anti-Fascist, had a 'far stronger' communist element than previously thought; many of its leaders were 'younger
men' and 'ambitious careerists swollen headed'. The Balli Kombëtar
was 'more influential than first estimated' but 'windy of fighting' due
to 'patriotic and vested and cowardly reasons': its leaders feared communism and 'losing their own positions to the new younger men'.[67]

Now, post-armistice, a fleeting belief, shared by Albanians and SOE
officers alike, that Allied forces might land to take advantage of the
Italian collapse saw the Partisans and Balli Kombëtar become further

Margaret Hasluck

Philip Leake

David Smiley (left) and Billy McLean at Biza, October 1943

Left to right:
Alan Hare, Peter Kemp
and Richard Riddell

Andy Hands

George Seymour

Bill Tilman

Myslim Peza (left)
and Baba Faja (giving
Partisan salute)

Mustafa Gjinishi

Female Partisans

Nexhip Vinçani (right)
with David Smiley

Balli Kombëtar
delegation at Biza

Arthur Nicholls

'Trotsky' Davies at Biza

Left to right: Frank Smyth, 'Trotsky' Davies, Alan Hare, Arthur Nicholls, Billy McLean and David Smiley at Biza, 23 October 1943

Cigarette case, sovereign and silk escape map carried by 'Trotsky' Davies and showing bullet damage and blood stains

John Hibberdine, March 1944

Ian Merrett

Reginald Hibbert

Muharrem Bajraktar

Abas Kupi (right)

Jerry Field

Giuseppe Manzitti

In the cave at Seaview: Nick Kukich (left) and Dale McAdoo

Men of Dukati visiting Seaview: Maliq Koshena (second from left) and Mysli Kali (second from right)

estranged, as both began scrambling to be in the strongest position as and when liberation came. Garry Duffy watched one early standoff, shortly after the armistice, when he entered a town in the southern Vjosa valley and found a combative Balli Kombëtar politician, Ali Këlcyrë, busily disarming Italians. 'There was very nearly a fight when one of the partisans with me picked up some kit.'[68] Later, after he had assured Duffy he would simply store the weapons, Këlcyrë was heard to have distributed them among his own people, most likely for future use against the Partisans. 'I will send a letter to him for full explanation and request either a meeting or delivery of arms,' Duffy told McLean, 'but he is a first class shit, no doubt.'[69]

As days became weeks and no Allied invasion came, tension continued to grow as the Germans, anxious to strengthen their grip, began to pursue a highly effective policy of divide and rule. While Mussolini had sought to absorb Albania into Italy's empire, this occupation was a tactical move to secure Germany's Balkan interests and flank, and the new occupiers were prepared to go to considerable lengths to win friends and reduce resistance. Union with Italy was dissolved; Greater Albania, incorporating most of Kosovo, was declared free and independent; and, in October, four prominent Albanians, each representing one of the country's four principal religions, were installed as Regents. Lef Nosi, an Orthodox Christian from Elbasan who had served as a minister in Albania's first government, was one. Another was Fuad Dibra, a landowning Sunni Muslim who had represented the country at the Paris peace conference in 1920. Anton Harapi, Franciscan prior of Shkodra, was appointed the Catholic member. Finally, to represent Albania's Bektashi Muslims, and as chief Regent, the Germans brought back a prize scalp, Mehdi Frashëri, a former Prime Minister and outspoken critic of the Italian occupation whom the Italians had interned. With the Regents in place, a new government followed, with Rexhep Mitrovica, another former minister, in charge.

Few elements of the traditional elite, with which the Germans were taking such pains to associate themselves, were aligned ideologically with Nazism. But once offered a level of self-rule not experienced under the Italians, and hoping to re-establish and reform the state, preserve Albania's ethnic borders and secure military assistance in countering the communist threat, significant numbers and personalities were quickly won over. So was the allegiance of many in the Balli Kombëtar: Nosi, Dibra and Mitrovica were all leading members; on

7 October, the Balli Kombëtar's Council officially instructed its supporters, if any were still fighting, to cease hostilities against the Germans. Soon joint German–Balli Kombëtar forces were fighting the Partisans. Not all in the movement were happy about this. Another prominent member, a young lawyer from Vlora called Skënder Muço, is thought to have been responsible for circulating in November a pamphlet denouncing both the Germans and collaborators. Such defiance, however, was rare.

Independently of the Balli Kombëtar, other Nationalists, to use SOE's catch-all term for non-Partisan Albanians, would work with the Germans. And yet others would choose to remain aloof, maintaining contact with SOE missions, collaborators, Partisans and even Germans until convinced of the best way to jump. One who preferred neutrality was Abas Kupi. Suspicious of the communists, he now split from the LNC, withdrew from the fight and set up his own little pro-Zog party, Legality. In December the LNC declared him a traitor.

All this left the Partisans, grouped in pockets mostly in the mountains near Korça and in the ranges south and east of Tirana, not only dominated increasingly by communists but also the Germans' only opponents. And SOE continued to arm and encourage them, since the LNC, despite the rising tension, was still proving itself capable of killing Axis troops. Bill Tilman, operating in October around Tepelena, Byron's old stamping ground, was on hand to watch the Partisans stop a German column from Greece on the road just short of the town. The fighting lasted days, during which the Germans shelled and burnt surrounding villages and Tilman directed two captured anti-tank guns to keep reinforcements at bay. Also in early October German infantry pushed into the hills south of Tirana and fell on the Partisans at a place called Arbone. 'They certainly did not appear to realize in what strength the Partisans were in this area,' George Seymour reported. He and McLean were there at the time; so were the LNC Council and a large combined force of Partisans and Italians. 'The Partisans held their ground and after a great deal of shooting on both sides the Germans retired to Tirana leaving some thirty dead and wounded.'[70] In fact the fighting had ebbed and flowed, with Mustafa Gjinishi, fast becoming a favourite of the British, making one gallant attack with hand-grenades on a German-held mill. After the battle McLean saw him 'riding on a donkey . . . wounded in hand and ear . . . in pain but happy, slightly annoyed that he had only managed to kill one German'. Few, if any, of the enemy wounded lived for long. McLean made a note of one 'Austrian boy, shot through stomach, lying in agony'. Partisans stood around him 'saying continuously "why don't we execute him"'.[71]

'ENDURANCE VILE'

THE Italian collapse, the rapid German takeover and reports of rising tension had little impact on British plans, laid prior to the armistice, to encourage greater resistance in Albania. With the country marked down as a field of considerable promise, preparations had been made to increase sharply SOE's commitment there and send out a British brigadier to take charge. By mid-October, David Smiley had crossed the Shkumbin into northern Albania, prepared a dropping ground at a spot called Biza, a remote and grassy bowl high in the Cerminika massif, and, with McLean, was standing by to receive him. East of Tirana, the peaks and beech woods and rolling karst country of Cerminika felt isolated and impregnable enough to be secure from sudden attack, but close enough to the capital and Partisan bases to promise reasonably frequent contact with the LNC Council and other groups.

Greece had had a brigadier, in the shape of Eddie Myers, for nearly a year. Two more were planned for Yugoslavia, to raise the importance of British missions working with Tito and Mihailović. Both were in place by the end of September. Whether Albania merited such a senior officer is a moot point. Certainly the scale of SOE's presence there that summer and autumn was small. By mid-October, it consisted of seven small missions, a total of twenty-four men, and the RAF had flown just a score or so sorties to supply them. By contrast, SOE had nineteen missions, well over a hundred men, in Yugoslavia, and more than forty missions, nearly two hundred men, in Greece. But SOE planning papers, dating from the eve of the Italian armistice, show that positive reports from the field had seen hopes rise among outside observers that the Albanian resistance would soon be large and formidable.

'The anti-Italian activities of Albanian guerillas are incessant, considerable and susceptible of great expansion; co-ordination and supplies are lacking' was the view at SOE headquarters in July, based on McLean's early reports. 'The conclusion is that these wants should be met in view of military possibilities by early infiltration of every British officer available, together with an adequate number of W/T operators.'[1] British officers were 'co-ordinating the activities' of fifty guerrilla bands, while the country presented good targets for sabotage: Albania, it was noted, produced enough chrome to meet all of Italy's requirements and 10 per cent of its oil.[2] By September, in London, senior intelligence officers privy to SOE reports and decrypted enemy signals agreed that Albania represented 'a promising field for guerilla activity . . . SOE officers concerned have made exceptionally good progress in a very short space of time'.[3] It was also known that the LNC was allowing McLean to train the first of three thousand men and that he expected to see them in the field very soon, and it was estimated that there was potential for twenty thousand. And although, by the summer, the rivalry between the Partisans and Balli Kombëtar was obvious and growing, it was not yet identified as a serious problem: 'approximately three-quarters' of all guerrillas sided with the LNC, while 'no open hostility' had occurred between the two.[4] As for the potential for division within the LNC, 'Communism of an apparently innocuous kind has recently made headway but it has not disturbed the unity of the guerilla elements,' an early message from McLean suggested. 'As a concession to the Communists all guerillas give the clenched fist salute, and in return the Communists wear the eagle of Albania in addition to the red star. The Communists represent only about 20% of the Movement of National Liberation, but make up for their lack of numbers by their activity.'[5]

The dispatch of a senior officer was also to be accompanied by a rapid increase in stores and personnel. In addition to the brigadier and a full headquarters staff, SOE planned to send a mission to work with the LNC Council, two to work with the Balli Kombëtar and eleven to work with LNC area commanders, while every mission already in the field would each receive one more officer and another w/t operator: a total, approximately, of two hundred men. SOE also intended to step up the number of supply drops: fifty sorties, over a hundred tons, were proposed for October and every subsequent month. The men were available, as SOE's recent recruitment drives had proved most effective, though whether SOE had sufficient resources to maintain them is debatable. In the end, changing priorities, terrible weather and a decline in resistance activity saw only a fraction of those numbers sent anyway and only a few sorties flown. This left SOE's missions in Albania looking rather top-heavy. Still, that autumn, SOE had certainly expected its brigadier to be dealing with a sizeable and powerful force both of guerrillas and British personnel.

Also, despite an added emphasis on urging rival guerrillas to unite, British policy was still to help any Albanian, whatever his politics, so long as he was fighting. 'You have been appointed as Officer Commanding the Allied Mission in Albania,' the brigadier's Foreign Office-approved directive read. 'The policy of His Majesty's Government for promoting and organising resistance to the Axis in Albania is to support all anti-Axis elements, wherever they may be, subject to the availability of aircraft and other resources, provided always that they continue to combat the Axis actively and wholeheartedly.'[6]

The brigadier selected was an energetic and experienced regular, forty-three-year-old Edmund Frank Davies of the Royal Ulster Rifles. Born in India, son of a bandmaster of the 4th Queen's Own Hussars, he was known universally as 'Trotsky', a nickname earned at Sandhurst not for his politics, one instructor recalled, but for 'a kind of disciplined bolshevism' in his character.[7] Commissioned in 1919, he won his first Military Cross the following year in Mesopotamia. Long service followed in Egypt and India. In Palestine in 1937 he was wounded, twice mentioned in dispatches and awarded a second MC. Davies was devoted to his battalion and, to his delight, given command of it in 1942.

Popular among his men, Davies was straight-talking, outgoing and tough and could display a frankness, one fellow RUR officer would remember, that 'did not always endear him to those who did not know him. Still below the surface there simmered a hatred of insincerity and of half-measures . . . and he had few equals in putting first things first and exceptional ability in finding a practical common sense answer to almost any problem. He was frequently unorthodox and forceful in his methods but nearly always effective.' He was also a fine sportsman. 'He was for several years captain of the 2nd Battalion [football] team and his stocky figure and bald head storming down the wing always drew a hearty roar from Regimental supporters.' In 1929 Davies led the team to victory in the All India Association Football Shield.

'Trotsky was then nearly 30 and the press comment on the final match of the tournament was "Davies, the right winger, who is well in the veteran stage, showed a rare turn of speed and a doggedness that knew no defeat." How true of the player and of the man!'[8]

How Davies came to SOE's attention remains unclear but the following August, while training at Hawick, he was called to London and asked to parachute into Yugoslavia to command its missions with Tito. Mystified at how and why he had been proposed for the job and sorry at the prospect of leaving his battalion, he was nevertheless attracted by the challenge and agreed to go. Flown out to Cairo, it was there that he heard he was being switched to Albania when it transpired that Churchill wanted his own man, Fitzroy Maclean, to go to Tito. Goschen, the brigadier already assigned to Albania, made way, returned to normal duty and was killed at Kohima the following May.

That autumn, while not training in Palestine or attending meetings in Cairo, Davies looked for suitable volunteers willing to go out to Albania with him. He tapped his own regiment for some. Others were plucked from the pool of officers and NCOs whom SOE had recruited at home for operations in any Balkan country and was sending, in batches, out to Cairo. But with the plan in place for a headquarters mission, certain specialists were required: Davies wanted a quartermaster, a medical officer, an intelligence officer and so on. Most of these were found in the Middle East.

One officer found in Cairo was twenty-four-year-old Marcus Lyon. 'I heard through a friend that there was a job going, but it was so secret he could not tell me anything about it. He sent me to an address and I was swiftly taken up to see a Brigadier, a small, thickset man with a decisive way of talking.' This was Davies. 'He questioned me astutely and I answered honestly except in one respect – I answered "yes" when he asked me if I was an athlete.'[9] In fact, though now fully fit, Lyon had had double pneumonia three times as a child which had seen him packed off to Switzerland at the age of eleven, after which he went to Stowe. 'To my chagrin I was still treated as a delicate child and not allowed to go on runs ... It was in reaction to this treatment that I determined as soon as I was off the leash to do some tough job.'[10] That led to a stint after school as a deckhand on a tanker to Texas and back and a territorial commission in the Warwickshire Yeomanry. When war broke out, Lyon, studying architecture in London, was mobilised immediately and shipped out to Palestine. In 1941 he volunteered for the Libyan Arab Force, a mobile unit working with tribes in the Western Desert. In 1942, having emerged unscathed from the retreat to El Alamein and keen not to miss out on Montgomery's coming offensive, he had joined the Yorkshire Dragoons and, as intelligence officer, pushed all the way to Tunis. Then the Dragoons went into reserve, a new colonel arrived and Lyon, once a captain with the Arabs, was 'back again as a troop leader which didn't please me too much'. Then the colonel sent him on a course, 'which he thought was an infantry course, INF, but he'd misread it and it was actually INT, an intelligence course, which was the second time I'd been on one', and that saw him in Cairo as Davies was seeking volunteers.[11] Davies now told Lyon that 'he was looking for a GIII (I) – a Staff Officer (Intelligence) – and my experience and courses would be useful'. Lyon asked if he should not tell his colonel and request a transfer. 'I have Churchill's permission to take anyone I want from anywhere,' Davies replied. 'I don't want you to get in touch with anyone.' Lyon left the interview 'like a small boy emerging from a cinema showing Bulldog Drummond'.[12]

By early October, Davies was trained and briefed and felt ready enough to go. Some of his staff, including Lyon, were still in training and would have to drop later. Six, though, were also ready. The most senior was Lieutenant Colonel Arthur Nicholls, earmarked as Davies' chief of staff. He was thirty-two, had been educated at Marlborough, the Sorbonne and Cambridge and, by 1939, was working in London as a stockbroker. A territorial commission in the Coldstream Guards soon saw him mobilised and posted to France. Brought out from Dunkirk, where he was ADC to General Alexander, he was sent to Staff College at Camberley and it was from there, in March 1942, that he had joined SOE, posted to work in its London headquarters. The following summer Nicholls asked to serve with one of the expanded headquarters missions proposed for Greece or Yugoslavia. Sent out to Cairo, he soon crossed paths with Davies who took him on for Albania. They became good friends. Nicholls, lean and six foot five, was a quiet, reserved, decent man, married with a six-month-old daughter; after the First World War he was the only surviving male on his mother's side of the family.

Of the other officers dropping with them, twenty-seven-year-old Major Jim Chesshire, another Marlburian and a chartered surveyor in Birmingham before the war, was Davies' sapper officer and joined the mission from an instructor's post at the SOE school on Mount Carmel. It was there, too, that Davies found his signals officer, thirty-year-old

Lieutenant Frank Trayhorn, an engineering graduate of Vienna University who spoke eight languages and was employed at the school as an interpreter and w/t instructor. Lastly there was Alan Hare, future chairman of the *Financial Times*. Then a twenty-four-year-old captain in the Household Cavalry, Hare was the youngest son of Viscount Ennismore, Eton- and Oxford-educated, and had served in the Mediterranean and Middle East since 1941. He was to be Davies' staff captain. Also going in were two NCOs: Sergeant Chisholm, once chief clerk at Mount Carmel, who, complete with typewriter, would deal with the mission's paperwork, and Bob Melrose, the young Scot from Penicuik, who would be Davies' signals sergeant.

Also dropping with Davies' party were two three-man teams, both earmarked for regular liaison work, and one Polish officer. Twenty-nine-year-old Alan Palmer, a major in the Royal Berkshire Yeomanry, led one of the teams. Great-grandson of the founder of the Huntley & Palmer biscuit dynasty, he had been educated at Harrow and Oxford, was on the firm's board when war broke out and had taken part already in an SOE operation in the Dodecanese. Victor Smith, a red-haired captain in the Lancashire Fusiliers, was his assistant and 'Jock' Huxtable, a short, dark, good-humoured Scot, the pair's w/t operator. The second team comprised Captain Jack Bulman and Lieutenant Frank Smyth, both of the King's Royal Rifle Corps, and twenty-one-year-old Harry Button, from Suffolk, a Royal Tank Regiment w/t operator. Lieutenant Michael Lis was the Pole. A colourful figure, older than most of the others, he had joined SOE with the help of Christine Granville, another of SOE's Poles, and been tasked with subverting any Polish labourers the mission might come across.

Davies, Nicholls, Chesshire, Palmer, Smith, Melrose and Button parachuted to Biza shortly after ten on the evening of 15 October. Hare, Bulman, Smyth, Lis, Chisholm and Huxtable dropped to the same spot the following night. Trayhorn followed four nights after that.

From the moment the mission arrived, Arthur Nicholls kept a pocket diary of its day-to-day doings. Whether such a record should have been kept is another debatable point: diary-keeping of any kind was against orders and, in Albania, a risky game to play. Had it been captured, the Germans would have made the most of it, as they did when Seymour's w/t log fell into their hands a few weeks later: a booklet, 'Major Seymour Informs London', was printed and circulated, designed to condemn the

LNC as a communist organisation. As it is, the existence of Nicholls'
diary has been virtually unknown for half a century. Only in 2002, and
in private hands, did a copy typed in the SOE office come to light.
Given the diary's detail and immediacy, the trouble taken to keep it
and the mission's significance and fate, it is quoted here at length; given
the appalling ordeals that awaited Davies' mission, it is astonishing that
the diary survives at all.

The HQ mission's first days in the field were devoted to settling in.
Huts and tents were erected. Latrines were dug. Kit was sorted and
weapons were cleaned. Mules were found and bought and muleteers,
servants and labourers hired. Patrols went into surrounding valleys, to
find potential hideouts and suitable dropping grounds and to mine a
couple of roads and blow the odd bridge. 'Long and weary trip,' Nicholls
recorded of one evening expedition with Palmer, Chesshire and Lis; 'no
moon, tracks a foot wide with crevasses, precipices and streams.' Next
morning, the sight, far below them, of German staff cars and motorcycles on the main Elbasan–Struga road 'made all trigger fingers itch'.[13]

Davies also spoke at length with McLean and Smiley and told them
he wanted them out to Cairo to report. Both were pleased to be off.
Having enjoyed six months' freedom from senior officers, neither man
was finding the new regime easy. Smiley wrote in his own diary:

> Thursday, October 20th
> The Brigadier, with a more military mind than either Bill or
> myself, has started a system called standing-to. This means
> we all get out of bed and dressed about one hour before
> sunrise and wait for an enemy attack or something. The first
> time he gave out the orders he asked Bill what time the sun
> rose. As neither Bill nor I seldom get up before about half
> past nine I could not help smiling as Bill had no idea and
> asked me. I vaguely said 6 so we all now have to get up at
> 5. Jenkins and Jones and our other NCOs are furious. I am
> afraid Arthur Nicholls saw me wink at Bill from behind the
> Brigadier's back when all this was going on.

But Smiley also noted how 'neither of us fancied hanging about this
new headquarters much. It seems most unsafe to me it is so large and
immobile.'[14] The pair said their goodbyes and left for the coast.

Though w/t contact with Cairo was soon made, Bob Melrose would recall that Davies' understanding of w/t was, at first, poor. The first message Davies gave him to transmit was a note to Mrs Davies sending greetings from Albania. Since Davies had told him nothing in North Africa about the mission's destination, this did at least tell him where they were; still, 'here was I, the wireless operator, being asked to send a message obviously breaking all security . . . My first reaction was to refuse but I decided to consider the possibility of this adorning the wall of some security office in the Middle East. I showed the Colonel the message and said would he inform the Brig.' In Cairo it had been drilled into Melrose that he might have to make himself unpopular if he was to do his job properly and, in later weeks, he was to clash again with Davies over w/t requirements and procedure. Once, annoyed to find officers wasting his batteries to listen to music and that Davies believed his signalmen could go on the air whenever they liked, he shared his concerns with Arthur Nicholls while sitting one night by a signal fire. 'He told me about his family . . . and [he said] he was sympathetic to my situation but the Brig was in charge. "But not of signals," I said. "I think he realises that," was the Colonel's answer.'[15]

Julian Amery, who never knew him, would write later that Davies was brave and fair but too much of a regular for this irregular role, and compared him to Colonel Blimp. It is true that Davies was fresh to guerrilla life and secret work and, when dealing with Albanians, would prove forthright and to the point. Certainly his standards and expectations were high. Possibly they were too high: soon after arriving, so Nicholls noted in his diary, Davies sentenced four muleteers to death for stealing from the mission's stores; the Partisans reduced the sentence. But he was also observant, hardworking, closely focused on his task of harnessing locals to the Allied war effort and, within days, building a picture of what was happening in Albania that, in the circumstances, was about as accurate as could be expected.

By the end of October, Davies had summoned to Biza and spoken to most of the other officers scattered about Albania. Tony Neel was the first to report, having come down from Mati, Abas Kupi country. Next, from Dibra, a couple of days' march to the east, came Andy Hands. With him was Major Richard Riddell, head of a three-man team that had dropped to Hands on 20 October. Riddell was twenty-seven, a regular officer in the Royal Horse Artillery and a talented sportsman: at Woolwich, after Ampleforth, he had won the Silver Bugle for athletics and scored the winning try against Sandhurst. After coming out of France via Dunkirk in 1940 and some quiet service at home, he had been posted to India and then to the Middle East. It was in Lebanon, in the summer of 1943, that he volunteered with Tony Simcox, one of his troop commanders, for SOE. The twenty-six-year-old Simcox, the son and grandson of distinguished clergymen, was now Riddell's No. 2 and had already seen a good deal of the war. After returning sick from France in the spring of 1940 he had been commissioned and posted to North Africa where his unit, the Essex Yeomanry, spent months besieged at Tobruk. In January 1942, with the siege over, the battery sailed for Singapore but events overtook them, Singapore fell and they docked instead at Rangoon to be swept up in the retreat to India. That summer, in India, the remnants of the battery were reinforced and it was then that he found himself serving under Riddell. Nineteen-year-old John Davis was the pair's w/t operator.

After bringing Davies up to date with what was happening as they saw it, Neel and Hands left with orders to explore Albania's north-west and north-east corners, while Riddell went with instructions to take over Hands' work around Dibra. Alan Palmer, taking Victor Smith and Jock Huxtable, also left, with orders to move south and work among the established Partisan bases in the mountains west of Korça, where McLean's mission had been for most of the summer. Peter Kemp then arrived with news of his own, plus reports from George Seymour. Taking Alan Hare, he was soon on his way again, this time to Dibra, where tension was growing between the local *bajraktars*, Albanian chieftain-type figures, and Haxhi Lleshi's Partisans.

Davies was also quick to begin dealing with senior guerrillas and political leaders and, on 26 October, while speaking at Biza with a member of the LNC Council, had an early taste of local friction when a Balli Kombëtar deputation turned up. 'A first class glaring match ensues, all hackles up,' Nicholls recorded in the diary, 'but no unfortunate incident as E.F.D. [Davies] determined to show he is approachable by anyone who is genuinely interested in extermination of Boche.'[16]

It was not long either before the mission began to realise how deep the divisions went. Davies' first meeting with Enver Hoxha and most of the LNC Council took place at Labinot on 31 October; Nicholls went with him. Davies spoke first, translated by Fred Nosi, an English-speaking Partisan who had been appointed liaison officer with the

British. He explained his orders and what the Allies were trying to do. 'Received very coldly.' The Council replied with a long account of the LNC feud with the Balli Kombëtar. 'Situation discovered to be more serious than known previously. Civil war, undeclared as yet, about to break out.' The two officers learnt that the 'LNC have issued orders for the Bali to be fought and disarmed wherever met. State that they can do this and in no way detract from effort against Germans.' Next day the discussions continued. 'E.F.D. stresses the supreme importance of denying to the Germans unmolested travel on the principal rds. They agree and promise to carry out a more energetic policy of sniping and ambushing.'[17]

Davies and Nicholls were not impressed. The Partisans' professed ability to fight the Germans and the Balli Kombëtar simultaneously was 'very much open to doubt'; they were also infuriatingly arrogant. 'Their conceit is unbounded and they appear, quite sincerely, to believe that there are four Allies, Gt. Britain, Russia, America and Albania, and of these the last is the greatest and has made the most notable contribution to the war effort and in fact can now sit back and relax.' Annoying, too, was the Partisans' 'colossal cheek' in demanding from the British 'all sorts of luxuries': a 'cynical disregard of the Partisan vow to live hard . . . The net result is that they live a damned sight better than we do.'[18]

On the evening of 2 November, the pair then rode over to the mountain village of Shengjergj, not far from Biza, to meet and speak with Abas Kupi who had arrived there a few days before. Talks began that evening and continued next morning after a night 'well and truly bitten by bed bugs'.[19] Kupi was still a member of the LNC Council, Davies reported afterwards, but had secretly formed his new Zogist party, claimed 'a huge following all over the country' and planned to propose union between the Balli Kombëtar and his own followers 'with the sole object of fighting the Germans'.[20] He also asked for arms. Davies agreed to try to get him three sorties, dropped in his own territory. Overall, however, Kupi, too, left the British unimpressed. 'A.K. [Abas Kupi] appears to be a sincere character but full of wishful thinking,' Nicholls noted.

> He appears, like all Albs, to have the same unflinching grandiose ideas, involving large formations and pitched battles. All this in a country which is God's gift to guerillas and for which the Albs are ideally suited as good long range shots. It's a disgrace that the Germans continue to have

uninterrupted use of the main rds, as E.F.D. repeatedly tells
them. I fear water off a duck's back'.[21]

As for Kupi's proposed alliance with the Balli Kombëtar, this, Davies
felt, would simply mean 'a big increase of Bal Kombetar strength' with
'a consequent aggravation' of local tension.[22] Davies and Nicholls
returned to Biza. 'Perfect ride back in hot sunshine, the beeches more
glorious than ever. Ending with a horse-race between E.F.D. and A.N.
[Arthur Nicholls].'[23]

It was time to speak with the Balli Kombëtar. Already, however, the
future looked grim. 'Incoming messages tell of widespread fighting in Cent.
Albania between LNC and Bali', Nicholls recorded on 6 November. 'The
former appear to put the extermination of the Bali before anything else.'
The same day, in 'torrential rain and soaked to the skin', Kemp and Hare
returned from Dibra with tales of fighting between the Partisans and Xhem
Gostivari, a proven collaborator with both Italians and Germans, who
had advanced on the town from Macedonia.[24] Riddell and Kemp had
done well to keep the *bajraktars* out of the battle, but the situation remained
tense. Kemp, taking Sergeant Gregson-Allcott, his paramilitary expert, was
soon on his way back to Dibra, en route to the far north.

With Sergeant Chisholm to take the minutes, Davies and Nicholls
rode out again to Shengjergj on 8 November to meet a high-powered
Balli Kombëtar delegation and, they hoped, persuade the movement to
fight the Germans and refrain from civil war. 'Some rain on leaving
but on the way is met a storm of rain and hail such as we have seldom
experienced. Even the horses refused to face it. Eventually, very wet
and bedraggled, we arrive in the village.' The men who met them
included the Balli Kombëtar's elderly president, Midhat Frashëri, the
Chief Regent's cousin. All were in for a depressing afternoon:

> After more than six hours of continuous discussion in what
> is sometimes a hostile atmosphere, the conference ends at
> 1930 hrs in a complete impasse. Surprisingly enough the
> subsequent dinner is really quite amicable.
>
> And so to bed – E.F.D. having striven most magnificently
> and [with] infinite patience and tact. The result cannot be
> laid at his door – no one could possibly have done more but
> the Bali appear to be determined on civil war.

Next morning, still at Shengjergj, the British awoke to snow: 'our first fall'. They were also in for a shock. To their 'surprised delight' and 'E.F.D.'s infinite satisfaction' the Balli Kombëtar delegation announced 'that they have decided overnight to give the signed declaration demanded by E.F.D. of their intention to fight wholeheartedly against the Germans. And to promise verbally to cease fighting the LNC. A really great triumph for E.F.D. – very hardly worked for.'[25]

That elation was short-lived. On 11 November, Hoxha and two other Council members, Spiro Moisiu and Dali Ndreu, came to see Davies. After lunch, Nicholls recorded, Davies told them about the Balli Kombëtar's 'written declaration to fight the Hun' and his own intention to have it broadcast by the BBC. 'And then the fur flew! Diatribes against E.F.D., the BBC, etc.' Hoxha said that he regarded the Balli Kombëtar undertaking as worthless and that he would fight them anyway. 'Civil War is most emphatically on,' the day's diary entry ends. 'No one could have tried harder than E.F.D. but to no purpose.'[26]

Over the next few weeks the mission's mood worsened. The weather closed in, preventing drops of both stores and personnel. Although the Partisans, in Peza and Cerminika, had now formed two new brigades, the 2nd and 3rd, each a few hundred strong, reports were heard of growing open conflict between them and the Balli Kombëtar. News also arrived that the Germans, with Albanian help, had routed the Partisans and British missions first around Peza, then around Dibra. Fears grew of further thrusts that might clear the LNC out of the north altogether. Reports were received, too, of British casualties.

Survivors from Peza began to arrive at Biza on 12 November. Jack Bulman, whom Davies had sent to work with George Seymour, was the first to turn up. With him was Tony Corsair, an MI6 officer, the only one in Albania, who had dropped in a few weeks previously: MI6 was never to be very active there during the war and for a long time, by agreement, SOE did its intelligence-gathering role. 'They had lost everything – kit, W.T. sets, gold,' Nicholls recorded. Seymour, Roberts and Jim Smith, the pair said, were still there, but Hill, Seymour's w/t operator, was dead. Three days later, Seymour and Smith staggered in, 'G.S. [George Seymour] suffering from malaria and both in pretty bad shape, having been chased round and round the Peza area for days after the battle'.[27] Supported by tanks, artillery and Albanian quislings, the Germans, Seymour explained, had launched a set-piece pincer attack on Myslim Peza and the new 3rd Brigade. Two days of 'serious fighting' had followed before Seymour's camp woke at dawn on 7 November to a pistol shot fired at close range. Thirty seconds later German machine-guns opened up and, as the British scrambled to get away, Hill was hit in the torso and head. Smith tried to reach him, a selfless act that won him a Military Medal, but it was too late. Sending Bulman and Corsair off to Biza, Seymour stayed in 'for prestige reasons' with Roberts and Smith until one night they were ambushed again.[28] He and Smith broke out; Roberts was captured. 'G.S. has shown the flag magnificently but the price has been very heavy.'[29]

Roberts, Kemp's w/t operator, 'a quiet young man, brave and intelligent', was not a prisoner for long.[30] Without his captors knowing he had kept his pistol hidden and later shot one of his guards and pushed the other over a cliff. Then he went on the run. By late November, however, when Seymour eventually found him in the care of a Partisan çeta, Roberts was very weak from sickness, exposure and lack of food. He died from pneumonia on 22 December.

Concerns now grew that the Germans might drive next into Cerminika. 'E.F.D. and A.N. burn all documents, telegrams and reduce vulnerable paper to the minimum. Rucksacks packed for emergency move.' Fears were confirmed on 16 November 'in the shape of desultory mortar and arty fire, heard all day'. That night Halifaxes were heard overhead: long-awaited aircraft carrying men and the mission's overdue supplies. 'Frantic dash and the fires are lit. Aircraft above cloud, which they cannot penetrate.' No drop was made. Half an hour later the Germans were heard to be close and orders were issued for everyone to leave Biza and make for the Martanesh hills, five hours distant, home to one of the LNC Council, the big, bearded, machine-gun-toting priest, Baba Faja. 'Frantic packing up and saddling mules and horses. Sgt Melrose does wonders with the W.T.' At three in the morning and 'in pouring rain' the column, sixty mules-strong, set off. 'The track very bad, loads slipping, mules falling continually. A nightmare undertaking.' But Martanesh was reached, primitive quarters were found and the mission relaxed a little: 'there appears to be little immediate likelihood of an attack upon us here and there are some reasonably stout partisans about who will give us some warning'.[31]

News then arrived that Dibra, held by the Partisans since the Italian armistice and where Richard Riddell's mission was thought to be, 'has been attacked by the Hun with inf, armd cars and arty. It looks as if he is flushed with recent successes and determined to break up the Partisans. In this he appears to be being notably assisted by traitors who, knowing the mtns and the tracks, complicate everyone's problems, not least our own.' On 20 November, Michael Lis, who had left earlier to see Riddell, reappeared at Martanesh, 'needless to say having in time lost all his kit, and horse etc'.[32] At length it was learnt that Haxhi Lleshi had been unable to hold the town and, with Lis, withdrew, while Riddell and his mission, together with Kemp and Gregson-Allcott, were forced into the hills. The Germans followed. All of the British had narrow escapes. Kemp was to write vividly of how he, John Davis and Gregson-Allcott were surprised one morning in the village of Sllova while staying in the home of Cen Elezi, head of the powerful Ndreu family. As the Germans attacked, the British had to flee, vaulting fences and sprinting across open ground as figures in grey closed in on all sides, Schmeissers chattering. Bound by custom to protect his guests, one of Cen's sons ran alongside while behind them his father could be heard fighting for his life. Nothing could be done, Kemp wrote, '[b]ut I felt bitterly ashamed each time Xhelal stopped to look backward, the tears running freely down his face'. Cen, in fact, though wounded twice, shot his way out and survived. But Kemp's gentle Italian servant was dead, 'shot through the heart at point-blank range as he ran out after us'.[33] Dead, too, were several villagers, including women and children, whom the Germans, after the attack, lined up against the school and machine-gunned.

As November wore on, Davies' mission settled down to more hard living at Martanesh, while German moves remained worrying and the weather become daily more wintry, which continued to prevent the RAF from getting in to drop stores. Fuel and food were now much needed, as were arms for the Partisans, not least to prove that the British really wished to help them. Nicholls' diary entries continue:

Tuesday, 23 Nov 43
The same appalling rain and hail continues . . . No wood, no lamps. We feel like explorers and go to bed at 9 p.m. to keep warm and save light.

Wednesday, 24 Nov 43
Another night of torrential rain and wind . . . Heavy rain

continues all day . . . E.F.D. and A.N. out for a walk hear volleys of rifle fire from the direction in which an attack is anticipated. Nothing transpires . . .

Thursday, 25 Nov 43
0715 Continued volleys of rifle fire . . . This sounds serious, so E.F.D. and A.N. rouse the camp. A.N. consulting Guri [the cook] is told that it is 'only a wedding'. What a country, what a people!

Friday, 26 Nov 43
Night of tremendous gale, sleet, snow and thunder. W.T. aerial knocked flat . . . Good news on the wireless of further RAF raids on Germany, bridgehead established over the Sangro R. etc. keep up our spirits. Petrol running low and no illumination – that is the most difficult thing to cope with, limiting all work and recreation . . .

Saturday, 27 Nov 43
Weather improves and we wake to sunshine on the snow-covered mtns . . . E.F.D. starts the morning off with a successful lice and flea hunt but A.N. has no luck, although undoubtedly tenanted. E.F.D. nearly distracted at night by rat gnawing the beam above his head . . .

Sunday, 28 Nov 43 – Albanian Independence Day
Much finer with snow during the night until just after dawn. Some sun nearly all day but more snow coming . . . Alarm and excursion in the morning at the sound of steady gunfire, well controlled, somewhere in the Shengjerg [sic] direction. Decided, after prolonged deliberation, it must be 'feu de joie' for Independence Day . . .

Monday, 29 Nov 43
0830 Warm sunshine and a clear sky. The first for weeks . . .

Tuesday, 30 Nov 43
. . . St Andrews Day duly celebrated particularly by A.N. and Sgt Melrose to a running fire of ribald comment from J.C. [Jim Chesshire], A.H. [Alan Hare] and Cpl Smith.

On 1 December, rumours arrived of more British casualties, this time in a little town north of Dibra. 'P.K. [Peter Kemp] is reported to have bumped into a German in Peshkopje, both fired together and both fell dead.' Another officer, 'thought to be Simcox', was besieged in a Partisan house for six hours and then 'stabbed to death with bayonets' when he went to remonstrate with the Balli Kombëtar outside. 'Feeling running very high in the area and the blood lust for BLOs and the prices on their heads being an added attraction to the fun of the fair.'[34]

Next day, after another stormy night, 'E.F.D. and A.N. start up at 0605 hrs, as a snowy dawn breaks, to the one sound they have dreaded to hear – rifle shot followed by the sound of automatic weapons and bombs! Out of bed in a flash and into breeches and boots.' Nicholls alerted the kitchen staff, 'who say that once again it is a wedding and that this is the season for them. A.N. raises hell and demands advance knowledge of all such celebrations. The strain otherwise is quite appalling.' Also that day the mission heard from Cairo that an aircraft bound for Albania with five SOE personnel was missing. 'The accumulation of bad news is getting rather too much.'[35]

The deaths of Kemp and Simcox were soon disproved: both were fit and healthy. The lost aircraft, however, was confirmed to have crashed after catching fire in the air over Greece. Killed with the crew were Major Ian Smart, from Aberdeen, twenty-six years old and recently married; Captain Jack Stephenson, twenty-six; Lieutenant Alan Toley, also twenty-six, a peacetime surveyor from Sussex; Gunner George McKenna, twenty-three, from Dundee; and Corporal Ian Kesterton, twenty-two, from Dartford in Kent. Bob Melrose had met Kesterton, a w/t operator, while waiting to drop in. Melrose was sorting his kit 'when a pair of legs, untanned and white as snow, appeared at the door of my tent'. Kesterton was to be his assistant and the pair worked together checking equipment for the field. 'He was quite a young soldier and well spoken. I liked him right away.'[36]

By early December, the plight of Davies' own mission was serious. Another move had been made, this time from Martanesh to Orenja, another remote Cerminika village: a good spot with a dropping ground where the mission had hoped to stay put for some time. It was now apparent, however, that the Germans had surrounded the entire area:

Davies and the LNC Council, based nearby, were thought 'very big bait', Nicholls noted. 'A very high price has been put on the heads of E.F.D. and his staff. With the large number of traitors about this adds an additional and unwanted complication to life.'[37] Plans began to be laid with the Council to break out and seek refuge in the mountains of southern Albania, if a way could be found of crossing the Shkumbin, now wide and fast-flowing from the rain and snow. And if that could be accomplished, Davies would try to get out of the country and back to Cairo to report.

For days the mission waited for the Council's word that it was ready to move. With German spotter planes now frequently overhead, it was an uncomfortable, anxious time:

Sunday, 5 Dec 43
. . . E.F.D. and A.N. have as near a bath as is possible under the circumstances – sectional washing – and a delousing parade. It is virtually impossible either to be or to feel clean. Our clothes are never off, even for sleeping, owing to the high degree of readiness and mobility which must be maintained at all times in this uncertain country . . . Poor A.H. has got 'worms' – not uncommon in this sort of life . . .

Monday, 6 Dec 43
Beautiful clear starlit night but no aircraft . . . Fiesler Storch over twice, taking an unfortunately active interest in us and our whereabouts. Much debate as to what this portends, as he has recently been carrying out detailed recce of Bixha [sic] and Martanesh. With so many spies and traitors about life is not very easy – and to this must be added the appalling Alb habit of gossiping and complete lack of security . . .

Tuesday, 7 Dec 43
In spite of a fine night no aircraft once again . . .
1430 E.F.D. and A.N. go out for a walk and to inspect the Partisan forces which have been coming into the village for the last forty-eight hours. Pickets are seen being posted on the surrounding hills, men running about – then suddenly, fairly near, three bombs, a considerable number of single shots followed by LMG fire. With one voice E.F.D. and A.N.

say 'Well, now we *are* off!' and return to HQ to be met by
A.H., who had heard the same, announcing that it was a
funeral . . . [Partisans] say this is the beginning of the local
Bajram festivities and we must expect a fusillade of shots for
the next three days. In the present circumstances this is
unhappy to say the least . . .

Wednesday, 8 Dec 43
We awake to a fusillade of rifle and LMG shots, bombs, etc,
which may be a dawn attack by the Boche or alternatively
only Bajram Festival! This continues throughout the morning,
to E.F.D.'s increasing rage, at least 500 rounds having been
expended before lunch and many bombs thrown.

On 11 December it was time to go and the Council, a Partisan battalion
and the British left together. Labinot, still within the German cordon,
was reached that evening. 'Fantastic performance then starts. An entire
battalion singing choruses, a huge bonfire, everyone smoking – all this
within sound and probably sight of the Germans – unbelievable!' After
an hour the column pressed on. '[C]loud covered sky but the moon
gives just enough light. Very bad going.' At three the next morning,
thoroughly lost owing to the Partisans' 'inadequate recce of the ground
and total reliance on the word of a peasant', the whole party turned
round and set off on a four-hour return trip to Labinot. 'Unload everything, get the horses fed, and collapse into an improvised bed.'[38]
    All next day 'the sounds of battle, rifles, SMGs, LMGs and HMGs'
were heard: clashes, it was said, between Partisans and the Balli Kombëtar.
In the evening, 'Enver Hoxha comes up to talk and discuss plans. He
is very ashamed of the nonsense they have made the night before.' Next
morning there was another louse hunt: 'E.F.D. catches a "Bajraktar".'
Then it was decided that everyone, Partisans and British, would trek
back to Orenja and wait there a few days before making another attempt
at getting out and over the Shkumbin. 'The river is no longer the trouble
but the area which has been thoroughly stirred up'; and for that, the
British felt, the Partisans were responsible. 'The LNC have made a proper
mess of things, having planned to cross and then have a parting crack
at all the Cerminike villages where there are Bali. But they haven't crossed
and have stirred up a hornet's nest.' Nicholls' diary entry for 15 December
ended 'with apologies to Louis MacNeice and his poem "Bagpipe Music":

It's no go the merry-go-round/ It's no go the muck up/ It's no go the Skumbini [sic] River/ It's been a proper F— up.'[39]

The return to Orenja was made on 16 December. 'In spite of delays caused by refractory mules and their loads and an apparent hang-over possessed by the principal muleteers, a quick trip is made.' Hare, left there in the hope that an aircraft might get in, met the exhausted party with the 'jubilant news' that he had had a drop, but of explosives, mostly, and a few small arms. 'Virtually no food, no clothing.' This caused some of the Partisans to refuse to accept what kit had been dropped. 'What unbelievable people they are!' By now the noose was tightening, however, and the outlook, Nicholls thought, 'very bleak':

> Thursday, 16 Dec 43
> . . . No local news but our appreciation is that the Hun will attack here any minute . . . There is virtually nothing between us and the Boche except some half-baked village idiots. The 2nd Bde and the Italians have withdrawn . . . and the remnants are dispersed all over the countryside and have lost such coherence as they ever possessed. E.F.D. holds a late Council of War and issues his order [for] Battle Stations and Stand-to tomorrow at first light. Sten guns and grenades, newly arrived by air sortie, are cleaned and issued. We should be able to give some account of ourselves at least.

> Friday, 17 Dec 43
> 0600 Stand-to for all HQ . . . Country almost uncannily quiet . . .
> 0800 Stand-down. Lovely sunshine but very cold.

> Saturday, 18 Dec 43
> 0600 Stand-to. Another perfect starlit night – brilliant dawn. Bitterly cold. Nothing happens but the moment we relax those precautions the Boche and/or the Bali will be on us. There is nothing between us and him to stop him doing what he wants.

Then, at two o'clock on the morning of 19 December, word arrived that the Germans were opening up a military road running through Cerminika. 'This is the real thing, as there are bound to be various other directions from which drives will come. The only question is from how many and how quickly.' After standing-to 'in another lovely dawn' another German Storch appeared, 'waggles his wings ominously right over our HQ and drops leaflets. These are picked up and prove to be calls to the Italian soldiers on the mtns to surrender and promising them a safe conduct and good treatment. All our Italians are not impressed saying the only welcome they would get would be from the business end of an MG.' Bread was baked and distributed. Davies prepared to send Cairo an emergency signal 'for food, arms and clothing'. As this was written, 'news comes in that the Boche are in Zdrashe, one hr away. A rapid departure is made.'[40]

'Everybody was clearing out and I was soon left alone,' Bob Melrose would remember. Davies had told him to bury the mission's gold. 'Outside the ground was very rocky, also the gunfire was very close so I decided I hadn't time to try and dig a hole so I went around to the side of the house where we had an outside toilet made up from a mule saddle and a parachute. I got hold of an empty bomb fin container and put the bags in this, put the lid on and immersed it in the toilet.' Then, after setting fire to the house, he was off, roughly in the direction he had seen the others go. 'I rode on and on getting more worried if I was heading in the right direction . . . At long last I spotted the tail end of our riders and made my way up . . . As I staggered on I became aware of the droning of aircraft and saw aldis lamps signalling above me. I got my lamp out and I had to tell them what was happening . . . I remember sending "Abort. Germans".'[41]

After abandoning Orenja, the British and Partisans rode and trekked seven hours to wooded hills behind Biza where the rest of the night, the first of many, was spent in the open. 'Very cold and sleep impossible,' Nicholls wrote; 'perpetual movement is required to keep warm. A scrap of meat is found and cooked under great difficulties, as we dare not show any smoke.' Next day the mission learnt that its mules had gone past in the dark. 'Very bad luck as there goes all our food, clothing, bedding, etc. We are likely to regret this.'[42]

Those now hiding in the woods totalled about 160 'with a large number of horses and mules for whom there can be no hope of getting food'. Davies spoke with Hoxha and 'finally' persuaded him 'to try to move to the south by breaking out of the Hun encircling movement in an easterly direction with a skeleton party'. An 'Advance HQ' of Davies,

Nicholls and Jim Smith would go with them. The rest of the British party was to stay in Cerminika and try to 'keep the mission flag flying'.[43]

Hoxha and Davies set off with their little group on 22 December. Soon enough a halt was called and men sent ahead to check the route. The rest stood around shivering:

> We are high up, the cold is intense and owing to it being day no fires can be lit because of the risk of discovery by smoke. To this misery comes driving rain and absolutely no food. Before leaving the others, our slender stock of chocolate had been distributed and each of us has five small squares. During the course of the day one of these is eaten. The only thing to be done is to keep walking round in circles and try and keep our circulation going.

After a night 'passed in abject misery and discomfort' the men sent ahead reappeared 'dragging a sheep'. This was killed and eaten; then the march continued, a steady climb 'getting into deep snow. And then the guide loses his way! We plough up and down steep and dangerous snow slopes – retrace our footsteps – E.F.D.'s torch is borrowed and exhausted to no purpose.' Eventually it was decided to stop and camp. 'Another appalling night of sleeplessness, cold and wet is spent, with no food or prospect of it.'[44]

Next day, Christmas Eve, the skeleton party set off again. '[A]fter a four hours' march, punctuated by a good deal of uncertainty on the part of the guide, a very wet and cold halt is made in driving rain near the outskirts of the village of Okshtun, where we are to spend the 48 hrs over Christmas recuperating from the appalling experiences of the past few days.' The British and sundry others were led 'quickly and surreptitiously into a peasant house on the edge of the village'. They were not to be there long:

> Fifteen people crowd themselves into the upper room, where a huge fire is soon blazing. The room is rapidly festooned with clothes and articles of equipment drying – we have been continuously soaked for days past and everything is in a dreadful state. Orders are given for the preparation of an evening meal and those who can settle down to sleep . . . amid a fascinating scene of the firelight playing on the festoons

of corncobs with which the ceiling is covered and the sheep bells of the sheep quartered on the ground floor. We are just thinking that we can spend Christmas quite pleasantly here – more particularly as some Raki has been obtained – when news comes that the Huns are 2 kilometres away. To our consternation and dismay the decision is taken to move at 0400 hrs next morning. A scramble ensues to prepare things for the morning and get what sleep we can.

Saturday, 25 Dec 43
0300 E.F.D. and A.N. stand-to. Others are more leisurely and typically Albanian, it is 0600 hrs before we are ready to move off and 0630 before we actually do so. By this time the sheep and chickens which should have been our Christmas dinner have been cut up and distributed . . . A very long steep climb brings us over the mountains to the East and thence down to the road which we are to try and cross by daylight . . . and to E.F.D. and A.N.'s horror the place selected for the crossing involves a march across a wide open plain both sides . . . By this time Cpl Smith is too weak to carry his greatcoat any further . . . At a halt when the woods on the far side are entered, the appalling discovery is made that the whole toe of one of E.F.D.'s boots has broken away, as a result of having been put too close to the fire by our host of the night before in his attempt to dry them . . . The climb is resumed over the high mountains to the East, making for a saddle. When half way up, 5 shots, followed by 3 more, are fired blind into the hillside in our vicinity. Fearing an ambush on the track over the saddle, a sharp rt hand turn is made, resulting in a truly appalling climb over the highest part of the mtn. It takes a great deal out of everyone, finishing as we did almost on our hands and knees. The route – no vestige of a track – then leads over the most terrible volcanic crater pocked country in which the guides have no idea of the way and involve us in much rock scrambling. As dusk falls, the party, excessively weary and cold, reach the top of the mountain above the village of Khorishte, which is supposed to be the next stage on our journey. Envoys are sent on to contact those who are supposed to be friendly to

us. An attempt is made, before the light finally fails, to follow them down but this has to be given up for fear of missing them in the dark. We have spent most of the day at approx 6,000ft and the cold is intense. E.F.D. and A.N. nestle in each other's arms in a vain attempt, like the Babes in the Wood, to acquire some warmth. A truly fantastic scene. Eventually the intense cold makes a withdrawal necessary to an area where fires can be lit. This is done and once again we crouch wet and very cold over a fire. What a way in which to spend Christmas!

The envoys returned after midnight with news that no one was going to help them. 'This is a bitter blow, meaning that having broken out of the encircling Hun movement, we must now re-trace our steps, re-cross the road and admit, temporarily at least, defeat.' The 'sad return' began but the guides soon lost their way, 'and only the gentle persuasion of E.F.D. and A.N. that their compasses should be used averts disaster. Already the guides had led us in one complete circle.' Before dawn another halt was called.

Everyone very exhausted and E.F.D.'s boot causing him a lot of trouble, as now are Cpl Smith's, the best part of both soles having disappeared on these appalling tracks and rocks . . .

We are all suffering badly, particularly in our feet which have now been consistently wet and frozen for more than a week. E.F.D.'s boots are causing him endless trouble and A.N.'s feet, due to bad circulation, are in a very bad way. Cpl Smith has broken his boots in the leg and they must now be cut to get them on.

After 'an appalling night of such cold as few of us have ever experienced' a fresh start was made. 'True to form the guide starts off in a circle and once again A.N.'s compass comes to the rescue.' Another long and agonising march followed in 'deep snow, cold so intense that our hands are burnt when they touch the metal of our weapons. Our clothes are board-hard and all feeling has left our hands and feet.' Okshtun was reached at noon: 'we crawl painfully into the outskirts . . . Some food of sorts is produced and everyone collapses into sleep. There is no real relaxation of tension, as all [villagers] are frightened of sheltering Partisans in view of the news of the Hun's activities.'[45]

At that point it was decided that Davies' little party should stay in Okshtun while the LNC Council moved on. 'We are merely extra people on the march to be fed and guarded.' And for the next week, waiting for some word from the Partisans, they barely left the room:

Tuesday, 28 Dec 43
. . . With our eight days growth of beard we are hardly spick and span British officers. Our clothes are falling to pieces and we have virtually no socks. A bad state of affairs. After the Partisans have gone, we settle ourselves in and relax. Feeding is going to be a problem, as no outside purchases can be made which would prejudice our security, [and] we must content ourselves with the very plain fare of the peasant, comprising chiefly beans and corn bread.

Wednesday, 29 Dec 43
Today is to be a day of cleaning-up and gradually our beards are removed. Unfortunately we all seem to be developing colds and coughs . . . Our washing possibilities are strictly limited as we only have the clothes in which we stand up and even then must share our clothing round as much as possible to ensure that all are clad more or less equally. The day seems very long, nothing to read, sleep difficult owing to the intense cold, the lack of any cover and the terrible hardness of the baked earth floor.

Thursday, 30 Dec 43
Another day of what E.F.D. calls 'Endurance Vile'. Our day is made up of the smallest things – this morning's excitement being a universal wash and louse-hunt . . . A very chilly but not entirely unproductive pastime . . . Food is a constant topic of conversation – dinners we have eaten in the past, meals we hope to eat in the future, favourite dishes and difference in ways of cooking them. The smallest incident serves as a peg on which to hang some reminiscences. Cpl Smith [is] in great pain from what we think must be a fractured vertebra at the base of the spine, done in the many heavy falls he

took. A.N.'s feet still very senseless and tending to become poisoned . . .

Friday, 31 Dec 43 'Hogmanay'
Another night of intense cold and discomfort got through somehow. A layer of corn husks under the mat on which E.F.D. and A.N. lie and share a coverlet does something to mitigate the harshness of the floor but not very much. This troglodyte existence is very trying for many reasons – not the least being the semi-darkness during the day. The sole illumination . . . is a glassless window 18″ square, through which a howling draught blows . . .

The old boy of the house – an old rogue to whom we are getting rather attached – goes off early in quest of news leaving us under the guard of a small boy of 8 or so. The children are unbelievably dirty and ragged and the degree of poverty quite appalling . . .

Saturday, 1 Jan 44 . . .
Cpl Smith's supposed 'fractured vertebrae' turns out on inspection to be a large and painful boil. Under the expert treatment of E.F.D. and A.N. acting as dresser, it happily is speedily cured. There now remains the fight which is being waged to get A.N.'s feet, which are in a very bad way from poor circulation and prolonged exposure to cold and wet, back into some sort of shape to enable him to withstand the long march which will be ahead of us once we do move. Belatedly with a couple of glasses of Raki . . . Christmas and New Year are jointly and very queerly celebrated. E.F.D. and A.N., the married men, toast 'Absent Friends – and Wives'.

Sunday, 2 Jan 44
The sixth day of our incarceration. We are all agreed that we are beginning to have enough of this . . . The family have now lost all sense of security about us and are madly 'on the make' . . . Another day of washing, shaving, delousing – very essential for the maintenance of self-respect and the passing of the days which seem age-long . . .

Monday, 3 Jan 44
A bitterly cold night and all are suffering from increasing
boredom and the restraint of being closeted for more than
a week in one small, dusty, smoky, smelly upper room of a
peasant house.

Then, that morning, unannounced, '4 thoroughly sinister men whom
on sight we dub Bali' walked in. 'The fool of an old man and his sons
had all gone out, leaving us completely unguarded . . . out we must get,
and quickly.' They made for Kostenja, Baba Faja's village, reaching it
that evening, and there, to their 'great surprise and joy', found Chesshire,
Hare and Sergeant Chisholm.[46]

Surviving with Nicholls' diary are three pages torn from Jim
Chesshire's own journal, describing the experiences of those left
behind among the Cerminika peaks while Davies and the Council
were trying to get out. 'No sign of food so a mule killed but not
eaten with much relish,' Chesshire scribbled on 22 December. 'Another
wet night,' he wrote the following day; 'No food . . . Majority of
horses and mules killed.' 'No food' again on Christmas Eve. Then,
that evening, 'Two machine guns opened up on us from about 75
yards – complete surprise – complete panic – hurried and disorderly
retreat. Sgt M. [Melrose] and Sgt C. [Chisholm] separated from self
and Capt H. and Roberto [the Italian interpreter] who after swim-
ming river stayed night in cave.' Next day, Chesshire, Hare and
Roberto made 'cross-country' for the mission's old w/t hut, found it
'unburned and unoccupied . . . took off all wet clothes and crawled
under bracken and went to sleep'. Later Chisholm turned up and for
the next few days those four remained on the move, hiding in shacks,
buying and stealing food. On 30 December they 'arrived safely chez
B.F.' in Kostenja and piled into another filthy sheepfold. Four days
later, Davies, Nicholls and Smith staggered in to join them: 'great
joy and exchange of stories'.[47]

By then, two of the British forced on the run in December were in
German hands. One was Frank Trayhorn. Sent to open a new dropping
ground, for a time he had accompanied John Davis and Gregson-
Allcott on their way to rejoin Richard Riddell, who had sent them
to see if Davies had a spare w/t set. As they struggled on, German

soldiers appeared. 'They were only a few minutes behind,' Davis remembers. 'Trayhorn was unable to run and unfortunately was caught.'[48] But of Bob Melrose, last seen when Chesshire and the others were attacked on Christmas Eve, SOE was to learn nothing for months. Word was sent to his family in Penicuik that he was missing, presumed dead.

It had been 'pitch black' and 'drizzling', Melrose recalled fifty years later, and he had been trying to fix a grenade to his w/t set when the machine-guns opened up and scattered Chesshire's party. 'The bullets pranged all over the place and I ran and I ran till I fell and it was then that I remembered my radio.' He walked back, pulled the pin on the grenade and fled; 'no one shot at me . . . the Germans must have thought I was surrendering'. When he finally stopped he was alone and hurt: 'a bit of rock embedded in my left leg above and to the side of my ankle, [while] my dagger had slit open the scabbard and cut into my right leg above the knee'. Then he met one of the mission's Italians, equally lost, who said 'he had heard an officer shouting my name . . . but that was ages ago'.

Together they made for Biza and, after hours of walking and being 'stared at' by locals, came in above the camp 'and looked down into what was a mess. The cabin and other huts were only ashes; my aerials were in pieces'. The Italian disappeared to find food. 'He returned with a tin of Irish Stew. These Italians had pilfered our stores when we were here and this proved to be one of the items that had been hidden for future use.' Now Melrose decided to make for the coast. He still had sovereigns on him and 'had in mind the possibility of hiring or buying some sort of boat to get across to Italy'. He and his Italian set off, buying a horse after a couple of miles, then rode on to 'a pretty rough-looking river' where a 'shifty looking character' appeared, guided them across and, on the far bank, led them into a rambling house. Melrose sat by the fireplace: 'the fire was playing havoc with my eyes and I knew it wouldn't be long before I fell asleep . . . next thing I remember it was daylight and morning. I roused myself and turned to get my gun but it had gone.' He also found his host pointing a pistol at him.

Melrose was 'pushed and jabbed' to the door and out to a road where he met a German field kitchen and 'two surprised looking Germans'. They approached, 'guns to the fore'. Melrose surrendered. '[T]o my right was a drop into a raging river, to my left a mountain.

I didn't have much choice.' In a hut by the kitchen a German officer gave him his chair and his dinner and asked who he was.

'2332263 Sgt Melrose.'
'English?'
'No, sir, British.'

Melrose was treated well. The officer gave him the same rations and cigarettes as the rest of his men and the soldiers took him for walks and 'were friendly enough, although they all said they couldn't understand how I could associate with people like the partisans'. 'Take advantage of being with front line soldiers,' he was told. 'You won't get the same consideration at our HQ.'[49] When the day came to take him down from the mountains, Melrose was put in the back of a truck and a circuitous drive began. In one village the truck stopped, the canvas above the tailgate was thrown up and Frank Trayhorn was pushed aboard. En route to Germany the two men were separated, being reunited briefly on a busy station platform in Berlin; an air raid was in progress and their guards had to rescue them from the attentions of an angry crowd. After some rough questioning and solitary imprisonment, Melrose was sent to Stalag IVB, a regular POW camp. Trayhorn ended up in Colditz.

For the surviving six Britons and their Albanian and Italian camp followers reunited in Baba Faja's sheepfold, life was to remain unpleasant. Next day, Nicholls recorded, after a 'fine sunny morning', the weather closed in. 'At dusk the sky clouds over and strong wind gets up'; at night the gale became worse, 'blowing snow into our semi-open hut'. Hunger was acute. 'A lucky purchase [next day] of some walnuts and quinces from a peasant woman provides our only food.' On 6 January a hen and half a loaf were shared out, 'small rations for 13 starving men'. Living conditions were now 'quite impossible . . . several men are suffering from bad eye trouble from the acrid smoke which fills the hut'. A minor improvement came when the party moved into Baba Faja's house. 'The night is passed in warmer conditions, but very hungry. The blizzard shows no sign of abating.'[50]

On 7 January another hen was found and eaten and 'the height of insolence' reached when Fred Nosi, still attached as the mission's liaison officer, declared 'that the present state of affairs is all E.F.D's fault for

not having denounced the Balkom earlier! After this staggering statement nothing they ever say again can surprise us.' Then Hoxha and
the Council rushed in. 'They are leaving us behind.' The British asked
them to send medical aid as soon as possible. 'A.N.'s feet have turned
septic and are in no state to march. E.F.D. tends them but with no
medical kit it is very difficult.'[51]

The morning of 8 January was spent 'washing and delousing' in
sunshine. Baba Faja's commissar arrived with an Italian colonel in tow
and orders from the Council that the British look after him. 'This beats
all previous records of their behaviour.' After lunch word arrived that
German soldiers were minutes away. 'A quick pack-up is made . . . We
cook all the meat we can either to get it inside us or in a condition in
which we can carry it.'[52] Then, standing outside, Davies was fired at.
At once it was apparent that they were almost surrounded: armed men
could be seen moving above them on three sides. The closest were six
hundred yards away.

Under fire, the party started up the mountain, climbing in single
file to break down the snow. 'There was no cover of any kind on this
side,' Alan Hare would recall; 'our dark figures showed up with
unpleasant clarity.' Progress was difficult: 'the mountain was very
steep, and the snow in deep drifts'.[53] The range shortened; the fire
became heavier and more accurate. Arthur Nicholls was a particular
target: bullets cut his belt and went through his cap and the skirt of
his coat.

Hare, at the rear of the column, then spotted two figures 'slithering
down the mountainside' towards him. One was Davies. 'When I spoke
to him he replied with some difficulty, said that he had been hit twice,
refused any offer of assistance, and ordered me to continue . . . After
a short period of indecision, I continued to climb.' More men fell out,
'some from exhaustion, some from wounds'. One was Sergeant Chisholm
'who said that he was too exhausted to go on, and lay down in the
snow despite all my efforts at persuasion'.[54]

Returning fire was ineffective, Hare remembered, 'as they were behind
cover and we were fully exposed'.[55] He and Nicholls agreed that the
survivors try, nevertheless, to make a stand on one of the peaks; but
their attackers reached it first and fired on them from twenty yards.
All surviving Partisans then scattered and, with Chesshire believed hit
and Sergeant Smith also missing, Hare and Nicholls, now alone, staggered for the cover of nearby trees. When it was dark, they set off

again. At six the following morning, after eleven hours of 'appalling experiences in snow drifts, freezing streams etc', they stumbled into the old w/t hut where Hare had hidden on Christmas Day.[56]

One of them, probably Nicholls, still carried the diary. Further entries tell the story of the next few days. The 'terrified' owner of the hut refused to let them stay, sold them some bread and, for another sovereign, sent them off in the direction of a village called Val. More sovereigns went on guides to get them across a ravine and on the right track, only for the pair to find the village burnt by the Germans. In one surviving home they were given some food and 'slept like the dead' before being 'rudely awakened' after an hour and told to get out, as 'spies' had 'denounced their presence'. More sovereigns were produced for the pair to be hidden and fed in another remote hut. 'Set off 1800 hrs on what is supposed to take 1½ hrs', the diary then reads. 'By midnight the guide has lost his way and an enforced stop is made and a fire is lit. The last thing to be wished for.' Both men were now 'in a very bad way' and Nicholls' 'septic feet and hands, which have been further frost-bitten, causing the greatest agony'. Next morning, in falling snow, a fresh start was made and the hut reached two hours later. 'A.N. and A.H. in the last stages of exhaustion. Some meat is cooked and bread eaten and all fall into an uneasy sleep. A.N.'s feet and hands in an appalling state.'[57]

They were to remain in the hut for five days. On the first morning, voices were heard outside and Fred Nosi appeared. Stories were exchanged and the British now learnt 'that there never were any Germans' at Kostenja: their attackers had been Albanian. 'It is too appalling to think that E.F.D. has been badly wounded, perhaps killed by the Albanians whom we have come to help against the invaders of their country. No news of Sgt C. or Sgt S. [Smith] but it is feared that both are probably prisoners even if not wounded.' Nicholls continued:

Tuesday, 11 Jan 44
A morning meal of corn bread and local butter. No water available except boiled snow which induces an appalling thirst. A.N.'s torch lost or stolen – a very serious loss. A.H.'s feet slightly frost-bitten. A.N.'s in a very bad state and his fingers covered with frost-bite blisters. Whether he will ever get his boots on again remains to be seen. At the most the stay here can only be for 4–5 days, nowhere is safer for

longer than that. Meanwhile news from whatever source it comes is anxiously awaited. The day passes somehow, the high lights as always being the preparation of meals, the eating of them – protracted as long as possible – and sleep after them.

Wednesday, 12 Jan 44
. . . A.H.'s left foot is in a bad way – the little toe being black with frostbite and the whole foot very swollen.

Thursday, 13 Jan 44
. . . Our underclothes are taken to the village to be washed, leaving us very cold. A.H.'s foot reported better, but A.N.'s are very much worse and climbing down the mountain from our present hideout is quite out of the question.

Friday, 14 Jan 44
A.N. much worse and the poison spreading.

It was now that Nicholls told Hare to leave him. Having heard that morning 'that everyone knows 2 BLOs are here', they decided to stay where they were for one more night, then Hare would take Nosi and Nicholls' pocketbook diary and strike out to the south in the hope of finding a British mission there.[58] Nicholls would move down to Val, hide for as long as he dared, then try to find George Seymour, last heard to be with Abas Kupi, about ten miles to the north. Next day, as planned, Hare and Nicholls split up. Over a final lunch they watched their ten hosts get 'thoroughly drunk' and squabble over the 'ethics of taking money from [the] British'. Then, at two o'clock, with 'the gravest misgivings', Hare watched five villagers carry Nicholls, 'both feet, one arm, both hands out of commission', down the hill towards Val.[59]

The following morning, Hare set off with Fred Nosi to search for a way across the Shkumbin and for treatment for the frostbite taking hold in his foot. For the next five weeks he wrote daily in the diary, his entries now a chronicle of one officer's experiences on the run, in the cold and snow, among a poor and fearful people:

Monday 17 Jan 44
. . . A.H.'s toe now gone septic but no sign of spreading . . .

Wednesday 19 Jan 44
. . . Foot worse . . .

Saturday 22 Jan 44
. . . Grave doubt as to how much further foot will carry
me . . .

Wednesday 26 Jan 44
. . . Foot now definitely starting to disintegrate and impossible
to walk, so start off for next house at about 1730 hrs on
diminutive ass. Travel for 1½ hours in blizzard when ass gives
up and I have practically to carry it . . . Serious decision has
now to be taken that must get medical attention before going
much further as otherwise no chance on tough journey . . .

Friday 28 Jan 44
Owner of house returned from wedding with much wind put
up him . . . Wants to be quit of us and quickly . . . Dismal
prospect ahead I'm afraid and this looks like the furthest south
A.H. will ever get . . . Moving tomorrow morning [to] neighbouring house to prevent present host getting heart failure.

Saturday 29 Jan 44
Move at 0530, about twenty minutes away and are received
after much delay . . . by new host who has had two wounded
Partisans on hands for five weeks previously and therefore
views me with grave misgivings. After uneventful day move
off by mule . . .

Tuesday 1 Feb 44
. . . Foot quiescent but will no longer take boot.

Saturday 5 Feb 44
. . . In perfectly vertical breeze am bundled off to Shengjerg
[sic] as Germans and Ballis reported about to attack . . .

Sunday 6 Feb 44
. . . Foot still stewing merrily . . . I must leave at once . . .
Germans hot on tail . . .

Monday 7 Feb 44

After a particularly unpleasant journey of about three hours, arrive at a house where we are taken in and warmed . . . To my unspeakable joy there is an Italian doctor in mountains about two hours distant and will send for him tomorrow.

Tuesday 8 Feb 44

Doctor sends list of medicaments necessary for foot but says not worth his while to come till we have them . . . We have plenty to eat but unfortunately I have slight fever which adds to the complications of life . . .

Thursday 10 Feb 44

[P]easant returns from Tirana in evening with harrowing news that medicaments needed by doctor for A.H. are unobtainable. However A.H. recovered from fever and now more or less impervious to slings and arrows . . .

Sunday 13 Feb 44

. . . Peasant has found super hideout with priest's hole thrown in, which from his description sounds like a mixture of the Ritz and the Waldorf Astoria. Agree to move there this evening as have been too long in present location. Start at dusk and have as usual bloody journey with some walking in deep snow, find new hideout to be slightly scruffier than any of the houses yet visited, only advantage inhabitants appear to be willing to keep us until the second coming as long as we pay one Napoleon per day . . .

Monday 14 Feb 44

Dirtiness, stupidity and general lack of recognisable human characteristics in the family with whom we now lodge is partially explained by fascinating typically Alb story. For the last ten years the family has had a blood feud with another of greater strength. During this period none of the adult male members have dared to go out of doors except short distances at night or accompanied by their wives which theoretically renders them inviolable to attack. For tilling their land and running errands they have to rely on their neighbours. As a result they are as batty a lot as I have ever come across and the time passes agreeably in endless arguments as they are obviously determined to bleed us dry.

Tuesday 15 Feb 44
Still no news of the outside world and day spent entirely on bargaining for food, wood and trying to explain politely to our family that they should not come in and sit around watching us eat as if we were animals at a zoo as they are far more like animals than we are.

Wednesday 16 Feb 44
. . . More eggs, more sleep, more Albanian lessons with more bad temper on my part.

Two days later, a letter, unheralded, reached Hare from George Seymour. 'States need for meeting . . . I reply in agreement stating my physical difficulties.' Then, on 19 February, 'another note from G.S. . . . He is only half an hour away. He sends over stores and bodyguard and A.H. feels guiltily he must have made himself sound much iller than he is.' Setting off the following evening, Hare reached Seymour within the hour. 'He makes A.H. extremely welcome.'[60]

Safe, warm and fed, and with medical treatment on hand, Hare found his health soon improving. But his joy at being found was tempered by news of Arthur Nicholls. After dispatching Hare to the south, Nicholls, in a terrible state, had remained on the move in an astonishing effort to locate Seymour's mission. Seymour reported later:

His means of progression in the first place was to sit on his overcoat and to be pulled down the snow-covered and rocky mountainside by his escort of two Partisans. He later succeeded in obtaining a small mule which, although it carried him, was extremely painful since, owing to his height, his mutilated feet were continually dragging in the snow. He was now unable to get his boots on and his feet were wrapped in roughly cured goat skins. Gangrene had set in . . .

On 14th January I had heard of his plight but not his location. I made every effort to find him but owing to lack of information and the fact that I and my party were ourselves 'on the run' after being attacked and chased, I did not find him until 26/27 January.

During this interval he had crossed a large expanse of mountainous territory which was continually patrolled by hostile bands. He had been compelled to move by night only. He had no money, change of clothing nor medical equipment. He was forced to hide in verminous sheep-folds by day and any food he had managed to obtain was almost exclusively rye-bread. He had no interpreter.

When I located him he was more than half-starved, verminous, exhausted, and gangrene had obtained a firm grip on his feet. He had also had an accident having fallen down a mountain side and his shoulder was dislocated.

His feet were in an almost unbelievable condition. Both were festering masses and the only indication of where his toes were was where bare bones showed through the gangrened flesh.

'In spite of his physical condition,' Seymour added, 'his fighting spirit was unimpaired . . . He began at once to discuss with me the re-organisation of the Mission and to plan for future operations.' Nicholls 'would not give in' though he was now 'so ill and in such pain that it was impossible for him even to ride a mule. He did not himself complain but fainted as soon as he was mounted.'[61]

Seymour undertook immediately to secure medical help and a safe and comfortable hideout. 'Am doing utmost get best doctors and hope may save his feet,' he signalled Cairo. 'How he kept going God knows. Has shown endurance and fortitude beyond all praise.'[62] Through Abas Kupi, contact was made in Tirana with Shefqet Ndroqi, a doctor, Osman Jounzi, a skilled surgeon, and Ihsan Toptani, an English-speaking landowner who had been a good friend to Percy and his gendarmerie inspectors before the war. Toptani, with Jounzi and an escort, then drove into the mountains, picked up Nicholls, whom Seymour had stretchered down gently to a village near the road, and took him to his home at Valijas on the wooded plain north of Tirana. Pettini, one of Seymour's Italians, went with them. Toptani wrote later:

We installed the Colonel in a guest room. The normal bed was too small for him and we made a special arrangement to lengthen it with a box and pillows. He said he was in a comfortable bed for the first time in several weeks and enjoyed it. Naturally the journey had been tiring and he felt rather weak. He ate something . . . and drank some coffee and rested. In the evening he asked for warm water and had a thorough wash aided by Pettini, sitting on a chair in the bathroom . . .

Considering his weakness, in the following days I kept the conversations short . . . I asked why he had not been able to prevent the frostbite. He said that for many weeks he had been wandering about in the snow in the mountains and had lived often in shepherds' huts built for the summer which had no fireplaces. In the beginning the frostbites had been insignificant . . . But they soon turned into open wounds which he could no longer touch . . .

Once he said that he was prone to his illness because of his height as the heart could not pump the blood to the fingers and toes easily and that he had already suffered once of a disturbance of the blood circulation.

Usually, he felt no pain except a little when Pettini dressed his wounds. He complained that he could not get warm. I gave him a woollen pullover and more blankets which helped somewhat . . . Also he did not sleep well which fact he thought the principal cause of his weakness. But his complexion and his appearance were good and he conversed with such interest that one cannot imagine even now, afterwards, that he was in such danger.[63]

On 2 February, Jounzi, assisted by Ndroqi, operated and removed toes from both feet. The result was thought satisfactory but Nicholls remained very weak. He died suddenly on 11 February, five days after his thirty-third birthday. Septicaemia was thought the cause. Toptani buried him in a barn near his home.

Nicholls was posthumously awarded a George Cross. Recommending him first for the Victoria Cross, Seymour wrote that he had 'set an example of heroism, fortitude, courage, leadership, the will to win, and devotion to duty which has seldom been equalled and never surpassed. He carried on far longer than could normally be considered humanly possible and this undoubtedly caused his death.'[64]

'I am convinced that no matter what medical aid had been immediately available for the treatment of Lt Col Nicholls when he was found the end result must have been the same,' agreed a senior SOE medical officer, reading reports of Nicholls' fate. 'The frost-bitten feet were only part of the picture. His general condition, due to exposure, frost-bite and severe pain from his shoulder during a period of over three weeks must have been truly appalling and makes it very hard to understand how he was able to survive even for as long as he did.'[65]

Although rumours soon reached Cairo and the surviving SOE missions that something disastrous had occurred, details of what had happened to Davies and his men were only confirmed as survivors were found.[66] Hare and the dying Nicholls were able to tell of the mission's destruction and the Albanian part in it, that Davies and probably Chesshire had been hit, that Trayhorn was thought to have been caught and that three British sergeants were missing. Then, in March, Chisholm turned up. Last seen lying exhausted in the snow, he was well qualified to confirm the Albanian involvement in the ambush as the Balli Kombëtar had taken him prisoner. An SOE officer who saw him after he rejoined Seymour's mission recorded in his diary how Chisholm 'had been stripped, robbed, escaped from Ballists by pulling up the floorboards of a lavatory, shot an Alb and lived for an age in filthy clothes in a stable with two horses'.[67] A scrap of paper found in OSS files adds that 'Sgt Chisholm was robbed by gendarmerie and about to be murdered but killed one and the other ran'.[68]

Confirmation of others' fates took longer to arrive. Only in July did the British authorities hear through the Swiss that Davies was alive and in German hands. Only on his release was he able to describe what had happened to him, down to the burst of machine-gun fire that had sent him spinning into the snow, shot in the stomach and heel with one bullet piercing a snuffbox and denting a sovereign before travelling through his body. The same burst had shot Jim Chesshire through the thigh, the Italian colonel through the neck and a Partisan through both thighs. Ignoring Davies' orders that wounded men must be abandoned, Jim Smith, with the help of two Italians, then dragged them inside a nearby stone hut. This, too, came under fire and, as the Albanians closed in, only Smith, with the last rounds of his .38 and his fists, could put up any resistance, first outside with bullets cracking round him, then in the doorway, then standing over his officers. All three British were taken prisoner. Next day they were given to the Germans.

Chesshire's leg healed quickly. Soon he and Smith were moved from Tirana to Belgrade, where they were imprisoned for weeks in underground cells, then on to Germany, where Chesshire was sent to Colditz and Smith to a regular camp for captured aircrew. Davies' wounds were serious. In Tirana he was told he would die. As his health improved he, too, was moved to Belgrade. After interrogation by the Gestapo and further moves, including a short spell at Mauthausen concentration camp which ended after a typically robust Davies demanded that he and other captured Britons be treated like soldiers, he joined Chesshire and Trayhorn in Colditz. All remained there until liberation. Later, for their work in Albania, Davies was awarded a DSO and Chesshire an MC. Smith, for his actions at Kostenja, received a Distinguished Conduct Medal, adding to the Military Medal for which Seymour had recommended him after the Peza battle.

5

'ENTHUSIASM AND ROMANTICISM'

ON 4 November 1943, Wing Commander Norman Hulbert, Conservative Member of Parliament for Stockport, asked in the House of Commons whether the Prime Minister might make a statement about the guerrillas in Albania and Britain's policy towards them. Churchill rose to his feet. 'Yes, sir,' he said. 'Thousands of Albanian guerrillas are now fighting in their mountains for the freedom and independence of their country . . . The Germans are employing the usual methods by which they seek to subdue the warlike peoples; already they have bombed Albanian villages and killed Albanian women and children; but the Albanian guerrillas continue to harass the enemy and to attack his communications.'

Churchill then made the first public admission that British officers, too, were in the mountains; and these, he said, had paid 'high tribute' to the guerrillas' 'fighting qualities'. Britain, he added, also looked to the Albanians' 'ancient war-like traditions' for future military gain. As for British policy, that remained as explained in 1942; 'that is to say we wish to see Albania freed from the Axis yoke and restored to her independence. The frontiers will of course be considered at the Peace Settlement.'[1]

Hulbert's question and Churchill's reply had been drafted after calls from SOE for some public acknowledgement of Albanian resistance. Signals from the field that autumn had suggested that a 'feeling of insecurity and doubt' existed among Albanians as to what the British wanted them to do.[2] The omission of any reference to Albania in the Prime Minister's recent and much-publicised speech at Quebec had not helped; nor, as McLean had fumed to Cairo, had some lamentable BBC broadcasting. Either Albania was not mentioned at all or the reports were grossly inaccurate. 'Not enough news of inside events and praise of Albanian suffering,' he protested to Cairo in late September.[3] 'The effects of these broadcasts have been very bad,' he complained again a fortnight later. 'The man in the street wonders why lukewarm Balli are praised and why some facts [are] distorted while others suppressed.' The result was reduced faith in the accuracy of other broadcasts and 'ill feeling' towards SOE officers and Britain generally. Some locals suspected that British officers were 'sending out false reports' or that the British Government wanted to 'meddle' in Albanian 'internal affairs' and support 'conservative elements' regardless of their attitude to the war.[4] In early October, while waiting in Cairo to go in and aware of McLean's concerns, Trotsky Davies called on Richard Casey, Minister of State in the Middle East, and urged on him the importance of a suitable public statement. Casey agreed that one would be helpful and undertook to approach the Prime Minister.

Shortly after Davies parachuted to Biza, SOE was informed that the Foreign Office also planned to rely 'to a large extent' on his reports when 'formulating future policy for Albania' and he was sent a list of questions to which the Foreign Office wanted answers.[5] How far was the LNC Council a body with which the British could deal now and after the war? How far was the Council communist, under Soviet influence and in contact with the Yugoslav Partisans and communist-backed Greek guerrillas? How closely was the Balli Kombëtar working with the new German-backed government? And how would the Albanians view the formation of a representative committee outside the country, perhaps with Zog involved? Unless Davies advised otherwise, the Foreign Office would continue to back both the LNC and the Balli Kombëtar, take no steps towards forming an outside committee and refrain from supporting Zog.

In November Davies gave Cairo his answers. The LNC Council, he considered, was communist, under the influence of Tito, not the Soviets, and in touch with its Greek and Yugoslav counterparts, while the Balli Kombëtar's Council, he felt, was indeed associated with the new government. He did not feel that an outside committee would help. Nor did he recommend that the British support Zog. But although the LNC was 'the only Council in Albania with which HMG could co-operate' he could not yet recommend exclusive support for it. 'Balkom have given me signed agreement they will fight Germans. Until I have evidence agreement false, propose continue contact.'⁶ The civil situation was depressing, however. Civil war between the LNC and the Balli Kombëtar 'already started, will increase'. The LNC was likely to win, 'being younger more aggressive with terrorist flavour'. The Balli Kombëtar 'intend resist L.N.C. fullest'; possibly 'Zogists under Abas Kupi' would assist. 'My estimate will take most winter to work itself out. Have personally done utmost with all parties to avoid civil war without success.'⁷

Then, on 17 December, two days before he went off the air, Davies transmitted fresh proposals. 'Now recommend a change,' his message began. 'Situation developed recently so much, imperative now denounce Regency Council collectively and by name. Also Balkom and Zogists.' Britain's failure to denounce the Regents was being employed as evidence of Allied sympathy, he explained, while the Balli Kombëtar and Zogists had failed to fight the Germans despite promises and 'many chances' to do so. Also all recent LNC actions had met 'mixed German Balkom bodies, well armed, German trained'. Recent fighting at Peza and especially at Dibra had shown 'ample proof' of 'closest collaboration'. Consequently, Davies concluded, 'recommend open declaration for LNC'.⁸

Six weeks earlier, Fitzroy Maclean, the British brigadier working with Tito in Yugoslavia, had recommended that the British make a similar break there: the Partisans, he proposed, should be given exclusive support at the expense of Draža Mihailović's Chetniks. On the day of the Kostenjë ambush, 8 January 1944, writing on Downing Street paper and enclosing a signed photograph, Churchill then penned a letter to Tito explaining that 'the British Government shall give no further military support to Mihailovic and will only give help to you'.⁹ Maclean parachuted back into Bosnia and delivered the letter in person.

It was a dramatic moment. The British were committing themselves to a powerful, communist-led guerrilla movement bent on being in the driving seat politically when the war was over; they were also abandoning a rival, royalist party with which they had associated for over two years. When SOE's first mission to occupied Yugoslavia stepped ashore in 1941, the plan had been to work with Mihailović, the small, bearded, bespectacled Serb colonel heard to have gathered round him in the mountains a sizeable force of guerrillas. Contact was made and help was sent. In 1943, formal contact was also made with Tito's Partisans. By the summer, although fighting between them had broken out, Britain was supporting Mihailović and Tito in tandem with SOE missions attached to both. And in February 1944, as Churchill had promised in his letter, the British broke with Mihailović.

The scale of Britain's wartime support for Tito was to confuse and anger many, including several SOE officers who had fought alongside the Chetniks. Some claimed that certain officers on the SOE staff, by massaging reports to higher authority and starving the Chetniks of supplies and favourable propaganda, had worked to deny Mihailović the help, recognition and respect he deserved. Great play was made of the presence of James Klugmann, who joined the Yugoslav country section in 1942 and rose to be the section's second-in-command. As a student in the 1930s, Klugmann had been a powerful force in Cambridge communist circles and counted Anthony Blunt and Donald Maclean among his friends.[10] Klugmann's accusers, however, have never produced a concrete case that confirmed he manipulated either policy or the outcome of events: all evidence was circumstantial.

With the declassification of his reports to senior officers, it is possible to confirm Klugmann's marked pro-Partisan stance and detect, occasionally, a picture of Chetnik achievement against the Axis that resembles only partially the one reported by SOE missions in Yugoslavia.[11] Also revealing are recently released MI5 records. These include a verbatim report of a conversation Klugmann had had in London in August 1945 with a senior member of the Communist Party of Great Britain. Picked up by MI5 devices hidden in the party's King Street offices, the conversation consisted principally of details given by Klugmann of his SOE career and subsequent work in Yugoslavia with the United Nations Relief and Rehabilitation Agency (UNRRA). Of his time in SOE he spoke at length of his 'political work' to secure support for Tito's Partisans at the expense of the Chetniks. He described in particular how he had sought to control and manipulate the intelligence gathered and reported by missions in the field. He had tried to influence the selection and destination of British personnel, he said, to ensure the best ones went to Tito. And when briefing officers before they left, 'that was particularly useful because everybody who went to the field had to go through me and I had to tell him what he would find, and you know that people often find what they expect'. He tried, too, to filter reports coming out of Yugoslavia to ensure that a picture emerged that was favourable to the Partisans, 'to see that what got back was satisfactory . . . to bring propaganda to aid arms; intelligence to aid propaganda'. Klugmann also admitted to passing information to the Partisans 'as guidance on general tactics vis-à-vis the British'.[12] Certainly Klugmann's admissions appear to fit the campaigns that the SOE staff were claimed to have waged; they also seem to fit several specific charges of manipulation that have been levelled against him personally. And MI5 was shocked. Sir David Petrie, MI5's Director, underlined Klugmann's 'betrayal of information' and 'most unforgivable offence . . . his efforts to secure that only Intelligence was obtained from the field which supported his policy of recognition for the Partisans and the discrediting of the Chetniks'.[13]

In recent years, however, the declassification of other wartime records, from Foreign Office policy papers and minutes of Chiefs of Staff meetings to secret transcripts of intercepted enemy signals, has shown conclusively that Klugmann had much less influence than was long supposed. If junior SOE staff were keen to support the Partisans, so were very senior commanders privy to important intelligence to which SOE had little or no access. Recent studies of decrypted enemy signals demonstrate that, in March 1943, when they authorised SOE to contact the Partisans, the Chiefs were well aware, from sources other than SOE reports, that the Partisans were causing the Axis serious problems. Top secret decrypts of enemy traffic had documented in detail, for example, the scale of a recent Axis offensive against the Partisans that stood as the largest anti-guerrilla operation Yugoslavia had seen for over a year. By June, when SOE was told to start arming the Partisans, decrypts also confirmed that Mihailović's forces were less and less anti-Axis and more concerned with confronting the Partisans; some of his lieutenants were even collaborating. As the Chiefs told the Foreign Office that month, it was clear from 'Most Secret Sources' that 'the Chetniks were hopelessly compromised with their relations with the Axis in Herzegovina and Montenegro'. The Partisans, meanwhile, were judged 'the most formidable anti-Axis element outside Serbia' and deserved 'the strongest support'.[14]

Churchill, too, knew from the decrypts about Tito's superior activity and Mihailović's failings. That July he noted from a long digest of intercepted material the 'marvellous resistance by the followers of Tito and the powerful cold-blooded manoeuvres of Mihailovic'.[15] It was also that month that he chose Fitzroy Maclean, a trained diplomat and

Conservative MP who had fought in the desert with the SAS, to be his personal envoy to Tito. Within two months of dropping into Yugoslavia, Maclean was pushing for extensive and exclusive support for the Partisans and his forceful reports went straight to the top without going through SOE's hands.

Maclean's reports, based mostly on Partisan sources, did exaggerate somewhat the Partisans' scale and value and he never met Mihailović. Some SOE officers who had worked with Mihailović were also to argue with passion and reason that, outside Yugoslavia, understanding of the factors forcing the Chetniks into inactivity, procrastination and even collaboration had been poor. Such was the fragile nature of his support, these officers explained, that Mihailović could not risk reprisals on the population by fighting the Axis in the way SOE demanded.

But in 1943, with the Allies busy planning the invasion of Sicily and the Second Front, arguments for backing the Partisans as a means of tying down enemy troops went a long way to overriding long-term worries and dispersing sympathy for men seeking Axis help to settle domestic scores. And the bigger picture revealed by the decrypts continued to provide Churchill and the Chiefs with strong enough evidence of the Partisans' superior worth and how compromised Mihailović was becoming. In November the Chiefs advised Churchill that support for Tito should be increased. The same month, the Joint Intelligence Committee recommended that support for Mihailović be brought to a close. By the end of the year, at the highest levels, frustration with Mihailović was widely shared and Churchill had resolved to support only Tito.

Albania was never to engage the attention of Churchill and senior ministers, ministries and commands to the extent that Yugoslavia did. Principally, of course, this was because Albania was much smaller and strategically less significant. In the winter of 1943–4, poring over decrypts in London, intelligence officers estimated that twenty-one German divisions were stationed in Yugoslavia in November 1943, rising to twenty-four in the first week of January.[16] Albania had a garrison of two. But the picture in London of events out there was also more confused, which explained the attention the Foreign Office gave that winter to the views of SOE officers like Davies. With MI6 almost completely uninvolved, these men were the British Government's eyes and ears on the ground.

When Davies' 17 December recommendations were received in Cairo, not everyone there wished to support them. Margaret Hasluck had been urging for some time that the British should be less keen to work with the LNC. In November she had tried to argue that, in view of the reverses the Partisans were suffering, SOE ought to stop encouraging them and thereby try to keep the Balli Kombëtar and other Nationalists on side. 'So here go the partisans of Peza, Berat, Valona and Kicevo,' she wrote to SOE in London. 'It does not look good, does it? I feel more strongly than ever, and hope you will agree, that non-intervention on our part is the only card to play now. Otherwise we get the Balkom and all the frightened people in the country against us.'[17]

Well aware of the potential long-term consequences of arming and funding the LNC, Hasluck, however, was facing an awful prospect. Albania was her home and for twenty years she had watched it become a place of relative peace and order and, though she did not think the order perfect and held no brief for King Zog, she had many close friends among the establishment. The closest was Lef Nosi. He shared her interests in antiquity and folklore – he had written the folk tale 'Kocamici' – and he had lived in Elbasan, where Hasluck settled in 1935 and built a home. Whether she had been Nosi's 'mistress' as insinuated after the war by Hoxha and others is impossible to say.[18] What is certain is that their relationship held great significance for her. When she was expelled in 1939 their paths parted, but in Cairo and Istanbul, while working for SOE, she followed his fate from intelligence reports and newspapers that passed across her desk. In 1942 she wrote to London of news, 'sad news for me personally', that Nosi, now over seventy, had been interned in Italy as a suspect trouble-maker.[19] Much worse was to come: in October 1943 he became a member of the four-man Council of Regents. Unease about how the Allies would respond to the Regents may well help explain both Hasluck's efforts to invoke understanding for them and her growing opposition to the Partisans, which in turn began to worry the SOE staff as to where her focus lay.

Hasluck's opinions may have been less of a concern had her duties not included compiling the Albanian section's intelligence summaries, which she used as a platform to express her own views. In her fortnightly intelligence summary of 15 December, for example, circulated as far as the Foreign Office in London, she argued eloquently that the

Regents' decision to work with the Germans should be seen as a patriotic attempt to secure order and stability, and concluded:

> The lines of the government's policy would meet with our warm approval if we were not at war with the country whose armed forces now occupy Albania . . . They have further appealed to the youthful to avoid civil war and to preserve intact the Albania with which they, the elderly men in the government, have done but which they, the young, are to inherit tomorrow. Indeed, these elderly men must be greatly pained as they watch the chaos into which the guerilla movement has plunged the country . . . They grew up to struggle for independence, many . . . by guerilla war . . . a few like Lef Nosi . . . by years of imprisonment, internment and exile. Independence achieved, they set their faces, Moslems as much as Christians, towards the West and they won for themselves and helped the younger generation to win a certain degree of western civilisation . . . Now they see the clock put back to 1920 or earlier, arms again in every man's hand, human life counted as naught, and anarchy rampant.
>
> They would be less than human if they did not ask if the benefit to the Allied war effort which accrues from the runaway tactics of the guerillas is worth the political and economic damage to the country which they cause.[20]

In other correspondence, Hasluck would underline, too, the significance of a secret Partisan circular brought out of Albania at the end of November. Printed a few weeks before and signed off by 'Shpati', heard later to be Enver Hoxha's *nom de guerre*, it instructed Partisan units to 'eliminate' the Balli Kombëtar and impress on the population that the party's treacherous actions demanded that they take this step. 'I maintain that, if we align ourselves with the men who produced this LNC circular, we shall do grievous mischief to our own war effort. The only policy for us is quiescence.'[21]

In London, the men now reading Hasluck's incoming letters and reports were Eddie Boxshall and David Talbot Rice. Boxshall, the son of a British vice-consul, was fifty-six and had lived most of his life in Romania; between the wars, in Bucharest, he had represented Vickers and MI6. Arriving in Britain in 1940, he was soon working for SOE and, by late 1943, was the first point of contact in London for Cairo's Albanian section. Talbot Rice, pre-war travelling companion of Robert Byron, was a distinguished classical scholar and archaeologist and, from 1934, Chair of Fine Art at Edinburgh University. In December 1943, after a period working in the War Office on Balkan-related intelligence, he had taken command from Jimmy Pearson of Baker Street's Balkan desk. Neither he nor Boxshall was an Albanian expert; but both men were aware of Britain's priorities and believed that winning the war was more important than the plight of Albania's Nationalists.

On 19 December, in a letter that both men read, Hasluck, having heard now of Davies' proposals, wrote to London disagreeing 'profoundly' with the idea of condemning the Regents. This was 'not because two of them [Lef Nosi and Mehdi Frashëri] have been for so long my friends, but because I think it would be the highest unwisdom to take such a step'. Once again she asserted that they were patriots and men of honour, but this time added that they must have been 'threatened with a German concentration camp' to have agreed to join the government. No reports or rumours appear to have reached Cairo that they had been coerced in that way, but Hasluck was adamant. 'The Germans are simply fiends incarnate. They have taken the best men in the country and forced them into the last possible position they would have chosen except under some dire compulsion.' She concluded: 'Germans or no Germans, I am sticking by my friends in their hour of trial.'[22]

Reading the letter, Boxshall highlighted that last sentence and, summing up the essence of SOE's position, commented against it in pencil: 'But does this really help our war effort!?' Passing it to Talbot Rice, he added: 'I am afraid that Mrs Hasluck's many years of residence in Albania render her unable to take a dispassionate and detached view of the problems arising out of the present position Albania finds herself in.' Talbot Rice agreed: 'I think we must abide by Brig. Davies' ideas rather than these.'[23]

In the event, the British decided not to do as Davies proposed. Sympathy for the Nationalists did not come into it. The decision owed everything to a sound assessment that the picture was simply too fluid, confused and disaster-strewn to justify, at that moment, supporting only the Partisans. That assessment owed much to the judgement of Major Philip Leake, head since the spring of SOE's Albanian section in Cairo, and his careful weighing of Davies' demands against policy requirements and the information available.

'Anyone who knew Philip Leake would have liked him and been impressed by his grasp of affairs and objective and unbiased approach,' remembered Marcus Lyon. All accounts support that view: Leake was very highly regarded. 'A gentle, kindly person with a nice sense of humour, a dry, cynical wit and that "transcendent capacity of taking trouble" which Carlyle equated with genius,' Peter Kemp wrote. 'He was a most capable officer, well fitted for his post as head of the Cinderella of the Balkan Country Sections.'[24] Born in May 1906, Leake had been a pupil at Dulwich College, where he edited the magazine and became school captain, and a scholar at Corpus Christi, Oxford, where he abandoned classics to read modern history and played a lot of rugby. 'Leake tackles very well,' the College Record reads: 'a valuable asset in a winging forward.'[25] Coming down in 1928 he went to teach at Dulwich College Preparatory School, where his father, the Reverend William Martin Leake, a former England rugby international, was headmaster. For a time, the son, too, ran the school but he did not warm to the post, and in 1939 gave up teaching and went to the Board of Education. When war broke out Leake was living in Southampton, working as a schools inspector for Hampshire and the Isle of Wight. Bickham Sweet-Escott, another Oxford man, who was to spend his war on the SOE staff, then recruited his 'oldest friend' in the summer of 1940.[26] A routine commission into the Intelligence Corps followed.

The intrepid Colonel William Leake, the British officer resident at Ali Pasha's court in the early 1800s, was an ancestor, a cousin several times removed, and Leake and his siblings were aware of his exploits. Another cousin was Arthur Martin Leake, the first of three men to win the Victoria Cross twice; he, too, had visited Albania, with the Red Cross in 1912, though not enjoyed it much. Philip, though he had holidayed in Eastern Europe before the war, had no experience or specialist knowledge of Albania, but the post of section head called also for staff experience and he certainly had plenty of that, together with a fine reputation as an intelligent and likeable man of balanced and careful judgement.

For his first year he had worked in Baker Street, assisting the heads of the Balkan and African sections. According to Kemp, he was then involved in Operation Postmaster, SOE's dramatic capture of two Italian ships off the West African coast in January 1942. But another officer's memoirs have Leake in a troopship leaving Britain that month for South Africa and playing a part in SOE's effort to spearhead the British capture of Diego Suarez.[27] Certainly SOE records show that by the spring of 1942 Leake had arrived in Durban and was working as assistant head of SOE's East African mission. From May, when the island was captured, until September, he was in charge of SOE's forward headquarters on Madagascar.

By February 1943 Leake was in Cape Town, running a joint intelligence centre, and it was in the Cape early that year that he met Peggy Prince. She was in her late twenties and had been brought up in South Africa, her British parents having settled there before the First World War. A shared interested in poetry forged a bond, for her brother was the poet F. T. Prince, and she and Leake became close. He helped her join SOE, which sent her to Cairo to work in the cipher office and then on to Italy. In both places they were able to keep in touch. He was 'very well-liked, very attractive', she recalled in 2001. 'Everyone liked him. He was *very* attractive.' She remembered his affectionate teasing when he found her in the mess ordering a large slice of cake, and she remembered his scholarly side, finding him engrossed one day in a history of the Jesuits in Germany. Once she asked him what he would do after the war. 'It was one of the few times he was being serious. He told me, "I want to re-educate Germany." He was quite serious. I'm quite sure he meant to go on in that line of work.'[28]

Leake took charge of SOE's fledgling Albanian section in May 1943. A few weeks had passed since Billy McLean went in, and, with the tempo of Balkan operations increasing and more missions planned, there was a need to address Margaret Hasluck's limitations, create a dedicated country section along more regular lines and appoint trained staff officers to appropriate posts. The new section was given the in-house title of B8: the Yugoslav section was B1 and the Greek section B6. Office space was found on a floor in Rustem Buildings. Gradually Leake took on a small staff.

One recruit was Jon Naar, a twenty-three-year-old Royal Artillery captain, taken on in November 1943 as the section's military intelligence officer. Educated at Mill Hill, the Sorbonne and the Universities of Vienna and London, Naar was fluent in French and German and already had two-and-a-half years' experience of intelligence and secret work.

Commissioned in 1941, he had responded to a call for French-speaking officers and soon been attached to Australian troops fighting in Syria and Lebanon. There he had been given the tasks of liaising with the Free French, directing propaganda against the Vichy French, advising the Australians on political matters and being employed in counter-intelligence; later he had been sent to the Turkish border to interview refugees from Eastern Europe. Since the end of 1941, except for six months sick in South Africa, he had been in Egypt: preparing stay-behind parties to resist any future enemy advance, seeing action at El Alamein and teaching at the Helwan intelligence school, outside Cairo. And while at the school, he recalls, 'I heard of an opening with the group that was organising resistance in the Balkans: MO4, one of the many code-names used by SOE.' Summoned to Rustem Buildings to be interviewed by Leake, 'I got the job because, he said, I was the first person to identify the map of Albania that he had on the wall behind him.'[29]

'He was extremely well organised [with] . . . a very quick . . . logical and linear mind,' Naar remembers. 'The thing that amazed me most about Philip was that he had the ability to compose a fairly long memo-randum to London or wherever in his head. He never seemed to have any written notes but he would sit there for forty-five minutes and simply dictate to one of the secretaries. I was very impressed by that.'[30] With the release of SOE's records, such memoranda now reveal Leake's opinions on policy at critical points and confirm his aptitude for the role of section head, his careful handling of reports from the field and his well-reasoned thoughts on policy. 'Leake was a schoolmaster by profession and in character,' recalls Naar: 'eminently fair in his judge-ments'.[31] His response to Davies' 17 December proposals is an excellent case in point.

According to Hasluck, Leake's initial reaction was of 'unthinking loyalty', much to her alarm. 'On 17.12.43 Trotsky signalled that we must denounce certain Albanians by name,' she wrote later. 'On receipt of this signal Major Leake paid me one of his rare visits and said that it only remained for us to obey Trotsky loyally. I replied that I was a civilian and owed my loyalty to common sense; that Trotsky had not been long enough in the country to judge fairly, and that I should fight his signal until more support came in for his view.'[32] But at that moment the section's job was to support any Albanian committed to fighting the Germans and not worry, unless told to, about much else, as Leake's

answers to an internal questionnaire, circulated among the Cairo country
sections three days before, neatly show:

> Q.1. *What is your military object?*
> Answer. The military object of [the] Allied Military Mission,
> Albania, as defined by [the Commander-in-Chief, GHQ
> Middle East], is to kill Germans.
>
> Q.2. *What political assumptions are you at present working
> on?*
> Answer. That HMG is not interested in Albanian internal
> politics and that the Mission is free to afford assistance to
> whatever elements it considers are resisting or are likely to
> resist the Germans irrespective of their politics.
>
> Q.3. *What political and military questions do you require a
> firm directive on in order to function without continual refer-
> ence to higher authority?*
> Answer. None. The present position is that the Head of the
> Mission's political views have been accepted by the Foreign
> Office who do not propose to change their policy unless he
> should so recommend.[33]

Support for Davies would have been entirely in line with that arrangement. Days later, however, sharing his thoughts officially with higher
authority, Leake argued that, while he agreed that the Partisans deserved
continued support, it was too soon for Britain to come out in sole
support of them.

Leake's argument is well set out in a paper drawn up on 24 December
summarising the pros and cons, as he saw them, of Davies' recommendations. The advantages, Leake felt, were that continued Partisan
cooperation would be secured, which was essential to the 'effective
execution' of SOE's tasks, and Britain's support shown to be genuine:
the Balli Kombëtar, he noted, was now definitely collaborating. On the
negative side, breaking with the Balli Kombëtar and Zogists would frus-
trate operations in territory they controlled and end hopes of a general
uprising at the war's end. Also, by supporting only the Partisans, 'we
shall be committed to a policy of intervention in a purely Albanian
conflict and to the support of a movement whose ultimate success and

popular backing are uncertain'. Leake therefore advised that while the Partisans should be given ongoing assistance, greater publicity and official assurance that the Balli Kombëtar and Zogists would be supplied only if they 'openly' adopted 'a policy of active hostility to the Germans', no break should be made with any party.[34]

Leake had drawn up his paper at the request of the Special Operations Committee, a new body in Cairo whose existence stands as a useful gauge of how the Foreign Office had reasserted its influence on Balkan policy and operations by the end of 1943. Policy was always meant to have been decided, after due deliberation, in London, while the local military command, GHQ Middle East, controlled operations in line with that policy. During the course of 1943, however, some observers in London, and the Foreign Office in particular, had come to feel that SOE in Cairo, with the encouragement of GHQ Middle East, had been supporting communist and anti-royalist guerrillas in Greece and Yugoslavia to excessive and unacceptable levels. After great debate it had been settled in September that the 'main policy' for SOE should be agreed in London between the Foreign Office and SOE and with reference, if necessary, to the Prime Minister, the Chiefs of Staff and other interested parties. But although GHQ Middle East was still to direct the execution of that policy in Greece, Yugoslavia and Albania, it would now receive political guidance about operations in those countries from a new committee in Cairo. SOE's Cairo set-up was also given a shake. Lord Glenconner, a civilian, had been in charge out there since 1942 and it was partly a reaction to the power that he and others had wielded that brought these changes and now forced his departure. Major General Billy Stawell, a professional soldier and former Deputy Director of Intelligence at the War Office, replaced him.

The new Cairo-based committee was the Special Operations Committee. Its members included local representatives of SOE and GHQ Middle East and the British Ambassadors to Greece and Yugoslavia, an arrangement that allowed the Foreign Office to keep a closer eye than previously on operations in the Balkans and the policy guiding them. In November, in view of SOE's growing presence in Albania, the Foreign Office authorised Kit Steel, Counsellor in the Cairo Embassy, to join the committee and to act for Albania in the same way as the two ambassadors were doing for Greece and Yugoslavia. Steel, a career diplomat, was also the permanent political adviser to SOE in Cairo: another new appointment to ensure that SOE had ready access to expert advice and that the Foreign Office was kept abreast of what SOE was up to. SOE, in fact, had agreed to grant him 'completely free access to files' and keep him 'as fully as possible in the picture in regard to all activities in the countries with which he is concerned'.[35]

On the morning of 29 December, the Special Operations Committee met in the War Room at Grey Pillars, the block of Cairo flats housing GHQ Middle East, and discussed Davies' proposed policy change. Present were Kit Steel of the Foreign Office and Leake and Stawell of SOE, plus representatives of OSS, the Political Warfare Executive and GHQ Middle East. Before them were the text of Davies' message and Leake's pros and cons paper. And as Steel told London two days later, the committee agreed unanimously that it was unwise to break with the Balli Kombëtar and Zogists. Though the Partisans had 'done whatever has been done against the Germans' they were 'really more interested' in fighting the Balli Kombëtar and their effort against the Germans was 'puny'. There were also clear operational benefits to be had from maintaining contact with the Balli Kombëtar, few of whose supporters seemed 'genuinely pro-Axis', while 'it must be remembered that Brigadier Davies is naturally rather under the impression of the LNC at whose headquarters he has been living'.[36]

In London, the Foreign Office, the War Office and SOE all fell in with the Special Operations Committee. Policy was duly confirmed in a directive drawn up by the committee, approved by the Foreign Office and issued on 24 January by GHQ Middle East. No break was to be made with any political or guerrilla movement. The British were to continue to endeavour to provide financial and military assistance 'to all guerilla bands, irrespective of their political allegiance, which are actively resisting the Germans or are genuinely prepared to do so'. In accordance with this, BLOs were to 'maintain contact with all guerilla bands and individuals actively resisting the Germans, or who may be induced to assist the Allied war effort in any material degree'.[37]

In practice, that directive meant that SOE officers were instructed to remain in touch with the Balli Kombëtar, Kupi and other Nationalists, even though the Partisans were the only movement doing any fighting. Given the information then available in Cairo, however, it is hard to see how any other course could have appeared wise on military grounds. If SOE was to maximise its chances of achieving anything in Albania, it had to keep its options open.

Leake was well aware that the LNC was communist-led and set on civil war. 'At the outset it was mainly composed of moderate nationalists with a small but disproportionately active communist minority,' he recorded in a long and widely circulated appreciation signed off on 14 December. That minority appeared to have 'increased rapidly in influence' within the movement, alarming more conservative elements and deepening divisions, while the LNC drew its support 'from the younger generation' which was 'particularly susceptible to the novel attraction of the apparatus and ideology of Russian communism'. Then, in early November, 'despite the efforts of Brigadier Davies to bring about an understanding, the LNC openly declared their intention of liquidating the Ball Kombetar [sic] before undertaking any operations against the Germans'. The aim of this, Leake went on, 'according to a circular published by them, is to seize power with a view to presenting an Allied landing force with a fait accompli'.

It was equally evident that the Partisans qualified on military grounds for British support. 'There can be little doubt that the LNC, faithful to their ideological formula of death to the Fascists, are uncompromisingly hostile to the Germans, and once assured of their internal supremacy, would be engaged in active hostilities against them. Recent drives against the partisans in the Dibra, Korca and Peza districts indicate that the Germans share this view.' The 'first line guerrillas' in the LNC's three brigades, each about six hundred strong, were, 'for the most part, well armed, partly with weapons infiltrated by ourselves but to a larger extent with material taken from the Italians after the armistice'.

By mid-December, however, as Leake also pointed out, 'heavy blows' had the LNC on its knees. The 2nd and 3rd Partisan Brigades were dispersed, offensive operations had ceased completely and the Council was preparing to retire from the centre and move south. So desperate was the situation that Davies himself had drawn up plans to ensure that, if the Albanians failed to take any action, the mission would remain active and could lay on 'small scale' operations 'independently of the local guerillas'. These plans, Leake felt, were 'clearly sound'. SOE's 'principal operational task' in Albania 'should be to prepare a scheme of widespread action' in the event of an Allied invasion or German withdrawal. 'The dispositions of the enemy should be carefully observed and plans laid for hindering their retreat, directing tactical bombing and causing the maximum disorganisation. One can but hope that when the Germans finally leave the country the Albanians will be prepared temporarily to sink their differences in order to speed the enemy on his way.' On these grounds, he argued, '[i]t is essential that Albania is covered by parties capable of maintaining and working up the proper contacts'.

That meant maintaining contact with the Balli Kombëtar and Zogists. Although it was presently inactive and heard to be collaborating, the Balli Kombëtar, Leake felt, was 'not naturally pro-Axis . . . If, on the Italian surrender they showed a greater reluctance to fight the Germans, this was largely due to German prestige and the relentless policy of reprisals to which their local organisation makes them particularly sensitive.' As for Abas Kupi, 'British Liaison Officers have found him affable and friendly' and he had 'impressed Brigadier Davies as a sincere patriot and his earlier record supports this judgement'. Kupi claimed to be able to raise three thousand men, albeit 'practically all drawn from the Mati district to the North of Tirana', and Leake felt that there was 'little likelihood' of him collaborating actively.[38]

Each of the concerns laid down by Leake had reflected a realistic analysis of how SOE could best do its job based on the information then available in Cairo. And Leake's recommendations and reasoning remained essentially unchanged, though condensed, in the pros and cons paper put before the Special Operations Committee two weeks later. As he explained afterwards to London, 'adoption Trotsky's recommendations would politically involve us in Albanian civil war possibly on the wrong side and from military standpoint necessitate abandonment important nationalist contacts in Northern Albania'. The Partisans had 'undoubtedly precipitated' the civil war but did 'not possess the same popular support as in Jugoslavia'. Their 'ultimate success' was 'by no means assured' and 'influence . . . virtually limited to Southern Albania'. In view of this, 'we felt obliged to advise SOC that no . . . open political declarations should be made unless considered absolutely essential for the continued existence of the Mission . . . Before reaching this conclusion we should of course normally have referred back to Trotsky but as you are aware contact with him was lost on December 19th.'[39]

It is arguable that Davies had taken his eye momentarily off the ball. In view of their anti-fascist stance and the Germans' concerted attempts to destroy them, the military argument for supporting the Partisans remained strong; it was equally clear that the Albanian government and elements of the Balli Kombëtar were working against them. But by 17 December Davies could not have been certain that continued contact with Kupi and the Balli Kombëtar could not have been of military value to the Allies, especially if the Partisans were wiped out. In his memoirs, Davies was not to mention his December proposals or that he had wanted to back the Partisans only. Today, with a clearer understanding of his perilous position that winter, it seems that a combination of frustration and fear of his mission's imminent extinction may have compelled Davies to recommend that day to Cairo that the Partisans must have exclusive and better support. There was no guarantee that he would ever make such an appeal in person. By mid-December, Davies and the LNC Council had been surrounded for a fortnight and he had had no first-hand contact with any Nationalist leader or party for more than a month. A German drive was also expected and the British were far from convinced they would emerge unscathed. They were also despairing at the absence of Allied broadcasts encouraging the Albanians to resist. 'Eden's speech in the House listened to with interest on the wireless,' Arthur Nicholls wrote on 15 December.

> Once again Jug and Greece are plugged but no mention of Albania. It's very heartbreaking and discouraging and each time our stock, so carefully built up, is sent crashing down. Distant sounds of MGs firing . . .
> 1400. E.F.D. has long walk and talk in the winter sunshine with Enver Hoxha. A good deal of ground is covered and E.F.D. stresses the vital necessity or his getting out [to Cairo] soonest poss.

'Every effort to be made to get and maintain max contact with Cairo over next few days,' Nicholls added two days later. 'Much to say which it is essential should be recorded in case we are killed or put in the bag.'[40]

One late diary entry, twelve days after Davies' mission went off the air, does suggest that, as the devastating effect of the German drive became apparent, minds may have changed. 'So far the news is that the whole of Martanesh has been burnt by the Huns, our mules and all our belongings captured and that the quarter of Orhenje in which we lived has also been burnt, including our base,' Nicholls noted on New Year's

Eve. 'If all this be true, it will be particularly difficult to make a fresh start, particularly if all the W.T. sets and equipment are lost. Anyway no village is exactly likely to welcome us with open arms as we are a sure draw for both Huns and Bali.'[41] In February, Nicholls then told George Seymour that he believed Davies' December proposals were 'out of date'.[42] Hearing of this, Margaret Hasluck wrote to Billy Stawell: 'This seems to vindicate my judgement, but where should we be if unthinking loyalty prevailed?'[43] In Cairo, however, patience with Hasluck was running out.

Certainly Leake and his staff had found her a mine of useful information when she was handled the right way and pressed on the right topic. Jon Naar worked closely with her in late 1943 and 'spent long hours going over maps and other documents in her flat'.[44] She was 'enormously helpful' in his allotted task of planning and plotting operations.[45] 'Leake and others said, "Get all you can because she is one of our few resources" . . . but she was generous with her information, and I got in some really specific discussions about terrain because we were looking for the kind of roads where ambushes might be carried out . . . She'd ramble on saying, "Oh yes, we had a marvellous picnic around that area," but I could get fairly specific information about not only the terrain, but what kind of people might be there.'[46] Yet Naar recalls, too, that Hasluck was 'very emotional' and 'hostile to anyone such as Leake who would even consider working with "those people" – i.e. the Partisans'.[47]

SOE records confirm that she remained vocal in predicting that support for the Partisans spelt doom for Albania's future. 'You will know already that I have little sympathy with the LNC because it lets itself be led by the nose by the Communist section,' she told London on 1 January.[48] Two weeks later she drew attention again to more Partisan propaganda directed against the Regents that contained untenable 'personal abuse of the character and patriotism of men who have been known to me for 20 years . . . It is now plain as a pikestaff to me that we can never satisfy the LNC . . . Personally speaking, I can never believe another word they say.'[49] But Hasluck's efforts to invoke sympathy and vouch for the Regents continued to fall on deaf ears and it seems that she knew it, as Naar remembers from one visit to her home:

She had a most incredible apartment: wonderful Victorian décor, full of bric-a-brac, I remember; wonderful art deco lamps; a real mishmash of stuff. She also had a parrot, which was very articulate, called Winston, always kind of butting in. I asked, 'Why did you call him Winston?' and she replied, 'It's the only time I ever get any kind of feedback from the Prime Minister'.[50]

Records also indicate that Hasluck eventually took to massaging intelligence in an attempt to suggest that the future had to lie with the Balli Kombëtar.

'The Albanian Civil War is ending, healing from within' declared her Fortnightly Summary of 9 January. 'Soon most of the country will go Balkom . . . We must, consequently, reckon with the Balkom for our war effort.'[51] One astute and informed recipient read his copy of that summary with amazement and alarm. Fifty-seven-year-old Harry Trevlen Fultz, the son of an Indiana farmer, had taken over from Dale McAdoo as overseas head of the OSS Albanian desk and routinely read reports received from missions in the field. From 1922, Fultz had spent eleven years in Albania as director of Tirana's Albanian Vocational School, working under the auspices of the American Red Cross, and it was on the basis of that experience that OSS had recruited him in March 1943.[52] He was a good choice. 'Worked incessantly,' one of his officers recalls:

> Was always called Mr Fultz, not Harry. Had a wry smile when you came in to see him. In my many months of working for him, we never had any social activities together, not even coffee. He was the Headmaster and we knew our place, not that he ever said anything to alienate us. His natural aura, very probably from years as the top gun of the American School of Tirana, made him a figure you admired, almost revered, but did not assume liberties.
>
> His grasp of the entire operation was phenomenal. He had two interpreters that were his constant companions, but they were in an outer office and did not seem to ever discuss any matter but their translations.
>
> He was fair in his dealings with his personnel. His attention was easily drawn to new intelligence, [he] thought it through, and then made his move to capitalize on the changed conditions, if any.[53]

Now, to his superior, Major Robert Koch, Fultz pointed out carefully how Hasluck's 9 January summary was 'directly at variance with reports' sent out of Albania by British officers. These confirmed that the Balli Kombëtar was collaborating, that Kupi was not fighting and that the LNC remained engaged 'in blocking roads and hindering communications of Germans'. The 1st Brigade, meanwhile, 'moves about in different areas and has no contact with BLOs', yet the Fortnightly Summary stated that it was 'immobilised' in the south-west. 'Whoever wrote the summary seems to have overlooked facts and come out strongly for Zogists and Balkom,' Fultz warned. 'Some of the alleged facts are based, it would seem, definitely on propaganda leaflets rather than on sober unbiased reporting of bits of evidence as it is collected . . . Almost the entire presentation seems to have been distorted in an attempt to make out a case for individuals and factions who do not have a very good case to date.' Koch raised the matter with his opposite number on the SOE staff, Lieutenant Colonel Bill Harcourt, who, a pencilled scribble reads, 'agreed with Mr Fultz'.[54]

In fact, moves were already underway to address the problem. 'The present situation,' Philip Leake told his Cairo commander on 18 January, 'is that Mrs Hasluck functions independently of the Section Head and is responsible without reference to him for compiling the fortnightly Appreciation and handling all matters concerned with propaganda, a state of affairs which is obviously absurd.' He recommended that he take over control of propaganda and compilation of the fortnightly summaries, leaving Hasluck as 'general advisor on Albanian affairs'.[55] Hasluck put up a brief resistance. 'I have been accused of bias,' she told Kit Steel and her superiors in early February. 'It exists.' The Partisans' slander of the Regents' characters, 'setting their young, excited views against reputations of seventy years' standing', and unfounded complaints about BBC broadcasts had convinced her, she explained, 'that the LNC were not trustworthy witnesses and must have all their information scrutinised critically'.[56] Next day she wrote to Eddie Boxshall that she was not prepared to give 'unthinking or "shut-eye" loyalty such as subordination to [Major Leake] would require. He does not suffer correction easily, and I think he needs a little. I am afraid I think stubbornly that, if there is to be one voice in B8, it had better be mine.'[57] For Boxshall this was becoming rather tiresome. 'Can you interpret what she is now groaning about?' he scribbled to the recently repatriated Oakley-Hill. 'Please vet the eruptions carefully.'[58] By then, however, Hasluck had decided to resign. In a final note to Boxshall she wrote: 'our association has ended . . . I could not reconcile my conscience to doing what was asked of me, so there was nothing to be done except to go.'[59]

As a note in her SOE Personal File reads, Hasluck's 'very intimate acquaintance with Albania led her to follow, perhaps somewhat too closely, her own ideas when they did not happen to coincide with HMG's policy'. Another note records her recommendation for an MBE for her two years' SOE service. 'Throughout,' it concludes, 'Mrs Hasluck has shown the most remarkable energy for her years and has devoted her gifts in intellect and knowledge unsparingly without regard to hours of work.' That assessment seems accurate also. When she resigned, Hasluck was seriously ill with advanced leukaemia and SOE considered privately that overwork might have made her condition worse.[60]

No sooner had Davies' December proposals been overruled than a new British initiative emerged: a plan first tabled when Billy McLean and David Smiley returned to Cairo in November. Leaving Trotsky Davies on the Biza plateau, these two had crossed the Shkumbin and marched south, then pressed west to the coast from where a British motor torpedo boat picked them up on the night of 17–18 November. There was a strong swell and the stony creek selected was too narrow for the ship to come in, so the pair paddled out in a holed and sinking rowing boat which left them treading water for a few alarming moments before finally being pulled aboard by the MTB's crew. 'I was sick after it all,' Smiley wrote in his diary, 'as the MTB rocked like hell while the crew hurled boxes of bully beef ashore . . . We arrived in Brindisi after three hours journey, still feeling rather sick. However the sight of the Albanian coast receding in the distance had cheered us up a lot.'[61]

Flown to Cairo at the end of the month, the two officers settled down to report on their experiences and share their thoughts on policy. Abandoning men like Abas Kupi would be hasty, they felt, as well as unjust, for the LNC was clearly set on civil war, and the pair suggested that the British intervene. 'Our policy should be to back the Partisans with all possible material aid as they are the only military force worth backing in the country,' McLean recommended in a long report circulated at senior levels in Baker Street and as far as the Foreign Office. 'At the same time, we should maintain contact with the Nationalist groups, and, if possible, try to stop the Civil War. We should try and ensure that the more anti-German Nationalists should either collaborate with or enter in the LNC movement.'[62]

Philip Leake shared the view that SOE should maintain contact with Kupi. In January SOE had been instructed to prepare for Operation Noah's Ark, a plan for operations to harass a German withdrawal from Greece, with D-Day set for April. The Albanian corollary to this was Operation Underdone and, by the end of January, Leake had drawn up a plan 'to stimulate the maximum guerrilla effort to harass and inflict the greatest possible damage on the German forces when they eventually withdraw from Albania'. The main effort, he proposed, would have to be concentrated against roads in the south. 'Since the German drives of November and December 1943 which disrupted three area parties and resulted in the capture of Brigadier Davies and his staff, the Mission has been without contacts in central Albania. It is doubtful if safe harbour can now be found in this area.'[63] By early February, however, George Seymour's recent reports suggested that that situation had changed. It remained clear, as Seymour pointed out, that 'partisans do not exist in north Albania and are finished in Central Albania as a coherent force. Some small bodies remain but they are mostly fugitives in the hills.'[64] But Kupi, with whom Seymour had been in contact since January, was now making encouraging noises, claiming himself capable of raising a national army many thousands strong. To Kit Steel, Leake wrote:

> According to our latest information Kupi, while still not definitely off the fence, is planning a national force embracing his own Zogists, the BK and moderate members of the LNC . . . An offensive plan is under consideration for a concerted attack on selected targets. Kupi has impressed the various BLOs who have met him differently but the consensus of opinion is that he is an upright patriot who would never collaborate with a foreign occupying power . . . In the interests of our BLOs, I should be grateful . . . that in pursuance of our tightrope policy, we go as far as we can to please Abas Kupi without committing ourselves. He is a figure of great importance for intelligence and operational purposes.[65]

Leake repeated that assessment to the Special Operations Committee. Kupi, he cautioned, was 'valuable but requires careful handling' and

he advised against granting his reported requests for arms, 25,000 sovereigns, Allied recognition of a Zogist government in exile and a broadcast
by Zog urging unity of resistance. 'It is impossible to depart from our
existing policy of political impartiality by declaring for Zog without
seriously embarrasing BLOs attached to the Partisans who continue to
be the only organisation fighting the Germans,' he explained. 'The BBC
is considered in Albania to be the mouthpiece of the Government. A
broadcast utterance by Zog would certainly be regarded as a mark of
official support.' Leake suggested instead that Kupi should be sent a
preliminary grant of 4,000 sovereigns and some token arms but otherwise a noncommittal response, and McLean and Smiley, who were in
London enjoying some leave and meeting senior diplomats and staff,
recalled for attachment to him at the earliest opportunity.[66]

But while he was keen to see what Kupi had to offer militarily, Leake
was never to be convinced of the wisdom of trying to reconcile Kupi
and the Partisans. His first assessment of the idea was in December
1943:

> It has been suggested that it would be practicable to attempt
> to widen the base of the LNC by inducing Abas Kupi and
> the Zogists to make common cause with the movement, and
> if possible, to persuade Zog to put pressure on Kupi for the
> purpose. If a really sincere and effective rapprochement were
> possible, the prospects of a speedy end to the civil war would
> be greatly improved and once this was accomplished, there
> is little doubt that both factions would be prepared to fight
> the Germans. However, it is more likely that, though Kupi
> might comply outwardly in deference to Zog's wishes and
> the Partisans in their present plight be ready to accept him,
> in fact no concrete result would be achieved.
>
> Though the nationalists of Kupi's party are not actually
> members of the Ball Kombetar, their views and interests are
> practically identical and their support for Zog is due to his
> value as an effective counter balance to the growing strength
> of the Partisan movement. It is possible, therefore, that the
> sole outcome would be endless procrastination and prevari-
> cation, leading to mutual recriminations and disputes. The
> opposition between Partisans and nationalists is too deep and
> fundamental to be overcome by an artificial 'combine'.[67]

Two weeks later, when SOE in London wondered whether Cairo should not support Davies' proposals on the grounds that German policy seemed to be to stoke the flames of civil war, Leake replied that the situation was far more serious than London could see. 'Even moderate nationalists such as Abas Kupi are strongly and probably irreconcilably opposed to the Partisans.'[68]

When told that McLean's plan was being considered in London, Leake summoned little enthusiasm. The Foreign Office had sent for Kit Steel's views on it and Steel had asked Leake for his. Leake told him:

> I do not consider it likely that Kupi would return to the LNC: it has far too strong a communist tinge and has openly declared against the Ball Kombetar nationalists with whom Kupi is in close sympathy. Kupi may and probably will succeed in detaching non-political elements from the LNC . . . [but] I am not quite sure how this will help us. The LNC will be reduced to a 100% communist organisation and the contrast between left and right be given added emphasis. Kupi may conceivably be able to negotiate a truce or modus vivendi . . . [but] it would be a very uneasy affair owing to the blood that has been shed and the sharp opposition of outlook and interests. In short, my view is that the left versus right contest must be fought out in Albania – the communists do not compromise.[69]

Replying to the Foreign Office, Steel echoed Leake's concerns. He began by explaining that he had discussed the 'political situation' with McLean when he had been in Cairo, so was familiar with his views. 'We all here regard him as exceedingly intelligent and level-headed.' McLean's scheme to 'broaden' the LNC, however, was 'now only wishful thinking'. It was true, Steel explained, that Kupi had recently made 'proposals of a superficially most encouraging nature for the creation of a national guerilla movement' and 'now appears seriously to contemplate active hostilities against the Germans'. But there was 'absolutely no evidence' that Kupi would work with the LNC. 'He is a staunch anti-communist and I am advised that he would be much more likely to attract the remaining non-Communist elements from the LNC to his own organisation.' Steel's conclusion was definite: 'I do not think we could attain any results by an ambitious political manoeuvre such as Maclean [sic] proposes which would be commensurate with the political difficulties into which we should be drawn.'[70]

While convinced that an agreement was unlikely, Leake was also conscious of the problems SOE had experienced when trying to inter- vene in similar situations elsewhere. In Greece in 1942–3 SOE had found itself supporting both the royalist guerrillas of EDES and the anti-royalist and communist-dominated guerrillas of ELAS. SOE had worked hard to persuade these rival groups to fight the Germans instead of each other and eventually negotiated an agreement by which ELAS and EDES agreed to coordinate their actions with the plans of GHQ Middle East. It did not last; and as civil war resumed and escalated, SOE officers, suspected of trying to intervene on political grounds, found working with ELAS increasingly difficult. Mindful of the paral- lels to the Partisan–Kupi standoff, Leake wrote to London in March that 'while we want to keep the two parties apart, it is important BLOs should not be maneouvered [sic] into the position of mediators. Experience in Greece shows what little effect the intervention of a British officer has on the course of Balkan politics.'[71]

Leake and Steel were not the only ones uneasy about McLean's plan. In February, in Baker Street, as the proposals were passed from desk to desk, David Keswick, Director of Mediterranean operations, likened the 'pattern of disunity' in Albania to that seen in Yugoslavia and Greece. If the British armed Kupi, he warned Colin Gubbins, SOE's Chief, 'we might . . . find ourselves tied to the same policy of backing the restoration Right Wing party and the Left Wing simultaneously with exactly the same results.' McLean and Smiley seemed 'very able and level headed', Keswick added, 'but they are very young, and are soldiers at present serving as BLOs with SOE without any experience or background of politics, and more especially Balkan politics. I am anxious that we should avoid, if possible, the difficulties we have experienced in Yugoslavia and Greece, and that our BLOs should not be given an intricate political task which they are not fully qualified to perform.'[72]

Bill Houstoun-Boswall, a Foreign Office official on loan as Baker Street's political adviser, also looked back to when SOE's support for ELAS had clashed with longer-term concerns. While SOE and the military had urged support for ELAS, Churchill, the Foreign Office and even SOE's Minister had come out strongly for the non-communist Greeks of EDES. Ultimately considerations of post-war politics were judged more important than the short-term strategic value of backing ELAS; and SOE, and Eddie Myers in particular, became scapegoats, accused of supporting ELAS to excessive lengths. 'We do not want a repetition of Greece,' Houstoun-Boswall warned Gubbins, 'nor do we want our officers to be blamed for showing too much sympathy to one particular resistance group . . . We should, I submit, tactfully put our point of view as strongly as we properly can to the Foreign Office indicating what we see to be the risks of allowing ourselves to be carried away be the enthusiasm and romanticism of Major Maclean [sic].'[73]

Even Leake's suggestion that Kupi be sent a few arms and 4,000 sovereigns went too far for some. While 'some slight support' should continue to go to the LNC, all other movements should be ignored, Keswick felt. If Kupi was armed, he told Gubbins, 'we may well have created just such another situation in other Balkan countries – an especially close parallel is Greece – and may well have fomented an acute civil war without in any way increasing the discomfiture of the enemy – if anything on the contrary.' Nor was Keswick taken with the idea of sending Kupi funds. 'I imagine that if one makes an initial payment of 4,000 sovereigns to an Albanian, that Albanian continues to behave as he imagines his benefactor would wish him to behave . . . until he has reached the bottom of the stocking, but what his action will then be is quite another matter. In business this is called an advance without security, and it has always been bad business.'[74]

Others, however, were less concerned and their voices carried greater weight. At a meeting at the Foreign Office on 18 February, Steel's warnings were brushed aside. McLean, who was present, considered that there was some force in the objections but felt his plan had a 50 per cent chance of succeeding and, if it failed, things could hardly get much worse than they were. The Foreign Office did not disagree and wheels were put in motion for McLean to return to Albania to work with Kupi. Approval was also given for Kupi to be sent 4,000 sovereigns.

In view of the strength of opposition in Baker Street and the objections of its own man in Cairo, it may be wondered whether the Foreign Office had hidden political grounds for pushing a plan that even its author felt had only a fifty-fifty chance of success. Leake was one who suspected such an agenda, remarking to Steel in February that he thought 'pro-Zog influences' were at work in London. Steel disagreed and was right to have done so.[75] The Foreign Office, though uneasy about arming communist-led guerrillas, was still averse to any commitment to Zog, which explains why it was so cautious about obtaining from him a letter for Kupi urging unity of resistance, and why, in fact, no such letter was ever sent. The fact that senior diplomats remained 'rather taken' with McLean's plan was a mark of nothing more than a belief that Britain had little to lose by trying to maximise resistance and minimise civil war by reuniting the Partisans and Kupi.[76] Yet the concerns expressed by Leake and Steel and senior SOE staff were prophetic. No agreement was ever reached. No agreement even seemed likely.

Down to April, when McLean was dropped in, George Seymour remained in touch with Kupi. Not that they saw each other often. Invitations were dispatched and meetings pencilled in but Kupi turned up only occasionally. From Seymour's reports and further entries in Arthur Nicholls' diary, which Seymour had taken to keeping after being handed it by Alan Hare, his frustration with Kupi's inaction is clear. So is his growing conviction that there was little chance of Kupi changing his position. Kupi had been repeatedly told that, to qualify for arms, he must commit himself to fighting the Germans openly and unconditionally. Even as Seymour urged him to act before the Allies closed the door on the prospect of future help, Kupi never demonstrated any intention of moving against the Germans or towards union with the Partisans.

Like many SOE officers, Seymour had warmed quickly to Kupi's personality. 'I was most pleasantly surprised at my reception,' he recalled of joining him in Mati in January.

> Abas Kupi himself came to meet me and I was at once made to feel that I was amongst real friends. I was most impressed both with Abas Kupi himself and the men round him who appeared fairly well educated, well disciplined and above all did not have that 'hang-dog' appearance which the Partisans always wore. Another point which struck me most forcibly was the cheerfulness of these men. The Partisans always regarded any form of humour or cheerfulness as directed against them personally, or against their ideals.

In early discussions Kupi also 'made no secret of his grave suspicions and mistrust concerning the Communists but said that he had no intention of joining in Civil War whilst enemy troops remained in the country'. And although it was hard to guess whether Kupi's grandiose plans for a national army would or could come to anything, 'I felt that, properly handled, Kupi could be organised and would fight.'[77] Also impressive was the assistance Kupi gave in finding and treating Arthur Nicholls.

Seymour saw nothing of Kupi from the end of January until the end of March. In that time Kupi apparently went off to tour the north and organise his supporters while Seymour stayed pretty much where he was, looking after Hare, still recovering from his winter ordeal, and generally trying to maintain a British presence in central Albania. Seymour based himself quietly in mountain villages on the southernmost edge of Mati, Kupi's territory, close to Cerminika. A little deeper into Mati were Jack Bulman, Frank Smyth and four British NCOs, whom Trotsky Davies had sent there before Christmas, plus Tony Corsair of MI6. Bulman and Smyth also had a w/t set, with which Seymour, who had lost both his own set and operator, kept in contact with Cairo.

For these two months the diary records a lot of bad weather, which continued to dog RAF efforts to drop stores, and paints a good picture of the frustrations and mundane activities of officers isolated from the outside world and without much to do:

Tuesday 22 Feb 44
The party remains split into three with G.S. and A.H. at Shengjin, F.S. [Frank Smyth], Cooper and Button with radio at Xiberi [sic] and J.B. [Jack Bulman] with Sgts Jenkins and Jones at Klos . . .
   Three English books arrive causing great excitement . . .

Friday 25 Feb 44
. . . G.S. had his hair cut by the eldest son of the house ably assisted with advice from all other members of the household. The result not nearly so weird and wonderful as might have been expected.
   The three books are now nearly finished and will then be sent on to F.S. and his merry men . . .

Monday 28 Feb 44
. . . We move [to a new village, Derje] and are safely over [the Erzen river] by 1830. At the point we crossed, the river was split into half dozen raging torrents girth high. All ponies

kept their feet in a remarkable way . . . A.H. has stood journey
well . . .

G.S. and A.H. have a very comfortable little room to themselves but we must do something about the smoke as there
is no chimney . . .

Wednesday 1 Mar 44
March certainly came roaring in like a lion with violent hail
and thunder storm nearly all day . . .

I.T. [Ihsan Toptani] produced for us a bottle of whiskey
(Italian medicinal but still whiskey) and a small tin of Liptons
tea. The rejoicing has been enormous.

That night a drop was scheduled, 'but God knows where it went to or
where it dropped the stuff. It certainly came nowhere near Xiber as
F.S. and party "stood to" all night.' The drop was meant to have
included the 4,000 sovereigns approved for Abas Kupi; also 'our longed
for mail. G.S. now had no mail since October and that was dated July
so he is feeling more than a little irritable.' Two days later it was learnt
that the drop had gone to Corsair, but 'at random' and 'over a wide
area – money containers falling into river'. To the mission's delight,
however, a little mail was recovered. 'G.S. and A.H. spend all evening
in complete silence over their mail, even dinner being ignored. Much
mail missing and some destroyed by water but sufficient arrives to show
all goes well at home.'[78]

By March, Seymour also knew of Cairo's desire for plans and action
in line with Underdone. This, and the 4,000 sovereigns, half of which
were apparently recovered, gave direction and urgency to his work and
increased his annoyance when Kupi kept delaying discussions. Seymour
recorded his anxieties and the disappointing outcome when he and Kupi
finally met:

Wednesday, 8 Mar 44
G.S. again sends message to A.K. for urgent meeting. Why
is it that one cannot find a single Albanian who appreciates
the value of 'now'? They all pin their faith on 'tomorrow'
and act accordingly . . .

Saturday, 11 Mar 44

A fine day which is a most notable event . . .
2200 Colonel Hyar Cha Ci [Colonel Yahya Chachi, Kupi's commandant] arrives on behalf of Abas Kupi and says latter has been called away and won't be back for ten days!

G.S. furious and spends much of the night wondering what to do . . . Cairo will be screaming for plans which cannot be given . . .

It will be difficult even to start an independent war of our own as locals will not only not help out but would oppose any attempt to do this – not by fighting us but by refusing us shelter, failure to produce guides and placing all those thousand and one obstacles in our way at which the Albanian is peculiarly [adept].

Sunday, 12 Mar 44
Col. H.C.C. arrives at 2230 hrs for discussion but finds that it is not a discussion so much as a monologue by G.S.

Opening remarks include fact that A.K. made many promises in past which he has failed to carry out; that A.K. is known to be at least in touch with 'bad' elements even if he is not actively working with them. G.S. points out that A.K. is an object of acute suspicion to the Allies and that only A.K. himself can allay those suspicions by prompt action. G.S. warns that if there is a sudden German withdrawal A.K. will be left in a queer position and promises of what he intended to do will carry no weight at all . . .

Monday, 13 Mar 44
0230 Col. H.C.C. departs with a worried frown and copious notes promising to do his utmost . . .

Friday, 17 Mar 44
. . . Letter from A.K. saying he will come and see G.S. on 22 March . . .

Wednesday, 22 Mar 44
. . . Very heavy snow and rain . . .
Today is the great day of the big conference with Abas Kupi. It is rather spoilt by the fact that A.K. does not arrive

and sends no word. G.S. getting very worried as Cairo will be getting restive. We can only wait but we are all getting more than a little bored sitting here doing nothing . . .

Friday, 24 Mar 44
A.K. has arrived . . . so now we may rpt may get somewhere . . .

He has said that he is ready to take action NOW and that his preparations are complete. He however declined to say what his plans are or with whom he is in contact. Has promised to give full details tomorrow. Hope he does. Meeting adjourned at 0200 hrs . . .

Saturday, 25 Mar 44
We woke to find it snowing like hell again.

A.K. comes in again in the evening. We hope that this time we are really going to hear all his plans. We ought to have known better!! We hear that whilst A.K. is now ready to fight he will do nothing unless the Allies recognise Zog and permit him to form a 'government' outside the country. G.S. keeping a firm hold on his temper tells A.K. that he is a B.F. to try and issue an ultimatum to [the] Allies and asks A.K. what he intends to do when the demand is refused as G.S. predicts it most certainly will be. A.K. says he will do nothing except look after the BLOs in his territory. G.S. now feels that A.K. has made this move as an excuse for not fighting and intends to wait for an opportune moment – when the Huns leave – to grab power by a coup d'etat . . .

Sunday, 26 Mar 44
A nice sunny day. G.S. worn out with his oratorical exertions and disgust of last night's meeting remains firmly in bed.[79]

Informing Cairo of the meeting's result, Seymour included his opinion that Kupi's real aim was to remain militarily inactive and seize power once the Germans had gone. He also reported a rumour that 'a pact of non-aggression' between the Zogists and the Germans had been signed on Kupi's behalf.[80]

Not much changed in April. Still Kupi did nothing, even when

Seymour told him of the possibility of a daylight drop by forty aircraft if he fought. 'If he can refuse 40 aircraft he is indeed in a very strong position.' And when Kupi complained about civilian casualties during a recent Allied air raid on Tirana, Seymour was furious. 'What are you grumbling about?' he replied. 'As you have never given us the targets we have asked for you are not in a position to grumble if our pilots fail to find [them].' In fact Seymour's views on Kupi's priorities were strengthened on 19 April when they met a second time. Alan Hare was also present; Kupi was 'charming as usual'. After dinner the conference began and Seymour decided to adopt 'a lighter tone' since he had given Kupi 'such a strafing' last time:

> [T]he whole conference was one long roar of laughter, jokes and badinage. A.K. in terrific form. Results as usual nega-tive. A.K. says he will not fight unless Allies recognise Zog . . .
>
> After real conference finished A.K., G.S., A.H. and Shaqir [Trimi, Seymour's interpreter] go into 'huddle' and A.K. being in exceptionally good form permits the cat to peer furtively out of the bag twice. He says:
> (a) He is preparing for Civil War after the Germans leave.
> (b) That there will shortly be a change or changes in the Govt as the present P.M. is considered by other Ministers (all Ballists) to be too lenient to the Partisans (Communists). The new P.M. is [to be] Fikri Din[ë] who is A.K.'s man.

Kupi asked Seymour for money and clothes for his men. Seymour asked Kupi 'why we should help him prepare for Civil War'. Why not? Kupi said. The British had helped the Partisans. 'This is fair and unanswer-able,' Seymour felt.[81]

On the night of 19–20 April, the moment of Seymour and Kupi's last conference, Billy McLean, now a lieutenant colonel with a DSO, para-chuted to Davies' old ground on the Biza plateau. McLean hardly recognised the place when it was revealed next morning covered in snow, mud and Vesuvius ash: the volcano had erupted not long before, winds had carried the grey dust east and the entire country was coated. Two men dropped with him. One was David Smiley, once again his

No. 2 and now promoted major. The other was Captain Julian Amery.

Amery's career had been a little chequered since he had last been involved with Albania. After returning from the Balkans in 1940 he had, to his disgust, found himself training in Torquay in the RAF ranks, before Hugh Dalton intervened and managed to have him rejoin SOE. Sent out to Cairo in 1941 he was re-employed on Balkan projects and, that September, went along for the ride in the submarine that dropped off SOE's first mission to occupied Yugoslavia. The same month he found himself in trouble again when it was discovered, so George Taylor told Cairo, that he was 'writing letters to his father dealing very fully with Balkan matters and the policy which, in his opinion, should be pursued . . . His father in turn is interesting himself in our Balkan activities and pushing his son's views.' Julian was 'seriously spoken to'.[82] The following July he returned to London.

In early 1943, Lord Selborne, SOE's new minister, then began to take an interest in Amery 'as his father is such a very old friend'.[83] By April Selborne was keen to see the son in Yugoslavia. SOE in Cairo was less keen. Lord Glenconner, then still Cairo chief, objected strongly, pointing to Amery's 'lack of experience and want of practical sense'. Also opposed were two of Glenconner's senior staff officers, Guy Tamplin and Bill Harcourt, who believed that Amery 'would at once become involved in political intrigues'. Both threatened to resign if Amery was foisted on them. Cairo 'must have confidence' in its men, Glenconner stressed, 'and in the case of Amery this confidence would be lacking'.[84] In May the issue was solved, temporarily, when a medical pronounced Amery physically unfit. In the autumn Selborne then began pressing to have Amery allowed to go to Greece with Eddie Myers. Amery was returned to Cairo but this time, to Selborne's growing irritation, Anthony Eden objected. Then, in London, in February 1944, Billy McLean told Selborne that he would 'warmly welcome taking Amery back to Albania with him'.[85] McLean, who had known Amery at Eton, had met him again in SOE circles and knew of his Belgrade work. Amery had even helped a little when McLean, after his first mission, had sweated in Cairo over his report and proposals. Destined at last for the field, Amery was delighted. 'Without you I might well have been left to rot in Cairo,' he told McLean after the war. 'I don't suppose I shall ever tell you quite how much your taking me meant to both me and – at that time – to my father.'[86]

Despite the fact that McLean and Amery had been issued linen parachutes, normally used for dropping stores, they and Smiley landed safely. Days later they joined Seymour and Hare in their cramped and bug-ridden house in Derje. Amery enjoyed seeing Hare: they had been friends at school and Oxford. The whole party, including Seymour's little group, then trekked to Xibër, deeper in Mati, arriving on 25 April. Soon McLean and Amery were in serious talks with Kupi. From these, from speaking to Seymour and Hare, and from a two-week tour of Mati, the pair saw themselves how vain was the hope of persuading Kupi to work with the Partisans. Kupi was 'very anti-communist', McLean reported in early May, 'and has stated unofficially several times that it is only his unwillingness to quarrel with the Allies that prevents him from attacking LNC immediately. No initiative is likely from Kupi though he would probably listen to overtures from LNC.' But McLean was 'very doubtful of the possibility of a real rapprochement' and feared that 'abortive talks now would only widen the breach. I consider, there-fore, that we should concentrate rather on preventing clash.'[87]

'A NIGHTMARE BEYOND
DESCRIPTION'

WHEN McLean dropped back in, his mission had three aims: to persuade Kupi and other northern Nationalists to fight the Germans; to encourage a reconciliation between Kupi and the LNC; and to reorganise the work of SOE missions in the north. The difficulty of the last became evident when the mission joined Seymour in Mati, where, not long after the survivors of Davies' mission had turned up, more exhausted British fugitives had started to appear. These were the men of the northernmost missions, driven down by fresh German drives and bringing news that SOE's set-up in northern Albania was now all but shattered. Morale was low and health was poor. One NCO, Seymour recorded, was 'completely off his head poor lad'.[1] Hard experience had also taught them that the British were extremely unlikely to see any Nationalist come out to fight.

Andy Hands was the first British officer to arrive in the very north since Oakley-Hill's ill-fated trek two-and-a-half years before. Hands' orders were to work up contacts and encourage locals to fight. By Christmas he had settled in the little village of Dega, high above the northern banks of the Drin, but managed little else. The only guerrillas he had found were a tiny band of ragged Partisans, mostly from Kosovo, who, though communist-led, had only slim links to those down south. They made their base near Hands' village and he gave them a few token arms. Their leader was Fadil Hoxha, no relation to Enver, whom Hands described as 'a young ardent Nationalist with some fighting ability, [who] has gained a reputation for bravery . . . He is, in general, honest, an idealist and trustworthy.'[2]

Peter Kemp, coming from Dibra, joined Hands at Dega shortly before

Christmas. So did Tony Neel, who, like Hands, had had a dispiriting few weeks. Neel had arrived in the north-west in early November, instructed by Davies to explore the resistance possibilities and establish whether Lake Shkodra might make a suitable flying-boat base. Since then he had seen enough to realise that there was very little chance of him doing much at all. 'Almost from the first it was quite apparent that it would be quite impossible to operate openly,' he explained later; 'the people were all very much afraid of the Germans and they talked of "Gestapo agents" being everywhere . . . It was impossible to travel anywhere by day unless disguised and most villages refused to allow me to stay . . . After about ten days I was advised . . . to move further away from Scutari as too many people knew of my presence.' So he had moved further inland, to the north-east, and in the village of Trun, on the southern bank of the Drin, met Ymer Bardoshi, a former army officer who had gathered around him about a hundred men 'and appeared quite willing to go into action against the Germans'. Neel found him 'most co-operative . . . he is practical and possesses much common sense'. Bardoshi was to impress all SOE officers who came across him, largely because he was friendly, helpful and had no obvious political axe to grind. As Neel remarked later, 'he is about the only Albanian whom I know who does not wish to involve one in political discussions'. But as Neel also commented, there was little chance of Bardoshi doing much fighting because the attitude of local villagers 'made this impossible. They made it quite clear that we were not wanted there, and should we have fought the Germans it would undoubtedly have meant fighting the local people as well.'[3]

When he joined Hands in mid-December, Neel, like Kemp, was on his own and had been out of contact with Cairo for weeks. His w/t set and NCOs were at Xibër with Frank Smyth, who had orders to receive a final sortie before pressing north and joining him, but the weather and German moves would intervene and Neel never saw Smyth again. Riddell and Seymour had also lost their w/t sets long ago and thus it was to Hands, the only mission north of Mati still in touch with Cairo, that Cairo decided to drop new sets and operators, both for them and for Kemp and Neel. These drops were scheduled initially for November. Poor weather and a backlog of sorties caused a lengthy delay. Then, on three successive nights in December, a pair of Halifaxes did make it to Dega. On each occasion the cloud was too thick to penetrate so the planes went home without dropping.

A fourth attempt was made the next night. Sitting in the aircraft among the bundles of clothing and boots were seven British personnel. Four, each with his set, were w/t operators: 'Roxy' Otter; Bob Elvidge, an ex-miner from Leeds; Ivor Clifton, a young Welshman; and Ray Goodier, who had been in the desert with the SAS. The other three were junior officers. Lieutenants John Hibberdine, Reginald Hibbert and Ian Merrett had all volunteered for special operations during SOE's recruitment drive in Britain earlier that year; all three had been interviewed and accepted there, then sailed for the Middle East and trained in Palestine. Earmarked to work as assistants to officers already in the field, none had been in action before or knew anything about Albania, save for what they had been told in Cairo.

Merrett, tall and dark, outgoing and occasionally wild, was twenty-four, had joined the Territorial Army in 1939 while working as a clerk and had spent the first year of the war in the ranks of an anti-tank regiment. He had then joined the commandos, becoming one of the first British soldiers to be parachute-trained. Commissioned into the North Staffordshire Regiment in 1942, he joined SOE in September 1943; his risky but characteristic bluff, that he had attended Rugby School and Pembroke College, Cambridge, went apparently undetected when applying both for his commission and for SOE. Reg Hibbert was twenty-one and halfway through reading history at Worcester College, Oxford. SOE's enticing circular appeared while he was in a holding battalion at Welbeck Abbey, a broken jaw having stopped him joining his regiment, the 4th Hussars, before it went overseas. John Hibberdine was twenty-three. After Christ's Hospital he had spent two years in London as a solicitor's clerk before being commissioned into the Cameronians in 1941. Days after joining SOE in August 1943 he was on his way to Cairo.

Bright and down-to-earth, Hibberdine kept a diary for most of his time in Albania that provides a most vivid account of the early experiences of young SOE officers catapulted into the field:

19.12. Sunday . . .
This was our fourth trip over the target area and as the weather was clear we were able to pick out many familiar landmarks in the darkness beneath – the German seaplane base on the south coast of Greece and the lights of Durazzo, Scutari and Tirana. As we turned overland we started to

dress up for the jump – not an easy performance for four people with the fuselage load and the crew in the way. At last however we stood about, four bulky figures, in our Sidcot linings, flying suits and parachutes. We arrived over the target at 2030 hrs with still no sign of the clouds which had kept us from dropping on the previous occasions and circled around while Ian's plane, which had arrived before us, made its drop. Then just before nine we ran in to drop our load. When all the containers had gone Clifton and I who were jumping first sat down on the edge of the aperture as the plane circled to run in for our jump. I was to go first and as the air brakes were lowered and the plane shuddered to a slower speed (about 140mph) I felt the familiar prickles up and down my spine and that empty feeling in the stomach. Far below, framed by the bottom of the aperture, I could see the ground-flares in the form of a Y, evenly spaced and burning clearly. A second or two later the red warning light flashed on, followed almost at once by the green and with the despatcher yelling 'Action stations, two, one, go!' I pushed myself off. The usual blast of air from the slipstream was softened slightly by the weight of my flying equipment and with 'chute fully opened, drifting down I was able to look about and enjoy the descent. Disappearing west over a line of mountains I could see the lights of the plane and behind and above me the dim white blur of Clifton's parachute. On either side level with us were the tops of the hills which enclose the valley of Deg. As we dropped below these all wind stopped. Directly beneath were the flares still burning clearly but now much closer. We reckoned afterwards that we baled out at 1500 feet . . .

As I hit the ground swarms of people gathered round gibbering excitedly and gesticulating. While some of them pushed forward to wring me by the hand, crying 'Partisan, Partisan, Partisan', others gathered up the parachute I had released and made off with it into the night. I never saw it again (enough silk to make goodness knows how many pairs of pyjamas). I was rescued at last by a tall figure appearing out of the gloom wearing a cossack hat, short Albanian coat and riding breeches. This was Peter Kemp and he led me

over to the fires where I was introduced to Tony Neel and
Andy. Ian was already there and we all watched the plane
run over again to drop Reggie and Elvidge.[4]

Hibbert would recall that it was frosty and cold when they landed, a
shock after the sand and warmth of the desert. Gunshots, as Hands'
Partisans, detailed to guard the dropping ground, blazed away at villagers
looking for loot, heightened the dislocation.

When all seven men were collected, they were led the few yards to
Hands' stone cottage. 'It is not an inviting place,' Hibberdine wrote,
before describing the sort of scene of simplicity with which all SOE
personnel in Albania were quickly familiar:

[It consists] of stables on the ground floor and an outside
wooden staircase leading up to the living quarters on the
first floor . . . There was a draughty loft just inside the door
used as a kitchen and servants' living quarters with the smell
of the stables coming up strongly between the wide gaps in
the rickety floor boards; and an inner room draughty and
badly lit, with a low ceiling and mud floor. The walls are of
mud plaster and three minute windows like those of a fortress
let in the light. Four rough beds, a table of canisters and
planks, a smaller table with a wireless set on it and canisters to sit on make up the furniture.

'In daylight – what daylight gets through the boards and dirty glass over
the windows in this room – our quarters appear even more filthy,' he
continued next day. 'This is not the fault of the people living here but
of the construction of the house, mud being the chief material. It is also
impossible to get hold of whitewash for the walls or boards for the floor.'
The house was 'really too crowded', Hibberdine added a few days later,
'and it is difficult to move round the room. We new arrivals have been
sleeping on the floor where we have collected many fleas and lice.' The
presence of five Italians, formerly of the *Firenze* Division, made life a
little easier. 'There is Orlando the waiter, Amerigo the cook, Angelo the
mechanic (for the charging engine) and Luigi and Ego who look after
the mules and do other odd jobs such as chopping wood. All are very
willing and hard workers and would be only too pleased to dress you
in the mornings if you would let them.' Less appealing were the locals:

21.12. Tuesday

It is now apparent that all our kit has been stolen by either the villagers or the partisan battalion here. Peter and Andy have made superhuman efforts to recover it, searching houses and railing at the villagers, but although much material has been returned no personal kit has come to light. The local inhabitants are dirty as well as dishonest (characteristics of most Albanians I'm told) and their clothes are such as a beggar in England would scorn. They stand about outside our house waiting for further pickings, spitting and blowing their noses between their fingers, all the while chattering away to each other like the monkeys on monkey hill.[5]

On top of the cold, the rain, the theft of their kit and the hours each man endured winding a hand charger to keep the w/t set working, the new arrivals learnt how depressing was the local situation. 'All our illusions about a colourful and lively guerilla war were punctured as we listened to Kemp and the others holding discussions with local leaders,' Reg Hibbert wrote later. 'No promising line of action seemed to be open in any direction.'[6] A redeeming feature, as ever, was the dramatic terrain. 'The country round here looks like the Highlands in autumn,' Hibberdine noted, 'except that the mountains in the distance are many times higher than anything one sees in Scotland.'[7]

One light on the horizon was Christmas. Couriers were dispatched to Kosovo to buy spirits and cigarettes, pork was secured from the Catholic north-west and, on Christmas Eve, Hibberdine recorded, 'we had a good party ... Raki, Cognac, Cinzano and Chianti have been disappearing all day and the room presents a spectacle of the wildest debauchery with half the occupants dozing on the beds and the floor'. Christmas Day 'did not go with such a bang', although 'Amerigo and Orlando produced a magnificent lunch for us which was a real achievement considering the uncomfortable conditions under which they have to cook', while in the evening some locals came in 'and the tempo of the party increased. One Alb seized Peter's bottle of tonic (it was carefully put in his way by Tony) and drained it off. It had the same effect on him as alcohol for he passed right out. Shooting then started, into the air, which is the typical sign of Alb jubilation.'[8]

After Christmas the missions split up. Hands, with Clifton and his own NCOs, moved to the next valley and made a fresh base in Berishte, another village above the north bank of the Drin. Tony Neel, with Merrett and Otter, returned to Trun, on the opposite bank, half a day's march from Hands, and made a new base of his own. Hibbert, taking Elvidge and Goodier, set off with guides to join Richard Riddell near Dibra. Peter Kemp, taking Hibberdine, left for Kosovo.

Throughout January, Neel and Hands remained in contact with local Nationalists and Partisans respectively. Not much occurred to alter their earlier assessment, summed up in Cairo on 1 January, that little could be expected from Northern Albania before the spring 'and that arms given to local bands will probably only be used in civil war'.[9] Over New Year, Hands did attend a meeting at Bujan, close to Kosovo, where Fadil Hoxha's force was transformed into the 'Kosmet' Partisans, short for Kosovo and Metohija, the full Serb title for the region, and promised him action against the Germans, but Hands felt few locals would support them. Neel, from his own experiences that month, felt the same. One mildly diverting development was when Nik Sokoli, a young Catholic chieftain, turned up at Trun, claimed he was leader of 6,500 Zogist followers ready and willing to fight the Germans and produced a letter of authority from Abas Kupi. Sokoli's claim to command so many was obviously bogus; George Seymour, who met him later, described him as 'of such feeble character that he was even scared of his own ceta [sic]'.[10] To be sure of the true position, Merrett, on 21 January, left for Betosh, Sokoli's village. But throughout the north, Neel reported later, 'everyone . . . was scared of openly opposing the Germans for fear of reprisals, and for the lack of support from the local people'. Also the 'anti-Partisan feeling was very strong and very noticeable wherever I went . . . It was obvious that the Partisans and not the Germans were considered the greatest enemy . . . in fact there was a very noticeable lack of anti-German feeling.'[11]

Kemp's experiences in Kosovo were a little different. When planning to open up the country, Billy McLean had told Cairo in July that a mission to go to Kosovo was 'most urgently required'.[12] Kemp, who saw the signal while in Cairo, told McLean on arriving in August: 'That's where I should like to go – it's bound to be interesting, that frontier.'[13] McLean was free to explore possibilities anywhere within Greater Albania, the entity created by the Axis in 1941 that included most of Kosovo, and would have known of the success the British had

had in securing support up there in 1940–41. He would have known, too, of important chrome and zinc mines in the region and the potential value of establishing links through Kosovo with SOE missions in southern Serbia. But neither he nor Kemp knew much more. When Cairo, in August, passed him rumours of some kind of Kosovar resistance and a report that two Albanian army regiments there might be persuaded to desert, McLean, though interested, replied that he had heard nothing from his own sources. 'I do not rpt not know anything of situation in Kossova area.'[14] Nor had SOE officers in southern Serbia learnt much, other than that the predominantly Serb Chetniks with whom they were working had very little local support in the province.

What Kemp did learn before setting foot in Kosovo was how emotive, for Albanians, was the issue of its future. And in September, anxious to make his mission a success, he asked Cairo for 'a declaration by the Yugoslav Government that the people of Kosovo would be allowed free choice between a Jug or Albanian Government in accordance with the Atlantic Charter'.[15] Issued by Churchill and Roosevelt in 1941, the much-publicised Atlantic Charter had proclaimed 'certain common principles' by which their countries would 'base their hopes for a better future for the world'. These included 'the right of all peoples' to choose their own form of government and a peace 'which will afford assurance that all men in all the lands may live out their lives in freedom from fear'.[16] But Kemp had soon become aware in Albania of 'the urgent importance of the Kossovo question' and the potential value of securing a more definite declaration. 'It is no exaggeration to say that it was a burning anxiety in the minds of all I met,' he reported later. Men of 'widely differing views', from Enver Hoxha and Mustafa Gjinishi to senior members of the Balli Kombëtar, 'all agreed on the importance to Albania of a just settlement of the Kossovo problem'. All agreed that such a settlement 'could only be secured by a return to Albania of Kossovo'. All pressed Kemp 'to obtain from the Allies a simple declaration, not that Kossovo would be returned to Albania, but simply that the future of Kossovo would be settled by plebiscite held under Allied supervision'. Alternatively, 'a declaration from the Jugoslav Government in London that they would consent to such a plebiscite'. But without any declaration, so Kemp was warned, 'the work of any BLO in Kossovo would be extremely difficult, if not impossible'.[17]

Assembling in Cairo, the Special Operations Committee considered Kemp's appeal on the morning of 13 October. As the meeting's minutes show, his request was dismissed out of hand. Aware of the priority the Foreign Office gave to assuaging Greek and Yugoslav concerns over Albania's borders, the committee dismissed the matter without pausing to consider the competing claims to the province or even refer the matter to London. Only Ralph Stevenson, British Ambassador to Yugoslavia, made any comment: 'that it was unlikely that the Yugoslav Government would accede to such a request, nor was it desirable that such a request be made. It had already been made clear that any questions regarding frontiers would have to wait until the peace conference.' The committee 'agreed that no approach should be made to the Yugoslav Government'.[18] SOE sent Kemp the bad news: 'Regret that prospect obtaining declaration from HMG or Jug Govt regarding future Kosovo or other disputed districts at present absolutely nil. You should therefore take line that such problems outside your competence as you are concerned with military matters only.'[19]

Based on Hands' headquarters at Dega, Kemp made two trips to Kosovo, the first in December and the second in January. Both times he stayed in German-garrisoned Gjakova, a few miles from the old border with Albania on the edge of the Kosovo plain. It was there that Oakley-Hill had spent his final night before marching into Albania in April 1941, and Kemp was to make both of his trips under the protection of Hasan Kryeziu, Gani's brother, who still lived in the family's home. Muharrem Bajraktar, the powerful chief from Luma, north of Dibra, had put Kemp in touch with him.

With guides sent by Hasan, Kemp left Dega on his first trip to Gjakova on the morning of 14 December. 'I reached Hasan Beg's house at midnight,' he reported later, 'after a very "musical comedy" entrance into the town, with my escort creeping through the streets and hissing at each other in a way that would certainly have got us arrested had there been any police about.'[20] For the next three days, as a guest in the Kryezius' grand Ottoman townhouse, Kemp held meetings with a succession of local notables whom Hasan brought to see him, from merchants and landowners to Gjakova's mayor and gendarmerie chief.

Retiring to Dega for Christmas, Kemp returned with Hibberdine on New Year's Day, sweeping down from the mountains 'in royal style': squeezed, with their guards and sub-machine-guns, into a two-man horse-drawn gig. Hibberdine 'half expected to be able to turn round and find we were being pursued by a pack of wolves'.[21] During daylight hours they hid, mostly in Hasan's house. Each evening they set out into the German-patrolled streets for secret meetings at various addresses. This time those whom Hasan had invited included the colonel commanding the Albanian Army in Kosovo.

Both officers were impressed by the risks the locals ran to hide and protect them and by the pro-Allied sentiments of many of the men they met. They were also soon aware of the intensity of ethnic friction. '[T]he scene of another Serb atrocity,' Hibberdine recorded of one home outside Gjakova. 'In 1941 when they were withdrawing north a Serb band of regulars called in here and forced the owner of the house (the elder brother of the present owner) to give them food and clothing. When they had eaten, in gratitude for his hospitality, they took him outside and shot him in front of his wife and children.'[22] Kemp told Cairo that in Gjakova he was shown an 'original Serb document, dated 1938, advocating wholesale deportation of Albanians from Kossovo and replacement with Serbs'.[23]

Ethnic hatreds also bred distrust of anything communist. As Hibberdine put it: 'Communism is not popular as communism means Tito and Tito means Yugoslav interference.'[24] And the officers saw very clearly how effectively Germany had minimised resistance by incorporating most of Kosovo into Albania and recognising Greater Albania's independence. 'The majority of Kosovars preferred a German occupation to a Serb,' Kemp observed. 'The Axis powers had at least united them with their fellow Albanians, whereas an Allied victory would, they feared, return them to Yugoslav rule.'[25]

The pair also heard about the Second League of Prizren, formed by prominent Kosovars in 1943. The chairman was Rexhep Mitrovica, head of the German-sponsored government in Tirana, but the League's popular appeal was not as a pro-German body but as a nationalist movement dedicated to preserving Albania's new borders. Kemp and Hibberdine never knew much about it, but it was clear that most Albanians they met sympathised with the League's central aim. Chatting with Ejub Binaku, their local bodyguard and guide, Hibberdine and Kemp were told: 'Rexhip [sic] Mitrovica is so far from being a collaborateur [sic] that if he came to Djakovica [sic] tomorrow Ejub would have no hesitation in taking us to his house.' Discussing locals in general, the pair concluded 'that it is not the large landowners in this part of the world who give the drive to the Irredentist movement, but the small people – shop owners, clerks, artisans; and these small people show a determination unlike any other Peter has seen in Albania.'[26]

From their talks in Gjakova the two officers also saw that few Albanians were prepared to put aside their priorities and risk all for the Allied cause. Hibberdine's diary provides something of the flavour of these tortuous discussions, with a long description of a meeting he and Kemp held in the town on the evening of 7 January. The mayor, Sulejman Bey Kryeziu, and a leading irredentist, Sulejman Riza, were present, as were the army colonel and Ejub Binaku. Kemp and Hibberdine had stressed already their wish to leave Gjakova and explore the rest of Kosovo and suspected that these men, whose help they needed to do so, were stalling. Hibberdine wrote:

> [The conference] started with promises to help us as much as they could, apologies for our prolonged stay here, and tales of the badness of the weather. We were told: it was only a matter of a week of two before the Irredentist group declared against the Germans and came out into the open prepared to fight; meanwhile they were willing to commence small actions of violence and sabotage at once. A conference was to be held of the Irredentist group to decide their position, the Albanian army [in Kosovo] is to prepare plans for attacking the Germans as they withdraw from the Balkans and is to start training irregulars in the use of arms. So far so good. But their plans with regard to our immediate future were far less pleasing. The weather, the political situation, etc, all so many arguments which we could not easily rebuff because of our lack of information were used to persuade us to withdraw to Dega until the weather cleared, and the political situation eased (although what exactly the political business is or has to do with it, I can't say). A great argument ensued, Sulejman Riza gesticulating wildly and pleading with us to have confidence in him ... the Colonel silent except for an occasional spasm of laughter and one or two short phrases, Sulejman Beg [sic] looking like a prosperous butcher and saying nothing, Ejub scowling and obstinate and saying plenty, [and] Peter and I getting more and more angry ... However we were beaten in the end, mainly by Sulejman Riza's generous gesticulating and calls for confidence. So now we are going to hang around the Kossovo area for a few days and then return to Dega. As one last

concession they promised us to arrange a conference of all
Kossovars willing to fight the Huns ... Some hope. Peter
wants to go home.

Except for the Partisans at Dega, most Albanians in northern Albania
and Kosovo who claimed to be willing to fight offered to do so only
as the Germans left. Men like Ejub Binaku, who promised 'immediate
and effective action on the part of his men', were rare and not nearly
numerous enough. Ejub's offer 'was most refreshing', Hibberdine noted,
'but we considered immediate action too premature'.[27] The attitude of
the gendarmerie and army commanders from Peja whom Kemp met
was more typical: both promised to keep him 'furnished with information about the Germans, but neither would commit themselves to
any military action prior to a German withdrawal or Allied invasion'.[28]

Kemp became convinced that 'no real military action' could be
achieved 'without some sort of declaration from the Allies, to the effect
that the people of Kosovo would be able to decide their own fate and
form of government after an Allied victory, by free plebiscite'. He
reported later:

> In several signals I impressed upon Cairo the urgency of this
> problem and the importance of a declaration, but each time
> I received the same reply – that there was no prospect of any
> declaration on the future of Kossovo either from HMG or
> the Jugoslav Government, and that I must take the line that
> such problems were outside my competence as a soldier. Such
> a directive could only have been given by people wholly unfa-
> miliar with the situation in the field. This political problem
> was so bound up with the military situation that neglect of
> it rendered sterile any attempts at military action ...
>
> I believe that the chances of organising some military
> activity against the Germans in Kossovo may still be good,
> given some Allied encouragement to the Kossovars ... True,
> the Irredentists would prefer to sit on the fence and do
> nothing until the Germans began to withdraw or the Allies
> to land in the Balkans but I think that, given such a declar-
> ation, we could have forced them into action. Without it we
> can expect nothing, since we are offering them nothing to
> fight for, and so we are leaving the field open for German

propaganda to convince them that, if the Allies win, they will revert to Jugoslav rule.

Cairo's advice that he 'tactfully avoid' questions about Kosovo's future was pointless, for 'it was quite impossible to avoid them, as they were invariably the first questions put to me by everyone I met in the area – of whatever party. I hedged as best I could, calling to my help the already overworked Atlantic Charter, but although I avoided committing HMG in any way I could not succeed in swaying the Kossovars on to our side sufficiently to take up arms for us. They did not trust our post-war policy towards them.'[29]

As Kemp and Hibberdine returned to join Hands and the others, however, dramatic news reached them: Gani Kryeziu had escaped from Italy in the chaos of the armistice and was now at his home in Gjakova. 'This was important because almost everyone with whom I had talked in Kosovo, of whatever political opinions, had stressed the influence of Gani Beg [Kryeziu] which was second to none in Kosovo; moreover, though he had his enemies, almost everyone admitted his ability, integrity and sympathy towards the Allies.' Kemp wrote to him at once, requesting a meeting. Gani replied, 'fulsome in his expressions of willingness to help me and the Allies in any way possible'. They met on 22 January in the village of Vlad. With Gani were Hasan, Said, who had escaped with him, and a certain Lazar Fundo, a former Albanian communist who had been in prison with Gani and Said, spoke 'fair English' and was known to Enver Hoxha. Kemp reported later:

Gani and Said seemed very ill with chest trouble – I thought TB. We received a most enthusiastic welcome from them, in a room almost crowded out with friends and retainers; we heard that some 3,000 people had already been to congratulate them on their escape. They had judged it wise to leave Gjakova and Hasan Beg had closed down the house there, and they were now in the hills 'for the duration'. It was here that I heard from them the story . . . of how Memet Konica [a veteran diplomat] in Rome had helped them escape from the Germans after they had broken out of their Italian concentration camp, and how they had travelled with false papers, in a German military train through northern Italy and Austria, and down to Yugoslavia.

Gani, Said and Fundo 'were most anxious to begin at once their efforts to unite all parties, including the Partisans, in one front against the Germans'. Gani said that he already had a hundred men but could easily raise 'ten times that number' and 'reiterated his willingness to help us and co-operate to the most of his power'.[30] He also undertook to organise at once the trip around Kosovo the officers wanted and, moreover, made no requests of his own. 'Our meeting was enthusiastic on both sides and we were soon in serious conversation,' Hibberdine recorded. 'What he said can be summed up in this remark: "We will make your journey. Give me five or six days to get things ready. There is nothing I won't do for you."' Kemp told Cairo on 24 January: 'Saw Gani and Said Kryeziu who escaped Italy . . . and now in hills . . . promised fullest help and fix our journey within week.'[31]

That evening, over Hands' w/t set, Kemp received the shattering instruction from Cairo that he must sever all contact with Nationalists in Kosovo. Stunned, he asked to keep in touch with Gani at least, but Cairo forbade it. Then Kemp asked for permission to leave Albania and report. This was granted. In early February he left Hibberdine with Tony Neel and began marching north, to Montenegro, aiming for an airfield held by Yugoslav Partisans at Berane. From there, in April, he was flown to Italy.

For fifty years, Kemp's memoirs have been the principal published record of British attempts to foster resistance in Kosovo that winter. They describe in detail his work with the anti-Serb and anti-communist Albanian majority, how much these men impressed him, and Gani Kryeziu most of all. Kemp also recalled his surprise and dismay at being told by Cairo to sever his contacts and claimed that British policy-makers, more anxious to maintain good relations with Tito's Yugoslav Partisans, had ordered the break after Tito protested against his activities. More specifically, Kemp felt that the Kosmet Partisans, reluctant to see him make headway with Nationalists in the region, had reported his activities to Tito, who then protested to the British mission with him in Bosnia, thus bringing about the decision that Kemp should keep out of Kosovo.

Though Kemp's experiences and exploits are recounted with modesty and wit, men who knew him have stressed his qualities as a coura-geous and experienced soldier and a perceptive and intelligent man. Andy Hands considered Kemp 'undoubtedly the best officer in the field', noted his 'keen brain' and admired the 'sound knowledge of both Albania and Albanians' he developed after arriving.[32] In January 1944, however, Kemp had been far away from the policy-making process and, today, SOE records show that his post-war explanation for his withdrawal from Kosovo is not correct.

For a start, no objection to Kemp's activities was received from Tito. The 'in' signals log of SOE's Yugoslav section in Cairo contains no complaint about Kemp either from Tito or from any British mission in Bosnia. What is recorded is a short and slightly confused message from Major Anthony Hunter, an SOE officer attached to the Yugoslav Partisans at Berane, referring to complaints made by an 'Albanian delegation here' and asking for 'information ref. British mission said to be intriguing with both sides' in Kosovo. Hunter wanted to know, too, about a British officer said to be working with Albanians 'co-operating with Fascists'.[33] It seems very likely that this was the protest Kemp thought later had come from Tito. The Yugoslav section sent a copy to the Albanian section and asked what it was all about. Philip Leake, aware that the Kosmet Partisans were in touch with Berane, explained that Peter Kemp was in touch with Nationalists in the region.[34] Kemp himself was told: 'partisans [at] Berane have been receiving unfavourable accounts [of] your activities – presumably from Kosmet'.[35]

Certainly the Kosmet had little liking for Kemp. 'Andy was a good man,' Fadil Hoxha remembered of Hands. 'He helped us a lot, with arms, money, clothing. Not like the other one, that other British officer. He did not want to help us; he did not want anything to do with us.'[36] But the man who was likely to have reported on Kemp was Mehmet Hoxha, again no relation to Enver or Fadil, who was working with the Kosmet in a sort of political advisory role. Hibberdine described him in his diary as 'a sleek stout man . . . who speaks French and looks to me like the personification of treachery'. Hands was none too keen on him either. 'He professes to be a Nationalist, but is in effect Socialist, his pose of Nationalist is only maintained to gain the sympathy of the Kossovars who are in the majority Anti-Communist. He is an opportunist and egoist and cannot be trusted.' Kemp, who had met Mehmet before and borrowed his suit to slip into Tirana, was convinced that the Kosmet had sabotaged his first trip to Kosovo, spreading news that he was in Gjakova in the hope that the Germans would arrest him.

Yet Hunter's message was not itself responsible for bringing Kemp's work in Kosovo to a close. It is now apparent that a greater impact

on minds in Cairo was made by Kemp's own w/t messages and by one
report in particular. On 9 January, sitting in Hasan Kryeziu's home,
he and Hibberdine had composed a summary of their discussions.
Before sending it by runner to Hands for transmission, Hibberdine
copied the text into his diary. The 'irredentists' were the 'strongest
group' in Kosovo, the pair explained, with 'much more guts than
mountaineers' and 'reps and sympathisers all parties' except the communists who were 'few and unpopular'. Tito wanted Kosovars 'as Alb
minority in Jug or autonomy within Jug federation' but 'all classes
here want Kosovo integral part Albania'. The Serbs provoked the
'greatest fear' but 'assurance' that the Allies would 'restrain Serb
forceful entry' would 'greatly increase effect anti-Hun action . . .
Kossovars won't fight for return Jugs under whom worst oppression
as evidence shows.' The pair had 'much hope' of organising 'anti-Hun
resistance', if not of immediate action: 'all tell us our presence boosts
pro-British feeling here as now feel not forgotten'. They added that
they would 'welcome any directive'.[37]

On receiving that message, decrypted in Cairo by 18 January, Philip
Leake drew up a paper for submission at once to higher authority,
setting out accurately the political and resistance scene and the state of
SOE's contacts in Kosovo as reported from the field. He emphasised
that the situation was 'extremely delicate owing to the existence of
strong racial as well as ideological feeling' and explained that 'Irredentist
feeling' was 'predominant and the majority of the population belongs
to Nationalist groups'. These were 'reluctant to take immediate action
against the Germans, as they wish to reserve their strength for the post-
war defence of Kosovo'. Nevertheless, several leaders had promised
help with propaganda and intelligence, while some action 'at the time
of the German withdrawal' remained possible. Support for the
Nationalists was likely 'to cause difficulties with the Jugoslav partisans'
while support for the Kosmet was likely 'to produce action but if
injudiciously supplied will precipitate civil war'. The Nationalists were
'anti-Partisan' but as yet there had been 'no fighting between the two
factions'. On 21 January Leake passed his paper to his Cairo commander,
stressing that 'owing to the delicate nature of the situation, a directive
is urgently required'.[38]

Leake's paper was duly discussed when the Special Operations
Committee's working body met at Grey Pillars the following morning.
As the minutes show, it was Kit Steel, the Foreign Office representative,

conscious of Kosovo's importance to Yugoslavia, who advised the committee to bring Kemp's efforts to an end.

> Mr Steel referred to the position of Kossovo which was a bone of contention between the Serbs and the Albanians, and which had been handed back by the Germans to Albania. We had at present a LO [Liaison Officer] both with the Nationalists in that area and with the Albanian partisans. It was important that we did not get involved in any disputes over this territory, especially in view of its sentimental value to the Serbs, and it was therefore proposed to withdraw the LO with the Nationalists.

The committee agreed that the 'LO with the Nationalists should be withdrawn'. SOE complied with the ruling.[39]

Kemp's impression that a pro-Partisan policy was at work was under-standable, given that Cairo told him that his contacts were having an 'undesirable' effect on Yugoslav Partisans and that relations with them were of 'overriding importance'.[40] And Britain's commitment to Tito by 1944 was certainly substantial, while observers in Cairo did feel that maintaining healthy relations with Partisans in and around Kosovo could benefit the British. The Kosmet were few and poorly armed, Philip Leake considered, as well as unpopular 'owing to the strong nationalist and conservative feeling which prevails in North Albania and particularly in the Kosovo area'. But he, Steel and the Special Operations Committee also felt that continued contact with them might ensure a friendly route into Yugoslav territory and that some forces were still on hand to attack the chrome mines, harass the Germans and provide intelligence. Also, there was 'no risk of this contact embroiling us with Jugoslavs over the Kosovo question' since the Kosmet 'repre-sent Jugoslav as well as Albanian interests'; severing it, meanwhile, might annoy Tito's Partisans.[41]

Cairo's signals to Kemp were misleading, however. British sensitivity to the issue of Albania's borders predated the emergence of Tito's move-ment. Moreover, neither SOE nor the Special Operations Committee wanted resistance in Kosovo regardless of its impact on local tensions. In his 21 January paper, Leake, well aware of the ethnic and political friction there, had advised strongly that 'all support and contact' be severed 'at the first sign of civil war'. In fact Kemp's withdrawal was accompanied by a ban on all SOE activity with any Albanians in Kosovo.[42] When told to stay in touch with the Kosmet, Hands was instructed to operate only 'within the old Albanian border' and 'break off contact at the first signs of further political complications'.[43]

As Kemp was picking his way towards Berane and evacuation to Italy, Hands, Hibberdine and the others waited for the Germans. Kemp had heard from the police chief in Gjakova that the Germans not only knew of the drop that had brought Hibberdine and the others but also believed that fifty parachutists had arrived. The Gjakova garrison had been reinforced by a thousand and an expedition against the British was apparently planned.

Locals, too, were becoming less tolerant. In January, fifty Germans appeared in Dardhe, a village two hundred yards from Hands at Berishte but fortunately on the far side of the Drin, impassable at that point. They stayed the night, quizzed locals, peered at Berishte through binoculars and stuck anti-British posters on walls. Next morning, having searched Neel's house in neighbouring Trun while he drank raki and watched from the hills, they left. 'The people of Dardhe, who were Catholics, recorded the Germans with all friendliness and when Hands went over there the next day to buy provisions, and started to tear down the German posters, he was very nearly murdered by the villagers,' Kemp recorded. 'It was not so much love of the Germans as fear of them that induced this attitude in the people. This very Sunday morning, when Hands and Neel went to the church above Dardhe for Mass, they were warned not to come again.'[44]

Also in January, Hands gave locals and Germans greater cause for concern with one of the most important acts of sabotage that SOE carried out in Albania. Hands had arrived in the country well briefed on the importance of chrome and soon confirmed, from close reconnaissance, that the mine at Kam, in the hills close to Kosovo, was a significant and sizeable concern. There were offices and barracks and the German garrison, he estimated, was 120-strong while 'slave labourers' numbered as many as four hundred. And when he reported that one hundred more soldiers and another four hundred labourers were heard to be arriving at the mine on the last day of January, SOE in Cairo suggested that a force of British parachute troops might go in to destroy it. Hands thought the plan a poor one. Such an attack, he felt, would probably succeed if made before February, but all the men not killed in the assault would certainly be captured. But if the attack was left until later, he warned, then the chances of success, given the larger garrison, the remote location and the wintry conditions, would be 'considerably diminished'.[45] For these reasons he decided to put the mine out of action himself.

Kam sat on a hillside, with the offices and barracks at the bottom. The shafts were sunk in several places and too difficult and too numerous for a small team to have destroyed with success. So, on the morning of 30 January, taking Brandrick, Clifton, two guides and a mule and three prepared packs of plastic high explosive, Hands set out from Berishte with the aim of destroying the mine's machine shed. Perched on the hill above the mine, this controlled the bucket way, a twin set of cables and buckets which carried the ore through the mountains to points where it could be picked up and transported more easily by road.

It was early evening and still light when Hands and his NCOs left their guides and, using the cover of trees and scrub, slipped past the guard patrols and edged their way towards the shed. Two more sentries were spotted and open ground lay ahead so the party hid until dark. At six o'clock the three men emerged, making for the shed and the sentries. Hands, brutally matter-of-fact, reported afterwards:

> The first sentry was despatched, his overcoat and cap were donned and his patrol taken over [and my] arrival at the machine shed coincided with the sentry there urinating [and] his despatch was effected without trouble. A knife was used on both occasions.
>
> Inside the shed there was a complicated pulley system with large drums of cables at one side, and a main engine, to the right there was an auxiliary engine. The Plastic was placed on the pulley system, cable drums and engines. Each pack was linked with cortex and 25 feet of Bickford [fuse] was used to enable me to get past the barracks before the explosion.

The fuse was lit. Hands and Brandrick left the shed, picked up Clifton who had been put on guard outside and, together, ran off. Minutes later 'the sky was lit by the explosion, the flame reaching 20 to 30 feet in the air. Signal lights were flashed and wild firing broke out, but by then we were well on our line of retreat.'[46] The Germans never returned the bucket way to effective use and, after trying to move the ore over the mountains by mule, gave up and closed the mine. Hands received the DSO. Military Medals went to Brandrick and Clifton.

For the next fortnight, reports were heard of reprisals around Kam but no Germans seen near Berishte or Trun. But with rumours growing, the weather deteriorating and life in general becoming daily more difficult, the strain on the British was beginning to tell. Hibberdine's diary reads:

2.2. Wednesday
Alarms and excursions today. Constant rumours of the Germans attacking or moving to attack Andy . . . Sounds of a/c over Berishte tonight and fierce firing from all directions. A 'drop' is in progress.

3.2. Thursday
We sent a man over to Berishte early this morning to collect our mail – if any. He arrived back with three for Tony and half a dozen Xmas greetings for me . . . After lunch we trekked over to see Andy and . . . found him sitting in utter despair cursing everyone. The drop was a shambles – inaccurate to a ridiculous degree and much thieving. He had to stop the drop and all he got was twelve rifles, one APT rifle (no ammunition) and fourteen canisters of emergency ration (chocolate). Also 1000 sovs. We relieved him of 500 of these. To crown it all he only received one letter – saying his bank have received no pay for him for eleven months . . .

6.2. Sunday
More rumours today of Germans approaching but as usual little truth behind them. We had some snow overnight but a brilliant sun today has made short work of it. Tony and I spent the morning making gigantic snow balls and then letting them trundle down the hillside. This caused much amusement to the Albs who however were reluctant to lower their dignity by joining in. Andy came over in the afternoon with news of future events and policy. I am now a member of Tony's mission and Ian a member of Andy's . . . I had my

third bath since I've been in Albania, standing in a container of warm water.

7.2 Monday
A cold day. Andy left in the morning on a mule. He is suffering from internal decay . . . and walking apparently makes frequent halts necessary. Tony's stomach has been giving him hell . . . This evening we had our third earthquake since I arrived . . .

9.2. Wednesday
It has started to snow again. All day it has been coming down and there is no sign of a break in the sky. Very picturesque but uncomfortable . . . We have been boiling all our water today in the hope that it will cure all the stomach trouble in the house . . .

10.2. Thursday
This has been a day of disasters. Otter arrived in the morning (not one of the disasters) bringing with him a charging engine. This was fine until we tried to get it to work . . . Just as our struggles were over aircraft were heard overhead and we had to sprint to the top of the hill and search under the snow for the fires. With the help of some petrol we managed to get them alight only to find that . . . Andy had lit his fires at Berishte and was getting all the drops . . . We all left the Dropping ground in a towering rage. To crown it all the dog peed under Tony's bed and Otter was found amid a dismantled wireless set trying to persuade it to work.[47]

Three days later, the Germans finally launched their drive.

Neel heard afterwards 'that a complete regiment was employed, together with many Albanian volunteers'. Alerted just in time that German troops were closing in, he and Hibberdine crossed the Drin, picked up Hands and were chased west, all the way to Nikaj Mertur, where they joined Ian Merrett and Nik Sokoli and spent 'a very uncomfortable two weeks there running away from the Germans. Nearly all the local people turned against us and would not allow us to stay in their houses or even in their villages, so we had to keep on the move all the time through very heavy snow and cold'.[48] The flight and the conditions are detailed in Hibberdine's diary:

13.2. Sunday

As we were about to sit down to breakfast a runner came in with the news that the Germans were at Vas Pas an hour away – 32 of them. Pandemonium on an Albanian scale broke out. In spite of this the Itis organised our stores onto the mules and Tony's horse in record time – before we were hustled off to the mosque . . . We spent two or three hours here after which a breathless boy arrived with the news of 300 Huns at Sakat – an hour away. He told us on questioning him that it had taken him an hour to get to the mosque. We ran. Seventy minutes later we arrived at Dardhe . . . crossed the river and arrived at Andy's in an exhausted state . . .

14.2. Monday

We all moved off from Berishte and marched with our sixteen mules to Krasintza via Deg (where we heard that the Huns were in Tropoje). We arrived at the bridge at K. after a hell of a walk 2 or 3 minutes before the Germans hove in sight. We turned left at the bridge and beetled (with our mules) into the hills where we found [Mehmet Hoxha], Fadil [Hoxha] and Sali Mani [Bajraktar]. The Germans attacked and Fadil decided to resist. Mehmet and Sali brought us an hour further into the mountains where we rested for a couple of hours. Then on again to another house through very deep snow [and had] another 2 hours' rest. Chased from here by rumours of the Hun approach . . . we struggled on – a hell of a journey till we reached Betosht [sic] at about 0600hrs. Ian met us. The whole journey was a nightmare beyond description.

15.2 Tuesday

In spite of our hopes of a long rest we were hustled on in the evening once more through deep snow to a shepherds hut higher up in the mountains.

16.2. Wednesday

We spent the day in our shepherds hut almost blinded [by

smoke from the fire] and very cold. Few of us slept last night owing to extreme cold.

17.2. Thursday
Sat about all day in our shepherds hut, the smoke and our tempers getting worse and worse. The cold is bad too. Very late at night we moved down into the valley again to a house [near Betosh]. All day news coming in about Jerry's moves.

18.2. Friday
In this game as soon as one thinks one is safe Jerry appears at your back door. Just as we were about to enjoy our supper this evening an excited Alb rushed in with the news that the Germans were at Nik [Sokoli]'s house [in Betosh]. In a minute we were ready to leave but the usual argument among Albs taken unawares broke out on the doorstep. When this had died down we left our house rapidly followed by German flares. We doubled down into the valley below Betosht [sic], crossed the river and climbed steeply at the other side on the start of an all-night march. We are still the same party with the addition of Ian Merrett, that is to say Tony, Andy, Self, Clifton, Brandrick, Otter and Smudge . . .

19.2. Saturday
This is mountainous country (very mountainous) and the snow is thick so going was very difficult. At one a.m. we reached a shepherds hut on the top of the pass where for reasons which none of us English can explain we stayed for two hours shivering around four or five twig fires. We moved on at last and after another halt in another shepherds hut reached Seraj at about 0700 hrs. Here we halted expecting at any minute news of the Germans on our tails . . . [Later] however a patrol returned with the news that the Germans had withdrawn from Betoshte [sic] and were not pursuing us . . . No sooner had the Germans desisted than the villagers demanded that we withdraw ourselves forthwith.

Having abandoned their mules, jettisoned their supplies and destroyed their w/t sets, the British were in a vulnerable state. And at that point Mehmet Hoxha announced that, for a price, he could get them out of the country by guiding them north to Berane. The British agreed to the plan and, reluctantly, to the cost: '50 sovs when we start, 50 sovs when we cross the frontier, 100 sovs when we have all reached Berane,' Hibberdine noted, although 'Mehmet seemed keen to get us off for personal as much as mercenary reasons. He told us that the inhabitants of this region are a wild and covetous race and know we are carrying much money [for which] . . . they will not scruple to kill us.'[49]

After a rethink, the British decided to head south instead and try to reach SOE missions there. Nik Sokoli would help with guides. This, too, was not a perfect arrangement. As well as demanding payment, Sokoli wanted at least one Briton to stay behind to guarantee the deal. Tony Neel, probably the most tolerant member of the party, agreed to stay. So did Hibberdine, who, more typically of the British, now found his patience with the Albanians almost exhausted. On 23 February he wrote:

> Today we again tackled Nik Sokoli about the journey south, saying it was most unlikely that Cairo would consent to drop material here and there was really no point in him keeping us back. He refused to see the point of this at all. He believes that anything a B.L.O. asks for he will get and says that anyhow even one aircraft will be enough as its effect on the morale of the people here will be terrific. I am sceptical about this as the attitude of the people to anything connected with the war is one of extreme disinterest except where it directly benefits themselves. And they have long ago made up their minds that the disadvantages of being on the wrong side of the Germans outweighs any advantage that may accrue to them through supporting the British . . . The only reason they tolerate our presence here, I believe, is that they hope at some time to catch us at a disadvantage and steal our money. They would not stop at murder to do this if they could find some excuse for it or some opportunity of putting the blame on the Germans. Naturally I am most unwilling to remain up here under these circumstances, but someone must remain here with Tony who has made up his mind to stay and appears quite indifferent to all the perils.

Nik Sokoli is a man who is too small for the position he holds, and is quite incapable of controlling his men. [E]very time he attempts to carry out an action he is confronted with a host of argumentative subordinate Bajraktars and as far as one can see comes off the worst. As for his six thousand five hundred pro-British fighters with whom he intends to make a drive on Scutari they just don't exist. I doubt if there are more than sixty. Even if they did, Nik is no more capable of making a drive on Scutari than he is of making one on the moon. I can't stand the way he keeps leaving the room to have discussions with men of his outside. I always imagine these men are stressing the advisability of killing us off.[50]

In fact, Hibberdine was not to stay with Neel and was earmarked instead for the party going south, although the plans changed again when fears grew that the Drin might prove impassable once the thaw began. Neel would still stay and Merrett and Hibberdine still leave for the south but Hands would take another group and try to get through to Berane. Hands, taking Smith and Brandrick, left on 1 March. Four days later, after celebrating Neel's birthday with a lunch of roast lamb and raki, Merrett and Hibberdine, guided by a nominee of Nik Sokoli's, set out with Otter, Clifton and the Italians to search for a way south.

Once again Hibberdine's diary tells of an exhausting and frustrating journey, of cold, rain and snow, of illness, alarms and scared and hostile locals:

6.3. Monday
News travels fast in this part of the world and the Germans even faster . . . We arrived at Zherba at half-past one in the morning but on reaching the house we intended to rest the day in we were told that a German patrol was in the village and that they had been beating up some of the civilians. In view of this Ram [Muja, the party's escort and guide] decided to take us to a house at the extreme end of the village . . . but the owner refused to take us in. He was too frightened of the Germans. We were all very exhausted and this setback made all our spirits sink noticeably. However we found a

wretched hovel nearby and all crammed in. None too soon
as far as I was concerned as I was on the point of collapse.

7.3. Tuesday
We spent the whole day in the hovel . . . started on again at
half-past six . . . reached Lleighan at two o'clock in the
morning . . .

8.3. Wednesday
We were not allowed to stop in this house after daylight so
at half-past four this morning we left to spend the day in
the woods . . . At 1445 we left on the next stage of our
journey. It is none too easy as these are snowy hills; much
mud, and for the first three hours no paths. At about half-
past ten we got to the foot of a very high hill and by this
time we were all exhausted. We were only just able to drag
ourselves up it. Just over the top was the house of one of
the guides who has been with us. We entered and fell asleep
quickly. The name of this place is Deminoll and we arrived
here at 0100 hrs. Ian not well.

9.3. Thursday
At four o'clock this morning we had to get up and go out
into the woods. We sat there all day overlooking Kukes,
watching the traffic passing over the bridge. At midday it
started to rain and later the rain turned to snow . . . Ram's
scouts returned from the river with the news that the
Germans were mounting a guard every night on the bridge
we were hoping to use . . . In the evening . . . we returned
to the house . . . After a meal we all lay down to sleep but
hardly had my head touched the pillow before Ram told us
that the local villagers knew of our presence and were threat-
ening to tell the Huns unless we left at once. So we had to
leave. We walked back down the hill it cost us so much
effort to climb, bitterly disappointed, until after five hours
we reached a house where we were able to resume our
sleep . . . Amerigo and Roxy are showing the effects of all
this sightseeing badly.[51]

Two days later, the party split up. Believing that there were now no British north of Dibra, it was decided that Merrett, with Clifton, would stay on in the region with the kind and friendly Ymer Bardoshi, in whose house they were then hiding, and maintain some sort of presence. Hibberdine, guided by Ram Muja, pressed on with Otter and the Italians and, that evening, found a ferry and crossed the Drin.

Though still several days from where missions further south were thought to be, Hibberdine now heard that one was not far away, about fifteen miles south of Kukës. Next day, in the deep Drin valley and in 'pouring rain', they reached Muharrem Bajraktar's fortress. Shown in, 'Otter and I stood like frightened schoolboys in the head-master's study, not knowing what to do with our kit, sticks, hats or steaming wet garments.' Muharrem, 'a tall, paunchy man very German to look at', told them that the nearby mission was Richard Riddell's, hiding out in an isolated cottage only four or five hours distant, which was indeed the time it took to get there the following after-noon. 'Here we found Riddell, Simcocks [sic] and Reggie in a minute room, living in conditions of great secrecy . . . We were made very welcome, although they have as little material as we have and nothing to spare.'[52]

Cairo was informed immediately over Riddell's w/t set that Hibberdine was alive and well. Except for a report that the Germans had driven the British from Dega and burnt to death the village priest, nothing had been heard of the missions up there since they went off the air a month before. And no sooner had Hibberdine left Riddell with directions to friendlier territory than Hands, Merrett and the remaining NCOs and Italians turned up. Hands had found the route to Montenegro snowbound and impassable so turned round, set off south and discovered Merrett and Clifton en route. Their safety was also confirmed to Cairo. Riddell fed them on porridge, bully beef, pickles and coffee, all dropped the previous night, then they, too, departed.

Hands, like Hibberdine, struck out for Xibër, in Mati. Hibberdine and Otter reached it first, on 21 March, to find Jack Bulman and five NCOs well provisioned and well installed in a tumbling wood-slatted tangle of hillside homes. Not far away, in Derje, were Seymour, Smyth and Hare. Hands arrived a fortnight later with Merrett, Clifton, Brandrick and Smith. Although photographs taken at Xibër show much relieved grinning, spirits were low and men were ill. Several went down with ptomaine poisoning. Hands, Seymour noted, 'looks very ill and is certainly due for a rest'. Merrett had flu and was 'vomiting lightheartedly'. But the worst case was Clifton, who was convinced that Hands' party had 'cut off his hands and legs' and now wanted to do the mission physical harm. 'He is with Hibberdine's party at Xhiber [sic] and his weapons have been removed. I hope to God he is OK.'[53]

That was the state that McLean found them in when he and his mission arrived in April. He decided immediately that most should be sent for evacuation. Hands, Smyth, Bulman and four NCOs, Brandrick, Clifton, Goodier and Smith, duly left for the south from where they were eventually shipped out to Italy in August. Seymour went north with Lis, Cooper, Gregson-Allcott and Chisholm and was flown out from Berane in July. A handful, judged fit enough to stay, joined McLean's mission. Thus Alan Hare, John Hibberdine, Ian Merrett, Sergeants Jones and Jenkins and Corporals Otter, Davis and Button were all retained. So was Lieutenant Roy Bullock, a Rhodesian in SOE who had narrowly squeezed through the German coastal defences after being put ashore, recently and unwisely, at Cape Rodonit, west of Tirana. Bullock's job had been to explore the possibility of shipping in stores for Kupi; warnings from Seymour that the coast was too thickly defended for that had failed to hit home at SOE headquarters. An American lieutenant, Jack Taylor of OSS, had gone in with Bullock and the pair had spent several days inching their way inland, creeping past strongpoints and machine-gun nests, licking the dew off leaves, before making contact with Kupi's men and being guided up to Xibër. Taylor, a dentist from Hollywood, stayed a few weeks, then left for evacuation with Seymour; later he parachuted into Austria, where he was captured and sent to Mauthausen.

With the exception of Tony Neel who remained alone, out of contact and with the ineffectual Nik Sokoli, Richard Riddell's was the only SOE mission active north of Xibër when McLean arrived. But Riddell, too, had lived precariously for months and, like Neel and the others, become ever more doubtful of the ability or likelihood of many locals putting up much of a fight.

As Riddell would recall, German activity around Dibra in November had convinced few locals that it was worthwhile resisting. It had also left the mission without a w/t link to Cairo, forcing it to lie low and rely on locals for shelter and protection. 'It was now [more] a ques-tion of survival than anything else, so Tony Simcox, Michael Lis and I retired to the house of a member of the Lita family who lived high up on the slopes of Mount Korab, and whose main livelihood was raiding into Kosovo for sheep.' Weeks passed with little to do. Riddell and Lis competed to grow the longest moustache. In the evenings they played cards and betted with sovereigns and mules; 'no accounts were ever asked for'. Christmas came, a boiled goat was produced – 'as guest of honour I had to eat one of its eyes' – and a tree decorated with bullets. 'All agreed that at every Christmas after the war we would put a bullet or cartridge on our Christmas tree. I did for many years.'[54]

In January, searching to the west for survivors of Davies' mission, Riddell found John Davis and Gregson-Allcott who had been on the run since Christmas. Then, when Hibbert arrived from Dega with a w/t set, the mission was back on the air. A drop, Riddell's first since November, was requested, and though, when it came, locals stole half the supplies, hopes of activity rose. By February Riddell and his offi-cers were once again working up contacts with local families, chiefs and tribes. Riddell was in touch mostly with the Kalloshi family, Michael Lis with the Lita family and Hibbert and Simcox mainly with Muharrem Bajraktar. After Hands and Hibberdine passed through, a joint force of gendarmes and Germans appeared in the valley, burning homes and asking about the British, and it was the turn of Riddell's party to be chased. By the middle of April the Germans had retired and Riddell and his men had gone back to work.

To the mission's mounting frustration, none of its efforts bore much fruit. Of Dibran families like the Kalloshi, for example, Riddell and Hibbert wrote later:

> The district of Dibra carries the complete anarchy of the rule of chiefs to its extreme. Close on a dozen of these chiefs control the district, each having his own sphere of influence, but always endeavouring to encroach on that of his neigh-bour. Self-aggrandisement in wealth and influence are the keynotes of their politics. They talk much of patriotism, but it is hard to find the slightest vestige of it in practice or in fact . . .
>
> Every Dibran will state his willingness to fight the Germans;

he will quote with glowing words his patriotism and, if they exist, any actions his family have done in the past. These will be exaggerated out of all recognition. He will give an estimate of the followers he can raise, and quote all his neighbours as being under his influence, and only too willing to follow him. Figures of 2,000 men have been stated, and facts have later shown no more than 50 to be available. He hopes by these means to get supplies from the British and thereby gather his following . . .

It has been said that to call a man a Dibran three times is the greatest insult in Albania; we have never come across this term in the country, but can well believe it. We would certainly be most insulted if anyone suggested that we were like Dibrans, but that would also apply if anyone suggested that we were like most Albanians. They build for themselves a colossal reputation for hospitality, they claim that while in their house all your property is safe and all your interests will be looked after. Major Riddell could cite numerous occasions of the theft of his personal property in a Dibran house, but if he did so his report would never end. What hospitality does exist is only in the interests of a chief who is with you and hopes you will serve his ends if you are well enough cared for. When in need of shelter, and on the run, without a chief's influence to help, a villager will bar his door, and, if necessary, shoot at you to make you go away.

SOE had long hoped to achieve something with Muharrem Bajraktar. Exiled in the 1930s for plotting against Zog, he had returned after the Italian invasion, raised a small band and, before McLean went in, was one of the few guerrillas whose name had reached the British. Since the Germans had arrived, however, he had done very little and, when the mission worked on him to act, he demanded outlandish subsidies of gold before action, enough to ensure that whatever force he created could survive the German response. 'Muharrem is no fool . . . He knew that if once the Germans had been allowed to devastate any Northern area in reprisals, the people, disillusioned, would have repudiated its chiefs.' Indeed, he could stand as 'the finest, the most complete example of the North Albanian chieftain'. He was also 'the nearest approach to a gentleman which this Mission found in Albania. He aided to his utmost every Allied Mission which passed through Luma, even in the winter, and never considered the Missions to be under any obligation to himself.' But he never fought, and, since supplies could be offered only to Albanians committed to fighting, all the British ever gave him were '50 sovs, a Bren gun and a Marlin SMG'.[55]

'THIS GOD-FORSAKEN, SAVAGE COUNTRY'

IN the hills above the bay and port of Vlora is the burnt-out village of Tragjas. Abandoned in 1944 and now overgrown, the ruined homes show very effectively what the Axis could do to communities suspected of helping and harbouring guerrillas and Allied missions. Not far away, a little further into the hills, is Dukati: Edward Lear's Dukhádhes. This village did survive the war, although the British and Americans sent to work on the coast had relied heavily on it to keep them hidden. Diaries, letters and reports describe vividly the dangers, strain and hard living endured by those missions that winter and spring as Davies, Nicholls, Hands and others were undergoing their own trials further north. They also record at close quarters the desperate choices facing many Nationalists as the war progressed, the communist threat grew and Allied help remained conditional on a belligerent stance that vulnerable communities like Dukati could not contemplate adopting.

Settling in the hills south of Vlora in late August 1943, Jerry Field's mission had been the first to reach the sea. It was from Tragjas, where he and his NCOs, Billy Eden and Austin DeAth, had moved into the mosque, that Field had gone down to speak to the Italian commander in Vlora and attack the Italian garrison at Himara. His principal tasks, however, were to target the coastal road and establish a secret sea base through which weapons and stores could be shipped in from Italy. Like all SOE officers he was also under instructions to arm only Albanians who were actively fighting the Germans. By the winter of 1943, that meant the Partisans, of whom there were a few hundred in the mountains close to the coast. What complicated matters was that Dukati, lying between Tragjas and the top of the Llogora Pass, controlled the region where Field was trying to exist and that Dukati's sympathies lay with the Balli Kombëtar.

'The Bal Kom have throughout not assisted in the war against the Germans,' Field reported after two months on the coast. 'Eden has been sent to destroy bridges and I have been to others myself and it has been impossible to carry out demolitions on account of Balliste [sic] opposition.' The party was also 'in complete control' of Vlora, arrested any Partisan going in and 'have led the Huns to the places where the N.F.C. [LNC] have hidden their arms and food dumps'. Most Balli Kombëtar leaders 'are with the enemy' and their anti-Partisan stance was 'clear enough' from propaganda pamphlets in his possession. As for Dukati, the village elders were just about willing to tolerate a mission in their territory but increasingly uncomfortable with the idea of him arming guerrillas who seemed increasingly keen to attack them. 'My work in this area has been uphill throughout, because the Bal Kom numbers here are very large, and their leaders wealthy.' Once they threatened to shoot him. Nor were local Partisans happy with Field's contact with Dukati, so they, too, proved awkward and obstructive. They were also increasingly inactive. When the Germans first arrived, the LNC 'fought well and hard'; now they could 'move in ones and twos about the country, their vehicles can go singly about the roads, and they can do anything they like without being molested'.[1]

At the end of October, Field's frustration with the Partisans turned to disgust. Local fears that 'the Germans might come and find our material and burn their houses' had forced him, by then, to exchange Tragjas for the bare mountainside above it. Space nearby seemed suitable for drops and on the night of 19–20 October he stood by for a sortie. On board the aircraft were a Royal Armoured Corps captain, Alfred Careless, and a young w/t operator called Rockingham, both set to work with Field. Sixty years later Austin DeAth still remembered the scream of the engines as the Halifax, coming in too low, tried, too late, to clear the mountain. When Field went down to bury the dead, the Partisans proved more interested in looting and 'only an Italian officer and 2 wop soldiers and 2 old men helped me'.[2] Field, DeAth recalled, was 'very disillusioned at the waste of British life on behalf of the Albanians who did not appreciate our sacrifice on their behalf. I don't believe he ever got over it.'[3] Certainly Field had had enough. Ten days later he wrote:

> The Albanians are lazy, liars and thieves and personally I
> think we are wasting our time doing anything for them. The
> partisans have stolen half my kit and all the kit of Eden and
> De'ath, except the clothes they wear and their bedding. When
> SAPLING 7 crashed they stood about and would not help
> me to dig graves for the mangled bodies I found . . . joking
> and grumbling that their material was lost and that there
> were no parachutes for them to buy . . .
>
> [W]e hate the country and hate the people. Food is almost
> nil – we have to rely entirely on the rations you send us. We
> shall, of course, continue to do our best, but if there is any
> excuse for another type of work and evacuation from here,
> we should jump at it.[4]

Not long afterwards, Field led his men through the ridge of peaks separating Tragjas and Dukati from the sea and into some caves overlooking the Adriatic. Infested with lice and black scorpions, these sat above a narrow, stony, doglegged creek that seemed suitably remote for bringing in stores and personnel and getting men out to Italy. Field christened the base 'Seaview'. Its isolation also meant that he and his men had even less food and were soon existing on mule meat and drinking rainwater from puddles in the rocks. When Billy McLean and David Smiley, en route to Italy, reached Seaview a week later, Smiley remarked in his diary how the fleas and lice were so bad that it was impossible to sleep, while Field 'won't have an Albanian near him and shoots at them all on sight'.[5]

When McLean and Smiley were withdrawn on the night of 17 November, five men were put ashore. One was Sandy Glen, last employed on Albanian projects in 1940–41, now working for MI6, whose orders were to collect intelligence and help organise further sea sorties. Another new man was Lieutenant 'Stan' Staniszewski, a Pole in the Royal Navy who had gone in to work with Glen. Staniszewski would stay a month and Glen about six weeks. The others were two Americans – Dale McAdoo, who had been running the OSS Albanian desk until replaced by Harry Fultz; and Corporal Don Orahood, a w/t operator – and an Albanian whom OSS was employing as an interpreter and agent. McAdoo scribbled a cheerful note, taken out on the next sortie: 'The landing was duck soup, except that we had all vomited ourselves to a mere shadow just before arriving. Maj. Field didn't know we were coming (!!!), but reacted quickly in admirable fashion and put us up in as nice a cave as one could ask for.'[6]

'This job here is no cinch. It's tough as hell and a terrible strain, even when we aren't sick,' McAdoo wrote to Fultz on 29 December. 'As of today, we have one man [Italian] dead of pneumonia (Christmas Day); two [Italians] to be evacuated, who we thought might die two days ago; and I myself have been feeling like hell.' Staniszewski, too, had been ill, with a temperature of 107 degrees. 'I had the same thing about Dec.23. What my fever was, I don't know because we hadn't yet found the thermometer. Anyway, I have had (1) dysentery – cured; (2) two bad colds – one still with me; (3) terrific rheumatic pains in both hips, which makes mountain travel a real agony . . . (4) conjunctivitis of left eye – seemingly cured.' The worst of these was the rheumatism 'and that is hell. The last time I did the mountain (1200 meters), one day over, next day back – much rain, some snow and ice, a wind so strong that when it comes you have to hit the ground or be blown away – it was terrific. But enough of this sick call.'[7]

Dale McAdoo was twenty-eight years old, New York-born, a graduate of Rome, Cincinnati and Harvard Universities, fluent in French and Italian, a former tutor of language and literature, and one-time associate editor of 'a small but good newspaper' in Chautauqua, New York. Leaving Harvard in 1941 with a Master's in Romance Philology, he had gone straight to work for the Special Defense Unit of the Department of Justice. In 1942 he moved to the Office of the Chief of Naval Operations and that July, in Washington, D.C., was appointed assistant to Earl Brennan, head of the new OSS Italian Section. The following March, Brennan gave McAdoo the task of running an overseas Albanian sub-section for OSS SI, its Secret Intelligence branch, broadly similar in its intelligence-gathering task to Britain's MI6. When other men proved unavailable, McAdoo had volunteered to lead the first OSS mission to Albania himself, 'pointing out specifically,' he explained later, 'that I did not want to get classed as an Albanian "expert", my real interest being Italy'.[8] Max Corvo, author of *The O.S.S. in Italy*, would write later that McAdoo, with whom he had worked in Washington, D.C., went into Albania against Brennan's express wishes. Corvo would make several unkind asides that OSS records do not confirm: the idea that McAdoo lacked drive, for example. In this case, Brennan did record in 1944 that he had 'disapproved in principle' of McAdoo's behind-the-lines assignment. He added, however, that this 'constituted no reflection on McAdoo and his capabilities': he was 'a key man in our activities' and 'doing an excellent job'.[9]

The OSS role in Albania was to be a limited one, despite the fact that Billy McLean, a week after McAdoo went in, told OSS in Cairo that he thought more Americans could well be of use. 'Major McLean suggests that whereas there are probably too many British officers in Albania on the Allied Military Mission, the addition of American officer personnel would be extremely helpful. He freely admits that the British are bearing the brunt of all criticism and would be delighted to share some of this criticism with Americans.' He also suggested that 'small groups of three or four demolition men' could be especially effective. 'It appears that Albanian personnel, regardless of what faction they are from, are extremely unsatisfactory in the field, and that one American or British soldier would be worth fifty natives.'[10] But in fact OSS was never to play a part in arming and training guerrillas or carrying out operations. Partly this was because it came to be felt that the British had that role covered and there were better opportunities for OSS elsewhere. Partly it was because the Americans were less involved in the Balkans anyway. In 1942, a 'treaty' between SOE and OSS had roughly divided the world into British, American and British–American zones. In the first zone SOE would have primacy and OSS play the junior role. In the second the reverse was true and in the third both organisations would work as closely together as possible. Since Britain was senior in the struggle against Hitler, OSS in Europe became subordinate to SOE. Many on the British side felt this was for the best. A particular worry was that the Americans might diverge from British views on which guerrillas to support, especially in the Balkans, thereby creating all kinds of problems at the operational and policy levels. In the end, with the fleeting exception of two officers from its Special Operations branch, all OSS men sent into Albania were from the SI branch, excluded, like MI6, from all spheres of influence treaties.

Suspicion of each other's secret duties and the policies behind them often strained the wartime SOE–OSS relationship and may well explain why, for some time, SOE kept OSS poorly informed of what it was up to in Albania. 'I don't think they have been sending anyone in,' McAdoo, in Cairo, told Brennan in July 1943, three months to the day after Billy McLean had been dropped into northern Greece.[11] Certainly some on the British side were cautious about independent American involvement.

'They are not under our jurisdiction and we wish to have nothing to do with them,' Arthur Nicholls remarked when news came through that the SI team had landed on the coast. 'They can only be a public menace.'[12] Bob Melrose also recorded his officers' reaction: 'What the hell are they doing here?'[13] And had SOE been more open, then OSS, for its part, might not have been so suspicious of British plans. 'WHAT DOES THIS MEAN???' Harry Fultz asked an OSS colleague on hearing that Trotsky Davies was hoping to leave Cerminika and move south. 'That having organised a Zogist Congress and started an amalgamation of Balkom with Abazi [sic] Kupi his mission has ended??? Does any one know exactly what the Brigadier's mission up there is or was?'[14] Six weeks later McAdoo wondered whether Mehdi Frashëri, the principal Regent, 'works for ISLD [i.e. MI6] or MO4. The presence of Nosi in the government and Fannie Hasluck in MO4 lends a bit of credence to the theory . . . MO4 refuses to denounce Mehdi and others, and maybe the Brig's [17 December] recommendations were just a smoke-screen.'[15]

By 1944, however, liasion was improving and suspicions lessening. This was helped by the fact that SOE and OSS officers in the field worked reasonably well together and, above all, by the fact that the Albanian policies of the Foreign Office and the State Department were much the same. Both governments would issue statements demonstrating their interest in Albanian independence, praising the efforts of the guerrillas and encouraging unity and greater resistance. Both would avoid making any commitment to Albania's borders and avoid, too, any commitment to any exiled government or internal group. 'I rather feel that it would not be appropriate to take up such a question at this time,' Roosevelt told the US Embassy in London in May 1943, after Zog, then living in Henley-on-Thames, had asked to resume diplomatic relations, severed when the Italians invaded. 'Please thank the King for the friendly sentiments expressed in his letter,' the President went on. 'He knows, I think, that we are looking forward to the day of liberation in Albania when normal relations between our countries may be resumed.'[16] A year later, the State Department was still noting that Zog's government must be considered 'as at least in suspense' and that 'factional strife has prevented other exiles from forming any group of a representative character. Unfortunately there is a similar lack of unity among the patriots at home.'[17]

OSS would also assist in shipping stores across the Adriatic. To be

nearer the action, both SOE and OSS had by then established a forward
headquarters in Bari, the Crusader port on Italy's heel, liberated a few
weeks previously. Both had also secured the use of port facilities there
and at Brindisi, seventy miles further south. Boats from the heel would
come to the Albanian coast much less frequently than the missions there
liked, with the weather and German activity proving formidable obstacles. Yet the fact that they plied that route at all meant that an unusually high volume of written correspondence took place between those
missions and headquarters and, indeed, almost every scrap of paper
produced or collected by OSS appears to have been kept and filed away
carefully. McAdoo's reports, written by candlelight in a cold, damp
cave, confirm him as a hardworking, thoughtful and perceptive man;
they also have a rather unmilitary tone: McAdoo was a civilian, not a
soldier, and the major's rank he held was an unofficial one. His reports
show, too, how much he thought of Fultz. 'It is a great comfort to
know that you are in Bari,' McAdoo wrote to him in December. 'You
can be sure that in every decision as to action which I must make here,
I shall ask myself "Is this what [Fultz] would do?" Even when I'm
beating a mule with a club!'[18]

McAdoo's original plan, agreed with Fultz, was to move inland and
link up with Trotsky Davies and the Partisan command. It quickly
became apparent that such a move that winter would be unwise. Davies'
location did not sound healthy and the journey there was thought both
slow and highly dangerous. Also McAdoo suspected that he could do
his intelligence-gathering successfully enough where he was. In the end
he spent three months living precariously in the caves and found plenty
to keep him busy. 'This whole damn thing is my entire life now,' he
wrote to Fultz in December. 'I work on it, actively or in thought, sixteen
or twenty hours a day.' Balli Kombëtar representatives came to Seaview
and impressed on him the delicacy of their position and concerns. He
crisscrossed the mountains on return visits and to meet local Partisans.
Helping him in all of this was Ismail Karapici, the Albanian agent who
had gone in with him. Karapici was a Marxist who had spent five years
in an Italian prison for an alleged plot to kill Mussolini. Plucked by
OSS from a displaced persons' camp in Italy, he spoke French and
Italian, came from Vlora and proved himself perfect for McAdoo's
purposes, rising above local differences to collect consistently good intelligence from as far afield as Tirana. McAdoo's correspondence confirms
the quality and objectivity of Karapici's work, his devotion to his job

and the risks he ran, how quickly he impressed McAdoo and how close the two became. 'I rely much on his basic judgement, his intellectual honesty, his loyalty to the United States and . . . his personal loyalty to me,' McAdoo told Fultz.[19] In his view Karapici was 'an outstandingly capable worker of great courage and intelligence'.[20] Nick Kukich, a tough, capable, w/t-trained Marine Corps gunnery sergeant sent in to join McAdoo in December, was impressed with them both. 'We need men like Ismail,' he wrote in January. 'I would go through hell and high water with him and the Major.'[21]

With Karapici's help, McAdoo was soon dealing more closely with the Balli Kombëtar than the British had ever done. He found local representatives 'singularly reasonable for Albanian politicos' and a young lawyer, Skender Muço, the most impressive: 'an intelligent, educated and thinking man. He is said to be sought by the Germans as well as the Communists.'[22] It was Muço who was heard to have printed anti-German pamphlets after most of the Balli Kombëtar turned its attention to the LNC. Such contacts made for excellent intelligence and McAdoo was soon aware, as he put it in one letter to Fultz, that he had been wrong in his early opinion that 'all Partisans were saints in white armor' and the Balli Kombëtar little more than collaborators. Mehdi Frashëri, the principal Regent, and Midhat Frashëri, the Balli Kombëtar president, were 'honest, patriotic men' and 'they know the Germans will lose the war, they sweat blood because of their present relation to the Germans and they want to get out of it if they can do so without being killed by the Partisans'.[23]

Had Margaret Hasluck read McAdoo's reports, she might have made much of them. As it was they went to Harry Fultz. For all the years he had spent in Albania, Fultz was aware that the United States was cautious about interfering in Albanian politics and he knew very well what he and McAdoo and OSS had been instructed to do. Reading the 'saints in white armor' comment and worried that McAdoo was losing focus, Fultz hauled him back to the task at hand:

> You mention your previous opinions of the partisans in which you considered them as saints in white armor – forgetting perhaps that human beings are human beings wherever you find them. They are not saints in white armor one day and devils in [sic] tails the next. There are no saints in white armor, you may be sure, whether among Balkoms, or

Partisans, or Americans. You weaken your position and distort your judgement when you labor under any such illusions. Moreover it has nothing to do with how many planes the Germans are flying out of Xhaf Zotaj or what ack-ack there is defending the Mati Bridge.

Your job and our job is not to determine which feudists wear white armor but as cooly and calmly as possible assay each of them for what they can contribute to the American and British Armies in their final drive to eject the Germans from Albania and the Balkans. What we do or do not do on that problem will be measured in terms of American and British lives. ABOVE ALL IT IS NOT OUR PURPOSE OR OUR JOB to slant American support to one faction or the other as against the claims of another . . . When we embark on diversions into the wilderness of Albanian politics we lose our perspective and the few simple truths that should guide us.[24]

Scribbling his response, McAdoo assured Fultz that his interest in the Balli Kombëtar was confined to the intelligence it could give him: 'my sympathies as a man are 100% against the BK, 100% for the Partisans in this moment, because LNC kill Huns, BK don't'.[25]

Fultz's correspondence and reports suggest a hard-headed realist focused closely on the task at hand and able to see through a good deal of the posturing, pretension and boasting which so confused many younger SOE and OSS officers. All factions had 'specialized aims', he pointed out to Washington that winter; suggestions that the Partisans provoked the present situation and were the only ones set on postwar power 'not only indicate considerable bias but also indicate a lack of understanding of what is really going on'. The Balli Kombëtar was set on destroying the Partisans; the Partisans were bent on liquidating the Balli Kombëtar. 'The LNC appear merely to be more bold and perhaps more honorable in announcing its intentions. That seems to be the chief difference between the policies and actions of the two groups.' So opposed to each other were the two organisations that he also doubted whether the LNC could be held 'solely responsible' for breaking the Mukja agreement. 'The truth probably is that both entered into the agreement with their tongues in their cheeks . . . An opportunity for an open break was not long in coming and it was hastened along by the arrival of the Germans in force and by their search for an Albanian group with which they could work.' But, in any case, trying to prove that the Partisans were the ones set on seizing power 'gets nowhere'.[26]

Again and again he would drill into his men the importance of being seen to stand aloof from internal Albanian squabbles and how the United States was interested only in winning the war. 'Listen to the baloney; give no sign as to whether you believe or do not believe but keep your eye on the ball, our ball, and do not allow too many diversions after their ball which more often than not may have nothing to do with fighting the Germans.' From time to time, McAdoo and those who followed him told Fultz that some of his old pupils with whom they were in touch were thrilled to hear that he was back on the scene and had asked for guidance. Fultz warned:

> Do not be taken in by any of this guff about Plak [Fultz's codename]:
> a. Plak can stop the civil war.
> b. Plak can ask the boys of Teknike to fall in and help and they will do anything, anything.
> c. Plak can do this, and do that.
> Back of all such palaver is a certain amount of nostalgia and a desire to say something that they think you would like to hear. In reality what is fermenting in their minds is something as follows:
> 'This bird is an American. I want to please him. He will be pleased if he thinks I like Americans. The easiest way to prove that I like Americans is to show that I know an American that he knows and to tell him what a grand fellow he is.'
> Something of that kind is more or less instinctive as a reaction and besides Americans are something fresh and new after the Fascists and the Nazis.
> Then again back of some of the palaver is the desire to live in a world of miracles and to look for some one person on whose shoulders can be laid the solution of all the vexing, damnable problems that have accumulated while they slept. That avoids all the hard work which the speaker can see ahead of him if he has to work out his own solutions.[27]

Although OSS was not in a position to dictate policy, Fultz was also in accord with Philip Leake and Kit Steel when it came to deciding which Albanians to help and whether it would be wise to interfere in their domestic affairs. When Washington wondered that winter whether help should be withheld from the Partisans until they agreed not to fight the Balli Kombëtar, Fultz replied:

> I do not believe that the Albanians are a kind of people who take kindly to being ordered about by any one. We do not get very far with them either by attempts at ordering them about or by veiled threats or the use of pressure of one kind or another . . .
>
> Were the policy [of withholding arms] placed into effect . . . it would [also] result in the LNC Partisans being denied arms and ammunition by the Allies while the Ballists would be operating under no such handicap. The Balkom receive arms and ammunition from the Germans. They would continue to receive arms and ammunition as well as technical assistance and training. If hard-pressed, undoubtedly they would receive the support of German troops. The Partisans on the other hand could expect to operate with steadily diminishing supplies of ammunition and of other essentials. In certain specific instances and areas there have been occasions when well-armed and well-supplied Ballists aided by German troops have swept over hungry, ragged Partisans reduced to their last few rounds of ammunition. Under such circumstances it would be superhuman for the Partisans concerned to love us for standing idly by with an apparent abundance of everything while they fought combined German and Ballist troops with bare hands and clubbed rifles . . .
>
> I agree fully with you that LNC may be 'ugly customers with which to deal at the time of the invasion and afterwards'. At that time it should not be difficult to look back and cite exactly the delays and procrastinations and the specific policies that had made them the ugly customers that they will have become. I am not at all sure that 'force' is the proper way to bring about a 'reasonable attitude'.

Were the Zogists and Balli Kombëtar offering any kind of resistance, Fultz went on, more German troops would have to garrison the country to keep order. 'Perhaps [the German units] that are not in Albania are today over at the Anzio Bridgehead killing Americans and British while we try to figure out ways to teach recalcitrant Partisans "a sharp lesson" . . . If we attempt to bargain for post-war tranquility on any such basis we will probably lose the very thing for which we seek.'[28]

Shortly after Christmas, 1943, Jerry Field's long and unpleasant vigil on the coast came to a painful end. Austin DeAth remembers that Field was fishing with explosives in the creek below the caves when he caught the blast diving in. According to Sandy Glen, Field had been standing over the creek when a stick he was hurling went off in his face. He fell thirty or so feet, bouncing off the rocks as he dropped, and was left unconscious with broken bones, wounds to his stomach and an eyeball dangling out which Glen, so his story goes, 'put back in with a spoon'.[29] Field came round, begging for morphine, and Glen, struggling to remember if a man with these injuries should receive it, pretended to give him a shot. Glen would also tell how, meeting Field for dinner in London years later, he had had to admit that in fact he had never given him any morphine, whereupon Field passed out cold across the table. What is certain is that Field suffered injuries that required expert attention and he was picked up by boat on the night of New Year's Eve, 1943. His replacement was Major Anthony Quayle.

Twenty-eight years old, tall and powerfully built, Quayle had volunteered for SOE just ten weeks before. Until then his war had been quiet. Commissioned in 1940 into the Royal Artillery, he had soon found himself on Gibraltar, where he served with the coastal artillery and as ADC to the Governor and was persuaded to produce the odd play: RADA-trained, Quayle was already an accomplished actor. In 1941, following the Governor home, he then began several rewarding months responsible for Northumberland's Auxiliary Units: teams of volunteers, mostly Home Guard, recruited to fight a guerrilla war if and when the Germans came. As the invasion threat passed he returned to Gibraltar as ADC to General Mason Macfarlane and it was from there, in October 1943, that he applied to join SOE, prompted, he recalled, by a desire to prove himself, not least to the woman he later married. 'Quayle is very keen,' Baker Street told its Cairo office. 'Is well known to SOE Gibraltar and two members of London Staff who confirm he is excellent type.'[30] Posted to Cairo in mid-November, he was taken on immediately for Albania. By December he was in Bari and earmarked to replace Field, who was now causing some concern. As Philip Leake wrote of Field that month: 'It seems that he has so low an opinion of the character and intentions of both parties that he refuses to have any dealings with either.'[31] Fresh, positive and in good humour, Quayle, with a w/t operator, Corporal Davies, stepped on to Seaview's tiny beach as Field, head wrapped in bloodstained bandages, was stretchered off.

Quayle reported later how he had found 'crammed into a few small caves' a host of 'bewildered and unhappy' British personnel, some Americans, some Albanians, jam, explosives and machine-guns, plus 'a great number of moribund Italians in inextricable confusion'.[32] His new colleagues found him impressive. 'Big, immensely reassuring, very amusing, patient, kind,' Glen remembered. 'In every sense a very good man.'[33] McAdoo also thought well of him: 'I feel he likes me, as I like him,' he told Fultz in January.[34] 'He has been very co-operative with me thus far, and I think will continue to be so. He is an actor and seems to want to do only one thing – get the war over with and get back to a much more exciting world than MO4 can offer. I think he will be honest and fair.'[35]

Quayle threw himself into his job. Seeing at once the need for a second base he recced another cove half a day's march to the south, called it 'Sea Elephant' and began moving most of the cave-dwellers there. Equally remote but larger than Seaview, it became better known to the missions as Grama Bay: the Albanians called it Gramata after the thanks and prayers that centuries of sheltering sailors had chiselled into the cliffs. Quayle also earmarked Austin DeAth and Billy Eden for evacuation: their six-month stint in the country was up. His next step was to meet the locals.

Climbing over to Dukati and sitting down with the village elders, Quayle found them friendly and 'by general and impartial consent they are brave men and good fighters . . . They apparently fought well against the Italians, but have taken no action against the Germans.' Their sympathies were certainly with the Balli Kombëtar, they told him, but they were 'not to be confused with the Quislings of Valona . . . They, the men of Dukati, merely had taken no aggressive steps against the Partisans, merely defending themselves against them when attacked.'

But while they also assured him they were 'disposed always to help the Allies' and agreed to spare some men to guard his bases, they were not prepared to fight the Germans. 'Small-scale attacks,' they said, 'such as they were capable of making, would advance the day of victory little and bring total ruin on the village.'[36] Two days later Quayle marched into Partisan territory and met the newly formed 5th Brigade, apparently 1,500-strong. 'To begin with I encountered a strongly antagonistic and suspicious atmosphere (old misunderstandings and quarrels with Major Field rankled deeply). I felt that they would greatly have preferred me to be a Russian, and were extremely sceptical of my giving them any help.' But after a day of discussions 'they were convinced, I think, of my sincere wish to help them' and seemed delighted with his offer to attach a British officer to them and look for a third sea base where the Balli Kombëtar had no influence.[37]

The following week more progress was made when the Partisans led him down to a beach near the coastal village of Vuno, a few miles to the south. Quayle thought it 'excellent' and agreed to bring in a sortie as soon as he could.[38] He also sent the young commando Paul Gray, who had been shipped in to join Field in December, to establish a British presence in the mountains behind. The spot chosen was the monastery of Stravidhi, hidden away up a stony track two hours' march from the beach and surrounded on three sides by vertical cliffs. From there, it was hoped, Gray could be on hand to land stores and liaise with the Partisans.

For a few weeks Quayle was upbeat about his chances of seeing the Partisans fight. That optimism soon faded: 'Political tension is putting a complete break on operations,' he reported at the end of January. Hamstrung by its fear of both Germans and Partisans, Dukati could do little more than it was doing already and Quayle was reluctant to jeopardise the mission's relations with the village by carrying out attacks of his own. 'An ambush would be childishly easy,' he noted, given the enemy transport toing and froing along the coastal road, 'but the German reaction would be disproportionate to the result achieved. I do not think, at present, that six dead Germans are worth the destruction of Dukati and our Balli contacts.' He had also seen for himself that the Germans were working with the Balli Kombëtar. One night while he was staying in Dhermi, a little village on the coastal road 'neither Balli nor Partisan, but endeavouring to steer a queasy middle path', six trucks 'carrying approx. 250 Balli and 20 Germans' arrived.

'All the men of Dhermi took to their heels. I was pulled along with them . . . their chief anxiety was that the Germans might find out that they had been harbouring a British officer.'[39]

As for the Partisans, it was a 'concrete fact' that they were 'the only party fighting the Germans, that they are suffering considerable privations, and that their needs, which are urgent, must be supplied quickly if they are not to be given the chance of accusing us of bad faith'.[40] Yet they remained uncompromising in their desire to attack Dukati and were extremely difficult, even unpleasant, to deal with. 'When Quayle arrived, he seemed disgusted with Field's anti-Albanian attitude, and especially his anti-Partisan attitude,' McAdoo told Fultz. 'He started out to see everyone – BK, LNC and anything else he could find. He returned full of conflicting ideas, but had apparently been very fair with everyone.' After a month, McAdoo went on, 'he is still valiantly trying to work with the Commies. They have been rude, selfish, inconsiderate and insulting; they have been met only with great patience on the part of Quayle.'[41]

By then, both McAdoo and Quayle also sensed that the missions' presence and their efforts with local Partisans might be becoming intolerable for the village. The first indication of this was on 23 January when the missions' ten Dukati guards were withdrawn without notice. Quayle summoned the elders. They told him 'that all able-bodied men were needed to defend Dukati, in view of the immediate danger of Partisan attack'. But it was apparent, Quayle noted, that a section of the village 'were convinced that I was supplying to the Partisans the arms with which to attack Dukati'. A fiery exchange followed. Quayle told the elders that they 'had better watch the company they kept, for if they were with the Germans they deserved to be shot'. As for the Partisans, he said, he had not armed them yet but 'certainly would in the future'.[42]

Relations with the village took a tragic turn shortly after that meeting. On 27 January, McAdoo's Albanian agent, Ismail Karapici, left Seaview to recce the coast around Cape Rodonit, north of Durrës. He took with him thirty gold sovereigns, with which to pay his way, and a youth from Dukati to escort him along the first leg of the trip: the walk from the coast to the village. Next day news reached Seaview that Karapici was dead: murdered, so his guide said, by two men they had met on the path. McAdoo was distraught. 'You can imagine how I feel,' he scribbled to Fultz. 'Ismail had become a real friend of mine. I am too sick to write anymore. I have only now received this news. Is Ismail's fate the fate of any man who tries to be honest in this God-forsaken, savage country?'[43] When Karapici's body was recovered he was found to have been shot three times in the back, once through the palm of his hand, indicating, it was thought, that he had managed to seize his killer's gun by the muzzle, and stabbed. He had also been stripped naked and his watch, pen, jacket, sovereigns and maps were all missing.

For a moment the missions suspected politics as a reason for the killing: a good gauge of how tense was the atmosphere and how threatened the missions felt. 'Our original thought,' McAdoo wrote, 'was he had been killed (a) by Balkom, for being a Partisan; (b) by LNC, for being a Balkom; (c) by non-political elements to rob him.'[44] McAdoo even suspected that one of his own men might have been complicit in the killing. By then, OSS had shipped over a few more Albanians plucked from DP camps; all were communists whom OSS hoped might be useful as agents; most joined up with the Partisans; one, Hasan Reçi, McAdoo wrote, had proved 'a tragic disappointment'.[45] While eager to help the Partisans, he was biased and dishonest, all 'reasonableness . . . hidden under the tragic rubbish left by years of suffering and imprisonment'. Once he walked past the mission's guards, 'whom he knew were Ballies', and gave the communist clenched-fist salute. 'Because he was in American uniform, they didn't kill him. His action was absurd and doesn't show anything good.'[46] Reçi also declared that Karapici was a traitor. 'Commies who change – he claims – never were Commies.'[47] McAdoo had found Karapici's thinking 'nearly invariably sound. His lack of bitterness, after five dreadful years of prison, was remarkable. As far as I could judge, his loyalty to me and to "Mr Fooltz", as he pronounced it, was complete.' But if Reçi had told the LNC he was a traitor, McAdoo suggested, then it 'would doubtless put into action its regular methods of furthering the interests of the common man'.[48] Nick Kukich heard later that a second agent, another passionate communist, had tried to justify the killing on the grounds that 'Ismail was no good because he worked for the Balli'.[49]

Suspicion eventually settled on Karapici's guide as the murderer and money as the motive. 'Conjecture as to Ismail's death,' Quayle noted in his diary on 29 January; 'Mysli Kali, his guard, says stopped by 2 unknown men and shot. A v. fishy tale.'[50] McAdoo agreed. 'The probable killer of Ismail was his guide, Mysli Kali, of the Dukat [sic] valley . . .

a youngster – perhaps 20 years old – and if he is anything particularly, he is a Balli. As a matter of fact, he is just a degenerate, shiftless and amoral chap.'[51] Dukati, too, felt Kali was responsible. He was arrested, tried and sentenced to death and the village guard detailed to shoot him. 'That night the commander of the village guard, who was to carry out the execution, received a deputation from the family of the murderer – who numbered, what with uncles, brothers, cousins, nephews, some thirty men,' Quayle reported later. 'These stated that if Mysli were not immediately released they would inform the Germans of the whereabouts of the British mission and of Dukati's relations with us . . . The village, therefore, shrugged its shoulders, released Mysli, and apologised to us, pointing out their helplessness in the matter.'[52] After that nothing more was done. As McAdoo explained: 'To shoot Kali now, as everyone would like to do, would almost certainly result in a chain of vendettas which would do no good.'[53]

By February, despite the second base, conditions for the missions by the sea remained poor. All men were verminous: Quayle had joined the others in shaving his head down to stubble, the better to reduce the lice. Moving stores any distance was now almost impossible owing to the state of the mission's twelve mules. 'Half are sick, all are badly underfed and becoming worse,' Quayle reported. 'None are capable of a long, hard carry without being a total write-off at the end.' Since fodder was unobtainable locally he had to turn them loose to graze and this, too, caused problems. 'I have lost several already at night from wolves, and also from thieves.'[54] Morale was not helped by the weather: it was to snow, sleet and rain with barely a break until the end of March.

Hundreds of Italian soldiers traipsing about the area were a further cause of concern. Quayle estimated in January that there were six hundred within a close radius of Seaview and another 750 a little further south; dozens kept arriving at Seaview and Grama in the hope of a trip home. 'It is unnecessary to stress the need for evacuating these men quickly,' he reported. 'They are consuming little enough, God knows, but still precious Albanian food: many are in danger of starvation, many are ill, and their presence is a danger to our present sea-bases. They know of their existence and position, and may possibly disclose them to the Germans if driven in extremity to give themselves up.'[55]

February also saw more SOE men shipped in: Captain Brian Ensor and Lieutenants John Young and Dare Newell, with two w/t operators,

Ashurst and Bowkett. They all came across from Italy on the night of
3 February. Ensor was from Dublin and another of Trotsky Davies'
Royal Ulster Rifles officers. Reg Hibbert, who trained with him, remembered 'a very likeable' and 'direct' man; another RUR and SOE officer
recalled 'a large physical presence and a strong sense of humour'.[56]
Young, assigned to work with Quayle, was twenty-five and another
North Staffs officer and Quayle was to find him 'of sterling worth.
He is untiring, conscientious and quite reliable.' Newell was twenty-
seven and, until 1941, had been working for the Forestry Commission,
a reserved occupation he had escaped by enlisting surreptitiously; 'apt
to become restless when out of action,' one confidential report on him
reads.[57] Captain Peter Rous arrived ten nights later. Son of the Earl of
Stradbroke, Rous was a regular soldier in the 16th/5th Lancers who
had joined SOE in December. 'A very conscientious officer, with a strong
sense of duty, and anxious to fight the enemy,' wrote Quayle, who also
detected in him 'a strangely unexpected streak of the morbid'.[58] Coming
in with Rous was Giuseppe Manzitti, the Italian lieutenant who had
helped Jerry Field as an interpreter and intelligence officer. Evacuated
sick with malaria on New Year's Eve, he had insisted on going back.

These men also appeared just as the Germans were beginning to take
an interest in what was going on. Quayle, at Grama, recorded:

Feb 5
Day of pouring rain.

Feb 6
Bad weather. Snow and sleet. Ice forming on the rocks . . .

Feb 8
Rain . . . Ensor and Newell left to recce Vuno . . .

Feb 9
Gale from South and pouring rain . . .

Feb 10
News arrived that detachment of Germans have taken up
their abode in Dukati. Much alarm amongst Albanians that
their co-operation with us (and God knows that is little
enough) will be discovered . . .

Feb 11

Ensor, Newell . . . returned from Vuno with depressing story. Huns in all villages, and patrolling coast including prospective pinpoint . . . Ensor reports . . . no hope of my getting in stores to the Partisans. Impossible even to contact them. At Dhermi his party was all but arrested by the village who, for fear of German reprisals if Partisans are found in the village, have a strong guard out to prevent any Partisan entering . . . At 16.30 alarm that Germans were half-an-hour away and were advancing towards Sea Elephant from the South. Took to the hills for the night.

Feb 12

Appears it was a false alarm, but clearly Germans could get within half-an-hour's distance in spite of our fringe of highly-paid guards. Decided to keep our eighty Italians out of camp for time being to ensure mobility. Had Germans come last night both we and they would certainly have been for it – they moved so slowly. Sent the poor devils to spend the day and night in next valley one hour away, in torrential rain.

In our brief absence [from camp] all personal kit and many stores looted by shepherds and by our own guards. Under pressure this comes dribbling in again during the day. Excuse is that it was taken to prevent it falling into German hands.

Feb 13

Sortie arrived just as we finished deciphering signal announcing its arrival. Sent for Itis who are in next valley, but it takes 2 hours before they can arrive. A dreadful night. Only a light surf to begin with but it increased during the unloading till the light canvas boats became completely unmanageable. Only two of us could row the ship's dinghy . . . Three Italians drowned when boat capsized. Evacuation given up when only fifteen embarked.

Five days later, John Young, whom Quayle had detailed to run the Seaview base, turned up at Grama with news of his own trials during the 11 February alarm, when he and his men had also gone on the run. 'In their absence Seaview was completely gutted by the shepherds, hardly one stone being left standing.'[59]

On 23 February there was another alarm, this time genuine. 'Abandoned camp and walked all night,' Quayle wrote. Two days later, still in the hills, he and his men watched four Germans pick their way down to Grama. 'A simple matter to kill them, but decided against it in view of reprisals on Dukati.' Quayle split his party into three and, that night, each section pushed slowly inland. 'Huns sandwiched in between our first and second parties during crossing of hill.' Forty-eight hours followed in a cold, wet cave, sleeping in pools of water, followed by another forty-eight hiding in the Dukati valley, fed and guided by Xhelil Çela, a loyal friend of the missions who ran considerable risks to help them. Quayle's diary continues:

March 1
Moved whole party to shepherd's hut . . .

March 3
Terrific firing in valley. Thought Partisans were attacking Dukati, but it proved to be only a 'feu de joie' . . .

March 5
. . . Rain and hail . . .

March 6
. . . Still raining. Peter has a fever . . .

March 10
. . . Peter's temperature 104. Covered with fleas and lice . . .

March 11
. . . Dukati wishes me move base again. All frightened. Might do so if it were not for Peter who is now 104.5.

Only then did the missions begin to trickle back to their old bases by the sea. Quayle himself reached Seaview on 14 March, 'where Young's party are living in conditions of great difficulty'. Shepherds had not only again looted all the petrol, food and blankets but now offered 'corn bread and goats, which they sell at fantastic prices, knowing well that we have no other food'. Days later, news arrived that Rous, still lying 'ill and semi-delirious' in the shepherd's hut, had been robbed of one thousand sovereigns which Quayle had hidden under his head. There was 'not the slightest doubt' that his two shifty-looking local guards, who had since disappeared, were responsible. 'Had Major Rous woken while they were in the act,' Quayle felt, 'they would not have hesitated to murder him.'[60]

By now Quayle's party had already lost one man. In early February, rumours were heard that Paul Gray, manning the monastery at Stravidhi, had been captured. Confirmation came through later that month. Quayle only learnt of the desperate fight that had taken place when Gray wrote to him after the war:

> You will undoubtedly recall 'Pavlo' the old man I had with me at the monastery, well, sir, he was killed – shot through lungs by machine gun [fire] in the fighting [that] ensued before we were captured. Perhaps you would like some details. Only hope they won't bore you.
>
> After I had been in the monastery a day or two and because of the increased Hun activity in the area I decided to post two sentries on the pass that overlooked Vuno and the main road, from dusk till dawn. This I did with two guards from the village. They usually finished their 'tour of duty' around six in the morning coming down then to waken me and make my breakfast . . . Well this morning they came down and were preparing the meal when suddenly from nowhere came a fusillade of shots. Georgie [the interpreter] rushed to the door and from [the] look on his face when [he] turned around I had no doubts in my own mind as to who was responsible for the shooting.
>
> With Georgie hanging on to me like a drowning rat lamenting to all his Albanian Gods, I managed to get my revolver on and load my machine gun. With the two boys and Georgie looking to me for confidence and leadership I decided the only thing to do was to make a bid for it, and . . . I say this because it was just how I felt, I the only Britisher present felt I had the prestige of my country and our mission in my hands. Silly really but I was amazed at the courage and fortification it gave. Pavlo all this time was coolly standing

there smoking and fondling his old Greek rifle like a child
as if to say don't fail me now and it didn't.

The 'Germs' [sic] were concentrating their fire directly on
the door so our only chance was to await a lull in the firing
and nip out singly. This we did Pavlo and myself going last.
We made the back of the monastery and tried to take cover.
By this time the Germs had us nearly surrounded and it
looked like a fight to the finish. Pavlo picked off two lying
up on the rock. Believe me it was wonderful shooting. I was
less fortunate. Then the fun started. They started using their
mortars on us and things became very hot. Then the rot set
in. Georgie ran out with the two boys and gave himself up,
and then the next thing Pavlo who was lying besides me got
his packet in the chest from a machinegunner who had
crawled up on our flank. The German officer then shouted
[at] me to come out or he would turn everything on me. I
felt it was the only thing to do, so I smashed my guns on
the rocks and walked in.

They treated Pavlo very well carrying him up to the
monastery and bandaging him up but old Pavlo's days were
numbered and he knew it. I admit here quite unashamedly
I cried, because I had come to like the old boy rogue as he
was.

They made me march to [the] village in my bare feet and
you can well imagine what they were like.

Gray was handed to the Gestapo and taken to Belgrade where he was
'held in solitary for seven weeks in a room without windows or light'
as they tried to make him talk; 'after that a period of being shifted
from one concentration camp to another'.[61] At Mauthausen he was in
the British party that Trotsky Davies had moved to a normal camp.
Eventually Gray followed Davies to Colditz.

Two others no longer with the party were Dale McAdoo and Don
Orahood, ordered out by Fultz to report. Both managed to scramble
aboard the boat that dropped off Rous and Manzitti on the night of
13–14 February, the same night that three Italians drowned in the surf.
Neither man would come back, though McAdoo had planned to. Poised
to return in March, he became ill and, recuperating in Cairo, was

transferred to Italian SO work. His absence meant that Quayle was left to speak alone with the Balli Kombëtar's Skender Muço, whom he and McAdoo had invited in February to come and see them.

Muço turned up at Grama, in between alarms, on 15 February. 'Physically delicate and frail looking,' Quayle wrote of him. 'Appears extremely tired. Not a very forceful personality but considerable charm.' Quayle, by then, had received orders to plan for Underdone and was interested in what Muço and his party could offer. Talks lasted three days. Like McAdoo, Quayle found him straightforward and his arguments honest and reasoned. 'He was very frank about the policy of the Balli Kombetar, admitting that they had aligned themselves with the Germans to defeat the increasing Communist and terrorist influence of the LNC. The Germans, he said, would one day be undoubtedly driven from Albania, but who would drive out the Communists?'[62] Nevertheless, Muço could make Quayle an offer: the Balli Kombëtar would accept British orders to give immediate assistance, but wished to send an emissary to Cairo to discuss representation in London and seek assurances on Albania's independence.

Word of Muço's proposals was transmitted to Cairo where the Special Operations Committee considered them on 26 February. Afterwards Kit Steel reported how the committee had agreed that the Balli Kombëtar was 'too loosely knit an affair for us to treat this offer very seriously. Moreover it is a death-bed repentance indeed and its motives – i.e. a realization of the inevitable Allied victory – are too obvious not to say barefaced in view of the hearty co-operation now existing between the Balkom and Germans who are attacking the LNC and our Missions in the South.' Steel added that 'Major Quayle, who is an able officer, is however convinced that the offer is sincerely meant and in view of the great potential advantages of Balkom co-operation during a German withdrawal we decided in favour of justification by works.' So SOE was told to give Muço the familiar line that 'our policy is to assist anyone who will resist the Germans' and that 'we are not interested in Albanian politics though we are always interested in promoting unity as a necessary condition of effective resistance'. Muço should be told, too, that the Balli Kombëtar must stop attacking the LNC; also that his request to visit Cairo had been refused, 'particularly as His Majesty's Government's intentions towards Albania had been made quite clear in public pronouncements'.[63]

News of the committee's decision reached Quayle on 19 March.

'Gave Muço verbal message,' Quayle recorded when he met him six days later. 'Inconclusive talks . . . Muço insists that the Germans are trying to arrest him. This is quite probably true.'[64] If it was not true then, it was certainly true later. In April German intelligence officers in Tirana recorded that Muço 'has indisputably contact with the English' on the coast.[65] In August they then told Berlin that fifty-two Balli Kombëtar members had been arrested in Vlora. 'In the course of the action Skender Muco and 2 men with him lost their lives. Albanian witnesses were not present at the affair. Fact is being kept strictly secret.'[66]

By April, SOE was still making little progress on the coast. Dukati was doing as much as it could, loaning Quayle at the end of March a forty-strong working party to help shift and hide stores, but its fear of both Germans and Partisans remained acute. As for the Partisans, these remained as ungracious and difficult as they had always been. 'After dinner a violent attack was launched against me for the non-appearance of promised help,' Quayle recorded, after he and Peter Rous went to see the 5th Brigade on 20 March. 'I put forward the obvious, and perfectly true, reasons – that by the time the stores were ready to be sent Vuno was in German hands and reception impossible . . . They refused to listen to any of these reasons, insisting that I should have been with them all the time instead of staying in Balli territory.' They cheered up a bit when he gave them Rous as a liaison officer.[67]

Orders to come out and report reached Quayle at the end of March. 'Welcome this,' his diary reads; 'it is time our policy re this area was cleared up.' And at that point, as he waited for a boat, he became seriously ill:

30 March
Another all night flashing session . . . NOTHING. And why the hell not? Conditions perfect. Slept night on cliff.

31 March
Climbed back to base feeling ill. Couldn't move all day. Vomiting. Crept down to beach, as this time quite certain boat must come . . .

1 April

Too feeble & ill to move off beach. Just lay there in the pouring rain covered up with ground sheets . . . 5pm moved to little cave. Can hardly walk.

2 April

Felt bloody all day.

Finally, on the night of 3–4 April, a boat did come and Quayle was taken out. On reaching Brindisi he was taken straight to hospital and diagnosed with malaria and jaundice. 'Oh dear Lord . . . And at the same time HEAVEN of bath, sheets & OVALTINE!'[68]

While Quayle was in hospital, Philip Leake came to see him. 'Told him I was prepared to return to same area if reqd,' Quayle scribbled in his diary. 'Mad??'[69] Before he was needed, a rapid increase in German activity and brutality saw the plight of the missions on the coast become so perilous that it was decided to pull them out. Quayle did go back, in late May, but on a lightning sea trip across the Adriatic to pick up the men left behind.

In a long letter to Quayle written in hiding in early May, Giuseppe Manzitti explained how it had all started on the morning of 5 April, when five German trucks arrived in Dukati and 120 soldiers 'surrounded the village and posted five heavy machine guns in the most prominent position. They then went through the village to the main square . . . fired a few shots from rifles and submachine guns and then scattered towards the houses of the village. Holding pistols they threatened women and children [and] arrested all the men they could.' Houses were searched, personal weapons collected and the villagers ordered to bring out certain men. None were produced.

Xelo Saferi, warned in time, was able to run from his house as the Germans entered it. His wife later told him that the Germans had taken his three little children to a room in the house where they were asked, not in a rough manner, in which room the British officers usually slept, how many biscuits and chocolates they had had from them and whether they were good men. The children, very wise, replied that they had never known of British officers and had therefore never had any chocolates or biscuits from them. Xelo Saferi, reporting this to me, smiled and added 'and to think, I once had Major Field to dinner and Major Smith [of OSS], too'.

Forty-five men were taken to the square and questioned 'in a wild and rough manner' about the British base and stores. Then a hole was dug in the ground and machine-guns put in position. 'They were told that in that hole they would all be buried, and after them and upon them the Allied officers.' In the absence of the headman, Maliq Koshena, who was away 'moving and hiding your stores', his deputy, Issuf Shehu, stepped forward:

> I bet he was wearing his usual trench-coat. The Germans on seeing him shouted that he was not an Albanian; that he was an Allied officer. I remember that . . . you suggested that he could well be French with his blue cap . . . Issuf's denial was heated, he had his papers and near him his wife and child . . . he showed them his house, but . . . the Germans decided that at least he was a spy, an agent of the Allies. He was very badly beaten and then his house was searched. They found some English books Issuf had from the Tirana school and a piece of soap with the impression 'Made in England' that his brother who lives in Cairo had sent him years ago. The books and the soap were proof of his liaison with the British!
>
> The Germans telephoned to Valona and a Gestapo officer rushed to Dukati to interrogate Issuf. They questioned him about Malik and the hiding place of the British Mission . . . Then he was asked if he was a friend of Skender Muco. This Issuf denied, saying that he had only met him a few times at nationalist meetings . . . Issuf was again beaten. This time by the Gestapo officer.

Next morning, the headman, Koshena, returned, explained that he had gone to the mountains 'to guard the village against the Partisans', and assured the Germans that the village knew nothing of any Allied soldiers. The men were released and had their weapons returned. The Germans seized 'food, sheep, lambs, eggs and bread' and then left.[70]

On 8 April, with men pressganged from Dukati, the Germans moved against Tragjas. Not much was left of the village after Italian reprisals but they searched it anyway, Manzitti told Quayle, 'and found a lot of British stuff, including many parachutes'.[71] All villagers were rounded up and quizzed and the following morning, Easter Sunday, the Germans burnt the surviving homes. Tom Stefan, a New Hampshire-born OSS officer whose father came from Korça, and who had been shipped over from Italy at the end of March, entered the village two hours after the Germans had gone. 'The women were lined up and pistols had been fired over their heads. The poor kids were terror-stricken even when I arrived.'[72]

The Germans were not away for long. On 17 April a force seven-hundred strong began sweeping up from the south and Manzitti, Kukich, Young, Bowkett and another OSS officer, Jim Hudson, who had come in with Stefan, found themselves trapped in the ridge of peaks between the coastal road and the sea. 'Every third soldier had binoculars and several were issued telescopes,' Hudson reported later. 'These latter sat for hours watching the mountains. At the sign of anything unusual a patrol was sent to the spot to investigate.'[73] On 22 April news came through that the Germans were taking hostages and had killed two local men. One was a young shepherd. 'The Germans forced him to guide them to the base,' Manzitti heard. 'He obeyed for a few yards and then suddenly jumped away towards some rocks; he was shot at once by a German patrol in front of him. They cut off one of his fingers the more easily to steal a silver ring.'[74] The other man was killed in Dukati for hiding an Italian thought to be working with the British.

It was then decided, Manzitti wrote, to drop down to 'the impossible swamp' at the southern edge of the Vlora bay. 'We went through the valley silent as shadows; and we had good luck. A German patrol of ten men missed us because Djevit, our guide, for no apparent reason changed direction.'[75] The swamp, Hudson wrote afterwards, 'was ringed in a quicksand like quagmire that would have engulfed us if we missed the right spot', so the party hid in a thicket until a safe way in was found. German patrols were all around and German voices heard. 'One of our guides was about to run but [Kukich] pulled a .45 and stuck it in his face.' When it was dark it was time for the swamp. 'We stayed in this muddy hell until the 26th. All day and night the mosquitoes swarmed over us.' There were other discomforts. 'We drank surface water, or should I say shared it, for snakes would slither in and drink at this little hole too. Because we couldn't make a fire it was impossible to boil the water to purify it.' When the Germans withdrew, the party went back to the mountains and cliffs and caves and 'Young came down with chills and fever. No one was surprised. We just wondered who would be next.'[76] A boat came in, Young and Bowkett were taken away and a British w/t operator, Jim Crane, sent to look for the others, dropped off.

No sooner had the Germans left than Dukati presented Hudson with a bill for six hundred gold sovereigns for the destruction and theft the village had suffered, payable by the end of May. 'The "or else" wasn't officially specified, but the undercurrent seemed to place the penalty at the betrayal of the missions to the Germans.'[77] When reports of this reached SOE and OSS headquarters the 'definite decision' was quickly made 'that such a claim for damages is unwarranted and should not be paid and that both American and British personnel should be withdrawn at the earliest possible time'.[78] Quayle and a young staff officer, Bryan McSwiney, organised the evacuation and sailed from Brindisi in a fast, Italian-crewed MAS boat on the evening of 24 May. Despite the nerves of the Italian skipper, rough seas and strong winds, they forced their way through to Seaview. 'Collected all the rest of the party off the beach, but narrowly missed being left behind myself,' Quayle told his diary. 'Back in Brin. by 7 a.m. A terrific night & a fitting last chapter.'[79]

For several months Hudson returned to the coast on a series of brief solo visits to gather intelligence and maintain contact with a handful of local agents. Among the packets and pouches of documents picked up were several letters from the Dukati elders appealing for the return of an American mission and offering unconditional help. 'It is true that Dukati and all of us in May have passed bad days because of the German strong operation', one read; but 'in a very short time we changed again the opinion of here in keeping the Mission'.[80] No contact was re-established. When one OSS officer suggested that the Allies take action against Dukati, however, Fultz urged him to understand the pressures at work on the village and how, in the past, it had helped when it could. '[T]he people over there are squeezed between two fires and all of them are beginning to realize that it is not at all a comfortable position to occupy.' They 'took a beating' and 'paid heavily' for that position when the Germans came to 'root out' Hudson and the others in April. 'Regardless of that none of them gave the show away . . . One does not bomb indiscriminately people of that kind.'[81]

'SECOND FRONT STARTED.
HUNS ALL AROUND'

'WHY do *you* have to go?' Peggy Prince remembered asking when Philip Leake told her he had decided to drop into Albania. 'Why don't they send someone else?'[1] Leake was then based in Bari, where the section had resettled from Cairo in April and set up office at 86 Via Melo, a modern apartment block on one of Bari's canyon-like boulevards. According to Julian Amery and Peter Kemp, who both passed through Bari that month, Leake hoped to act as a mediator and try to persuade the Partisans to reach an agreement with Kupi: a corollary to what McLean had been sent to do in the north. Possibly Leake also felt that he ought to experience what life out there was like. Kemp recalled him saying that 'for a year now I've been sitting on my bottom, sending other people into the field. Now I feel I must go in myself – and apologize.'[2]

There was more to Leake's decision than that. In the north that winter the Partisans had suffered severe reverses. In the south, however, although the Germans and Balli Kombëtar had come after them hard, they had managed to survive and, by the spring, were recovering and returning to the attack. Enver Hoxha and the LNC Council were also on hand to motivate and lead them, having escaped the German–Balli Kombëtar cordon that had closed round Davies' mission. And in the light of impassioned reports from SOE officers working among the Partisans' mountain bases, it had seemed in Italy that some encouragement to Hoxha was now deserved and needed and someone suitably informed should be sent in to meet him.

Most of the British who had watched what was happening in the

south had been earmarked initially to join Trotsky Davies in the north.
Terrible weather had then intervened, leaving them stranded and frus-
trated in Libya. Senior among the men hanging around was Lieutenant
Colonel Norman Wheeler of the Royal Ulster Rifles, a twenty-eight-
year-old, staff-trained, professional soldier with long experience as a
quartermaster, most recently in the Sudan and Eritrea. Davies had now
wanted him as his own quartermaster and they knew each other well:
Wheeler had been one of his subalterns when the regiment lined the
Coronation route at Piccadilly Circus. Rifleman Pickering, assigned as
Davies' bodyguard, was another RUR man in Wheeler's party: a tough
Ulsterman and a crack shot who, Jack Dumoulin recalled, 'liked to pick
fights in Cairo pubs'.[3]

Dumoulin, the young doctor who had qualified barely twelve months
before, was another of Davies' specialists. Arriving in Cairo, he and
another medical officer, Bill Felton, had been set various written intelligence tests and put in a joint effort, cribbing each other's answers.
Dumoulin came top. Davies had said he would take the man with the
best score, so Dumoulin found himself bound for Albania and Felton
went to Greece. 'Aquiline, dark, with very clear blue eyes,' remembered
Marcus Lyon, Dumoulin was to prove 'immensely well qualified for the
job, because not only was he a very good doctor, but he was completely
calm in the most difficult circumstances.' Lyon, the intelligence officer
whom Davies found in Cairo, was also waiting in Libya. So was Major
Gordon Layzell, thirty-one, recently married and from Kent, who had
worked before the war in the clothing business. Lyon remembered 'a
quiet and very likeable man who was coming in to be GII'. Last among
the officers was a regular BLO, Tony Northrop, a young lieutenant in
the London Irish Rifles. Four NCOs were also going in: two w/t operators, Tommy Clayden and David Carpenter; one paramilitary expert,
a Lancers corporal-of-horse called Charnley; and Private Loftus,
Dumoulin's orderly, 'a tall, serious man with quiet good manners'.[4]

As the party waited in North Africa, nerves were not helped when
Lyon and others saw off the five men whose Halifax, bound for Albania,
caught fire in the air over Greece and crashed, while Lyon and
Dumoulin's first attempt to get in was almost another disaster. Hit by
flak over northern Greece they still made it to the dropping ground
but saw no fires and turned for home. On the return journey the crew
explained that they had burst a tyre on take-off and everyone might
have to jump into the desert or the sea. 'All the equipment was chucked

out and we crash-landed in Libya,' Dumoulin remembered, 'wheels up and with one engine out and a large hole in the fuselage but everyone OK. Not a lot of fun.' Days later, still planning to drop to Davies, Dumoulin tried again. The Halifax made it to the dropping ground, saw nothing through a thin layer of cloud and returned to Libya. 'That thin layer probably saved my life. Otherwise I would have dropped to Trotsky and I couldn't have left him with a bullet in his liver.'[5]

After much delay and more attempts to get in the decision was taken to drop instead to Alan Palmer and Victor Smith at Krushova, in the south, in the mountains west of Korça. Lyon, at his third attempt, with Northrop, Charnley and Carpenter, finally parachuted to Palmer on the night of 7–8 December. 'I remember shouting as the "go" light came on, "Albania here I come!" – and slipped through the hole to be hit by the slipstream and carried away.'[6] Dumoulin followed to the same spot on the night of 15–16 December, dropping safely with Wheeler, Layzell, Clayden, Loftus and Pickering.

Lyon's arrival coincided with the fleeting appearance at Krushova of an extraordinary group whose story deserves a few lines here. 'We all slept solidly,' Lyon recalled, Palmer having seen the new arrivals bedded down for the night, 'but my dreams were invaded by girls' voices that seemed to be getting nearer. I woke up as the door of the hut opened and a number of apparitions appeared. Long shapely legs seemed to fill the light coming through the door and a voice said "Gee! Aren't you boys up yet?"'[7]

A month earlier, on the morning of 8 November, an American C-53 transport had taken off from Sicily bound for southern Italy. On board were thirteen US Army flight nurses, all female, and seventeen men: thirteen medical technical sergeants and the four-man crew. Five hours later, having become hopelessly lost in cloud and with fuel running low, the pilot crash-landed in a field south of Elbasan. Except for bumps and scratches, nurses, sergeants and crew were in one piece. Only on asking the oddly garbed natives did they learn they were in Albania. One local with a smattering of English then led them to Berat, where, he said, the whole party could hide and find help. But a few days later German troops attacked the town, with aircraft bombing and strafing to clear the way, and the Americans scrambled out in such a hurry that three nurses were left behind. Those who made it out went back to moving between mountain villages.

It was in the village of Lavdar, at the end of November, that Victor
Smith found them. They returned with him to Krushova where their
location was transmitted to Cairo and the British distributed boots,
socks and warmer clothes and prepared to try to get them to the coast
and out by boat. On 8 December, in the charge of Garry Duffy and
Corporal Bell with his w/t set, the party then left on the first stage of
the journey: a long march south to Bill Tilman's base at Sheper, keeping
to the mountains for safety all the way. The second stage would be the
swing westwards through the mountains to the sea. Tilman was reached
on 14 December. Four days later, still miles from the coast, Duffy went
ahead, alone, to check the route. He found it crawling with Germans
and, for the moment, impassable.

It was then that the C-53's pilot proposed to Cairo that a swift pick-
up by air might be possible from a German airfield in the valley below
Gjirokastra. Duffy was not sure about this: it sounded very risky, the
weather was poor and his orders were to make for the coast. But since
the way to the sea was still unsafe he led the group to a village overlooking the airfield, settled down to assess the option properly and
waited for word from Cairo as to whether an attempt might be made.
On 27 December he reported that the party was ready to go and he
would state a definite time when the weather improved.

By then, however, senior Americans outside Albania were alert to
the crisis and taking a personal interest in the nurses' fate. Jon Naar,
working hard at headquarters at coordinating the British response,
received constant telephone calls 'urging us to get them out and "save
the flower of American womanhood"'.[8] And on 29 December, without
waiting for word from Duffy as to whether it was safe to proceed, the
Americans attempted a daylight pick-up.

The weather was better, the landing strip dry and the strength of
Allied aircraft that appeared over Gjirokastra impressive: three dozen
P-38 fighters, two C-47 Dakotas and one Wellington bomber, the latter
to land first and turn its machine-guns on any ground opposition. But
this overenthusiasm almost proved disastrous. Hours earlier, a large
German force of tanks, trucks and troops, probably preparing to clear
a recent landslide that was blocking the main road nearby, had halted
by the side of the airfield. The situation was extremely dangerous and,
as the circling aircraft searched vainly for a signal to bring them in,
Duffy refused to give it. Willie Williamson, whom Tilman had attached
to the group for evacuation, described the scene in his diary. 'Planes

arrived 12.20,' he recorded. '4 times the transports attempted to land – it was a marvelous sight, but with Jerry in position on the road it was impossible . . . so the planes went off amid the girls' wails. Morale went down to zero.'[9]

On 2 January Duffy cancelled the pick-up idea: the weather was again bad, two nurses were sick and the Germans were still in Gjirokastra in strength. It was decided to give the coast another go. This time it was quieter and the party reached Seaview on 8 January, making contact on the final stretch with Captain Lloyd Smith, an OSS officer sent to collect them. Evacuation to Italy was made that night.

Duffy, brought out with the party, would report that there was 'quite a reception' when the boat docked at Bari: 'Dozens of official army photographers and a fleet of brand new cars.'[10] Amid much flashing of cameras, the Americans got into the cars. Duffy, Bell and Williamson climbed into a fifteen-cwt truck and were driven away quietly to the SOE office.

One or two published accounts of the episode present it as almost comical, but the risks had been real and the strain considerable. Within days of the crash, the Americans were shifting nightly from one village to another and traversing on foot the first of hundreds of miles of dangerous and difficult terrain. Not all coped well. The American men, the British felt, struggled most. 'I saw one of them one day in the mountains and he was crying his eyes out,' Williamson remembered. The girls, on the other hand, 'were the finest women I've ever met. They walked for miles, powdered their faces and were so smart.'[11] As one SOE report concludes: 'it is a tribute to the leadership of the BLO in charge of the party and the fine courage of the American nurses that the party was brought to Italy without mishap'.[12]

The dangers were underlined when, in early January, Alan Palmer and Victor Smith tried to rescue the last three nurses cut off and left behind in Berat. These had remained hidden, waiting hopefully for someone to come for them, and the British knew they were there, but local sympathies lay with the Balli Kombëtar. Narrowly escaping an ambush, Palmer and Smith returned to base empty-handed. Six weeks later, friendlier Balli Kombëtar contacts were persuaded to help and the nurses driven from Berat to the coast and handed to Lloyd Smith, who then escorted them out to Italy.

Had the main party still been in the mountains in January, the outcome of that story might also have been very different. That month, after dispersing the Partisans north of the Shkumbin, the Germans went after those in the south. The Partisans suffered casualties and, to escape, were forced with the British missions to abandon their camps and embark on long, gruelling marches through the snow that not all of the American nurses and medics might have survived.

For the British at Krushova, Christmas and New Year had been quiet. The new 4th Brigade, about six hundred-strong, was the local force and relations were excellent. The British thought especially well of its commander, Nexhip Vinçani, a lawyer before the war. 'He is young (about 27 years), extremely capable, an enemy of the Germans,' Victor Smith reported. 'He has always been a great friend of the mission, has never been secretive and even seeks advice from us on occasions . . . He is NOT a politician and detests red tape, etc.'[13] Although most of Vinçani's men were inexperienced they were increasingly active and, by early January, were mining roads and attacking convoys and had captured the town of Këlcyra. Cautious of German reaction, Norman Wheeler moved his men and stores to Lavdar, deeper in the mountains, where Jack Dumoulin busied himself with setting up a hospital in a local house. 'Plenty of snow on the ground,' Dumoulin recorded in his little pocket diary, 'plenty of patients but complete chaos . . . no beds & very dirty.'[14] Then, on 9 January, German units began moving out from Korça and westwards into the mountains, picking their way up towards the 4th Brigade and Wheeler's mission.

Soon Partisan casualties were pouring into Dumoulin's hospital, mostly machine-gun and rifle-bullet injuries. For the next two days some forty cases were treated; 'very busy . . . Hospital full.'[15] Heavy firing could be heard and local villages seen burning. Palmer and Smith returned from trying to reach the three nurses in Berat but there was concern for Northrop, Huxtable and Charnley, left behind at Krushova to receive two final sorties. Eventually they turned up, with news that Krushova was in German hands. Charnley was wounded with three bullets through his knee.

By the night of 11 January it was clear that the Germans had the Partisans and British almost surrounded. The decision was taken to try to break out and get south to the town of Përmet, in the Vjosa valley, thought to be in Partisan hands. Rejoined by Dumoulin and Loftus, Wheeler's party prepared to move, whereupon the Partisans stole almost all of its mules. Consequently, fifty mule loads of stores, including farrier, saddling and veterinary stores, motorcycles, welding equipment, food, spare w/t sets, charging engines and all of Dumoulin's medical kit, had to be abandoned. At three o'clock on the morning of 12 January, after smashing as much as possible and loading the five remaining mules with essential w/t equipment, 15,000 gold sovereigns and Charnley with his leg in plaster, the mission left Lavdar and joined a Partisan column two to three thousand-strong. 'The snow was about 18" to 2' deep', Wheeler reported afterwards, 'hard frost, very slippery . . . Our route was extremely roundabout and the column stretched for miles.'[16]

That night the column slipped silently through a narrow gap in the enemy lines at Leshnja. Others trying to flee Lavdar were not so lucky. As the Germans closed in, the Partisans had evacuated Dumoulin's hospital, where there were '28 in-patients with severe bullet wounds' and more with lesser injuries. These were loaded on the mules stolen earlier from the British but next day the mule train 'walked straight into the Germans, who proceeded to kill all the patients'.[17] The Germans also burnt the hospital and, it was heard, shot the Bulgarian doctor with whom Dumoulin had been working.

The flight from Lavdar lasted for days and, for the first forty hours, as Lyon's diary records, with barely a break:

12 January 1944
March all night. Long climb uphill. See bear prints. Unload some kit onto Italians . . . Lunch etc in woods . . .

13 January 1944
Saw ghosts (extreme exhaustion). Took Benzedrine tablet . . . Food on top of hill. March again . . . Arrive in village. Sleep. (43 hrs march)

14 January 1944
Feel 100% better after rest. Early morning, sun shining, clean arms, sit in circle, partisans sing. Move before dark. Long march. Guide loses way. Arrive small village (Lapan). 24 sleep in a room. V cold.

15 January 1944
Chicken supper at 0200 hrs. Lovely day . . . set up in house with two rooms. Dear old lady. Drink whisky and eat eggs.

That day, believing the German drive over, the Partisans turned back. Wheeler, less certain this was wise, continued south, aiming for Bill Tilman's base in the village of Sheper where the mission might be able to recover and re-equip.

On 18 January, with its mules, guards and helpers, the party dropped down to the Vjosa. Përmet, a town fought over many times, was still held by the Partisans. All seemed quiet. Wheeler, Palmer and Smith climbed up behind the town and into the neighbouring valley and found Tilman. Gordon Layzell took the rest to a village near Përmet and waited for orders to follow. 'Cross rickerty [sic] bridge,' Lyon wrote in his diary. 'Stay night in good house. Sleep in sheets but won't take off trousers.'[18] On 24 January, when Wheeler and Tilman returned to Përmet to attend the inauguration, planned for the following day, of another new brigade, the 6th, word arrived that German armoured cars had appeared on the road at one end of the Vjosa valley. Wheeler told Layzell's party to get over to Sheper at once but now German soldiers and Balli Kombëtar troops appeared in Tilman's valley. 'It was obvious that a concerted drive against Zagorie was about to take place,' Tilman reported later, '[and] it became a question of whether we would be able to get out.'[19] He and Wheeler went back to Përmet, to find that German armoured cars had skirmished with Partisans outside the town and Layzell's party had failed twice, owing to snow and the toughness of the climb, to get over to Sheper. With villages beginning to burn, Wheeler now led his mission and Tilman's back to the mountains west of Korça, though the terrain was now about as hazardous as the threat the Germans posed. At one point the party came to a frozen torrent that had washed the path away. 'To get the mules across this gap in the path with its icy shoot we had to leap the gap and literally heave the mules across,' Lyon remembered. 'They mostly managed it, even the one carrying Charnley, but one misjudged his step and skidded over the cliff. He bounced and rolled down the slope with his precious cargo of one of our radios.'[20] Suspecting that the new German drive had petered out, Tilman returned to his valley, arriving to find the Germans and Balli Kombëtar gone but much evidence of 'varying degrees of ferocity. In some cases whole villages were burnt and in Hormove thirty-five men were shot, but the pillaging was universal.'[21]

Wheeler's party finally halted in Staravecka, a village high on the side of Mount Ostravica. With the chase at an end, mules were unloaded, two houses occupied and a fresh headquarters and dropping ground set up. But the mission had hardly arrived before the village became the setting for a terrible day and night. It began on the afternoon of 1 February, Lyon recalled, when he and Gordon Layzell were sitting upstairs in one of the houses:

> Suddenly Gordon said: 'My God, I think the house is on fire!' Smoke was coming through the cracks in the mud wall. I got up and ran downstairs to find that Antonio and Pepini had lit a large fire . . .
> 'Is alright Capitano – only chimney on fire – is alright – we put out.'
> Gordon had been hurriedly collecting his kit and had slung his Schmeisser submachine-gun on his shoulder. I yelled up to him: 'Crisis over Gordon, it's only the chimney on fire!' Then I heard a gun go off upstairs and ran up.
> Gordon was lying on the floor, a bullet wound through the back of his head. Jack who had heard the shot came running up the stairs and immediately took over.

In throwing a haversack over his back, Layzell had struck the Schmeisser's cocking handle, causing it to fire. 'The back of his head was shattered and I doubt if the greatest brain surgeon could have done anything for him. He seemed still conscious but Jack assured me that he was not aware of what he was saying or doing. He died within a few hours.'[22]

By then there had been a second disaster. That evening a drop was scheduled and as the Halifax came in on its third circle, Wheeler recorded, it 'began to lose height and crashed into the hillside . . . We reached the aircraft in ½ hour and found 30ft of fuselage incl rear turret had snapped off and been hurled 30 yds away, upside down.'[23] Inside the turret was the only survivor, Flight Sergeant Baker. Lyon remembered that although he was unhurt, 'someone had reached him first. He had been knocked out by the impact and someone had removed and stolen his boots.' The dead airmen were buried at the site of the crash. Layzell was buried in the corner of a meadow near the village: 'a very beautiful place,' Lyon recalled; 'part of nature and a happier place than the regimented graves of a cemetery . . . We stood around the grave and Norman read a prayer.'[24]

Staravecka was to remain the mission's base until June. During the first few weeks, despite the mountains being largely weatherbound by rain and snow, Wheeler sent men to recce and blow a few roads in line with Underdone and make contact with nearby Partisan units. Contact was also made with Enver Hoxha and the LNC Council. Having escaped the fate that befell Davies and his mission, the Council had managed to get south and was based not far from Staravecka in the village of Panarit, where a new hospital, too, was set up. Jack Dumoulin, there and elsewhere, found he had plenty to do, distributing stores, advising and reorganising, and, when possible, performing surgery, including one double below-knee amputation on an eighteen-year-old Partisan with frostbite, using a carpenter's saw drenched in disinfectant.

Dumoulin, in fact, was much in demand. 'Doctors are few and folklore handed down from father to son is the chief guide to medical treatment,' he wrote later.

> Cupping was the most popular general treatment for all ills; sometimes this was combined with bleeding when many small incisions were made over the area before the cups were applied. A sick person with as many as twenty red or bronze circular patches on back and chest was a common sight . . .
>
> One of the more insanitary but popular forms of treatment more especially for chest conditions was to apply to the body in the form of a jacket the warm skin of a newly-killed goat or sheep on top of which were worn four or five layers of clothing. The sick man would be so left for several weeks.
>
> It was pitiful to see whitlows of three weeks duration which had received no treatment save the daily application of wet leek leaves. An original idea was provided by a keen guerilla fighter whose friend received a thro-and-thro wound of chest. He found his 'pull-thro' with a piece of 'four-by-two' of handy if unorthodox use for first-aid treatment.[25]

'I think one of the best jobs done in Albania is that of Captain Jack Dumoulin,' Tom Stefan told Fultz in June. 'Everywhere that he has gone I find that he is very popular. A man of his caliber and ability is needed [here].'[26]

As the weather cleared, the mission then watched as the LNC recovered its strength and began to expand rapidly to levels far outstripping anything known before: old brigades were reformed and reinforced; new brigades were created; divisions were formed. Training and stores provided by the British aided the recovery to some degree, especially as improving weather and the availability of Italian airfields meant supplies could be dropped more frequently. By March 1944, more than a hundred aircraft were devoted to supporting Balkan resistance groups – three times as many as the previous summer – and, in all, between January and the end of April, seventy-nine tons of weapons and kit were dropped to missions with the Partisans. Maybe another dozen tons or so reached them through Seaview and Grama Bay.[27] These were very modest amounts compared to what was going, for example, to Tito's vast movement in Yugoslavia, where, between January and the end of March, three hundred tons were dropped and more than 6,300 tons sent by sea.[28] It was still a good deal more than had gone to Trostky Davies and other missions in recent months.

Gold, too, helped. In December, the Special Operations Committee had approved a grant to the LNC Council of 15,000 gold sovereigns: this, the largest single amount sent in at one time, was infiltrated with Lyon's and Wheeler's parties in December and carried safely through the German encirclement in January. Wheeler now handed it over and, again, it was not insignificant: the previous summer McLean had estimated that to feed and maintain three thousand guerrillas for a month in the mountains would cost 1,500 sovereigns.[29] Also helpful was a decline that spring in anti-Partisan activity, partly as a result of the German occupying forces becoming rather overstretched. In March the 100th Jaeger Division was withdrawn. To replace it, elements of the 181st Infantry Division, then in Montenegro, moved into northern Albania, the 297th Infantry Division extended its commitments into southern Albania and several battalions of *Osttruppen*, Eastern European and Central Asian troops, many of them former Red Army soldiers pressed into German service, were required to fill the gaps.

But the chief factor in the Partisans' rapid growth was an incoming flood of volunteers. The pressures forcing Nationalists to stay neutral or work with the Axis had left the Partisans, less cowed by fear of reprisals, as the only organisation in Albania that could hold itself out as genuinely, unconditionally and patriotically antifascist. Set against the death and devastation spread by German and Nationalist forces trying to destroy them, the Partisans' propaganda found it easy to exploit the Nationalist position. Eager to join the fight against the

Germans and all 'traitors' and attracted by promises of future change and reform, thousands of young disaffected Albanians joined the Partisans in the spring and summer of 1944. Few were convinced communists, but they swelled the Partisan ranks and, ultimately, would provide Enver Hoxha and his lieutenants with the manpower and popular support with which to seize power.

With more men on which to draw, the Partisans also returned to the offensive. Skirmishes and ambushes increased. In March the 4th Brigade fought its way back into Mokra, the 1st Brigade was heard to have pushed back briefly into the north and thirty-two Germans were rumoured to have been killed in a battle south of Korça. In April, near Berat, another hundred were reported killed and prisoners were also taken; further south, roads were harassed; in all, that month, SOE officers estimated German casualties at four hundred killed and captured.

Partisan claims often seemed ridiculously high and could be impossible to confirm unless the British were on hand to pick over the battlefields and actually count the bodies. Prisoners, though, were impossible to fake and provided concrete proof of growing Partisan activity. That summer Marcus Lyon reported that although for a long time 'the Partisans were shooting prisoners very soon after capture' they eventually agreed to have them interrogated 'before disposal' and, in May, 'when the Partisan forces and organisation had increased greatly, POW cages were started'. All this applied to German prisoners. 'Italian prisoners who have been with the Germans are usually shot without being questioned.' 'Traitors', meanwhile, risked a grisly fate at the hands of a Partisan butcher, while 'Bastanardo [sic], it is believed, is used on Balli Kombëtar spies to make them talk before they are shot.' By comparison the Partisans treated their German prisoners fairly well. 'Their food and accommodation is probably no worse than that of the average Partisan. Their hands are tied with cord in front of them so that they can eat or smoke a cigarette without difficulty.' There were exceptions. During the winter one Austrian 'was marched for hours through deep snow without boots before being shot. When he was seen several hours before he was shot, he was already too exhausted and frightened to give any intelligible answer to questions.'[30] Years later Lyon would recall 'the silent horror' with which the British heard of the fate of one German corporal, 'an intelligent young man and far more sophisticated than most of the people we were meeting'. After a failed attempt to escape he had been thrown in a pigsty 'and the butcher sent in to deal with him'.[31]

By the middle of March Norman Wheeler had seen and heard enough to convince him that Cairo 'had little conception of what was going on'. He asked permission to report, took Pickering and left for the coast, hoping for quick evacuation to Italy. Bad weather and German activity on the coast, not least the hunt for Quayle's party in early April and Hudson's and Young's in May, meant it took him more than two months to get out, during which he had the opportunity to see much more of the Partisan recovery. He reported at the end of May:

I have had experience of the 1st, 4th, 5th, 6th and 7th Bdes. They are all roughly the same size – approximately 1,500 men. All armed with a personal weapon, amn, and grenades. In most Bdes there is now an LMG per approx. 20 men. In addition we have trained a limited number of mortar crews.

The Bdes are sub-divided into varying numbers of Bns 200–300 strong. There can, of course, be no comparison with regular troops, but what the Albanians lack in knowledge they make up for in enthusiasm and incredible endurance. They are immensely interested in weapons of all kinds. Their tactics are simple and definitely 'guerilla'; when the Hun carries out his drives the Partisans are obliged to disperse into the mountains and re-appear on the enemy's flanks, re-disperse and so on . . .

There are very few Commanders with any real military knowledge; a number served with the gendarmerie or in Zog's Army, but their conception of war is elementary. However, as with the men, what they lack in knowledge they make up for in enthusiasm . . .

I do not consider that the Partisans are capable of holding defensive positions against trained troops, but there is no doubt that they are the largest, best equipped and best trained armed body in Albania, and in the event of direct conflict with any other party they would have no difficulty in quelling opposition.[32]

May also saw Wheeler on hand to watch the new 6th Brigade drop down to the sea, hold a bay called Borsh outside Balli Kombëtar territory and bring in the largest single supply of stores the Partisans had yet received. 'Since November my refrain had been "Only wait till the Sea Service starts" and to the LNC the Sea Service was much the same as "Jam Tomorrow",' Bill Tilman wrote later. 'However, once Borsh and the road had been secured events moved quickly.' First Wheeler and Pickering blew the coastal road either side of the bay, then 'the LNC laid on a thousand mules and on the 22nd thirty tons were brought in by LCT, cleared from the ship in an hour, and cleared from the beach by dawn'. Two nights later a second sortie came in and another thirty tons of stores carried swiftly and efficiently away: given that a total of forty tons, a fraction of which had reached the partisans, had gone to Seaview and Grama between November and May, this was a great success. Tilman and Wheeler went out on 22 May; with them went Charnley, Pickering, Dawson and Ashurst. 'It was astonishing to me that the cutting of the coast road provoked no enemy reaction at the time or up to the time of writing (May 30th),' Tilman recorded in Bari. 'The only explanation seems to be that they have not the troops.'[33]

By then Wheeler had also met a series of officers who agreed with him that the Partisans deserved better support and, as well, that the fresh British effort with Kupi was flawed and also harmful to what they were trying to do. One of these officers was Tilman, who had received news in March of McLean's planned return to Kupi. 'Naturally, I did not inform the local HQs of this, but the Central Council were soon aware of it,' he reported. 'On 18th Lt Col Wheeler arrived on the way out. His views and mine on the wisdom of sending MacLean [sic] to one whom the LNC mistrusted so much were the same.'[34] When Tom Stefan, on his way inland, heard from Wheeler in April of the proposed 'Kupi LNC merger' he wrote to Harry Fultz: 'a most ridiculous thing you ever heard of. These reds will fight til death if Zog is foisted on them.'[35] Feelings ran high, as Brian Ensor, back from six months with the Partisans, explained that autumn:

> My briefing before infiltration consisted of a statement that 'on all possible occasions I was to use British material and Partisan manpower to kill Germans'. I am deeply grateful to those who arranged and supplied me with all that they were able to procure to enable me to carry out these orders, but I believe that until the entry of the late Major Leake into Albania, the support BLOs received to help them to gain the

full cooperation of the Partisans was criminal . . . [I]t seemed to us that until the latter months our efforts were being deliberately hindered by our own countrymen . . .

[T]he Partisans were, and would always be, the most effective fighting machine, provided they were not deprived of weapons and supplies to continue their fight against the Germans to the advantage of any doubtful resistance elements whose only claim to recognition consisted of empty promises and idle boastings . . . It is easy enough to be wise after the event, but my signals of April and May prove that I was always a staunch supporter of an immediate change of policy, because it was not possible to carry out my orders properly . . . The Partisans believed that no military commander or political leader could be responsible, so BLOs must be reporting adversely and falsely on Partisan activities, and thus for a long time we were not trusted, and co-operation between BLOs and Partisans was very difficult . . . We were held responsible for a policy with which we did not agree, and which was inhibiting Partisan resistance to the Germans, and preventing us from carrying out our briefing orders, i.e. harassing the Germans.

What had not helped at all, Ensor added, was the Allied response during 'the dark days of last winter' when 'the enemy was most active, conditions at their worst', to the 'treacherous attacks by Albanian collaborationist quisling elements' on the Partisans with whom he was working. 'The fact that these Albanians belonged to the Balli Kombëtar party who were being treated as harmless naughty boys by the British made us ashamed.'[36]

'It has been proved beyond a shadow of a doubt that the Tirana Govt, and the Balkom, are collaborating actively against the Partisans with the Germans, and the rest of the country, by sitting on the fence, are collaborating passively,' Wheeler reported when he finally arrived in Bari. 'It can be appreciated, therefore, that it is exceedingly difficult to explain to the Partisans the reason why the Allies not only do NOT denounce these collaborators but give them supplies . . . and continue to maintain Military Missions with them. During the past six months, together with Major Tilman and [Major] Palmer, I have asked for a change in policy and submitted recommendations accordingly. The position has remained

unaltered.'³⁷ Tilman, in Bari, argued the same point. 'I was as convinced
when I left as I had been for some months previously that our policy of
backing the LNC was honest and expedient, they being the only party
in Albania with the same war aims as our own, who are willing to make
sacrifices for them . . . They realised we were doing our best to help them
materially, but the good effect of that was more than offset by our helping
equally other parties, if not with money or material, then with encouragement.'³⁸

When Wheeler left Albania, weeks had passed since he had dealt first-
hand with Enver Hoxha and the Partisan general staff, or 'Shtab' as it
was known locally and the British were coming to call it. In that time,
to the British officers still attached to them, senior Partisans had
continued to complain, as they had since the winter, about the lack of
recognition of their fighting record and the amount of stores coming
in. They continued to point out that both Greece and Yugoslavia had
representatives in Italy, that Trotsky Davies had promised them representation as long ago as November and that a British general had been
attached to them then. The general was Davies: in Albania the word
'brigadier' suggested a lowly rank, so McLean had advised that the
Partisans call him general-major, the German equivalent of brigadier.

   Now the Partisans' highest-ranking Briton was Alan Palmer, who
had taken over as senior officer with the Partisans when Wheeler set
off for the coast. He was an excellent choice. 'Personality strong, amiable
and impressive,' reads one confidential report. 'He is quick and skilful
at sizing up an intricate political or military situation. An extremely
capable leader of men both in and out of action.'³⁹ Marcus Lyon thought
him 'ideally suited for this job; he was courageous, physically tough,
and had the gift of getting on with everyone, of whatever nationality
or class. His obvious and transparent honesty as well as his constant
good humour in all circumstances was disarming even to his would-be
adversaries.'⁴⁰ Palmer, who had studied modern languages at Oxford,
was also able to converse with Hoxha and other French-speaking
Partisans with relative ease. His relationship with Hoxha suffered badly,
however, when it was heard that McLean was returning to work with
Kupi: 'the signal,' Victor Smith recorded, 'for a furious onslaught on
us by all members of the LNC'. The mission's 'defences were obviously
weak': 'an insignificant amount of material was being sent to the
Partisans; the propaganda effort . . . was shockingly poor; and (most

important of all) the existence of a Lt Col in the North, whereas our Senior Officer was a Major'. He and Palmer 'were attacked constantly and vigorously from all directions. We resisted to the best of our ability, our personal relations with individual members and especially military commanders remained good, but finally . . . Palmer realised that a serious breakdown was inevitable unless HQ policy changed radically.'[41]

Among SOE staff officers and other observers in Italy, these concerns were beginning to hit home. As the staff in Bari explained to Baker Street on 1 May, no Partisan would be brought out for political discussions since it was 'not our concern' to 'interfere [in] Alb internal politics'; it had been decided, however, to send in Philip Leake 'to explain our policy'.[42] Days later, Harold Macmillan, now resident minister at Allied Forces Headquarters in the Mediterranean, agreed that it was unwise to receive a Partisan delegation but wondered whether someone from the SOE office might be dropped in to meet Hoxha and report generally on the situation.[43] From Bari, the new Foreign Office adviser to the SOE office there, Philip Broad, who was working with the country sections as Kit Steel had done in Cairo, told Macmillan that Leake was already earmarked to go. 'I know the officer in question personally and feel sure he will successfully carry out [any] functions suggested by you.'[44] Another career diplomat, Broad was forty-one, had been in the service eighteen years and fitted this advisory role well, having worked closely with SOE and its predecessors since 1940 when he became assistant to SOE's chief executive officer, the Foreign Office's Gladwyn Jebb. It was to Broad that Tommy Davies had written in 1940 to ask about Malcolm Burr; it was also Broad who had recommended that year that Julian Amery be removed from the Balkans.

News that Leake was on his way and of Palmer's official appointment as senior officer with the Partisans did ease the crisis.[45] But as Leake was tidying up his affairs in Bari and preparing to parachute to Palmer it was still not resolved, as Major Johnny Shaw, another Royal Ulster Rifles officer, discovered after dropping to Staravecka on the night of 4–5 May. Shaw, short and fair, was an experienced regular soldier, quiet and professional, who had been sent to replace Bill Tilman. He was taken at once by Victor Smith to meet senior Partisans in neighbouring Helmës. 'They appeared to be intelligent and reasonable in their views,' Shaw reported, but also badly aggrieved and 'pressed their cause for two and a half hours with Major Smith on the following lines, which involved constant repetition which I found somewhat tiresome: 1. When were

they going to be allowed to send delegates to the Allies? 2. What was
the object of Lieut Col McLean being infiltrated to the North when they
were the only party fighting the Germans?'[46]

That Leake intended at least to try to persuade the Partisans to reach
an agreement with Kupi is evident from his last letter to London, written
in Bari on 9 May, his thirty-eighth birthday. But the letter also confirms
that Leake had weighed reports of Partisan strength and intentions
against those of Nationalist weakness and inactivity and recognised the
implications for Albania's immediate future. It confirms, too, Leake's
steady conviction that Britain should remain uninvolved politically even
if civil conflict increased.

'In my opinion we are now embarking on the final phase in Albania
– the end of German resistance and the beginning of [renewed] civil
war,' he wrote. 'As the pressure of the Germans is relaxed, so the offensive attitude of the LNC towards the Zogists and the Nationalists in
the North will increase.' And the Partisans, he considered, were well
placed to succeed:

> The military quality of the German troops in Albania has
> recently declined considerably. The LNC have shown a corre-
> sponding expansion and now apparently feel in a strong
> enough position to attempt to impose their will on the whole
> country. On the military side they are beginning to organise
> divisions. On the political side they are preparing to form a
> provisional Government. In both these actions, they are, as
> always, keeping closely in step with the Jugoslav Partisans.

Kupi and his movement, Leake went on, 'will, in my view, find themselves in an extremely awkward position' made 'all the more difficult'
by the fact that Kupi had nothing like the support he had long claimed
to have. 'Either he will be forced to collaborate or he will find himself
isolated.' Leake felt Kupi was 'unlikely to collaborate, except in the
last resort', since it would discredit Zog's cause in the eyes of the Allies.
But though Kupi might agree in principle to reconciliation with the
Partisans, whether the Partisans would agree to some arrangement with
him was quite another matter. Leake's letter concluded:

> Our problem is of course, to decide what policy we are to
> follow in view of the situation which is now developing. In

my opinion we are in an extremely strong position to put
pressure on Kupi to induce him to make an approach to the
LNC regarding a possible modus vivendi. Such an approach
would place the LNC in a slightly embarrassing position as
if they refuse they will show their hand as fomenters of civil
war, and accordingly strengthen our position in relation to
them. On the other hand they may be susceptible to the argument that an understanding with Kupi is worth while since,
by broadening their political base, they are more likely to
obtain definite political supremacy and possibly even recognition. It would then be up to them to liquidate the Zogist
party, if they felt so inclined, at a later stage . . . This, for
what it is worth, is the line we are proposing to take.

Leake's final thoughts were on policy once civil war escalated. 'I feel
that the time has come for us to reduce to a minimum our personnel
in the field, so that if civil war breaks out and the military effort of
the LNC and Zogists is devoted wholly to slaying Albanians, we can
withdraw from the scene easily and gracefully.'[47]

Leake dropped into Albania on the night of 10–11 May 1944, safely
and alone. Eliot Watrous, one of his staff, sat with him on the short
flight from Italy and, from the aircraft, watched for his signal on landing.
'I was very disturbed to see the letter "O" flashed so far away from
the dropping ground,' Watrous wrote in a letter dropped a few days
later. 'I hope you are OK and that you will see as much of the country
as you can.'[48] By then, as reports and signals show, Leake was already
working hard, learning a lot and getting results. Victor Smith reported
that as soon as Leake arrived, holding the acting rank of lieutenant
colonel and bringing permission for Alan Palmer to hold the same, relations with the Partisans 'took an immediate change for the better'.
Moreover, when Leake went over to meet Hoxha and his staff at Helmës,
Leake's 'obvious grasp of the situation impressed the LNC greatly'.[49]

Two conferences, one political, one military, were held with the Shtab.
From these and from speaking with Palmer and other officers Leake
quickly confirmed the dramatic growth in Partisan strength and activity
and his fear that Kupi's future was grim. On 15 May Leake told Bari
that it was 'clear' to him that the 'value' of the Partisans had 'greatly
increased since last year'. Recent actions, witnessed by British officers,

showed that the Partisans' 'fighting qualities and skill' had improved significantly and that they were now capable of coordinated 'offensive action' and 'resisting drives' and posed an effective threat to enemy lines of communication. The decline of the Balli Kombëtar, meanwhile, meant that the 'bulk of fighting' was now against the Germans.[50] On 20 May Leake then recommended a policy change. The 'chief factor' he had identified since arriving, he explained, was the 'rapidly increasing strength' of the Partisans. This, he felt, made a 'clash with Kupi likely' in the near future. Therefore Leake proposed that the Allies should condemn the Albanian Government and demand that Nationalists like Kupi sever their links with it and 'openly' fight the Germans. If this demand was not met, then the missions with them should be withdrawn.[51] A few days later, Leake and Palmer also recommended that Kupi be set a time limit within which he had to act. They thought the end of June a suitable date.[52]

How far Palmer and his officers were convinced of the Partisans' increased strength and potential is evident from the briefing Johnny Shaw received from Victor Smith a few days before Leake arrived. Shaw recalled that Smith told him that Bari was 'out-of-date with the situation'. The Partisans, Smith said, 'were the only party fighting the Germans' and their strength 'was about 10,000 men' and 'nothing could stop this figure increasing'. They were also 'not communists' but 'had a genuine desire to free their country from the Nazis and . . . after the war, they would allow the people to choose their own Government'. Soon they would set up 'a Provisional Government in Southern Albania, chosen by the people'.[53]

Revised estimates later that month put Partisan numbers even higher, at twenty thousand men organised in twelve brigades plus sundry units with 'numbers growing'. Shaw cannot have been correct if he meant that men like Smith really felt that all Partisans were not communists, for commissars, red stars and clenched fists were everywhere. But it was certainly true that Alan Palmer, like Leake, did not recommend that the British should take issue with the Partisans' politics, even when it was obvious that the Partisans were bent on attacking Kupi. Palmer would report later that he, Leake and Tom Stefan, who had now arrived from the coast, 'were all agreed' that the newly formed 1st Division, with the experienced 1st Brigade at its heart, was being prepared to spearhead the coming Partisan push into northern Albania and a direct assault on Kupi.[54]

That Leake gauged them purely on the basis of their military value may be qualified by how unlikely he was to have warmed to the temper of many of the Partisans with whom he was dealing. As his signals to Bari show, Leake, like other officers, found negotiating with senior Partisans wearisome and difficult. Hoxha he described as 'more temperamental than systematic' in his 'complaints' and 'demands' and the Shtab as 'inclined [to be] dilatory and oriental'.[55] Leake's policy proposals also came at a time when relations with the Partisans were again starting to sour. Hoxha and his lieutenants had started to demand the immediate withdrawal of British missions from the north and acceptance of Partisan representatives in Italy. They also wanted written confirmation that Leake was the accredited representative of Allied Forces Headquarters and Palmer in charge of all British missions in Partisan territory. Leake and Palmer had demands of their own: Partisan cooperation with Allied plans to harass the enemy; Partisan agreement to meet Kupi and accord a military pact with him if he attacked the Germans; and Partisan permission for Leake and Palmer to move north and meet McLean. When the Partisans forbade the British from leaving their base until their accreditation was produced, Palmer told Bari to suspend all supplies until movement was restored. In Smith's words, by 21 May, when Hoxha and the Shtab left for Përmet to proclaim their provisional government, 'things looked pretty black'.[56]

Relations improved with the arrival by parachute of official letters confirming Leake's and Palmer's positions and authority. And in Përmet on 5 June Leake, Palmer and Smith held their first meeting with the new government. It was a success. All missions, Smith reported afterwards, 'would have complete freedom of movement'. The Fronti Nacional Çlirimtarë, or FNC, as the LNC had been renamed during the congress, would attack specific 'military targets as given by Lt Col Palmer, conforming to Allied strategy'. Leake would return to Bari and then visit Kupi 'in order to put certain suggestions to him'. Also, the FNC 'agreed to union with Kupi, providing he fought the Germans', though 'one or two actions were not to be sufficient . . . continuous warfare by Kupi against the Germans [was] essential if union [was] to be agreed'.[57]

The suggestions Leake proposed to give Kupi were likely to have included the FNC's conditions for union and, if authorised, the deadline idea. And although no mention was made in this rather rushed agreement of the Partisans' request to send representatives to Bari, it is possible that Leake had promised to raise the matter when he returned. Smith observed how, after impressing on Leake their strength, the Partisans did 'gain satisfaction on the questions of representatives and the bogey of the North'.[58]

With the discussions over and agreement reached, the meeting broke up. All eyes, British and Albanian, turned to what the Germans were doing. Worrying reports of German movements had been coming in for days and the signs were not good: something large and dangerous was afoot. The British felt, in fact, that fear of a major German offensive probably helped explain why the Partisans climbed down so quickly from their earlier demands.

Palmer now guided Leake over the mountains behind Përmet and into the Zagori valley: the first stage of Leake's journey to the coast for a boat back to Bari. They arrived the same evening at Sheper, where Johnny Shaw, who had now taken over from Tilman, had pitched his tents among the stones and scrub on the edge of the village. Palmer left at once to rejoin Victor Smith at Përmet and begin their own journey back to Marcus Lyon and the others. Leake stayed with Shaw and began planning his route to the sea.

At five o'clock on the morning of 7 June, two German fighter-bombers dipped into the valley and attacked Shaw's camp, bombing and machine-gunning for thirty minutes. As Shaw reported later, Leake, due to leave that day for the coast, was 'the only person out of bed at the time' and the only casualty, killed instantly by the first bomb.[59] He was buried that morning with Partisan military honours in the village's Orthodox churchyard.

News of Leake's death reached the Germans. 'New partisan camps were reported in the valley of Sheper,' recalled General Hubert Lanz, wartime commander of the German 21st Mountain Corps, while he languished after the war in Bavaria's Landsberg prison. 'Two twin-engined fighter planes of the ME 110 type attacked the tents high up in the rocks. A high-ranking British officer is said to have been killed in the attack, which proves that the Allies valued this particular area very highly.' In 1944, Lanz had planned the June offensive against the Partisans that had claimed Leake's life. Codenamed Gemsbock, it was a major undertaking, and its aim, he remembered, was simple: the 'annihilation' of the Partisans in southern Albania. Escape routes to Greece and the north were to be blocked, the southern peaks and valleys bombed and strafed and then, sweeping in from the east, trained troops unleashed to 'encircle the enemy' and 'push him into the sea'. Assigned to the front line was the crack German unit in south-east Europe, the 1st Mountain Division, with instructions to 'follow the partisans into the remote and steep rock formations and engage them in battle there'.[60] It was the first time since the winter that the Partisans had been targeted like that and the scale of the offensive was far larger and the quality of the opposition much higher than anything encountered before. It was also to make a significant impression on Allied observers both inside and outside the country.

For the SOE and OSS missions camped on the upper slopes of Mount Ostravica, directly in the path of one of the main German thrusts, the first hint of what was afoot was some unwelcome aerial attention on 3 June. 'ME 110 circled us this a.m., which means trouble brewing,' Jack Dumoulin wrote in his diary. 'Plane over again,' he added the following day.[61] Then, at dusk on 5 June, as Marcus Lyon recalled, 'suddenly, swooping low over the mountain behind us and diving straight onto us, came two German planes machine-gunning.' Running for his tent and weapon, he was forced instead by the hail of fire to dive for a half-dug trench:

> The planes were taking it in turns to dive down on us and then circling round to attack again and again. After each attack I looked around to see how people were faring. I saw Tom Stefan sprinting towards the deep latrine trench which had just been dug being literally followed by a row of bullets hitting the dust behind him . . .
>
> One of the planes came once more and made a direct attack on me in the middle of the camp. I lay in the slit trench on my back, my head as low as possible, my knees up higher than I would like – as if sitting in a bath too small for me. They were using some tracer bullets and they hit the earth just above my feet and set fire to the tent just beyond.[62]

Eventually the aircraft gave up and were gone. No one had been hit, though Stefan, in the open throughout the attack, had had a narrower escape than most: 'I thought it was the end,' he wrote afterwards.[63] With Alan Palmer still away at Përmet, Lyon was in charge and he evacuated the camp. This was just as well, for another ME 110 attacked the empty tents the following morning. 'Just as the first rays of dawn were showing there was a heavy roar from an airplane which woke everyone up, then a sound of machinegun fire [and a bomb exploding],' Tom Stefan's two NCOs reported later. 'When we went up to the tents we found bomb fins around that stood up a good two feet.'[64]

Palmer, fresh from leaving Leake with Shaw and picking up Victor Smith, rejoined Lyon and the others that evening. German mortar bombs were dropping on a village an hour away, so Palmer gave orders to get rid of all excess clothing and food, pack a few essentials and bury what was left. A hole was dug in a cornfield and a mass of kit thrown in; then, at midnight, with German soldiers heard to be fifteen minutes away, he told everyone to run. It was the night of 6 June. Although minds in Albania were on more pressing matters, news had filtered through by then of the Allied invasion of France. 'Camp got completely shot up last night & this am,' Dumoulin scribbled in his diary. 'No one fortunately hurt. Second Front started. Huns all around.'[65]

Dawn on 7 June, the moment of Philip Leake's death, revealed enemy aircraft again overhead. With no organised Partisan force between them and the advancing enemy, Palmer split his party into three, for better safety from air attack, and gave instructions to keep moving west and regroup deeper in the mountains that night. For a while, Smith stayed behind, monitoring the progress of German patrols as, below him, they picked their way forward village by village. It was obvious, he reported later, that they were 'advancing very quickly' and that 'the situation was undoubtedly serious . . . [They] were carrying out their usual burnings though on a far greater scale than I had seen before, to the extent even of destroying the standing crops.'[66] By evening Smith had joined the others at Frashëri. It was no place to hang around. 'Heavy mortar and artillery fire could be heard behind us,' Tom Stefan wrote, and many villages, including his father's, were seen burning.[67]

In Odriçan, reached next morning, they found the Shtab 'doing a good ostrich act'. Already Partisan units were 'falling back through us' but Hoxha, recalled Smith, seemed 'unaware of the situation and quite happy. I advised him to be ready to leave.'[68] Not long afterwards, as mortar bombs began bursting outside the village, the Shtab fled. To the disgust of Palmer's party, they went without saying they were off. 'We were sitting in a room at the bottom of the village cleaning our arms,' Lyon remembered, 'when an excited partisan came in and told us that the Germans were at the top of the village. The Shtab had left without telling us and were well out of the way.' Lyon, who had his Thompson sub-machine-gun stripped down on the table, was last out. 'With rising panic but absolute determination not to be left without my arm I eventually managed to put it together after three or four attempts and bolted out of the house and followed the tracks of the others, missing the Germans, I imagine, by minutes.'[69] When they caught up with Hoxha he told them vaguely to rendezvous in Fratar, a village two or three miles away, but Palmer and his party had no guides, Smith recorded, only a growing trail of 'secretaries, women and children, none of whom knew anything at all'. In the event, though the British and Americans made it, stumbling into the village at midnight, the Shtab did not: 'we had no idea where they had gone'.[70]

Palmer split his party again. Stefan and Northrop went to explore the possibility of slipping through the German cordon at Përmet; Palmer, with Smith and Huxtable, would wait for them. Lyon was sent ahead with the rest to try and get over to Tepelena. On the morning of 9 June, after another all-night march, Lyon's party dropped on to the road and into the gorge that led down to the town. 'There was precious little cover,' Lyon recalled, 'and we felt naked in the daylight as we made our way along it as fast as we could. The hard surface of the road and the pace we had been making were beginning to take their toll of our feet, and some were limping. Any moment we expected a plane to come down the gorge machine-gunning – we could hear them circling, looking for us.'[71] They made it to Tepelena and so did Palmer, Stefan and the others, who turned up that night with news that there was no way out through Përmet: the partisans had abandoned it and the Germans were moving in.

With German columns now closing on Tepelena, Palmer led his men away on an another strenuous trek to the west. 'Left at midnight and marched to 7.30 am,' Dumoulin recorded, 'terrific hill climb & very tired . . . Had some bread and cheese & set off again.'[72] The goal was to squeeze through to Peter Rous and the 6th Brigade, thought to be holding out on the coast: 'the only possible chance of escape,' as Smith put it.[73] That evening, in the hills above Borsh, the exhausted party ran in to Rous's second-in-command, Dare Newell, heading off to blow the road at Tepelena and delay the German advance. It was too late for that, Newell was told, so he scrapped the plan and led the group down to the sea.

One of the jewels in Albania's southern coastline, Borsh is where the mountains break to create a low-lying bowl of olive groves and scrub

and a white strip of pebbles sloping gently into the sea. To men who
had spent the last six months surrounded by mountains and the last
seven days on the run, it was quite a sight. 'What a wonderful place
to finish a flap,' Dumoulin wrote.[74] And there was another moment of
relief on the morning of 11 June, when, as they moved down to the
bay, 'a figure appeared,' Lyon remembered, 'wearing a very shaggy
black sheepskin cloak, a bushy beard, a sort of astrakhan type of hat
and carrying a gun. He looked and smelt evil – a bandit perhaps?' It
was Peter Rous. 'His cheerful character and welcome certainly helped
our morale.'[75]

At Borsh they also found the impressive Tahir Kadaraja, commander
of the 6th Brigade. Kadaraja was a former army officer and he and his
men, Smith reported, were 'obviously fighting a good battle'. They were
also fighting with their backs to the sea, and, with the Germans clearly
keen to wipe out this awkward pocket and a powerful assault considered imminent, Kadaraja was 'not overconfident' that he could hold
the enemy off forever. Nor was Palmer, who signalled Bari for a boat
to get some of his men away. 'Many of the party were tired, some
could hardly walk, and were, therefore, not even useful in the event of
a fight.'[76] But when Bari replied that no ship could come, a final stand
on the beach seemed likely.

Shortly before midnight on 12 June, unannounced and out of the
dark, a Royal Navy motor-torpedo-boat suddenly ran into the shore.
Two hours later, with most of the British and Americans aboard, it
pulled away. Among those left behind were Palmer and Stefan. Both
sent out letters scribbled hastily for Bari that explained their decision
to stay and summed up the present dangers. 'The situation here seems
to be worsening with the Huns advancing from the north and mending
the roads, etc,' Palmer's letter read. 'This Bde is magnificently armed
due to sea sorties and morale high; but they are no match for 1st Mtn
Div.' With Newell, 'who was fresh and knew the country', Huxtable
and Stefan, he would remain with the 6th Brigade, report developments
and hopefully call in air strikes. 'Please do all you can to get the latter
answered rapidly as the battle may be moving pretty fast.'[77] 'Germans are
making every effort to close the base,' Stefan had written to Fultz; 'we
are in a helluva spot.' The Partisans were 'holding off at Shen Vasil in
the south and north of here just this side of Himara,' but the Germans
were repairing bridges and massing, it seemed, for a major attack. 'We
are all heavily armed and will fight if we have to.'[78]

Smith, Lyon, Rous and the others reached Italy the following morning. 'Very stormy trip & very sick & miserable,' Jack Dumoulin's diary reads. 'Arrived Taranto at 5.30 . . . amazing to be back in civilisation again. Tired but great welcome & pleased to be safe.'[79] From Taranto the British in the party were driven up to the village of Castellana, in the hills not far from Bari, where SOE ran a rest camp for men bound for and back from the Balkans. From Castellana some of the officers moved down to Bari, by then a great hub of Allied activity with a heavy British and American presence, and took rooms in the Imperiale, a modern hotel on the front. Haircuts, food, parties and sleep were much on the agenda for the next few days. Minds were never far from what was happening on the far side of the Adriatic. Officers spent hours with the SOE staff, socially and in the office, and heard that news from the field was not good. By 18 June the Germans had broken through to the sea at Borsh and Palmer's w/t link was dead. Not long afterwards Shaw, too, went silent and, with that, Bari lost contact with southern Albania. 'No news of Alan or Johnnie,' Dumoulin wrote a week later; 'very worried.'[80]

Shaw reported later that he had been forced out of Sheper on the night of 9 June. He had then spent several days dodging Germans and 'wandering around the mountains' before returning to Sheper and receiving eighteen sorties of supplies in a week.[81] Shaw's was the only dropping ground in southern Albania now able to receive drops and, aware of the Partisans' plight, Bari had crammed them in: though out of w/t contact, Shaw was still able to light fires and signal aircraft. One, an American Dakota, crashed before dropping. The remains of the crew were recovered from the wreckage, carried down to Sheper and buried beside Leake. On 25 June the Germans again forced Shaw to leave the village. Shortly after that he regained w/t contact with Bari. 'Johnnie came up on air yesterday,' Dumoulin recorded on 29 June; 'surrounded but sounds cheerful. We have almost given up hope for Alan.'[82]

Palmer did survive, although the coast remained dangerous for some time. Brian Ensor, in the mountains behind Borsh, had joined his party on 17 June as it was picking its way inland. 'I learned from Lieut Col Palmer that the bridgehead was broken and the Germans were proceeding in five directions in an attempt to surround and annihilate the Partisan 6th Brigade,' he reported later. The position was 'considered critical' and, by 20 June, Tahir Kadaraja had decided with Palmer to try to break out. 'The plan was to advance up the line of the river Zur i Kucit until contact with the Germans was made, and then attack with all force one small section, make a gap and pass the whole Brigade through it into the free territory beyond.' As the force moved up the valley, however, Dare Newell suffered a bad attack of malaria. Palmer, Stefan and Huxtable pressed on with the main body; Ensor and his NCOs, Corporals Blake and Still, waited with Newell, intending to continue the climb if the breakout was successful and when Newell felt better. Suddenly Germans 'flooded the valley from five directions' and Ensor, with his little group, ran:

> I decided to make for the mountains above Vuno, but due to our slow movement the Germans caught sight of us and moved some troops into position on the path in front of us, unknown to me. I had with me three mules, one carrying Lieut Col Palmer's wireless set and extras, one carrying some food and personal kit, the other carrying Captain Newell. I was ahead with Captain Newell, Cpl Still and Cpl Blake; behind followed a few Partisans with the other two mules.
>
> The Germans opened up with three Spandau machine guns at close range, but fortunately our party was able to dive into cover and get away up the hill with the mule carrying Captain Newell. The other two mules were captured by the Germans, the Partisans with them being killed, with the exception of one who eventually joined us.
>
> We continued to the top of a mountain where a mist descended at nightfall and as it was too dangerous to continue I decided to stay until light. We stayed on the top of this mountain for four days and nights. We managed to purchase a sheep but it was not possible to procure any water. We found some snow, proceeded to boil it and drink it. It caused the illnesses of all three – Captain Newell, Cpl Blake and [Cpl] Still – to get considerably worse.

On the fifth day they learnt that the Germans were climbing up to get them so tried to join some locals fleeing further into the mountains. But with Newell weakening, the British party was left behind and instead went down to hide in bushes by the side of a river. 'We lay doggo during the day and all our movement (exercise, and fetching of water) was by night. The Germans were some 500 yards away.'[83] On 1 July, with the offensive petering out, the Germans packed up and moved off. Next day Palmer and Huxtable appeared on their way back to Borsh having found it impossible to break out; Tom Stefan had decided to try to slip inland by a more circuitous mountain route: 'Borsh is hot as hell these days,' he told Fultz.[84] On 4 July another boat came in, dropped off a new w/t operator for Ensor, Corporal Hibbitt, and took away Palmer, Huxtable and the sick Dare Newell. Ensor, with Hibbitt, Blake and Still, rejoined the 6th Brigade. Days later, Albert Blake's health became much worse. Several attempts were made to evacuate him but bad weather and German movements made it impossible. Seriously ill with malaria, he was finally shipped out at the end of July but died in Brindisi the following day.

'COLLEAGUES IN CONSPIRACY'

ON a warm June night in 1944, at a spot called Gjoles on the main road north from Tirana, David Smiley blew up Albania's third largest bridge. As an operation it was a great success: the Germans had been sending five hundred trucks over the bridge every night; now they had to use a longer route more vulnerable to air attack. It was also daring: after slipping past the guards, Smiley and George Jenkins had scrambled down to rig the spans with explosives while German transport rolled overhead; a pause was necessary while a staff car changed a wheel and one occupant relieved himself over the side. Smiley was to receive a bar to his Military Cross and Jenkins the Military Medal and, since a covering party of Abas Kupi's men had been lurking in the darkness while Smiley set his charges, Kupi, McLean felt, now qualified for arms.

Those weapons were never sent. Within ten days, the Partisan 1st Division, which had escaped the brunt of the Germans' June offensive, had pressed north, pushed into Kupi's mountain stronghold and attacked him. Kupi fought back and in Bari the decision was taken to suspend all drops to Albania. In early August, however, McLean and his men learnt to their alarm that arms and ammunition were once again going to the 1st Division. Nor was the mission impressed by an apparent 180-degree change of opinion in Bari when, in September, in the last weeks of the occupation, Kupi opened a small campaign against the Germans. Days later, Bari told the mission to do nothing to encourage him to fight and that no weapons would be sent. 'He had fought, but now there were to be no arms,' Julian Amery wrote in his memoirs; 'we felt as if we had been stabbed in the back.'[1]

Amery wrote, too, of the mission's further dismay when Bari refused to evacuate Kupi. He justified sympathy and support, the mission felt, and, since Partisan victory in the civil war seemed only weeks away, should be saved from liquidation. Here, it seemed to Amery, was a clear instance of the 'appeasing climate of Bari'. And on arriving there in October he found 'responsible staff officers' revelling 'with indecent, almost masochistic, glee' in the demise of Nationalist forces. 'Never before had there been so many British observers in the Balkans, and yet never can responsible Englishmen have cherished so many misconceptions and illusions about the problems of that blood-stained region.' The treatment of men like Kupi, Amery felt, had been dishonourable and wrong, for 'we knew that to support only the Partisans was to surrender Albania to the Russians. They were our allies; but this surrender was none the less a defeat for the British Empire, and the cause of it lay in some defect either of understanding on the part of our statesmen or of vital strength in the imperial body politic.'[2]

In other memoirs, more British officers echoed Amery's views; some even claimed that certain staff officers had wantonly undermined the efforts of missions working with the Nationalists. Smiley wrote of the section staff suppressing McLean's messages to Eden and drew attention to Lieutenant John Eyre, who, he believed, was a communist. Sandy Glen went further and suggested more sinister trickery, claiming that well-placed colleagues of Kim Philby had ensured that men like Kupi were defeated and betrayed.[3] First expressed in memoirs, these allegations have been widely reprinted. So has speculation that McLean's mission was crucially deprived of a sympathetic ear and a steadying hand at headquarters when Philip Leake was suddenly removed from the scene.[4]

Certainly Leake's death was a terrible blow to those he left behind. Peggy Prince was working in the SOE office at Monopoli, down the coast from Bari, when someone came to see her saying she brought bad news. 'I said, "The canteen's not on strike again?" and she said, "No, Philip Leake has been killed." We heard his family couldn't believe it. I felt the same. It was a ghastly shock, a terrible shock.'[5] Bickham Sweet-Escott, passing through Bari that month, wrote to Leake's mother:

As far as I am concerned, it will be a loss which can't ever be replaced and I am sure Doris will find with me that a part of our life has been torn away. As you know, there was nobody of whom we saw so much as we did of him.

It may, perhaps, be some consolation to you to know that, in the last few days, I have been seeing some of the officers who worked for Philip . . . and that it astonished me rather to think what feelings of loyalty and devotion Philip inspired in them. Philip was always, it seemed, a rather retiring sort of person, but he became a real leader, and several of the chaps who had been working for him were almost in tears when they spoke to me of him. I hope you don't mind my writing to you like this, but, as I have said, I have lost the best friend I have ever had, and I can therefore guess what you must be going through.[6]

'I need not tell you how charming I found him and how much I admired his mental qualities,' Billy Stawell wrote. 'He was most interested in the various problems which continually faced him, and when the story of this organisation is told after the war it will show how much was owed to Philip. I have lost a good friend and a loyal and most capable officer.'[7]

It is impossible to know how Leake would have responded to the Partisans' assault on Kupi and there is no record in SOE's files of any planning by him for that event. Possibly he may have wanted to pull out every SOE mission. Possibly, after appreciating at first hand the Partisans' increased strength and military value, he may have sought to continue arming Partisan units still in action against the Germans, as Alan Palmer was to recommend strongly in July. Certainly Leake and Palmer worked together closely and well. 'A word about Philip,' Palmer wrote to Bari a week after Leake's death. 'It was one of the greatest tragedies in the rather tragic history of B8. He did splendidly here and I got on extremely well with him. We were in agreement on all points and he fell in most readily with any points I had.'[8]

What is quite clear is that Leake was convinced on the eve of his death that the Partisans, though communist-led and set on securing power, were fighting the Germans well and that, on military grounds, they deserved Allied support. It is also clear that Leake had long been convinced that Britain should pursue an impartial policy of promising support only to Albanians genuinely resisting. And this does make it rather difficult to believe that he would have supported the radical new plan for a late Nationalist rising that McLean and Amery, that June, came to propose after seeing themselves how unsuited was the north to sustaining much of a fight.

That plan was transmitted to Bari under McLean's name on 18 June. 'Nationalist leaders who represent the existing social order can only maintain operations in so far as they can adequately protect their society against enemy reprisals,' he and Amery explained. 'Failure to provide protection leads either to the rejection of the leader by society or to the radical modification of the social order on which the leader's power is based.' Thus a last-minute general rising as the Germans withdrew, the pair felt, would be 'a more productive use of Nationalist strength' than small-scale action or a long campaign. If support were obtained from Kupi and other prominent leaders, the rest of the north would follow. And since the revolt would rely on surprise and begin 'near its peak' it was 'essential' that the British provide cash and stores 'before action': 25,000 sovereigns plus 'small supplies' of light machine-guns, mortars and ammunition. 'As a military venture I have no doubt the insurrection would be value for money but of course it raises political issues which I am not competent to judge,' the report concluded. 'I would, however, hazard opinion that unless there is a Nationalist insurrection and the Nationalists derive its consequent moral and material advantages they will stand little chance of preventing the LNC from seizing power by force of arms in the Civil War which after the German defeat only foreign intervention may avert.'[9]

That analysis of the factors forcing Nationalists to remain inactive matched that made and reported by missions in the north and on the coast throughout the winter and spring. Leake would surely have agreed with it: the Nationalists' stalling and steadfast refusal to fight the Germans had been obvious for months. He would have agreed, too, that the prospect of an agreement between Kupi and the Partisans was extremely remote. But arming Kupi before he had fought and building the Nationalists up to counter-balance the Partisans would have marked a complete departure from the policy Leake had long advocated of arming only those committed to fighting the Germans. Taking sides in domestic squabbles, he had argued, would aggravate local tensions, damage relations with genuine resisters and hamper the Albanian war effort. Leake's last letter to London and his signals from Albania demonstrate that, even though progressively more convinced of the precariousness of Kupi's position, he never recommended that Britain should intervene to protect it. Given the deadline idea that he and Palmer proposed, Leake seems also to have felt that Kupi's time was almost up: it was hard to believe that, once the Partisans attacked him, any agreement would be reached or Kupi would be able to do much more than defend himself.

Still, SOE records today do suggest that, after Leake's death, the Albanian section in Bari may have checked the progress to SOE in London of several of McLean's w/t messages. That spring, London had instructed the section 'to repeat by telegram all signals of interest received from MacLean [sic] until further notice'.[10] In June, McLean had then transmitted a series of messages that the section chose instead to send by sealed bag, with the result that they reached Baker Street many days later than if they had been forwarded instantly by telegram. This happened twice.

The first bag, sent under a covering note of 26 June, reached London on 4 July. It enclosed Mclean's long 18 June report in which he and Amery assessed the pressures on traditional leaders in the north, asked for arms for Kupi and suggested a Nationalist rising at the right moment might save Albania from the Partisans. The section explained the eight-day delay since McLean had first transmitted it as due to 'many corruptions and the necessity for checks and repeats'.[11] That is perfectly feasible given its length and the workload of the SOE w/t and cipher staff, but fails to explain why, once decoded, it was not sent on by telegram. The second bag, sent under a note dated 1 July, reached London on 11 July and enclosed four messages. One, dated 5 June, stressed the potential value of obtaining encouragement for Kupi from Zog. The rest, all later, related to McLean's confidence in a last-minute Nationalist rising if arms and funds were made available.[12]

When the second bag arrived, officers in London were not impressed. 'We cannot but express our surprise that you should not have repeated to us at an earlier date Lt Col MacLean's [sic] telegrams dated 5, 10, 21 and 24 June,' Boxshall complained to Bari on 12 July. 'Whilst appreciating that parts of these might have been corrupt and that you had to ask for repetition, we believe that you could have passed the gist on to us, which was of considerable interest at the period you received them.'[13]

Quite possibly these were the w/t messages allegedly suppressed in Bari.[14] The source of that allegation was one of the secretaries in the

Bari office who, in October, told David Smiley that messages from McLean to Eden and others in London had deliberately not been sent.[15] According to McLean's signals log, the mission had transmitted two messages for forwarding to Eden. Neither, however, was delayed or suppressed. The first, sent in May, passed along Abas Kupi's request for Zog to send him a personal message of encouragement.[16] This went through all the proper channels and arrived in London on time: a telegram was sent at once to SOE in London, which then sent a copy to the Foreign Office; Bari also informed Philip Broad and he, too, telegraphed London.[17] Reluctant, as ever, to commit to Zog, the Foreign Office and Chiefs of Staff turned the request down.[18] The second message meant for Eden, transmitted on 25 October, was a last-minute appeal to have Kupi evacuated; again it was passed at once to Broad, who sent it to Macmillan, who sent it to Eden.[19] It was not SOE's fault that Eden did not respond until after the mission was withdrawn.[20] Cross-checking the signals log against messages passed from Bari to London, to Broad and to other commands suggests that all other messages were dealt with swiftly and appropriately. The exceptions were those sent to Baker Street by slow bag in June and it is not impossible that the secretary was referring to the fate of those.

SOE files also record another officer's doubts about the section's objectivity. Flown out of Montenegro in early July, George Seymour shared the view that the Nationalists were poorly suited to sustained resistance and felt strongly that the British had not taken adequate account of Partisan aims and methods. He also felt, as he reported later, that British officers in southern Albania had been taken in by Partisan propaganda:

How much it had added to our difficulties I did not appreciate until I returned to Base at Bari where I found the entire Albanian section biased to an unbelievable extent on behalf of the Partisans. They were not even prepared to listen to the Nationalist case and views. I attempted to explain this case but when in the office I was called a Fascist I realised that the position was hopeless. I applied to be sent home to state my case there and was informed by Major Watrous, the head of the Albanian section, that I would be sent home but not immediately, because at that time a policy was being decided in London and, if I went home then, it might alter the whole policy. A truly remarkable statement to be confronted with after one had spent eleven months working with and studying both Partisans and Nationalists. That we achieved but little is hardly surprising.[21]

When Seymour's report reached London, Talbot Rice noted that passage. 'You will remember that at the date to which it refers,' he told David Keswick, 'when Seymour complains that the Bari office adopted a rather dictatorial attitude, we were complaining bitterly at this end of the lack of information which we received from our overseas headquarters.'[22]

Although, in post-war accounts, Philip Leake, John Eyre and Eliot Watrous are the only three section officers identified by name, the section was much larger than that. By the summer of 1944, in addition to the section head, there was an intelligence sub-section of two officers; a staff captain; more officers responsible for operations, welfare and conducting; a dozen or so FANYs and NCOs in various clerical and secretarial posts; plus one officer in Cairo.

Jon Naar and John Eyre made up the intelligence element. Frank White was the staff captain. He was thirty-two, had worked before the war as an insurance claims inspector and came to SOE in July 1943 after service on the staff of the Sudan Defence Force. Captain George Cowie ran the operations side. Thirty-two and a Scot, he had joined SOE after three and a half years with a field artillery regiment followed by six months on the staff of the 51st (Highland) Division, which he followed from El Alamein to Sicily. Before the war he had been a solicitor and Assistant Secretary of Aberdeen University; after it he became Secretary of Queen's University, Belfast.

Working under Cowie were Bill Squires and John Stubbs. Squires, a twenty-six-year-old Royal Tank Regiment captain, had been in the army ten years and in Bari since the winter, helping organise sea sorties to the Albanian coast. Stubbs, a twenty-eight-year-old Royal Army Service Corps captain and an accountant before the war, had taken charge in March of air matters: planning and preparing drops and generally arranging and coordinating air support for what missions in the field were trying to do.

Captain James Herratt was the section's welfare officer. He was twenty-nine and, like Squires, had volunteered for operations and slotted into a staff job while waiting for deployment. When war broke out he had been studying catering and psychology; in 1940 he had served with a motorcycle reconnaissance unit in France; after that he had joined the commandos. His duties, many and various, all concerned the well-being of men in Albania and of the families waiting for news of them at home. He censored letters, sorted out wills and pay, sent books, mail and other comforts to the field and tried to deal with endless minor crises like finding and dispatching spectacles to replace pairs lost or broken. He also kept relatives informed that husbands, fiancés and sons were at least alive. Helping Herratt for a time was thirty-four-year-old Lieutenant George Campbell, a schoolmaster before the war in County Durham. When the Albanian section moved to Bari, Campbell was left in Cairo as liaison with SOE's Greek section.

Conducting officers made sure that men bound for the field attended their briefings and had the right kit and were sent off on time. These duties were ones that several officers took on from time to time: White, Herratt and Watrous had all done their share. Herratt, while loaned to the Cretan section, had paddled Captain Billy Moss ashore when the latter went to help Major Patrick Leigh Fermor kidnap the island's German commander: *Ill Met by Moonlight*, Moss' account of their deeds, was later made into a film. Hugh Munro, working in Cairo over the winter, had also done a spot of conducting. Busy in the role that summer was Bryan McSwiney, the young captain who had helped Quayle bring out Hudson, Young and the others in May, though it still left him time to help with welfare and other office work.

By the autumn the section had been joined by Lieutenant Nora Galbraith, a South African FANY, to help with welfare, plus Robert Stevenson, an Intelligence Corps captain, to work on provisioning and operations, and Captain W. G. Bisset, another Scot, as a further conducting officer. None of these officers was posted out before the fighting in Albania was over but Leake was not the only casualty among them. In September, Jim Herratt was rushed to hospital dangerously ill with poliomyelitis. He died five days later.

Such was the roll call of SOE's Albanian section during the summer and autumn of 1944. It was Watrous, though, who had been given temporary command of the section when Leake had left for Albania. With Leake's death the post became permanent and Watrous remained in command until the section was closed down in February 1945, three months after the German withdrawal. Until then, as Leake had been, he was its principal mouthpiece, the representative with whom higher authority chiefly dealt and corresponded; he was thus in charge throughout the period when the section has been accused of an excessive, pro-Partisan bias.

Watrous' accent left some thinking he was American. Actually he was naturalised British, born in Johannesburg to an American father, a lawyer engaged in opening African markets for the Texas Oil Company, and a New Zealand-born mother. The family moved to London in 1931 and, when war broke out, Eliot, educated at Westminster, had been working in the Pall Mall offices of his father's new travel firm. Commissioned into the Royal Artillery in 1940, he came to SOE in the summer of 1943 after two and a half years on Malta and a short staff course in Haifa. That November, after a period on planning and conducting duties, he moved up to Bari to run the advance branch of the section, develop the sea sortie link to Albania and hold and brief personnel while they waited there to cross. The following May, when he became acting section head, he was still only twenty-two. Some thought Watrous rather young for the role, but he was a logical choice; by then he was well established and well known in the town, while his qualities and commitment had certainly impressed his superiors. A confidential report that spring remarked that he was 'very keen, reliable, energetic and intelligent' and 'of well above average ability'. He was 'willing and capable' of more responsibility and an 'excellent' promotion prospect.[23]

SOE records give no indication that Watrous was ever considered difficult or a problem. Nor do they suggest that his views and opinions had ever conflicted with Leake's. In March, for instance, when Norman Wheeler had urged that the Allies condemn the Balli Kombëtar, Watrous was firmly in favour of the current policy of fostering resistance from all quarters and only denouncing certain leaders known to be collaborating. Writing in Leake's temporary absence, Wheeler's proposals, he told Kit Steel, would create 'an impossible situation' for SOE officers still working with the Balli Kombëtar. While the LNC was 'the only movement at present actively co-operating', the Balli Kombëtar was 'more representative of Albanian opinion than the left view of the LNC'. Denouncing them would also increase hostility between the two and 'certainly affect our present relations with Kupi which, at the moment, are of paramount importance'. Steel scribbled on the letter: 'I entirely agree with the arguments and the proposed action. It is exactly what we have all felt here before.'[24]

By the summer Watrous was more sceptical about Kupi's value, but his doubts seem to have developed at the same pace as Leake's, as reports brought home the reality of superior Partisan strength and how urgent was the need for policy-makers to appreciate its implications. 'From your recent cables,' he wrote to Leake in late May, 'I think I can see why Norman was so emphatic that we did not see the Partisan point of view and the very changed situation in the South. There appears to be no doubt that the Partisans are now reaching their peak and I feel that they will strike in one direction or the other very shortly.'[25] To Eddie Boxshall in early June he wrote that the 'LNC have, without doubt, increased enormously during the last few months; they now represent a strong, well-equipped and well-organised guerilla force, capable of taking offensive action on a scale hitherto not thought possible . . . Further attempts to support Kupi's movement would lead possibly to civil war and certainly cause the Partisans to discontinue operations against the Germans.'[26] Soon he was passing along Leake's and Palmer's recommendation that Kupi be set an ultimatum; 'we now have to wait for the big brains above us to absorb and digest them before final decisions are reached,' he told Palmer. 'I am pressing daily for decisions and hope shortly to have authority to hold the pistol to Kupi's head.'[27]

From Watrous' covering letter to McLean's 18 June report it is also obvious that he did not share McLean's enthusiasm for a last-minute Nationalist rising. Watrous told Baker Street that although the report gave 'a very clear picture of the position in North Albania', he doubted whether support for McLean's proposals would be worth the effort, risks and repercussions involved. A rising would probably begin at its peak, he agreed, 'but in rather an amateurish way. "Small supplies of LMGs and mortars" would not, I feel, be sufficient; large sums of gold would probably be necessary; probably large sums of both would be essential.' Other factors, he added, ought also to be borne in mind: the FNC's obvious value and superior strength; the 'distinct possibility' that the FNC would overrun the Nationalists; the FNC's refusal to meet representatives of Kupi's movement until he had openly fought the Germans, 'hence our present inability to arrange any kind of working agreement'; and the potential results to be derived from supplying the Nationalists when the section only had a gross allotment of seventy tons a month. Watrous also worried about the impact on relations with the FNC if the Nationalists were armed before an agreement had been reached: he observed that these were strained already and a change in the present 'tightrope' policy needed in any case to be made. Furthermore, in view of the Germans' imminent withdrawal from the southern Balkans, arming both sides would increase the chances of civil war 'which, if it came about, would result in a loss of LNC resistance at a time when it is most needed'.[28]

By then, SOE officers who remained or had been recently at close quarters with the Partisans had long abandoned hope of any agreement and, moreover, were deeply sceptical about the wisdom of maintaining a mission with Kupi. At the end of June, when Alan Palmer came back on the air, details were sent to him, too, of McLean's apparent confidence that 'Kupi will fight the Germans when supplies are sent, after which there will be a good chance of collaborating with FNC'. From somewhere in the scrub and rocks above Borsh, a startled reply came back:

> Cannot believe Kupi has been asked to re-enter FNC. Think First Partisan Division expressly formed to attack Kupi and if his troops resist the Partisans will attack and succeed rapidly if there is no [intervening] German drive. Any understanding between FNC and Kupi is out of the question at such a late date even if he fights the Germans. At the end of May Leake and myself recommended targets for Kupi and a time limit end of June . . . It is too late now . . .
>
> Arms must not be sent [to] Kupi as they would only be used against the Partisans and aggravate the situation. Surely by now Kupi's unwillingness to fight the Germans is clear. There is no time for Kupi to take action against the Germans before he is attacked by the Partisans.

Palmer concluded by recommending the 'immediate withdrawal' of missions with Kupi. 'Their retention can only aggravate the civil war and be a real danger to BLOs there.'[29]

It was at about that moment that McLean's 18 June report and a few related w/t messages were sent to Baker Street by bag; days later, George Seymour was incensed at Watrous' apparent reluctance to let him explain the pressures at work on Nationalists to remain inactive. Billy McLean claimed later that Watrous, as section head, had sought to push the communists' cause, but the memories of men who knew him better than did McLean do not support this. 'I really do not think he was very left wing,' remembered Marcus Lyon, who found Watrous 'very pleasant, enthusiastic and helpful . . . quite clever too'.[30] Jon Naar, who worked alongside him for a year, also finds the accusation strange, although Watrous did suffer by comparison to Leake:

> Philip was very dedicated and totally at ease in doing what he did and he did it very well, running the Section, recruiting people. He really did practically the whole job . . . He was a good manager, a good organiser, and a schoolmaster, and I don't mean that in a derogatory sense. He was very fair. And he made that terrible mistake by not keeping his head down, but it's easy for me to say because I survived . . .
>
> Leake was the person you miss terribly when they're not there. Fairly low profile. A lot of these other people – Smiley, McLean, Anthony Quayle, Tilman – they were kind of larger than life. You almost had to be to volunteer for that kind of stuff. Whereas Leake was softly spoken and pretty cool, which was just what we needed. And so after he got killed there was a terrible vacuum and his replacement never got sorted out. Watrous got bumped up from GIII (Operations).[31]

But SOE files do show how Watrous' changing views and proposals reflected openly and consistently those of men like Leake and Palmer. Like them he placed the emphasis on war-fighting considerations and acted on what policy dictated as urgent: action against the enemy. Like them he worried that efforts with Kupi threatened to hinder SOE's chances of causing the Germans the greatest discomfort. It is also evident that Eddie Boxshall, unable at such a distance to keep up with events, expressed alarm at suggestions in June that Britain might have to consider dropping Kupi.[32] So perhaps the reason why the flow of information to SOE in London may have been briefly slowed was an anxiety in Bari that men should not push plans that seemed increasingly irrelevant to policy requirements. Whether it was proper to have sought to slow that flow is another matter, of course.

That said, McLean's methods and Amery's keen interest in saving Albania from communism did have an abrasive effect on other officers. 'Julian was put forward, and put himself forward, as an especially well informed sort of political guru with a thorough understanding of the communist menace and Britain's strategic interests in keeping it at bay,' recalled Reg Hibbert, who crossed paths with the pair that summer. 'The rest of us were treated as common soldiery who thought that fighting the Germans was all that counted and did not understand the higher subtleties which made the Soviet Union and the CP's of Eastern Europe the real, long-term enemies.'[33] Contemporary signals also reveal a certain friction that autumn between McLean's mission and Bari. Through SOE and OSS channels, Bari had heard that McLean was allowing Amery, a captain, to wear major's crowns and tell locals he was the 'counterpart' in Albania of Randolph Churchill, the Prime Minister's son. Churchill had been sent recently to Tito as a semi-official envoy of his father's. The decision to send Amery to Albania, however, had had no such diplomatic impulse or authority behind it. An exchange of w/t messages resulted in which McLean was told directly that this act on his part had made the work of officers with the Partisans 'extremely difficult'. Already the Partisans interpreted Amery's presence as British 'political support' for Kupi, McLean was informed; Amery was just a 'straightforward' BLO and by telling him to assume his majority 'you have exceeded your powers and he must revert to his proper rank'.[34] Hibbert, reaching Bari in October, 'received the impression' that staff officers there were certainly irritated with McLean and Amery's efforts to keep the Kupi and Zogist cause alive. And if the mission found these staff officers 'unfriendly', he reflected, 'it was probably because they did not take kindly to being upbraided for losing a battle against communism when they thought they had just won a victory over Germany'.[35]

Jon Naar's recollections of life and work in Bari may reinforce this picture. Half a century later, learning, for the first time, of many of the post-war charges against the section, he found them startling. 'If there was a Communist conspiracy in Bari, as alleged by Amery and his supporters, it certainly fooled me.'[36] But there was a 'schism between the pro- and anti-Kupi factions', he remembers, and the personalities and politics of individual officers did contribute to it. 'Most of us on the staff and in the field were open as to our political sympathies . . . Personally, I was openly pro-socialist as were almost all of us who had served in the Eighth Army.' Amery, by contrast, was known to be decidedly conservative and Naar recalls a sense in Bari that 'Amery and company had their own anti-Partisan, anti-Communist agenda . . . and very strong connections with the FO (rather than with SOE London) and were able to continue for some months with a policy that was very divisive'.[37]

Naar's own politics were more than a product of the desert. In 1936, as a young Jewish sixth-former at Mill Hill, he had clashed with Mosley's fascists in Cable Street; as an undergraduate he had joined the University Labour Federation and marched in protest against German and Italian aggression. After Spain he had little time for communism but in any case, he stresses, the post-war 'polarizing' of people in Bari as procommunist or anticommunist is 'totally misleading'. As the section's military intelligence officer, his own duties had been chiefly to 'debrief bodies who came back from the field, translate and evaluate captured documents, and then co-ordinate this information with BLOs who were beginning to start operations'. Of the men coming back, 'almost all of them were extremely helpful and interested only in getting the job done of attracting and pinning down as many German divisions as possible'. What mattered most both in the office and in the field was that it 'made sense from the military viewpoint' to support Hoxha. 'Did the Pzns in Albania indulge in terrorism and other civil war operations against their enemies within what was originally a common front? Of course, they did. But on balance and when it counted . . . the Albanian resistance was 90 per cent or more Partisan-supported and organised at great personal loss to themselves.'[38]

The significance of the delayed messages should not be overstated. Nor should the significance of the apparent suppression of what, that summer, George Seymour had to say. For a start, Philip Broad was well enough informed of all reports from the field. And not only did he receive a prompt copy of McLean's 18 June report but he also forwarded it in a telegram that reached the Foreign Office days before the bagged copy reached Baker Street. Moreover, neither Broad nor Baker Street nor the Foreign Office was particularly keen on McLean's plan when they read it. Broad praised McLean's 'excellent description' of Kupi's position but warned that arming him before a working agreement with the Partisans was reached would damage relations with the Partisans and any chance of united resistance; Denis Laskey, Albanian desk officer at the Foreign Office, felt much the same.[39] So did senior SOE staff. 'I am against increased support for Abas Kupi,' David Keswick wrote to Gubbins. 'Our political unwisdom has got us into the most unholy mess in the Balkans . . . We do not want bigger and better civil wars, and this eternal tinkering with both sides in order to match them up one against the other will in my opinion prove disastrous.'[40] Gubbins, too, writing in July to all directors and regional and country section heads, felt support for Kupi was 'not warranted'.[41]

More importantly, SOE's work in Albania was then harnessed more closely to short-term military needs than at any point before. That spring General Sir Henry Maitland Wilson had succeeded Eisenhower as Supreme Allied Commander in the Mediterranean and taken direct responsibility from GHQ Middle East for special operations in Yugoslavia and Albania. Wilson's orders from the Chiefs of Staff were very clear. His principal tasks were to defeat the Germans in his theatre, stop as many as possible from reinforcing other fronts and encourage the enemy to believe that major Allied operations were planned for the Eastern Mediterranean. He was not told to interest himself in trying to control communism; on the contrary, the Chiefs considered guerrilla warfare in the Balkans to be one of his principal tools. And in June, in view of the increasing importance and tempo of Balkan operations, the Chiefs then allowed him to establish a subordinate command in Italy to coordinate all operations across the Adriatic. Air support was identified as central to the command's success so the new body was named the Balkan Air Force and a senior RAF officer, Air Vice Marshal William Elliot, placed in charge. Housed in offices close to Bari castle, Elliot and the Balkan Air Force were soon firmly in control of the flow of arms and ammunition across the Adriatic. And from the start Elliot's orders were exactly in line with Wilson's. The 'primary object' of his new command, as the in-house history of the Balkan Air Force puts it, was to 'contain and destroy as many enemy forces as possible'. In relation to Albania, this meant:

(a) To endeavour to unite the resistance movements in Albania to take concerted action against the Germans.

(b) To afford such air support as was possible for operations by the Albanians against the Germans.

(c) To carry out a series of harassing raids by British forces on the Albanian coastline in order to further the efforts of the Albanians themselves in containing and destroying German forces.

(d) To continue sending supplies to Albania by air and sea and to try to open up an area on the Albanian coastline for the sending in of supplies by sea.[42]

To discuss political issues, Elliot chaired and was advised by a policy committee, much as GHQ Middle East had been since 1943. Its members included representatives of Wilson's Allied Forces Headquarters, the Foreign Office, the State Department and SOE, and, when terms of reference were drawn up, it was decided that SOE activities in Yugoslavia and Albania should be placed under the committee's direct supervision. When post-war accounts have attacked decisions made in Bari after Leake's death, the distinction has not been made that the responsible authority there was the Balkan Air Force policy committee, not the SOE office or junior SOE staff officers. Moreover, these decisions were always in line with Elliot's instructions. As records of its meetings make clear, uppermost in the committee's minds was always the 'primary object' of inflicting the maximum damage on the Germans in Albania. So were a realistic view of the contrasting capabilities of the Partisans and Kupi and a dwindling hope of seeing unity of resistance. As the minutes also show, the members who did most of the talking whenever Albania came up for discussion were the chairman and the men representing SOE and the Foreign Office.

As AOC Balkan Air Force, Bill Elliot was a sound and suitable choice. A former Royal Flying Corps fighter pilot, he was forty-eight and had solid experience of staff work, including a recent spell in Whitehall on inter-service planning. As a member of the Joint Planning Committee he had also attended several of Churchill's conferences with Roosevelt. Consequently, as the Balkan Air Force history puts it, he was 'well versed in inter-service matters and the interplay of military and political problems essential for waging war in the Balkans. Moreover, from his attendance at the inter-Allied conferences, he was necessarily familiar with the outline of Allied world strategy and how the Balkan theatre fitted in to the general design.'[43]

The FO's man on the committee was Philip Broad, while representing SOE was the head of its Bari set-up, Lieutenant Colonel the Viscount Harcourt. Grandson of a Liberal Party leader, Bill Harcourt was thirty-six, Eton- and Oxford-educated and a managing director of Morgan Grenfell. He was also very familiar with SOE's Balkan work. Soon after joining SOE in 1941 he had been sent out to the Cairo staff; by February 1943 he was deputy director of Cairo's country sections and had been appointed MBE. That October he moved up to Bari to run the new forward headquarters. By May 1944, by which time the Albanian and Yugoslav sections had resettled in Bari, he was chairing the weekly

Albanian meetings at HQ Special Operations Mediterranean (SOM), a new Anglo-American special forces command directly under Wilson to which the sections reported. For the rest of 1944, although Watrous attended the occasional policy committee meeting to give background information or explain a certain point, Harcourt was more closely involved in decision-making over Albania than anyone else on the SOE staff and, in fact, seems to have shouldered some of the burden of running the Albanian section after Philip Leake was killed. All of the section's plans and proposals had to be approved by him and he worked very closely both with the staff and with officers returning from the field. 'He has a very thorough grasp of the political background in the Balkans, particularly Greece and Albania,' Billy Stawell wrote of him; 'a very definite and forceful personality and commands respect'.[44] It was Harcourt, Watrous' superior officer, who reproached McLean about the major's crowns incident; and he himself chose personally and deliberately that summer not to send certain documents to London 'as they could not have failed to be extremely misleading'.[45]

It was obvious to observers in Italy, even before Palmer and other fugitives from Gemsbock arrived to bring them up to date, that, militarily, the Partisans in Albania were doing a good job and were a much better bet than Kupi. 'Partisans during April and May have greatly increased their strength numerically, have reformed their organisation and generally seem to be in the strongest position which they have ever occupied,' Harry Fultz told Washington on 12 June.

> Reports state that they have formed as many as 15 brigades with several independent battalions. Their total armed strength is placed at from 20 to 25 thousand men which incidentally I am inclined to think is an exaggeration even though it is confirmed by both our own and British sources. They seem to have convinced finally both the Germans and the British that they are an organized factor that may well upset the plans of either. The British as you know all during February and March seemed to be banking a great deal upon what Abas Kupi would do at the same time sending out cock and bull stories of the men that he could raise, some 25 thousand I believe. Their recent reports tell quite a different story . . .
>
> They do better with the military information. Below I am

quoting one of their military summaries for the week just ended:

'. . . The many reports indicate that the present German attacks against the Partisans are the largest and strongest so far undertaken. There appear to be three main reasons for the German operations. Firstly, to ensure that lines of communications from Greece are clear in order to permit withdrawal. Secondly, to disrupt Partisan formations which certainly hinder any attempted withdrawal. Thirdly, to clear the coastline and in particular close the bridge-head, thus making it more difficult for the Allies to invade or attempt a diversionary invasion thrust. The quality and strength of the troops used by the Germans for these operations and the methods employed show clearly that Partisan resistance has not been underestimated.

Further attacks against Partisan units, HQs and Allied missions can be expected for some time. It is difficult to say at present how many of the German drives will be held but it is certain that Germans will be killed and MT [motor transport] destroyed by the combined effort of ground forces and the RAF. Should German opera-tions be successfully concluded it will be necessary for them to leave a large force in southern Albania to ensure that the area is kept under control.'

This I think is a sober statement of fact which has evidence to back it up. The Bridgehead referred to is one which the Partisans have been holding open for the past two weeks down along the Himara coast near Borshi [sic]. It will prob-ably go although the Partisans seem to be putting up a fight to hold it. In fact around here we have been surprised that they have held it as long as they have.[46]

Ten days later, HQ SOM declared that 'the fact that the enemy has seen fit to launch an offensive on a considerable scale against the Albanian partisans is proof of the value of their operations and of the importance which the enemy attaches to the elimination of their br[idge]head, the disruption of their forces, and the reopening of the two main routes North from Epirus'. Ongoing support for the Partisans was recommended 'for from a military point of view it is paying a good dividend'.[47] Wilson, too, who was extremely keen at exactly that moment to have the Germans suspect a major threat to the Balkans and so keep them away from Normandy, was impressed by it all.[48] The Albanian Partisans, he told the Chiefs of Staff that month, 'are rapidly growing in strength and organisation and are already an effective instrument for action against the enemy in the south where his main commitments (the defence of vital road communications from Greece) are placed'.[49] At the end of June the Balkan Air Force policy committee recognised the Partisans as the only movement actively resisting and agreed that it might be a good idea to invite representatives to Bari for discussions on operational matters.

As for Kupi, it was also clear by then that he had far less support than had long been believed. He had once said that his followers numbered up to 50,000.[50] In February he told George Seymour that he could raise 25,000.[51] In May Julian Amery estimated Kupi's strength at 5,000 poorly armed men.[52] In June McLean had asked Bari for arms for 2,000.[53] To onlookers in Italy this did not look impressive and stood in stark contrast to the thousands of Partisans already under arms in the south. As Harcourt noted on 20 June, Kupi's movement appeared 'immature and without support' and was not yet 'a military factor'; the Partisans, on the other hand, were 'the only party which has continuously fought the Germans' and deserved support as they were 'organised, pro-Allied, and willing to take offensive action'.[54] In Bari there were doubts, too, about Kupi's contribution to the demolition of the bridge at Gjoles: was it really enough to warrant sending him weapons? 'Whilst in no way detracting from Major Smiley's outstanding success in this operation,' Harcourt recorded, 'the conclusion was reached that it could not be considered a whole-hearted attempt by Kupi to throw in his lot with the Allies.'[55] By then, Wilson in Italy and the Chiefs in London were also agreed that Kupi ought not to be armed before he and the Partisans had reached an agreement. The Foreign Office had asked the Chiefs of Staff for their thoughts on whether Zog should be asked to send Kupi a message of encouragement. The Chiefs, reluctant to send Kupi supplies that 'might be more profitably used elsewhere', were not enthusiastic, but sent for Wilson's views.[56] He replied on 16 June that reconciliation was 'an essential prerequisite': otherwise arms sent to the Zogists 'would mainly encourage civil war'. He was 'doubtful', however, whether an agreement was possible.[57] Although reluctant to abandon the Kupi effort, the Foreign Office fell into line and, thereafter, was never able to elicit any kind of support from military commanders for any policy favouring Kupi.

Conscious, like Leake and Palmer, of the need to resolve this matter, Harcourt supported at once their proposal, passed swiftly along by Watrous, that Kupi be set a deadline. Kupi was still 'unwilling to show his hand either on one side or the other', Harcourt explained to Philip Broad and others. The time had come 'to force Kupi's hand' or 'drop him'. He must agree to 'immediate action' coupled with 'a declaration of wholehearted sympathy and non aggression to other resistance movements' and be warned that 'any signs of sliding back into a collaborationist policy will cause the immediate abandonment of all support and the withdrawal of all Allied officers with him'. The Partisans, Harcourt noted, were 'beginning to show signs of impatience with the British policy of maintaining officers with groups which appear to them to be purely collaborationist. If Kupi cannot be forced into action in the near future, there is grave danger of our losing the Partisan support at a time when it is most needed.'[58] Broad, already aware of the proposal, agreed, telling Harold Macmillan earlier that month that it was time to 'intimate clearly' to Kupi 'that unless he is prepared to do something we shall not continue to support him'. Kupi, Broad noted, was 'much weaker than was originally believed' while the FNC was 'the only party in Albania at present offering any active resistance'.[59] In the end, although the Balkan Air Force policy committee also wanted it, no deadline was set, owing to Foreign Office concerns about the consequences should Kupi actually meet it. Britain might then find itself committed to supplying Kupi with weapons he would 'probably' use against the Partisans, Macmillan argued; a Kupi–Partisan agreement had to be in place before any decision was taken to arm Kupi.[60] The Foreign Office agreed: the 'first aim' should be the reconciliation.[61]

It has been suggested in the past that the Partisans, after they attacked him, were resupplied because the authorities in Bari believed Partisan lies that Kupi was working with the Germans.[62] Certainly Bari knew of Kupi's open dealings with outright collaborators. It was known, too, that these associations became a military alliance when the Partisans pushed into the north. A broad front was formed in which Kupi allied himself with Gjon Markogjoni, who had worked with the Italians, Mustafa Kruja, who had worked with both the Italians and the Germans, and Fikri Dinë, appointed Prime Minister in July. 'It is more than possible that he personally never conversed with a German,' Harcourt

wrote in late 1944, 'but collectively his organisation, which boasted
the inclusion of high-ranking Officers of State, was tending more and
more to collaboration.'[63] It is also clear that his quiet attempts that
spring to build a stronger anti-Partisan front, in exactly the way he had
explained to Seymour in April, were documented in decrypts of intercepted enemy signals read in Baker Street and, apparently, in Bari. 'It
is certain that similar information will be in possession of our people
in Italy,' Archie Boyle, SOE's security chief, told David Keswick in
July.[64] Decrypts showed, too, how the Germans had expected Zogist
forces to support the coming Gemsbock offensive 'to take the
Communists in the south by a pincer movement'.[65] In the end Kupi did
not take part and it does seem that, even after the Partisans attacked
him, he remained cautions of dealing too closely with the Germans. In
fact German assessments of Kupi's strength and stance did not differ
significantly from SOE's: that spring, German Intelligence had numbered
Kupi's followers at between five hundred and three thousand and
described them as 'biding their time'.[66] And although Kupi did approach
the Germans through Mehdi Frashëri that summer to allow 'a force of
some hundreds of his supporters' to pass through Tirana, the Germans
still regarded him 'with suspicion'.[67]

Whatever allegations were doing the rounds, however, a charge of
collaboration was not the reason why the Partisans were resupplied; in
fact, Kupi did not figure in the decision at all. When news filtered
through that the Partisans were attacking Kupi, the policy committee
had suspended supplies, dispatched Victor Smith to tell him to avoid
clashes and instructed Johnny Shaw to try to persuade Hoxha to leave
Kupi alone. Shaw made little progress. 'From the beginning it appeared
to me that Enver Hoxha had no intention of withdrawing from his
plans and his attitude, though cordial, was to delay the issue until such
time as his Divisions were engaged,' Shaw reported later. 'I asked Hoxha
to by-pass Kupi's forces pending negotiations and put it forward to
him that he would be in a better position afterwards whether negoti-
ation failed or not. His answer to this was that, though he would like
to do this, the forces of Kupi were barring their way to the North and
to the Germans whom he wished to fight.'[68] But when Alan Palmer,
with Marcus Lyon, dropped back in on 14 July and took over from
Shaw, he then heard from Hoxha that Partisans in the north were being
attacked by the Germans and needed help. Palmer signalled Bari that
if SOE officers confirmed this, then 'consider situation on which my

mission based completely altered. No longer civil war and recommend most urgent consideration given to sending material.' If supplies were withheld, 'future co-operation' with the Partisans would be impossible: the Partisans would 'feel abandoned' in their 'hour of need'.[69] At that moment, reports began to arrive in Bari from Richard Riddell of German forces massing to attack the 1st Brigade, which had pushed up to Dibra where he and his mission were based. The Brigade was in desperate need, Riddell told Bari; 'Pzns must have supplies for this battle.'[70] The policy committee assembled, discussed the appeal and, as Bill Harcourt recorded, 'decided, on the information available from all sources, that the value of the FNC actions against the retreating Germans was such as to render the cessation of all supplies to the FNC impolitic'.[71] The decision was also taken to allow a Partisan delegation to proceed to Bari to negotiate directly on military matters. Both steps were in line with policy, which was still aimed squarely at supporting Albanians committed to resistance, and reflected the realisation that if supplies to the Partisans were cut then action against the Germans stopped.

The arrival of the FNC delegates, shipped to Bari with Palmer at the end of July, and the subsequent military agreement reached a month later marked the start of a major commitment. Though the delegates' demand for political recognition of the provisional government was turned down, the Balkan Air Force agreed to recognise the FNC as the only movement actually fighting. Targets were agreed, greater cooperation was promised and drops and sea deliveries were stepped up. Two sea sorties, totalling 140 tons, came in during August; 160 tons were dropped by air. September saw 200 tons shipped in and about 100 dropped by air. In October another 140 tons came in by sea and more than 200 tons by air. More stores were sent to Albania during those three months than in all the months preceding them and almost all of that material went to the Partisans.

The decision not to arm Kupi after he finally fought the Germans in September was also taken by the policy committee. McLean and his men were shocked and angry and believed they had been misled, but the apparent inconsistency, though unfortunate, was not a deliberate deceit. With the German withdrawal from Albania well underway and Kupi faring badly against the FNC, events by then had overtaken what McLean had been sent to do and complicated, in Kupi's case, the simple fight-and-receive-arms approach. During the decisive committee meeting Philip Broad had noted that 'we had originally given a general undertaking throughout the Balkans to support all those forces which were attacking the Germans'. But it was for consideration, he said, whether this 'belated and half-hearted change of front by Kupi' had 'any real military value' and whether supplies sent to him 'might only be used for carrying on civil war'. Broad also wondered whether the actions carried out 'were no more than small sabotage attacks made by some of Kupi's followers under British officers'. Elliot agreed, remarking that 'we appeared to be under no moral obligation to supply Kupi', and highlighted two 'strong arguments from the expediency point of view against our sending supplies to him'. One was the 'half-hearted and last minute' nature of Kupi's recent actions; the other was that he seemed to occupy a small pocket near the coast where little effective action against the Germans was possible.[72] As Broad told the Foreign Office afterwards, the committee agreed that this recent activity could not be seen as 'a serious attempt by Kupi to undertake genuine action against the Germans'.[73]

In fact Kupi could still operate against the main road north from Tirana, while some of the actions carried out were more than acts of sabotage, albeit of varying value and with varying degrees of Albanian help. The first, on 6 September, was an attack on the tents of a small, remote camp, an artillery battery headquarters, when ten Germans, not a hundred as Amery would remember later, were killed and the mission's twenty-eight Tajiks, all recent deserters from German service, did most of the fighting. 'Albanians were very keen on the attack but "the spirit was willing but the flesh was weak", which resulted in an unimpressive action,' McLean reported.[74] The second action, a convoy ambushed on the night of 9–10 September by a joint force of Zogists and Balli Kombëtar, was more impressive. Afterwards Ian Merrett picked through the remains and counted three trucks destroyed and fifteen damaged and thirty-five Germans killed. The following night George Jenkins mined the same road and the next night he and Smiley blew up a bridge, blocking it for two days. The last action put before the committee for consideration was another ambush, this time by a Zogist force with McLean, Amery and Jenkins attached, that destroyed nine vehicles and killed a few more Germans.[75] Perhaps more valuable than all of this were the reports the mission received in September, through Kupi, from an Austrian corporal working at the headquarters of the 21st Mountain Corps which described in detail German positions and plans for withdrawal. But it was clear enough to Bari that Kupi's decision finally to fight had come extremely late in the day, that he remained preoccupied with the Partisan threat and that his actions were a last-gasp attempt to reinsure.

That awkward episode would have been avoided had the advice of the policy committee been taken weeks earlier and McLean's mission withdrawn on the grounds of Kupi's shortcomings. But despite Broad's efforts, the Foreign Office continued to cling to outdated hopes that contact with Kupi might yield an agreement with the Partisans or otherwise prove fruitful. A report sent by Eden to Churchill provides a typical illustration of the Foreign Office view that summer. Churchill had seen a telegram of Broad's that remarked on the 'definite German threat' facing the Partisans at Dibra and that the situation now was 'no longer a straight issue of civil war'.[76] Churchill had minuted to Eden: 'Let me have a note on this, showing which side we are on.'[77] Eden's reply, drawn up three weeks after the Partisans had pushed north and attacked Kupi, noted, accurately, that the FNC was a 'left wing' movement 'with a strong communist element' and 'the only organisation in Albania which is doing any serious fighting against the Germans'. It added, less accurately, that the FNC's influence was 'confined to the south' and reconciliation with Kupi remained possible.[78] And when Broad reported in early August that the situation might demand McLean's withdrawal, the Foreign Office remained stuck in the past. 'At this stage of the war we don't want to commit ourselves too deeply to one side or the other and I am against withdrawing the BLOs from Kupi,' minuted Armine Dew. Sir Orme Sargent, Deputy Under-Secretary, agreed.[79] Only in September did Eden finally concede that the Foreign Office had nothing to gain from a mission with Kupi. 'Surely it is asking for trouble to leave our officers with him. Better get them out.'[80]

As for Bari's refusal to evacuate Kupi, for which some hold the SOE office responsible, this was in fact insisted on by Philip Broad. As Broad told Harold Macmillan, he was unconvinced by McLean's claim that Kupi had been of 'considerable service to the Allied cause'. In recent months Kupi's record 'has not been such as to justify us in saying that he has been of any help whatever'. He had 'consistently failed to carry out requests for action' and what he had done 'amounted to a few minor rebuffs of no practical importance' when it was clear that the Germans were leaving. 'On the other side of the balance sheet there are reports that certain of his lieutenants have been working with the Germans.'[81] It was also Broad's idea that steps should be taken to ensure that

McLean, when he and his mission were brought out, complied with the decision. McLean should be given 'categorical instructions' not to bring with him any Albanians and the captain of the MTB picking him up should be told the same.[82] Harcourt and Elliot agreed and the orders were duly sent. When McLean and his mission were evacuated at the end of October, Kupi was left behind.

Others in London still unimpressed by Kupi included David Keswick and Colin Gubbins. Kupi, Keswick felt, had remained on the fence 'until the last possible moment, when it was too late and the country had been almost completely overrun by the FNC. His contribution against the Germans is negligible, and chiefly remarkable for the body-guard which he gave to Smiley on one of the latter's more daring bridge-blowing efforts'.[83] Gubbins agreed.[84] When word reached Eden of McLean's wish to save him, however, the Foreign Secretary was sympathetic. Here, Eden considered, was a man whom Britain had supported 'and against whom the most serious charge is that of inactivity against the enemy'. While it was 'undesirable that HM Government should be identified with steps to rescue Abas Kupi, I do not think we can escape the moral responsibilities'. Broad was instructed 'to consult with McLean as to ways and means of getting Kupi out of the country without it appearing that HM Government have been involved'.[85] Hearing of this, Bill Elliot objected strongly and, for a moment, believed he had had the order withdrawn. The problem solved itself. In November a British destroyer found Kupi adrift in the Adriatic in an open boat. He was picked up and landed at Brindisi.

Kupi was not the only man McLean had had to leave behind. Bari had also told him not to bring out the mission's interpreters, Italian camp followers and Tajik deserters. Although there has been some confusion about the reasons for this, SOE records show, once again, that there was nothing sinister behind it. The Royal Navy, after a terrible experience picking up Tony Neel three weeks before, had simply refused to evacuate anyone other than British and American personnel. Trying at night in heavy seas to collect Neel, Roy Bullock and Neel's w/t operator, Harry Button, plus one German deserter and forty-odd assorted Italians and Tajiks, one assault boat ferrying men to the MTBs capsized and sank. Button and two Tajiks were drowned. 'When I left him on the beach, Button was heavily clothed, with also a haversack on his back,' Bullock reported afterwards. 'It was only when he was missing that I recalled that earlier in the evening he had mentioned to me that he could not swim.'[86] Lieutenant Commander Tony de Cosson, captain of one of the MTBs, advised that future evacuations of such numbers in such conditions should not be attempted. 'At this stage of the war it would seem madness to imperil British lives in order to evacuate large numbers of non-Allied personnel.'[87]

In February 1944, two months short of his twenty-sixth birthday, Lieutenant John Eyre joined the staff of SOE's Albanian section. A head-and-shoulders photograph pinned to his personal file shows a pale young man in steel-rimmed spectacles and a shirt that needed an iron. He was to work in the role of political intelligence officer until the section closed down twelve months later; by then he had been promoted captain. It is his presence in the section that has long been the central plank in the argument that left-wingers and communists at SOE head-quarters had helped condemn Albania to communism. Whatever the political opinions of junior SOE staff officers, it is evident today that the staff did not lead policy-makers astray. Nevertheless, one or two charges levelled specifically against Eyre are of such seriousness that they do require some attention.

As a glance at the literature shows, however, the case presented against him in print has to date been extremely thin. Peter Kemp, who met him in Bari in 1944, wrote later of 'a serious young Communist whose courteous manner could not altogether conceal his disapproval of my Albanian record'. Kemp had just arrived after months with Nationalist elements; Eyre was a 'newcomer' to the section. 'Like his co-religionist, James Klugman [sic], he was his Section's intelligence officer,' Kemp recalled, 'and like Klugmann and so many other Communists he had great sincerity combined with charm.' Kemp added that he saw little of him in Bari but 'heard a great deal about him later, when I was in Java [in 1946]. There, while attached to the 5th Indian Division in Soerabaja, he landed himself in trouble for editing a sedi-tious newspaper for the troops; in consequence he was sent home by the GOC, General Mansergh.'[88] David Smiley claimed that Eyre was a communist agent, had had a hand in suppressing a message to Anthony Eden, so a secretary had said, and was overheard calling Smiley's mission 'fascist'. Smiley heard later that Eyre had also stood as a communist candidate in the 1945 general election.[89] That is as far as the evidence goes, but it has not stopped others from broadening the speculation to include bold statements in print that Eyre, while in SOE, was a

Communist Party member and even a Soviet mole.[90] Still, care should be taken not to dismiss every claim against him.

Thirty years after the war, in 'a bare little room' in Glastonbury, Eyre sat down and wrote his own book. His appearance had changed a bit since 1944. He had 'long silky hair to the shoulders and an enormous grey beard' and wore 'flared jeans, a little torn and faded, with a pentacle adorned in colour on one knee to hide a hole'. As he wrote he could hear 'a guitar, Bob Dylan's voice on *Blood on the Tracks*, the inevitable sound of a flushing toilet'. The fact that the existence of *The God Trip: The Story of a Mid-century Man*, a slim memoir published in 1976, has gone unnoticed for so long is not surprising given the book's principal subject matter. Just five pages deal with the first fifty years of Eyre's life. The rest, in his words, recounts the subsequent experiences

> of a middle-aged professional man who brought his marriage to an end after twenty years and dropped out of society. For the past six years I have been travelling through different countries following the hippie trail, living in caves in Crete, in drop-out colonies in Israel . . . After a year roaming around India . . . I ended up barefoot and in rags . . .
>
> I have earned my way unloading rolls of barbed wire off lorries, selling my blood, painting houses, teaching English, mending people's clothes. I have entered the world of psychedelics and hallucinogens, acid trips and pot, mysticism and UFOlogy.

Eyre described his book as 'putting together factually a series of paranormal events which started for me in 1967 . . . a case-history of interest to both believers and disbelievers'. The brief passages devoted to his earlier life were included 'as a way of indicating the yardsticks for measuring the phenomenon of my existence'.[91] Yet he wrote revealingly of his youth, of his growing independence and self-awareness and of his political activism both during and after the war.

His childhood was unhappy, dislocated and 'curiously Victorian'. Cousins on his father's side were the Crosthwaite-Eyres of Bradshaw: 'the most solid upper crust'. Eyre's mother was the daughter of Thomas Rome, 'chairman of the Mersey Dock and Harbour Board'. She died when Eyre was six months old and his father, a vicar, on remarrying moved from a rich Liverpool parish to a mining village near Burnley 'where class distinctions killed friendships'. Eyre was sent to live with an aunt. Boarding school followed and in 1931 he won a scholarship to Marlborough. He remained unsettled. Twice during his teens he ran away from home, 'leaving a suicide note on my pillow to frighten them'; at seventeen he ran as far as Paris. At eighteen he was 'persuaded' to enter St Peter's College, Oxford, to train as a priest 'but dropped out to go to the Maddermarket Theatre, Norwich to become an actor, an aborted priest'. Before long he had swapped Norwich for 'the Unity Theatre, run by left-wing political militants in Mornington Crescent'. It was in the context of his own politics that he referred to his time in SOE:

> I came to accept the class basis of society during the war years when I was working with Special Operations Executive responsible for economic and political intelligence coming from our missions in occupied Albania. I was trained in parachute jumping and sabotage, preparatory to being dropped into Greece, but the plan was abandoned. Instead, on the staff of the Albanian country section I saw the Marxist-Leninist thesis working out under my very eyes. Julian Amery and [Billy] Maclean [sic], my colleagues in conspiracy, were battling against the winds of change while I and others in our wisdom or ignorance helped to stir up the hurricane. I had the honour of drawing up the list of Albania's quislings.

Eyre wrote, too, that he did join the Communist Party, though only on returning to Britain after finishing his military service in the Far East. Back in London he spoke on street corners as 'a complete scientific and dialectical materialist'. He also stood, he wrote, as a communist in North Kensington both in local elections and in the 1951 general election. He helped found the Ex-service Movement for Peace and, to further his 'ideals', worked for four years as a postman. He finally left the 'orbit' of the Communist Party when the Soviet Union intervened in Hungary. By 1966, when he 'dropped out', Eyre was assistant editor of a London-based architectural magazine. By the summer of 1967 he was experimenting with various mind-altering drugs and attending courses run by the Spiritualist Association.[92]

Much of this account can be confirmed by other sources. University records show that he went up from Marlborough to St Peter's in 1936. When joining SOE he added that he had studied English Literature for a year and won a blue at fives. Possibly he may have tried to make his past sound more respectable than perhaps it was, for he also told SOE that after Oxford he had become a schoolmaster and published three novels; no mention was made of acting. But *The God Trip* says nothing about pre-war teaching or writing and no published novel can be found in his name. In 1937, however, as the records of the Maddermarket Theatre show, he had indeed turned up in Norwich, where he acted in several productions between September that year and May 1938.[93]

SOE files also provide an outline of Eyre's wartime service. Joining the army in December 1939, he had been commissioned within a year into the Royal Artillery and joined SOE in August 1943 after service with an anti-tank regiment in Iraq, Syria and the Western Desert. Recruited in Cairo and earmarked for operations, he underwent parachute, paramilitary and signals training before being posted on to the staff of the Albanian section in February 1944. The description of his duties in *The God Trip* also sounds about right. Eyre's main tasks were to collect and collate information on political conditions, factions and personalities, and circulate it to other offices and commands. Sources ranged from w/t messages and SOE officers returned from the field to newspapers, propaganda pamphlets, captured documents and OSS reports.

Colleagues in the section would remember Eyre as something of a loner, if they remembered him at all: neither Marcus Lyon nor Tony Northrop, two BLOs who spent several weeks in and around the office in 1944, could recall him. Richard Riddell vaguely remembered Eyre as 'the one who was very interested in how the partisans dealt with the villagers in the areas they controlled, and the role of the commissar'.[94] Bryan McSwiney, one of the section's conducting officers, remembered 'a thin, white-faced and fair-haired' young man who was certainly 'left-wing' but also quite 'distant'.[95] A report from Eyre's paramilitary course describes him as 'sound and steady with plenty of common sense' although more a 'good co-operator' than a leader. 'Takes a good, quiet, sober interest in things. Not a ball of fire intellectually or socially but a solid, sensible, companionable man to have around.'[96]

'Scruffy; bright, of course,' Jon Naar recalls.[97] 'He was doctrinaire in his socialism, leading one to think he was a communist.'[98] But even Naar, who worked in the same office for a year, remembered him chiefly as 'rather odd . . . It's a terrible thing to say, but he didn't wash.'[99] Naar is also certain of one thing. 'No one, except possibly Eyre, would have called any of our BLOs Fascist, because we had too much respect for their courage even though at times we disagreed politically.'[100] And although there is no indication in Eyre's personal file that he was ever considered a security problem, an incident is recorded that suggests he was capable of delivering rather intemperate abuse. That summer he had learnt from the Army Pay Office that there had been an overissue of pay into his home bank account and that steps were being taken to recover it. Eyre wrote back objecting strongly to this: he was in no position to examine his statements, he said, and had told his bank to advise him should payments be reduced. Eyre finished his letter: 'your assumption of guilt without defence appals me, and the fact that you have apparently already commenced docking makes me want to vomit'. This 'highly injudicious phraseology' was brought to the attention of the War Office and Eyre's superiors were instructed to 'ensure that he does not again adopt such a tone'.[101]

It is not impossible that a note may be found one day in some Soviet archive or currently classified MI5 file proving that Eyre had worked at some point for the NKVD. But although an Oxford communist cell had existed in the 1930s with which he feasibly could have flirted, a nineteen-year-old actor in Norwich would have made an odd agent to run. And while there was a Soviet presence in Bari with which he could have been in contact, and Eyre would almost certainly have known James Klugmann, it is not at all clear what the Soviets could have wanted him to do. It is possible, of course, that he would have been prepared to leak information had they asked for it, but there were plenty of opportunities for them to learn less covertly about Britain's Balkan operations and policies. Soviet aircraft, based in southern Italy, were then taking part in drops to SOE and OSS missions and Naar remembers 'several boozy sessions at the Imperiale Hotel with our Soviet comrades. The sharing of military and political information with them was what I would call "normal" and certainly not in any way subversive.'[102]

As for pushing the Partisan case for support in the ways that Klugmann seems to have pushed Tito's, there was little that Eyre could have done to make the military case for Hoxha much more obvious than it was already. Leafing through the summaries and reviews he produced it is possible to detect something of where he stood on key issues. In August, asked by Bill Harcourt for his thoughts on action now that Kupi was embroiled with the Partisans, Eliot Watrous produced a paper recommending that the Allies break with Kupi and withdraw McLean's mission. If this were done, he said, then Allied approval of the 'military effort' of the Partisans would be obvious and other Nationalists encouraged to join the Partisans.[103] Loose in one file is a sheet of points supporting that argument: some are typed, others are in Eyre's handwriting. 'Hang on to this please – we may yet have another Kupi crisis,' Watrous had scribbled to Eyre across the top of the page.[104] And although inaccuracies, corrected in London, in some of his early papers are merely those of an officer unfamiliar with his subject, it is possible to detect occasionally in later papers a slightly excessive pro-Partisan slant.[105] As Dennis Laskey of the Foreign Office commented in July of one of Eyre's recent situation reports: 'Rather too favourable to LNC, to whom no political objectives are attributed.'[106] But by then, as that comment suggests, it was obvious to the Foreign Office that the Partisan leaders wished to replace the old order. Moreover, whatever Eyre's opinions and politics, the key decision-makers had a solid enough picture of Britain's priorities at that moment and of what was happening in the field.

Given the disarming honesty of *The God Trip* and his evident pride in his past and beliefs, it might be wondered whether Eyre, if he felt he had led an exciting and effective double life in Bari, would not have resisted the temptation to say so. For while the brief passage quoted above is all Eyre recorded of his time in the Albanian section, he was effusive when describing his subsequent service and political activity in the Far East and clearly considered that later period worthier of note. 'Towards the end of the war, independently and without any political affiliations, I began working secretly with the nationalist movements in Burma, India, Malaya and Indonesia, as indeed were many in the armed forces at that time. We were consumed with the vision of one world and one people, without exploitation of man by man, a world at peace.'

He wrote a booklet entitled 'Why Burma?' and had it circulated among British troops 'to prevent our forces being used politically to crush the nationalist movement'. He spent many evenings 'in the rattan-walled home of Thakin Than Tun, General Secretary of the Communist Party of Burma . . . I smuggled Thakin Soe into India as my interpreter to meet P. C. Joshi, General Secretary of the Communist

Party of India, in the days before Soe formed his own party.' It was in Indonesia that Eyre felt he achieved 'the climax of these covert activities':

> Here I was public relations adviser to Generals [Christison] and Mansergh, master of all I surveyed in psychological warfare and Far Eastern publicity, answerable to no one. For a while I was in charge of Radio Djakarta, responsible for broadcasting programmes on two world wavelengths, with five different orchestras at my command. With a total monopoly in Surabaja – all the printing works, and newsprint stocks were in my hands; I was publishing all the newspapers; I had a radio broadcasting station built to broadcast exactly what I pleased – what was to stop me? I caused the mutiny of a British artillery regiment and the withdrawal of an Indian brigade. I published Mao Tse Tung's thesis on New Democracy in three languages from a copy smuggled out of China . . . I spent half a million pounds of Japanese banana money in four months to help the cause.
>
> I was aged twenty-seven and not even an official communist . . . My final venture was a daily Digest quoting world news picked out of the air by a radio-monitoring service manned by Dutchmen, Eurasians and White Russians whom I had found in the Japanese concentration camps. Every scrap of disastrous news, every report of a further collapse of the capitalist system in France, Holland, Italy, all round the world, I featured for the benefit of the English-speaking officers, NCOs and headquarters staff. My Digest rattled with the sound of tumbrils and doomsday.

But Eyre had 'over-reached' himself. 'I was summoned by General Mansergh, who explained with the utmost courtesy and patience that sometimes democracy must be withdrawn in order to defend democracy. He ordered that from now on everything I was putting out must be censored first by himself.' This was 'too much' for Eyre. He was 'long overdue for demobilisation' and had plans to marry a girl he had met in Indonesia, the survivor of a Japanese concentration camp. There was also 'the world of social revolution and socialism in Britain to explore'. So he 'got hold of an aeroplane' and flew to Singapore, where he married by special licence and was demobilised 'in full honour since no one knew what I had been doing'.[107]

Again SOE records corroborate some of this. In April 1945 he arrived at the Ceylon headquarters of Force 136, SOE's Far East section. A report that June has him in Burma as a political warfare officer attached to the British Twelfth Army. 'This officer has made a good start'; he seemed 'hard-working and conscientious'. Another note that September recorded that Eyre had been promoted major and was leaving SOE to join a Psychological Warfare Division team attached to Allied forces liberating Java.[108] Dutch records confirm that, from October 1945, a 'Major J. Eyre' of 'PWD' was in command of Allied Forces Radio in Batavia. Both PWD and the Far Eastern Publicity Detachment, into which it merged, were criticised habitually by the Dutch authorities for their apparent sympathy with Indonesian nationalism.[109]

As for Eyre's later life, he did stand as a communist in North Kensington, both in a by-election in 1949 and in a general election, although that was in 1950, not 1945, as others have supposed, or 1951, as he would remember it. His growing interest in spirituality and mysticism are also confirmed independently in print. In 1970, the journalist and psychic investigator Dennis Bardens employed Eyre as a case study in a published discussion about various spiritual and mystical matters, and described him as a writer married to a Dutch woman whose brother had been killed by the Japanese.[110] Although Bardens lost contact with him after that, Eyre remained active for some time in new age and spiritualist circles. He died in 1988.

10

'WHY SHOULD WE ATTACK THEM NOW?'

SOME post-war accounts of SOE's work in Albania paint a picture of total Partisan inactivity as the Germans, from the summer of 1944, in line with their gradual withdrawal from the Balkans, began to pull their men out of the country.[1] Like the image of a betrayed Abas Kupi, this is some way wide of the mark. Despite the fact that elements of the 1st Division had been detached from the battle and launched against the Zogists, the Partisans maintained effective pressure on the Germans well into the autumn. 'Communist attacks on German vehicles even in the immediate neighbourhood of Tirana,' a German intelligence officer in the city told Berlin in August. 'Losses of men and material. There are shootings here every night.'[2] A month later the situation was worse. 'Central and Southern Albania completely dominated by Communist groups apart from a few traffic roads . . . Attacks all the time . . . Red bands are fully mobilised . . . Please ring up Prague 75835 and tell them I'm all right.'[3] What remains clear is that the Partisans did become progressively less willing to expend bullets and energy on an enemy which would, very shortly, be gone; for the British, they also became increasingly difficult to deal with.

The Partisans became noticeably more awkward after the sudden arrival in August at Partisan headquarters of a two-man Soviet mission. This had dropped into northern Greece and marched north and, though the mission held no brief to bring in stores, the Partisans were thrilled to have it. 'The Ptz [sic] began to fire every available weapon they had on hand for a period of two hours,' Nick Kukich, whom OSS had dropped back in, wrote of the mission's reception: 'at first we thought that the war had ended.'[4] In command was Major Ivanov, an electrical engineer before the war and very much a soldier. 'In most of his speeches he urges the Partisans to keep up the fight and keeps off the subject of politics,' Marcus Lyon reported. 'I would not say that Major Ivanov is playing a very deep political game or, if he is, he is a very good actor. He impresses one with his frankness and his open friendly manners, and he always swears he is not a politician.'[5] Still, as Stefan informed Fultz, once Ivanov and his w/t operator had arrived the Partisans made 'every effort' to extol 'the deeds of Russia and the Red Army' while noting British and American successes only 'in passing'.[6] Relations between Ivanov and SOE and OSS officers were excellent, as they were with a small Yugoslav liaison mission, under Colonel Velimir Stojnic, which arrived a few weeks later.

One particular stumbling block with the Partisans concerned the deployment of small units of British raiding and reconnaissance troops. Looking on from Italy, Brigadier George Davy's Land Forces Adriatic, a sub-unit of the Balkan Air Force, had been keen for some time to send in small teams of Special Boat Service and Long Range Desert Group (LRDG) troops to block and harass German units withdrawing from Greece. Hoxha was reluctant to let them operate, however, and, when he finally allowed them in, was unwilling to help them much. 'Apparently they feel that they might be shown up,' Stefan told Fultz, after he and Palmer discussed the matter with senior Partisans. 'Furthermore I am of the impression that they do not want the Huns to be destroyed too soon. At least not until they get the maximum amount of arms.'[7]

What caused the greatest tension and suspicion of British motives, however, was the continued presence of SOE missions with Kupi and other Nationalists. Barely had the FNC delegates in Bari reached their military agreement with the Balkan Air Force in August than Hoxha issued a formal demand that McLean and Smiley leave the country at once. If they did not do so and the Partisans captured them, he warned, they would be tried as 'agents of foreign reactionaries who are organising the fight against the Pzns'.[8] Under pressure from Bari and SOE officers with him, Hoxha withdrew his allegations and threats but McLean and his mission remained uneasy about whether this was enough to ensure their safety. 'Reports from Nat sources persist that Partisan patrols have received orders to shoot all BLOs with Kupi,' McLean reported in September.[9] Bari's reply that 'Hoxha would be risking too much if he attempted anything but correct treatment' did little to quell concerns.[10] Already, by then, Hoxha's men had overrun Alan Hare and Ian Merrett's mountain bases: Hare was disarmed, marched away and passed into the care of SOE officers with the Partisans; Merrett, with Jenkins and Jones, escaped to rejoin McLean and the others. Rumours soon reached McLean that the Partisans had orders to shoot them if they found them; Merrett felt compelled to ask Bari for permission to fight 'should Partisans attempt take BLOs and material under protection'.[11] Further north, Tony Neel, who had been rejoined by John Hibberdine, was hearing Partisan stories 'that Captain Hibberdine and I were exiles from England and we had taken an aeroplane and come into Albania on our own initiative. That we were with Nik Sokoli because we were afraid to go anywhere else, we were Fascists and traitors, and that we should be killed.' A little later 'we received an unsigned letter written in English, saying that we called ourselves Englishmen, working for the Allies, but we had worked only for the Fascists and should we fall into the hands of the Partisans we should expect no mercy. We would be treated as traitors and not only killed but also tortured beforehand.'[12]

After the war, in speeches and in print, Enver Hoxha would claim that British officers in Albania had worked with the Germans; Tony Neel, he said, had even proposed 'that they should fight together against the partisans'.[13] The claim is absurd and typical of Hoxha: his memoirs are shot through with lies and fantasy. Still, it is not impossible that this allegation had its root, albeit twisted, in rumours that reached the Partisans of Neel's genuine contact in 1944 with a German called Fred Brandt. It is a remarkable story in its own right and merits a few lines here.

Neel had made contact with Brandt in April, after hearing from Nik Sokoli, in whose remote village he was then living, that there was a German soldier in the mountains who had learnt of Neel's presence and wanted to meet him. The German was keen to desert, Sokoli said. Neel agreed to a meeting and, on 11 April, was in Sokoli's home, playing cards with his interpreter, an Italian soldier called Napolitani, when the door opened and in walked a German lance-corporal, tall and fair with a moustache and jutting jaw, accompanied by two Tajiks in German uniform. 'They were all armed with sub-machine guns which they placed on the floor,' Neel recorded. 'Brandt was carrying his cap and he smiled and offered me his hand which I took. He was dressed in khaki drill tunic and service grey slacks and his cap was Afrika Corps drill . . . [T]he ribbon of the German Iron Cross [was] in his top button-hole.'[14]

Everyone sat down. Neel produced some cognac. 'Conversation was rather difficult because Brandt would speak to Sokoli in Serbian, Sokoli, whose Serbian is very bad, would translate into Italian, which was worse, and Napolitani spoke to me in English.' Neel asked Brandt 'his name, number, rank, regiment, etc, and what were his intentions'. Brandt explained that he was a Leningrad-born Baltic German, had served in the Brandenburgers, an elite unit attached to the Abwehr, Germany's military intelligence service, and was now commanding a small Tajik unit in the mountains not far away. 'He gave me to understand that he was prepared to desert at once with four soldiers, but if I wished he could return to his unit and try to get many more . . . He said he was an entomologist in private life and as "proof" he produced a glass bottle from his pocket in which were a few "specimens".' After an hour and a half the meeting broke up and Brandt and his men departed.[15]

Two weeks later, they met a second time. Brandt reiterated 'that he was very anxious to remain with me and give all the help he could'. He chatted again about butterflies, said he had an uncle in London and impressed Neel as 'a very intelligent man of good education'. He also said that although his superiors, stationed in Kosovo, wished him to capture the British heard to be with Sokoli, he had no intention of doing so. Another fortnight passed. Then, with an Albanian bodyguard supplied by Sokoli, Neel visited Brandt's camp, a strongpoint a few miles away. 'We talked for a while, had a drink or two and a little food and he showed me his collection of butterflies.' Neel also noted how well equipped was Brandt's little group. 'Each man had an S.M.G. and a pistol and Brandt had binoculars, compass, maps, complete clothing with waterproof capes and the food we had was of good quality. They also had two Bren guns, a 1½" mortar and ammo.'[16]

In late May, Neel marched south for a meeting with Billy McLean and, at McLean's request, brought along Brandt and two Tajiks. Also present when the parties met were Julian Amery and John Hibberdine, both German-speakers, and Amery would recall how open and frank Brandt had seemed. When he had been conscripted into the German Army, Brandt said, his command of several Central Asian languages, acquired while an entomologist in pre-war Persia and Afghanistan, had soon attracted interest and seen him join a mission to Afghanistan to win over the Fakir of Ipi. When that mission failed he had returned to Germany, been assigned as an interpreter to the Tajiks and found himself posted to the Balkans. And now, he explained, since Germany's war seemed lost, he wished to desert. 'At the end of it all,' Neel reported, 'we all decided that Brandt was, on the surface, genuine enough and that it was unlikely, although of course not impossible, that he was still an active agent.'[17] McLean noted in his diary how the Tajiks, 'in the rather dim candle and lamplight, looked sinister and interesting. Both were continually smiling.'[18] Discussions over, Neel, taking Hibberdine and Harry Button, returned to the north and set up a fresh forest camp. Brandt, with fifteen Tajiks, joined him there in July.

In Bari, reading Neel's signals from Albania, British field security officers were less trusting. 'The German opposite number to SOE has always been very much more interested in and successful at political subversion than physical sabotage,' one officer warned SOE's Albanian section in August. 'Moreover, German intelligence services have had a great deal of experience in the running of double-agents and penetrators of various types. They are prepared to run considerable risks and to pay out handsomely in the form of information and even acts of sabotage if they see some ultimate larger gain in prospect.' It was quite possible, he thought, that Brandt was being employed 'with the object of compromising Neel locally with undesirable and reactionary elements among the population'.[19] Jon Naar, who had worked on counter-intelligence operations in Syria and Lebanon and instructed on the subject at the Helwan intelligence school, shared these concerns. While there was certainly 'a variety of disenchanted Volksdeutsch and other "unreliables" in Albania, it was extremely rare for a "true" German soldier or officer to desert,' he remembers. 'I warned Neel's mission as to the likelihood that Brandt was a German agent and that he should be handled with kid gloves for any suspicious behaviour. We also took care not to send Neel's mission sensitive material that could fall into enemy hands.'[20]

After sending to Cairo and India for help in corroborating Brandt's tales, field security in Bari heard back 'that at any rate up to the time of his adventures in Afghanistan' Brandt had worked as an Abwehr agent. 'His position appears to have been more important than that merely of interpreter and, according to one source, he held in 1939 the rank of Colonel in the Luftwaffe.' SOE was now urged to invite Brandt

to desert and come to Italy forthwith. 'In view of his past career and
certain aspects of his present activity . . . there are strong reasons for
supposing that he may still be acting as an Abwehr agent.'[21] More
warnings were sent to Neel, who recalled years later:

> I was sending back messages on our radio which the other
> chaps brought up, saying I'd made contact with this German,
> and then one day my wireless operator, Button his name was,
> Corporal Button, he came in and he said, 'Got a message
> for you, sir.'
>   I said, 'What is it?'
>   He said, 'This man, Brandt, who you've contacted. Is he
> about five-foot-ten? Ginger-haired?' and so on and so on.
> 'Because if he is, he's a colonel in the Abwehr.'[22]

Neel told Brandt what Bari had said. Brandt agreed that it sounded
like him and offered to go at once to Italy. On the night of 12–13
October, in the rough seas that drowned Button and two of the Tajiks,
the party was taken out. Brandt was handed to field security, interrogated thoroughly, then flown to London under the name Fred Green
for further questioning by MI5. The belongings that followed him
included a rucksack, pins and tweezers and two sealed boxes 'containing
butterfly specimens'.[23]

Thirty years later, Brandt wrote an account of his Albanian
experiences that has been reproduced widely in books about the
Brandenburgers. In this he explained again how his pre-war knowledge
of Central Asia had seen him sent by the Abwehr to Afghanistan and
later assigned to the Balkans for work with Tajik troops. He also wrote
of being in touch in Albania with the British, though made no mention
of having orders to catch them or of any desire to desert. He was a
simple NCO, he said, dispatched to win friends among the mountain
tribes, and, when local leaders had implored him to persuade the British
to help them fight the communists, he had gone to Bari to plead on
their behalf.[24]

German records confirm that Brandt was not and never had been
an officer.[25] From his interrogation reports and the testimony of SOE
officers, however, it seems very clear that his orders in Albania were
indeed to capture any British he came across. 'Brandt's manner under
interrogation is open and helpful,' his interrogators in Bari observed.

'He considers he has had a raw deal from Abwehr and SD, does not regard himself as a true German, and therefore sees no reason why he should be reticent. He likes to lead an active, outdoor life and to work on his own, rather in the Lawrence tradition.'[26] He freely admitted how, as early as March 1944, after hearing from locals that a small British party was trying to get out to Montenegro, he had had every potential crossing point 'patrolled day and night by Tajiks'.[27] He also explained how rifles and ammunition had been distributed among local leaders and money offered as a reward for any British officer captured. Later, once he was in touch with the British, his commanders, whom he kept well informed of his progress, pressed him repeatedly to get on with rounding them up. And when John Hibberdine gave him three rolls of camera film, with the warning that they contained shots of British personnel, and asked him to develop them on his next trip to Shkodra, Brandt had two prints made of each negative and kept a secret set of copies for himself. Brandt also claimed that his Tajiks had become increasingly difficult to control, so keen were they on capturing the British.

'This account makes me shiver,' John Eyre wrote after reading Brandt's interrogation transcripts; 'our ALOs [Allied Liaison Officers] like sheep among wolves.'[28] Brandt's interrogators noted, though, how 'his motives and intentions are open to question and may even have undergone a change as the war progressed less favourably for Germany and his liaison with the British Mission became closer'.[29] One officer observed that while Brandt had had plenty of opportunities in Albania of 'either murdering or capturing the British officers with whom he was in contact' he had instead 'confided in them and came over to the Allied side'.[30] Another felt that Brandt seemed 'to have devoted his efforts almost exclusively to avoiding unpleasant jobs and to being left in peace in the mountains with his collection of butterflies and Tajiks'.[31]

As senior Partisans became more hostile to the British, they also became more focused on securing their route to power. In August 1944, while on the march with the 1st Division in northern Albania, Mustafa Gjinishi, the young communist with whom the British had first worked in 1940, was ambushed and killed. Victor Smith was with him when it happened. 'Mustafa and self separated from escort, ambushed by Hun patrol at range 10 yards,' he reported. 'First fire wounded Gjinishi but while assisting him to cover second burst killed him. Self unhurt.'[32]

Smith, whose cap badge was shot off in the ambush, did not believe that Gjinishi had been murdered, but it is generally believed today that the attackers were Albanians and that Hoxha, conscious of Gjinishi's popularity and wary of his relations with the British, had had him killed.

Not long after Gjinishi's death, the Partisans went after Gani Kryeziu. That summer, in contrast to Abas Kupi, Gani had come out to fight the Germans in exactly the way the British wanted. He did not lead the general revolt that some SOE officers had hoped for in 1940–41 and 1944: preoccupied, as ever, with the threat posed by the Partisans and unwilling to risk damaging reprisals, no other Nationalist leader was prepared to fight alongside him. Compared to the efforts of Hoxha's Partisans to the south and Tito's Partisans to the north, Gani's campaign was also tiny in scale. In consistency and commitment to Allied war aims, however, his efforts rivalled those of any Balkan guerrilla and impressed all on the British side who saw or heard of them. They seemed to confirm, too, the promise SOE had identified earlier both in Kosovo and in him. Gani was 'the outstanding political figure' in Kosovo, Peter Kemp had reported in March; he was 'very pro-British and seems a most able and intelligent man with a sound grasp of statecraft. I think he could do a great deal for us as he has great influence . . . and – what is rare in the Balkans – a high degree of integrity.'[33]

The fact that SOE ever re-established contact with the Kryezius was due partly to Billy McLean's renewed effort that spring to encourage Nationalists to fight. Since the ban on SOE operating in Kosovo remained in place, it also owed something to Gani's decision to base himself in the mountains of northern Albania. It owed most, however, to the fact that Gani, unique among Nationalists, was already committed to fighting and, when McLean met him in June, pledged himself willing to do anything the British asked. 'The Kryezius live as outlaws, publicly denounced by the Huns against whom they have recently fought two actions, killing seven and wounding four: they are thus the only Nats now fighting,' McLean told Bari. 'At present Gani has mobilised one hundred men, lacking means to maintain more.'[34] He had also circulated round Kosovo a declaration that 'our friends are the Allies and the only way to gain their favour is to fight now. In no other way can we hope to gain future independence and inclusion of Kosova [sic] in Albania. Let us unite regardless of party, clan or religion to show the world that we want our independence by helping the Allies to fight those nations who wish to domineer the smaller nations.'[35]

When Gani asked McLean for a British officer to be attached to him, McLean sent him Tony Simcox, who became as convinced as Kemp and McLean of his qualities. 'Gani, as an individual, has a most striking personality,' Simcox reported, 'and gives one the impression of genuineness and honesty. He is well educated, has travelled the world and is a perfect gentleman . . . What has really happened is that a very influential, well educated person has called together the true patriots . . . for the purpose of fighting the Germans in order to free his country, and at the same time gain for his country the right to receive a hearing in the Peace Conference.'[36]

Joining him in June, Simcox was quickly aware, as he wrote to Richard Riddell, that Gani was 'at war with the Huns'.[37] In a recent reprisal for earlier attacks the Germans had taken hostages, all relatives of Gani's men, from a village not far away; on 17 June, when another patrol returned to take more, a party of Gani's men, concealed outside the village, were waiting. Simcox was with them and watched as the patrol was ambushed and five Germans, or Russians in German service, were shot. Days later the Germans began hanging hostages and swept through the area with a larger force and set fire to a hundred homes. On 28 June, with another party of Gani's men, Simcox then dropped down to blow a bridge on the main Gjakova–Prizren road. A convoy of vehicles appeared just as everything was set, 'so the safety fuse, timed to last five minutes, was ignited', Simcox recorded. 'As luck would have it, the first lorry, containing the usual protective platoon of soldiers, was crossing the bridge as the explosion occurred.'[38] Eighteen were killed and others wounded. Two days after that, an attempt to surround and destroy Gani's mountain base left more than seventy German and quisling troops dead, wounded or missing.

'G.B. [Gani Bey Kryeziu] is very active and has killed some Huns in offensive raids and there is no doubt that he ought to receive some assistance,' Simcox told Tony Neel a week later. 'In the meantime he is spending his own fortune in supplying and maintaining about 100 men . . . It is difficult for him to carry out another raid until he can get the munitions . . . the last raid used all the rounds for the Bren and the men were forced to buy from the villagers of Deg a further supply.'[39] When Roy Bullock joined him in July with two thousand gold sovereigns and a w/t operator, Bill Collins, Simcox was able at last to re-equip Gani with stores

bought locally and request arms drops from Italy. In all nine sorties would
be sent. By the end of the month Gani was continually in action and
Simcox reporting a 'series of planned and successful actions which not
only proved Gani's genuineness but also gave him widespread publicity'.[40] In August raids and ambushes grew in scale and frequency, German
reprisals became ever more brutal and, despite the reprisals, Gani's force
doubled in size. Attacks on Simcox's dropping ground and Hasan Kryeziu's
camp were repelled. Gani's men overran the chrome mine at Kepenek,
destroyed the facilities, killed or captured more than fifty German and
quisling troops and freed seventy Montenegrin slave-workers. In response
more homes were burnt, more villagers murdered and more men hanged
in Gjakova. The Germans brought in a thousand Albanian volunteers
and several hundred troops of the SS 'Skanderbeg' Division, a short-lived
Albanian unit, raised mostly in Kosovo and of very limited ability, but
these apparently refused to fight Gani; some even deserted and joined
him.[41] By early September Gani had round him more than 1,500 men.

Decrypts, captured documents and other German records confirm
that Gani was considered throughout this period a genuine and active
threat. As early as April the Germans had put him and his estimated
three hundred supporters at the top of a list of 'Hostile Bands'.[42] In
June, pulled from an ambushed German staff car, a report by the
commander of the 297th Infantry Division described Gani as 'a pro-
British leader' who had attacked the Germans north of the Drin.[43] The
same month, German Intelligence heard that Gani was rumoured to be
preparing 'to destroy the chrome mines near Gjakova'. The Skanderbeg
Division and other quislings were being employed 'to liquidate the
guerilla band'.[44] And in mid-September Billy McLean reported the
contents of a bag of documents, found among the remains of an
ambushed German convoy, which included a warning from intelligence
officers in Prizren of an imminent attack by Gani on Gjakova itself.[45]

In September Gani did attack Gjakova. On the night of 10–11
September, from his bases in northern Albania, he and three hundred
men began the assault by over-running the strategic German camp and
mine at Zogaj, close to the border. Simcox went with them. 'I set our
only "long range" mortar up and bombarded the enemy camp and
positions (it was reported, later, by workers who left the mine, that the
first bomb killed four Germans) and our forces advanced from two
directions, under considerable fire. It was a very brave advance (such
as I could not before credit the Albanians for) under heavy enemy

mortar and M.G. fire and had the effect of causing the enemy to withdraw in disorder.' By the evening of 12 September Gani's force had
dropped down to the plain, forced the Germans back into Gjakova
and reached the town's edge. 'Two mortars were set up and with captured
ammo we bombed the enemy outposts. Soon after nightfall our forward
troops announced their arrival on the outskirts of Gjakova by setting
fire to the barracks [and] petrol and ammo dumps.' Next morning 'a
savage counter attack' by heavy German reinforcements 'using several
75mm guns and mortars and countless M.G. 42s' forced Gani back
into the mountains.

As Gani rested his men and planned for a second assault, Simcox
left for his own camp to call in more supplies. But on the heels of the
German withdrawal, elements of the Partisan 1st Division had arrived
in the mountains nearby and now these set about bringing Gani's efforts
to an end. Its first step, to sever his contact with the British, led to a
remarkable confrontation on the morning of 19 September when a
forward party 'armed to the teeth with British L.M.G.s, rifles, etc'
walked unannounced into Simcox's camp. The commander instructed
Simcox to leave at once 'for identification' by senior Partisans in the
south. 'I replied that I intended to do no such thing and that if he
thought his precious staff thought I would do my duty better with their
permission then they must send the authority to me by courier.' When
the commander insisted, Simcox told him he took orders only from his
superiors 'and that should I receive orders from these to proceed south
I would do so, but I did not wish to be escorted by a crowd of hooli-
gans such as were commanded by him. This made him almost as angry
as I and had the effect of making him issue the threat that I WOULD
be ready in two hours and WOULD accompany him south.' Simcox
retired to his tent.

When the time limit had expired, the commander, now feeling
very bold, entered my tent, where I reclined on my bed,
reading old messages. He asked me if I had prepared everything for the journey, and, on receiving the reply that I had
not, and had not any intention of making any journey,
stamped out of my tent and very angrily issued orders in
Albanian. In an inconceivably short time, I found myself
sitting in the ruins of my tent and when I eventually extri-
cated myself I was met with a scene of much activity. My

whole camp had been struck and was swarming with
Partisans, some hastily eating my lunch, others generously
helping themselves to the supplies from the cook house, and
the reserves of comforts and my supply of raki, while others
were bundling material together to load on to mules. I made
feeble attempts to stop this chaos as did my Italians and
Albanians, but had to give up and attend to the salvage of
my personal belongings. It was fairly obvious that these gang-
sters intended to carry out their threats and I must move
south – with the hope that they, at a later date, would be
made to pay for their amusement.

Roy Bullock escaped the roundup but Bill Collins, Said Kryeziu and
Lazar Fundo were also at Simcox's camp and forced to follow him
south. The march lasted days. Simcox was forbidden to use his w/t set
and had his kit looted and his mules stolen. When a stop was made,
heavily armed Partisans surrounded him 'in case I should try to break
away'.[46] Another time Lazar Fundo was hauled out, tried as a rene-
gade communist, and, in front of Simcox, stripped, stretched across a
rock and flayed to death. Eventually Simcox and Collins were turned
over to SOE officers and evacuated safely to Italy.

Said Kryeziu, too, was given to the British and taken to Italy. He
was fortunate to get out. In early 1945, Hasan, the third Kryeziu brother,
still in Kosovo, was among several of Gani's followers in Gjakova who,
with the Germans long gone and the communists in control, were
rounded up and murdered, their bodies being tipped down a well. As
for Gani, for some months the British heard only continued Partisan
claims to be willing to do business with him and the occasional story
that he had joined a Partisan brigade. Philip Broad, watching events
from Italy, wondered hopefully: 'if it should go well with him it will
be an indication of the sincerity of the FNC's professions that all men
who have taken a patriotic stand against the Germans are welcome. It
will also show that a conservative leader can, without fear, offer his
allegiance to the FNC.'[47] Only in April 1945 did a credible report reach
the British that Gani was a prisoner of the Yugoslavs.[48]

The British response was immediate. Ralph Stevenson, Ambassador
in Belgrade, twice pressed Tito personally for information, first in April,
then in May, before extracting an ominous statement in June. Gani was
indeed in prison, the Yugoslav Foreign Ministry admitted; he was also,

technically speaking, a Yugoslav citizen.[49] The implication was clear: this was a domestic affair and the British should mind their own business. 'In these circumstances do you wish me to press the matter any further?' Stevenson asked London.[50] 'I agree that [the] extent to which we can intervene is limited but I do not wish to abandon Kryeziu's case without making a further effort on his behalf,' Douglas Howard replied. Stevenson should explain that 'Kryeziu has rendered us considerable services and we know that he has worked wholeheartedly for the Allied cause. We cannot remain indifferent to his fate since it is not our practice to abandon our friends. We hope therefore that his case will be dealt with promptly and that if the Yugoslav authorities have charges to make against him these will be investigated without delay and that his record will be taken into account in his favour.'[51]

Stevenson spoke to the Yugoslavs. Nothing happened. Months passed. Then news filtered out that Gani was to be tried for murdering Serbs, collaborating with the Germans and causing unnecessary deaths during his assault on Gjakova in 1944. Not long afterwards the British Embassy heard that he had been sentenced to five years' hard labour.[52] The Foreign Office protested. Evidence challenging every charge was obtained from Simcox and other officers and plucked from old SOE files and forwarded through the Embassy.[53] Again nothing happened. In May 1946 the Embassy heard that 'it was probable that in about six or twelve months Gani would be amnestied'.[54] In 1948 the Yugoslav Foreign Minister declared that Gani was not in fact going to be amnestied.[55] In Kosovo it is thought that Gani died in prison in 1951.[56]

'We have let the Nationalists of Albania down,' Simcox wrote on arriving in Bari, 'especially Gani Kryeziu, who has fought well and is sacrificing more than any communist . . . Allowing the communists to kill, attack, or provoke their political enemies with our supplies is as bad as doing it ourselves.' The British, Simcox argued, should have stopped sending supplies to the FNC 'the moment they used them against their political enemies' and promptly 'increased supplies to people like Gani'. If that had been done, he felt, 'the nationalists of the north would have ranged themselves behind Gani, fought the Germans well without interfering with the FNC and then claimed to be recognised as a government'.[57] Such proposals, though, assumed too much of the willingness of policy-makers to shift their focus from military gain to political intervention: the decision to continue arming the Partisans that summer was no less pragmatic than that taken in January to bring

Kemp's work in Kosovo to a close. Reading Simcox's report, David Talbot Rice remarked that 'there is no doubt that Kryeziu was a far more attractive individual than were most of the FNC leaders and he was prepared to take action without any long term political ends in view but we should, I think, consider the big picture of successful FNC Partisans operating in the south . . . and of Tito and his Jugoslavs, operating to the north. This, I think puts the situation into a truer perspective, however one may sympathise with Simcox's attitude.'[58]

Another feature of the summer and autumn, as SOE was withdrawing its missions from the Nationalists, was an influx of SOE officers and NCOs to strengthen existing missions with the Partisans. Captain Bertie Wright, another of Trotsky Davies' Royal Ulster Rifles officers, who had been in for a month before the German June offensive swept him out, returned in July. A carpet salesman from Belfast, whom Marcus Lyon remembered as 'a fiery little man with an RAF moustache', Wright was soon busy among the peaks southwest of Korça, calling in air strikes and blowing up roads.[59] Dare Newell, too, came back in July, while Hugh Munro was dropped in August with Jack Dumoulin, the latter to organise a hospital above Borsh and Munro to work on the coast with Newell, and Captain E.C.G. Harlow parachuted in to work with Johnny Shaw. In September, Mike Thornton, a Royal Tank Regiment major with an MC won in North Africa, was dropped to replace Victor Smith as senior officer with the new Partisan 1st Corps, comprising the six brigades of the 1st and 2nd Divisions; Smith moved south to rejoin Alan Palmer. Major Philip Oliver was sent in the same month for attachment to the 1st Division, Lieutenant Rowland Winn was dropped at Biza, breaking his leg on landing, and Lieutenant Tony Andrew parachuted to Alan Hare in the Peza hills. Lieutenant Peter Payne of MI6 was also dropped in September, joining Palmer and Lyon in the south; the MI6 presence was still tiny: Payne and his w/t operator were effectively it. Three more captains, Eric Bishop, J.P. Durcan and Bill Squires, and Lieutenants Wilkinson, Whyte, Raynbird and Lawson all arrived in October. By then, with most outlying towns in Partisan hands and the final garrisons shrinking, several of the new arrivals found there was little fighting to see or do. Winn's injury prevented him from seeing or doing much at all; it would not, however, stop him from becoming a vocal critic both of the Partisans and of Britain's support for them.

Certainly some FNC units were of poor quality. Trying that summer to blow a stretch of road at Barmash, Johnny Shaw, attached to the reformed 2nd Brigade, saw the Partisans at their foot-dragging and fat-headed worst. The road at that point had been a target agreed with the Partisan delegation in Bari; the plan was for Shaw to lay his explosives while the 2nd Brigade destroyed a nearby German garrison and held off reinforcements until his job was done. But weeks of quibbling over minor points of detail convinced him that the brigade 'did not like the idea at all' and, in fact, the attack never came off. The brigade's aversion to fighting was underlined, he felt, by its pathetic record for August of 'four Germans killed, one mail lorry captured and one civilian lorry destroyed'. He also challenged the brigade's claim to have fought a series of later actions. 'One night the Second Brigade put the Vickers machine guns into position 2,000 yards away from Leskovic, and let off about a belt each into the town. They sent a communication to General Staff that the forces of the Second Brigade had attacked Leskovic but that enemy casualties were not known.'[60]

Other brigades, however, were more impressive. In July, shortly before he appealed to Bari for arms for the 1st Brigade, Richard Riddell had watched one of its battalions attack the town of Peshkopi, held by a joint force of German and quisling troops. 'It was apparent at once that they possessed good organisation and discipline, unknown in the old days' he reported.

> The distribution of ammunition was quick, every man was fed, and then at the pre-arranged time the leading company formed up into squads, was checked and moved off. Every company commander had a whistle, and used it to summon his company. This discipline was all the more impressive as the battalion was entirely in rags, practically no men had boots, and many had nothing on their feet at all. They had had little to eat and were exhausted after many days forced marches and recent heavy fighting . . .
>
> At about 3pm the fighting started and continued until dusk when the Partisans withdrew according to plan. Until this time they had maintained their positions against continued attack, without apparent worry and little expenditure of ammunition; until they withdrew they suffered no casualties, during the withdrawal they had one killed, one wounded.

The opposing forces suffered 26 killed or wounded. One
could see at a glance that these partisans were experienced,
steady fighters.[61]

In the subsequent battle for Dibra, in which the 1st Division, with aerial
support from the Balkan Air Force, took the leading part, the Germans
may have lost as many as four hundred killed by the end of August,
when the town finally fell to the Partisans.

The standard of some of the enemy units engaged ought also to be
noted. 'The German soldier in Albania is no less good than the rest of
the Wehrmacht,' Brian Ensor felt.

He fights with great courage and success. He is very well
disciplined and never considers the position lost. He
is extremely fit physically, well clothed and equipped. He is
master of all his weapons and uses them to their best advantage . . . Like all dangerous bullies he is physically brave and
now that the day of retribution is drawing near he is fighting
a last desperate battle no less bravely than before.

Punishment battalions and non-Germans pressed into German service
were also encountered. These did show the effects of poor health, imprisonment and maltreatment and did not fight as well as the regular
Wehrmacht, but nor were many deserting or giving themselves up
without a fight. Fear of reprisals on their families played a part but if
'a non-German is in a trench with Germans he must in self-defence do
his best. If the Germans are fighting hard and he makes an attempt to
give in or even hesitates, he will be shot.'[62]

Ensor was on hand that summer to watch a British commando raid
both underline the enemy's quality and give effective encouragement to
local Partisans. The aim of the raid was to destroy a German garrison
dug into the hills behind Himara, an operation, it was hoped, that would
stimulate and encourage local Partisans and compel the enemy to reinforce the coast. The British force, mostly from 2 Commando and the
Highland Light Infantry, sailed across from Monopoli and landed at a
concealed cove south of Himara on the night of 28 July. The attack went
in the following morning. Although the German positions were eventually overrun, British losses were seventeen killed and sixty-one wounded,
testimony, George Davy wrote later, to the 'extremely difficult country'

and the 'ferocity of the defence'. The German troops encountered had been in excellent positions, well dug in and well armed. 'Their morale was high, and they fought with fierce determination, refusing to surrender, dying at close quarters. It is noteworthy how many casualties were inflicted by hand-grenades.'[63] The Germans, men from the 297th Infantry Division, the principal force in southern Albania, lost forty killed and more than thirty wounded; twenty-five were captured. One commando report noted that they were 'for the great part young and of good physique' and their 'morale and bearing were of a high order. The quality and dash of our own troops is reflected in the degree of success they gained against such determined and well planned opposition.'[64] British methods, meanwhile, had 'dumbfounded' the watching Partisan 12th Brigade, Ensor observed.

> The way the British managed by night to take up positions so close to the enemy and then suddenly appear at dawn was new and, until they saw it happen, considered impossible by them. The bravery, discipline and excellent control shown by the British caused much admiration, as indeed it should. The Partisans were astonished at the way the British troops advanced in a perfect line, standing erect and oblivious of the intense fire. They considered the operation a masterly exhibition of how to fight . . . The effect was a tremendous boost of Partisan morale and obvious improvement in their methods of fighting.

When the British left that evening, the surviving Germans withdrew into woodland where the Partisans killed or captured them all. By the end of the day the whole area was under Partisan control and thirty-eight more German soldiers had been taken prisoner, almost all of them 'slightly wounded, very shaken and bewildered'.[65] When the German garrisons in Vlora and Saranda dispatched strong columns to retake Himara, the Partisans resisted three drives before a fourth broke through; after further Partisan attacks, this, too, withdrew.

A second raid took place in the autumn, beginning on 22 September, when 2 Commando, 40 (Royal Marine) Commando and support units began landing in a sheltered bay just north of Saranda. The plan was to be ashore for thirty-six hours, seize the port, harass the Germans and sever the road inland. In the end the force stayed for a month.

Fresh plans to isolate the German garrison on Corfu were largely
responsible for the extension but constant enemy shelling, awkward
terrain and terrible weather also caused problems and delays: 'over
130 personnel had to be evacuated to Italy suffering from exposure,
exhaustion and trench feet', one commando report reads. Nevertheless,
when the main assault was made on 9 October, results were judged
excellent and there was good Partisan–British cooperation. After 'fierce
street fighting' and the loss of fifteen commandos killed, the port was
in British hands and 750 prisoners were taken. Partisans of the 12th
and 14th Brigades were on hand to assist and did their allotted jobs
well. 'No special difficulties arose,' the commandos noted, 'and the
Partizans carried out whatever they undertook to do, with none of
those last minute changes of plan which this Bde has experienced
from Partizan forces in previous ops in this theatre'. Supported by
British artillery they attacked their targets 'with the utmost determination'.[66] Also impressive, on the eve of the final assault on Saranda,
was a Partisan attack on a strong German motorised column that had
set out from the port to eliminate a commando reconnaissance party:
the column was driven back with confirmed losses of well over one
hundred.

The length of time that that force remained in the country heightened Partisan suspicions about its presence and put relations under
further strain. That the British managed to keep the Partisans harnessed
at all to the wider war effort had a great deal to do with Alan Palmer's
success at maintaining an effective working relationship with Hoxha.
It was no small achievement. In late September, Palmer, then still with
the Shtab but about to leave for Italy for a rest, scribbled a letter to
Bari that gives some sense of the difficulties:

> This business over special troops is quite fantastic. The present
> game is to play for time – it's a game I'm rather impatient
> over. If nothing starts happening tomorrow I shall 'get in
> there' again. I'm fast getting in the mood in which I may say
> or do almost anything, so you have been warned . . .
>
> When I saw Hoxha on 22nd he said 'I have a protest to
> make'. I replied to the effect that this was nothing new and
> what was it this time. Imagine my surprise when he said
> 'we understand you are leaving Albania'. They don't miss
> much . . .

I am at the moment speechless with rage at Hox [sic]. As the direct result of his hanging fire over SBS we have missed the boat over Barmash again and now the Huns are streaming through. I had a cosy chat with him this morning. He claims to have ordered all out action up the road. We shall see . . .

I have sent Marcus to Perat to establish an OP so I hope we shall be passing some hot messages on the emergency skeds. The Pzns have made a balls-up over sending the telephone wire to the wrong place – pure carelessness. So I've pinched 2 of their No 22 sets for our own w/t link Perat to here. That may teach them to be more careful . . .

I had a long heart-to-heart with Johnny S. [Shaw] . . . He has the misfortune to have a very moderate Bde (2nd) with him which is rather discouraging for anyone. He wants to go [to the Far] East when he can and I suggest that, when the Korca road ceases to be quite so important, he should be given the opportunity to pull out even if his 6 months here is not completed. His feelings may have changed by then. They do sometimes . . .

Your signal that the commando raid on Saranda was NOT taking place was a bit inopportune. I passed it on to the big boys just ½ hour before they got their own report that the [landings] had taken place. Can you please persuade Davy not to put me in such embarrassing positions more often than necessary? What happened?[67]

'I think Alan Palmer has not been fully recognised as the remarkable man he was,' Marcus Lyon reflected. 'All who worked with him admired him tremendously. He was wise, caring, diplomatic, but great fun. There was never a dull moment when he was around.'[68] Palmer's superiors also thought highly of him. 'By now you will have had ample opportunity to talk to Alan Palmer whom I am sure you will have found interesting,' Bill Harcourt wrote to Talbot Rice in late October, by which time Palmer had come out and been flown to London on leave. 'Although latterly he has been at very close quarters with [the Partisan] General Staff, he has managed to keep a sense of proportion which is very creditable and I consider that he has the soundest views of any of our BLOs in the country.'[69] Colin Gubbins, who had met Palmer a fortnight before, was also impressed: 'such a nice, sensible chap. He has

done a really good job and in my opinion deserves a DSO.'[70] The award
came through in 1945.

Written up at the end of 1944, the experiences of Tony Northrop
provide a good illustration of how, in the final months of the occupation, though the military results from continued contact were mixed,
SOE remained able to secure Partisan assistance and carry out operations.

Half-Irish and Heswall-born, Northrop was the young lieutenant
who had been dropped with Marcus Lyon in December 1943. Then
barely twenty-one, he was probably the youngest officer sent out to
the country but colleagues found him impressive. 'Tall and physically
very strong,' he seemed to Lyon 'the typical athlete' and 'the perfect
SOE type'.[71] Withdrawn from Borsh in June and promoted captain,
Northrop had parachuted back in at Leshnja in July. Alan Palmer then
charged him with leading a team in to eastern Albania and the mountains and valleys of Mokra, to liaise with Partisans there and to do
what he could to harass the retreating Germans as they passed through
on their way north from Greece. With him went Lieutenant Tommy
Renfree, a twenty-five-year-old South African from the Natal Mounted
Rifles who had played top-flight rugby before the war, and a young
w/t operator, Corporal Cole of the Royal Tank Regiment, both of whom
had just arrived by parachute. Mokra was thirty miles away. Three
days of hard marching followed, much of it in torrential rain. In one
village en route they spent the night in the graveyard, 'as the only
houses available were buggier than usual'.

In Mokra the party based itself in the little monastery near Llenga
that had been home to Andy Hands and David Smiley the previous
summer. Signals were sent to Bari requesting explosives and weapons
and seven sorties safely received. Contact was also made with the
Partisans of the nearby 15th Brigade. From the start talks were awkward.
Northrop asked for their help in destroying his first target: a stretch
of road among the hairpin bends twisting up to Qafa e Thanës, a mountain pass high above Lake Ohrid's western shore. Blowing the road at
that point, it was hoped, would hobble the German withdrawal by
severing a principal route to the north. But though the Shtab had
approved the action and the brigade's participation, the brigade
commander demanded confirmation. He also wanted arms: 'far more
than was necessary'. Northrop also had problems with the commander's

commissar, whose 'whole attitude was one of anti-co-operation . . . On several occasions he made disparaging remarks regarding our aid and tried to tell me that I was there as a Quarter-Master just to receive stores for the Pzns.' Once assured of air support, the brigade finally agreed to help.

On a late August evening, 'straining our ears and praying the RAF would arrive', Northrop, Renfree and the Partisans were in position. 'At 1815 hrs we heard them. Beaufighters. What a roar went up from the Pzns.' With the nearby German barracks on fire and the Partisans 'in the highest spirits', the two officers took twenty men down to the road. Ten small beehive charges, staggered ten yards apart, were placed in position and blown, making small holes in which Northrop placed and blew ten more. Picks and shovels then made the holes deeper. For the 'big blow' three twenty-five pound tins of Ammonal explosive were put in each hole, rigged with primers, linked with Cortex and detonated. By then, alerted by the exploding beehives, nearby German posts were machine-gunning the road and Northrop was having difficulty keeping the Partisans at work. First some of the digging party withdrew; then the protection force moved off without telling the men on the road, leaving Northrop and Renfree sitting there as the Germans poured down it 'a veritable hail of MG fire'. Later, crossing another road on their way back to camp, they were fired on again. This time the Partisans fled 'in such panic' that Northrop was knocked down. 'This was the nearest I had been to being hurt during the whole night.' The only men for whom he had any praise were a commissar 'who worked exceedingly well on the road' and a battalion commander who 'told the men who had rushed back from the road what they had done was disgraceful for Pzns, and what would the English think of them'.

Eighty yards of road had been destroyed, though a blow like that was never likely to be permanent as enemy engineers were always expected to make repairs. Still, since the Partisans had repeatedly assured Northrop that no repairs on the road had yet started, it was a shock when the brigade commissar reported three days later that the Germans were already reusing it. 'He would give no explanation as to why we had been told a pack of lies, and after a few more words on his part as to why BLOs were in the country he left.'

September was spent blowing the Korça–Ohrid road in various places and with better Partisan cooperation. At the end of the month, hoping to blow it where it curled round Lake Ohrid's eastern shore, Northrop

found boats and sailed across with kitbags packed with a ton of explosives. On the far side he found no Partisans to help 'and at first the
situation looked most unpromising'. But after cobbling together a few
villagers and finding a guide and some picks, shovels and mules, he
managed to achieve quite a lot:

> After half an hour's marching I was asked by the guide how
> near to the road would I require them to go. When I told
> them that they would be working on the road they imme-
> diately stopped and refused to go any further. He said they
> had been told they would only have to accompany me to
> within sight of the road. I argued with them for almost half
> an hour and it was not until I produced gold that some of
> them consented to come . . .
>
> I had decided on the following plan, 8 holes 25ft apart
> with 100lbs of Ammonal in each, and by midnight I had the
> men started. They dug fast and well, and except for frequent
> interruptions by the men I had posted to act as sentries every-
> thing ran smoothly. By 0330 they were down in some of the
> holes to 5ft. Whilst my interpreter put the explosive in the
> holes I unrolled the Cortex leads. By 0415 everything was
> ready, and I blew the road at 0419 just after dawn. I distrib-
> uted propaganda stickers on trees also copies of Soldaten
> Nachrichten.

The results, Northrop noted, were excellent: fifty-five yards of road
and part of an embankment destroyed, all of which took the Germans
two days to repair. And not bad at all, he thought, for such an irregular force. 'We had no weapons whatsoever in the party apart from an
antiquated Turkish rifle, mine and my interpreter's revolvers. Considering
that there were two enemy posts above and below us I think these men
acquitted themselves extremely well.'

Back across the lake he was soon reacquainted with how infuriating
regular Partisans could be. The 20th Brigade had taken over in Mokra
and in general Northrop found it 'most helpful and co-operative'. Even
its commissar 'did everything he possibly could to help me'. Trying to
persuade some 20th Brigade men to mine a road, however, he was told
that they would help him 'only if I took up the mines the following
morning. Of course I refused to do this and after much argument the

following statement was made and this I was to hear again: the Germans are leaving our country so why should we attack them now?'

In October, in the wet and cold that badly hampered the commandos on the coast, Northrop found it impossible to do much at all and his last major demolition took place in early November on the main road to Elbasan. Thousands of Germans were then collecting around Ohrid and seemed certain to use the road to press north. Taking mules weighed down with two tons of plastic explosive, Northrop and Renfree set off to stop them, 'marching night and day through most miserable and difficult weather'. On arriving they chose a spot 'excellent from every possible point of view . . . the road ran alongside the Shkumbin with a drop of 15ft straight into the river and rock wall on the other side. The most important factor however, was that across the river from this point and directly above the Pzns had absolutely first class positions from which they could easily cover with fire the point we were to blow.' Holes were dug and plastic explosive packed in and detonated, 'destroying most completely 60yds'. On 8 November an enemy column some four thousand strong began moving out from Ohrid and on to the road to Elbasan. It was delayed nearly two days at the stretch just blown, though could have suffered more, Northrop felt. All the way from Ohrid 'the Pzns held outstandingly commanding positions from which they could have covered the road with fire, and made the Hun withdrawal a very costly business'. As for the spot across the river from the blown stretch of road, this 'could not have been bettered, and I am sure that had they been determined to stop this large fleeing German column they could have done so . . . As it was the Hun repaired this blow which held him up for 42 hours and continued his march . . . with very few casualties at a point which should have been a German graveyard.'[72]

As the German withdrawal from Albania reached its final stages, SOE officers found the Partisan 1st Corps, circling and probing Tirana, similarly awkward to deal with and reluctant to engage. 'I found the individual Partisan was keen to fight and that when given some specific task to perform carried it out conscientiously and with a high standard of personal courage,' Philip Oliver reported. 'Certainly there was a high proportion of men of this calibre in the 1st Brigade which, when employed on its half hearted attempt to take Tirana in the early days of the entry, convinced me by the very absence of individual effort that its punch was being pulled.'[73]

At the end of October, without the Partisans knowing, Oliver slipped into the city, hid among houses in the eastern quarter and watched the Germans skirmish with forward troops of the 1st Division, now commanded by Mehmet Shehu. He noted the German positions and estimated the garrison's strength at three hundred: 'Shehu had spoken of 3,000.' The only enemy reserve Oliver spotted was 'a small mobile squadron consisting of two tanks with several armoured cars and carriers'. And although the Germans were employing this 'with great skill and success, emerging from the perimeter and clearing any area where the Partisans appeared to be concentrating', the Partisans, he felt, were making 'no real effort either to attack or to harass the enemy'. They had 'strong superiority in firepower' and greatly outnumbered the Germans, who had withdrawn to prepared positions in the centre of the city, yet the front line was static. 'Several times we saw a party of five Germans with a machine gun on a lorry hold up groups of a hundred Partisans supported by a dozen light machine guns.'[74]

After much arguing with the British and assurances of air support, the Partisans did attack the capital in strength. A discussion between German and Partisan officers appears to have taken place beforehand when the garrison was offered the chance to surrender. This was refused, so OSS records state, 'on the grounds that the commanding [German] general was in Scutari and only he could make a decision'.[75] Then, on the afternoon of 11 November, the assault began. It was not the epic struggle portrayed in communist accounts but the city was soon encircled and, according to SOE reports, 'fierce hand-to-hand fighting took place and the Germans suffered heavy casualties in numerous attempts to win back lost positions'.[76] Allied aircraft flew two hundred sorties, rocketing barrack blocks and positions, machine-gunning enemy motor transport, bombing bridges on roads to the city and maintaining fighter vigil.

Perhaps the most significant action took place outside the city. As the battle began a strong German column of up to 1,500 men, with tanks, moved out from Elbasan and on to the road to Tirana. Its likely intention was to raise the siege and continue north. But a few miles short of the capital the column ground to a halt, an LRDG patrol having blocked the road by blowing a twenty-foot bridge. The hills around were full of Partisans and for three days the column came under sustained sniping and attack. The LRDG, watching all of this, reported afterwards that, when the Germans finally repaired the bridge, 'masses of equipment, MT and horse-drawn vehicles' were left behind, while 'no sooner had the column started forward' than Allied aircraft arrived to bomb and strafe it. 'The result was a rout.' Survivors tried to keep going on foot, only for the Partisans to attack them again. 'Very few, if any, of these troops reached Tirana, and all vehicles and other equipment were either destroyed by the aircraft or captured.'[77]

Surrounded and now with no chance of relief, the garrison became desperate. Some units did break out and retreat north but OSS reports describe how many doomed defenders 'battled grimly to the end and at times refused to surrender even when cornered'. Dwindling hope and 'heavy drinking' also saw them became 'more ruthless'. In one home, German soldiers found a mother and her three daughters and eighteen-year-old son: 'The son was stabbed to death before the eyes of the women and the house was then ransacked.' In another, they 'turned the guns loose' on two families found inside. 'Of thirteen, twelve were killed on the spot. Only a small child escaped.'[78]

By the morning of 17 November the fighting in Tirana was over. Hundreds of Partisans swept in. When, two days later, the 1st Corps commanders finally permitted SOE and OSS officers to follow, the missions found the Partisans well in control. Mike Thornton reported on 22 November that in five days there had been eight hundred arrests: 'mostly political . . . certainly not all collaborators'. A curfew was in place, property was being seized, only party newspapers were allowed and the Partisans were 'dragooning' locals to attend political meetings. 'This might be any capital city one week after [the] arrival [of the] Nazis.'[79] 'Arrests continue,' he added on 27 November. 'Prisons full.'[80]

At Berat there were different scenes. Hoxha's new government greeted news of the fall of the capital with celebrations 'only equalled by the reception of the Russian Mission', wrote Marcus Lyon, deputing as senior British officer in the absence of Palmer and Smith. 'One bullet among the millions which were flying about came through the window of the room in our house in which I was standing; another burst of fire brought down the electric light overhead cables on Huxtable's head. For once I think they had good reason to celebrate.'[81]

Albania's national day, 28 November, was set aside for the official Partisan entry into Tirana and the celebrations started early when six Halifaxes flew over from Italy, swept low over the capital and dropped food packets and leaflet greetings. Hoxha and his government, having been rafted across the Shkumbin and driven in trucks to the outskirts, then walked in at half-past ten to a twenty-one gun salute. Behind them marched Lyon, Stefan, Ivanov and Stojnic, followed by a mass of Partisans. 'The road as we entered the town passed through streets shattered by shelling,' Lyon recalled.

> I remember particularly a mosque badly damaged with its minaret still standing and German traffic signs, some splintered, standing awkwardly against the sky. As we neared the centre of the town the crowd grew. Young girls in peasant costume with flowers in their hair were cheering. The noise became greater and greater. We entered through Skanderbeg square and down the long central main road towards the Government Buildings.

Photographers worked busily, although in many shots taken that day it is Lyon, six-foot four and sporting a pristine white duffel coat, a last-minute find among the mission's stores to cover the 'battered battledress' he had been sleeping in for weeks, who stands out. 'I am not sure how pleased Enver Hoxha was that I was so conspicuous, but he said nothing about it.'[82]

Outside the Dajti Hotel a podium had been erected and here Hoxha halted, saluted the Albanian flag and turned to address the crowd of thousands assembled in the boulevard before him. 'Women's colourful ancient vest- and pantaloon-costumes . . . mingled with modern battle dress,' reported a watching American journalist flown in for the event. Standing in front of the podium 'was a little pink-cheeked girl hardly more than ten, carrying a man-sized rifle and ammunition belt around her waist. Hoxha appeared to look directly at her as he reviewed the fierce struggle of the Albanians during the last five years.'[83] Speeches over, columns of Partisans began to file past. Each unit carried the Albanian flag. One displayed the hammer and sickle. At least one battalion of Italians went by. Photographs confirm Lyon's memory that the parading Partisans, though 'ragged by our standards', displayed 'great spirit'.[84] Tom Stefan noted the reaction of the crowd. 'For the most part it appeared as if the people were almost stunned,' he transmitted to Fultz the following day. 'What cheers I heard sounded almost forced by the occasion. There was not the usual enthusiasm shown in the south.'[85]

*   *   *

Anthony Quayle, February 1944

(Above and below) The first ten nurses reach Bari, January 1944

Marcus Lyon

Johnny Shaw

Jack Dumoulin

Brian Ensor (left)
and Gordon Layzell

Norman Wheeler

Alan Palmer

Left to right: Alan Palmer,
Myslim Peza, Philip Leake
and Enver Hoxha, at Permet,
5 June 1944

(Above) Tony Simcox en route
to join Gani Kryeziu
(Above right) Julian Amery (middle)
and Billy McLean (right)
(Right) Fadil Hoxha, Tony Simcox,
Gani Kryeziu and Lazar Fundo

Front row, from left:
Fred Brandt, Tony
Neel, Harry Button.
Back row: Tajiks

Eliot Watrous (left)
and Victor Smith

John Eyre

Jon Naar

Bill Harcourt

Billy McLean, Julian Amery and David Smiley, summer 1944

Partisan column moving off to attack Peshkopi, July 1944

Tony Northrop (left) and Tommy Renfree

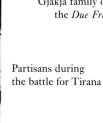

Hugh Munro and the Gjakja family on board the *Due Fratelli*

Partisans during the battle for Tirana

Enver Hoxha enters Tirana, 28 November 1944. Marcus Lyon marching behind in white duffel coat.

The British military cemetery in Tirana, 1946

The last German units left Albania in December 1944 and, with that, SOE began to pull out its remaining men. On 28 November there were still forty of them there. By 1 January 1945 twenty were left. By the end of February all had gone, save for a handful seconded to a new British military mission. The withdrawal had to be gradual. A British presence needed to be maintained until the Allied relief and military missions, which had been preparing for months to go in, were ready to cross from Italy. There were also plenty of other tasks to be done. Tons of non-warlike stores – food, fuel, clothing, medical supplies – had to be brought in and dispersed. There were mines and booby traps to lift and clear, roads and bridges to help repair and hospitals of sick and wounded to equip and oversee.

Throughout this final phase there was also the new government to watch, as it tightened its grip on the country and became progressively more intolerant of the remaining British and Americans in its midst. In speeches Hoxha and his lieutenants heaped passionate praise on the Soviet Union and made less and less mention of Britain or the United States, except when they wished to belittle them. In the light of recent developments in Greece, where British troops had been sent to stop the Greek communists seizing power, Britain was singled out for particular attack. Mehmet Shehu declared himself 'Anti-Churchill' and that 'the British had discarded the Atlantic Charter'.[86]

The regime's worst excesses were seen in the north, where sporadic local resistance to the Partisans dragged on. Tony Andrew and James Durcan, clinging on in Shkodra despite the Partisans exerting 'every conceivable pressure' to make them leave, reported the town's prison as 'bursting with political prisoners' and that the corpses of the executed were on display in the streets.[87] 'Spoke to painter, shop assistant, nun, labourer, draper, schoolmaster, hotel proprietor, librarian, tailor,' the pair transmitted to Bari on 11 January; all had told them: 'We cannot go on like this, why don't the British come . . . ?'[88]

Tirana was quiet by comparison, but the movements of British and American personnel were now strictly limited, their contacts and visitors arrested and questioned and their dealings with the government delicate and difficult. One American, who had worked in Albania before the war and recently returned to join the small OSS mission, reported:

> During my second day in Tirana I met a few of my former
> colleagues . . . They all wanted to talk to me at length but

did not dare lest they found themselves in prison the next day. Technically, we Anglo-Americans are free to see anyone we wish in Tirana, but in reality it is dangerous for most Albanian civilians to visit us or to have us visit them . . . None of us is allowed to visit any place outside of Tirana without a permit and a 'guard' from the Shtab . . . A former student of mine rushed to greet me, but he was off on his bicycle as soon as he realised we had a 'guard'.[89]

Tom Stefan's relatives in Korça were among the hundreds, probably thousands, detained, while Hoxha refused for weeks to permit any new OSS team to enter the city. 'I am beginning to hate that son of a bitch's guts,' Stefan wrote of him in February.[90]

The Allied missions also tried to do what they could to help the thousands of destitute Italians still in the country. Alan Palmer, who returned to Albania in December, persuaded the Government to let the sick ones leave. Hugh Munro, bringing in supplies at Vlora, managed to get a few of the fitter ones out on boats back to Italy. But neither SOE nor OSS could do very much for the hundreds of German prisoners scattered about, half-starved and at the mercy of the locals. Officers and men were treated the same and 'their existence is a Hell on earth,' reported Tommy Renfree. 'They are badly fed, deprived of most of their clothing and worked like slaves.'[91] George Wilkinson told Bari:

Their clothing and footwear (. . . bits of leather and felt strung together with odd lengths of string . . .) are in rags and the quantity of even these rags is grossly inadequate for a winter in this climate . . . They have no blankets or other covering to help them keep warm during the night . . . Until canvas chutes were available from [the] British mission, PsW working on roads slept by their work without any shelter in all weathers . . . I am told that PsW who died in the country are buried where they fell.

Wilkinson sent out a list of a hundred Germans who had died 'from hunger, cold and gross neglect' in recent months. 'It is difficult to comprehend how a nation with any claims to civilisation could tolerate such a state of affairs, although I appreciate that the Albanians have no cause to love the Huns.'[92]

There was also no shortage of Albanians anxious to leave. In November, from Tirana, Mike Thornton had joked drily to Bari that he could do a 'lucrative trade selling seats on planes to Italy'.[93] In reality there was very little the British or Americans could do. At a time when they were trying hard to maintain a working relationship with Hoxha's government, it was unthinkable that they would openly evacuate locals who loathed and feared it. Already the new regime demanded the return of many who had already fled, and felt that the British had been complicit in Kupi's escape. Tom Stefan told Bari in November: 'Members of Shtab sarcastically remarking how many more of the traitors now gathered at Durres are the English going to evacuate.'[94]

As the last SOE missions were withdrawn, however, one evacuation was attempted. It was probably SOE's final covert act in the country and was also entirely irregular, with little trace of it recorded in official files. Drawing on his memory, diary and w/t signal logs, Hugh Munro recalled that it all started when Philip Oliver came down to Vlora on the afternoon of 6 January 1945:

> He brought the latest news from Tirana; the situation wasn't improving and Hoxha was beginning to throw his weight about, giving the Brits orders; insisting his own people should supervise the arrival of all supplies, and that the British Mission in Tirana was too large, etc. Oliver confirmed that many people were on the run from the Communists, and that, indeed, was why he had come to me. He knew schooners were due in Valona soon and there was a job he wanted me to tackle.

Munro found himself given the task of spiriting out of the country two women, one with her husband and child, who, Oliver said, had helped the British in Tirana. Both were also desperate to leave and already on their way to Vlora. Munro was warned that all this was 'quite unofficial'. If anything went wrong the mission in Tirana 'would deny all knowledge of it: it would be entirely my idea and "my baby" . . . I said I understood.'

The first fugitive appeared on Munro's doorstep in Vlora 'on a wet, blustery night'. Her name was Mary Çelo. She was Russian, once married to an Albanian and had lived in the country for ten years, working latterly as a schoolteacher and for the Albanian Red Cross. She also had a son but was leaving him behind. Munro hid her in his house. Two weeks later the fleeing Gjakja family turned up. The mother was English, the father Albanian and their daughter, Vera, three years old. They checked in quietly to a local hotel.

Getting them away was never going to be easy. A departing British boat was the only means of shipping people out but Vlora was thick with Partisans who crowded its tiny pier when any boat came in to offload. The weather, too, posed problems: throughout January the winter wind and rain prevented any British ship from reaching the port. But in early February the weather cleared and the *Due Fratelli*, a requisitioned schooner, put in at Vlora. As Partisans set to work carrying off its cargo of drums of diesel oil, Munro sent the Gjakajs a torch and a map to a secluded spot among the marshes south of the port.

Next came the more inventive part of his plan. A fortnight before, Munro had arranged for local craftsmen to make 'a flat box, sturdy, with a few knot holes in it, with a couple of locks and rope handles'. Now, inside his house, Mary Çelo climbed into it and lay down, the lid was locked and Munro's unsuspecting Albanian servants, thinking it was full of his kit, carried it out: Munro, too, was leaving, having received instructions from Bari to pack up and return to Italy. By now a 'great crowd' had gathered; Munro had been popular and many locals and Partisans had come to wish him well. At the pier the Partisans carried the box to the schooner and laid it on deck and Munro, stepping aboard, casually threw his duffel coat on top. Night was falling and it was time to go. With shouted farewells the schooner pulled away 'and soon I was unlocking the box'.

The schooner's captain, a British sergeant called Bridges, had been briefed by Munro on what to do next. Out in the bay, a safe distance from the port, he blacked out the lights and steered back towards the shore while Munro, through binoculars, scanned the marsh for the Gjakjas' torch. When the schooner scraped the seabed, Munro and Bridges launched a rowing boat and went in closer. 'I don't know just how long we kept going back and forth, maybe 1½ to 2 hours and I was beginning to get really worried.' Finally they saw flashes. 'Bridges and I got out and waded ashore. Gjakja said "Thank goodness you've come".' Munro, with the child in his arms, hurried the family to the boat. Back on board the *Due Fratelli* they wrapped themselves in old parachutes as the schooner, 'its main sail billowing, battled across the Adriatic'. They docked safely in Brindisi next morning. Mary Çelo and the Gjakjas were taken away for processing. Munro, job done, went to report to the SOE office.[95]

EPILOGUE

THE impact on Albania and its people of the communist rise to power was profound and long lasting. Standards of health care and education improved. So did the economy, briefly. Advances like these came at a horrible cost. The one-party state, with the cult of Hoxha at its heart, was all-powerful. Zog never returned, dying in Paris in 1961. Pre-war leaders who had stayed behind and survived the war found themselves executed or imprisoned or otherwise stripped of their assets and influence. Religion was forced underground. The press was placed under rigid control. Thousands who protested or looked likely to object were given little quarter. International isolation, largely self-imposed, robbed Albania of foreign investment and soon saw the economy struggle: it was long Europe's poorest country.

That outcome is clear enough. The idea that Britain was responsible for it is less convincing. By 1945, according to SOE records, the British had sent in 7,000 rifles, 5,000 sub-machine-guns and 1,800 light-machine-guns, together with 16,500,000 rounds of ammunition, 240 mortars with 25,000 bombs, and 25,000 grenades, plus a few PIATs and pistols and sixty medium-machine-guns. Also there was a good deal of kit, ranging from 28,000 sets of battledress and 57,000 pairs of boots to 14,000 blankets, 390 torches, 6 jeeps, 24 shovels and a motorbike. Most of the arms were of British and American make; most of the bullets were Italian and German for use with weapons already in the country; almost all of this went to the Partisans. So did 33,000 gold sovereigns and hundreds of tons of food.[1] Certainly this assistance helped the Partisans survive and expand and dispose of domestic enemies, but the British contribution to the communists' success should not be seen in isolation. The vast bulk of this material was sent in during the summer and autumn of 1944, by which time the Partisans had recovered already to a position of very significant strength. Captured weapons and stores and even Italian soldiers, post-armistice, played their part in boosting that strength. So did the guerrillas' ability and willingness to endure hardship. Most significant of all were the local conditions that helped the communists secure the popular support to carry them to power. Partly these conditions were created, as elsewhere, by the terror and destruction spread by the Axis and by widespread disaffection with the pre-war regime. But partly they were created by the basic inability of the old order to do much more than collaborate or stand aloof rather than resist.

As for the charge that the SOE staff, after Philip Leake's death, had worked against the SOE mission attached to Abas Kupi, it is certainly evident from wartime diaries and reports that SOE officers back from Albania recorded their concerns at the time. It is also apparent from their own accounts that the politics of some staff officers were pretty left wing, while SOE files suggest that attempts may have been made to tamper with the flow of information from the field to higher authority. Yet care should be taken not to assume that ideology motivated the staff to back the Partisans or to exaggerate the significance of what seem to have been attempts to prevent London from overstating the military value of rival groups. The key decisions that favoured the Partisans in 1944 were taken above the heads of junior SOE staff and on predominantly military grounds that reflected overwhelmingly the short-term interests of Allied strategists.

These decisions were also based on accurate assessments of the various guerrilla bands' starkly contrasting military worth. Until the spring the situation in Albania was still too confused to justify all-out support for the Partisans. By the summer the picture was clear enough that the Partisans were the only Albanians causing the Germans significant discomfort. Most eye-catching of all had been the pocket that the Partisans, armed and encouraged by the British, carved out on the coast in May and June and the powerful German offensive, involving crack mountain troops, that followed. Speaking years later in Oxford, Alan Palmer, who had survived that drive by the skin of his teeth, considered it 'the greatest compliment' paid to the Partisans and a good marker of 'what effect on the war' they had. 'But partisans being formed militarily the way they are, they disperse, disappear, reform. And so it was only a month or less after that operation that they were again formed up in groups and being once more supplied by air in greater quantities and operating still.'² Hubert Lanz estimated that German casualties during the drive were 120 dead and 300 wounded, and it is clear today that, after the offensive petered out, the Partisans continued to cause the Germans problems. Careful SOE estimates of enemy losses in Albania, albeit inflicted partly by SOE missions, the SBS, the LRDG, the commandos and the Balkan Air Force, put German dead at between 6,000 and 7,000.³ Post-communist Albanian studies have sought to suggest that the figure might be around 2,400 dead, with another 1,000 missing.⁴

A case might be made for claiming that some on the British side understood little and cared less about the factors that compelled many Nationalists to refrain from resisting. Margaret Hasluck believed that to be the case during the winter of 1943–44; Amery and McLean felt the same during the summer and autumn of 1944 and for a long time afterwards. Contemporary records do suggest that a number of SOE officers, both at headquarters and in the field, had little time for the plight in which many Nationalists found themselves. That June, for example, Eliot Watrous, echoing sentiments expressed recently by Norman Wheeler, remarked in one letter to the SOE office in London that nationalists like Abas Kupi were aiding the enemy merely by their neutrality. 'This war appears to have reached the stage when a neutral attitude, of assistance to the enemy, can no longer be tolerated; vide Turkey, Spain, Sweden. It is this attitude of Kupi's which the Partisans so strongly condemn, alleging that by it he is prolonging the war.'⁵ Of course, as Watrous implied, an alternative route was open to Kupi: fighting the Germans in the way SOE demanded. This was the route taken by Gani Kryeziu that summer. But it is impossible to dispute McLean's and Amery's own analysis that Nationalist society was poorly suited to prolonged and large-scale action against the Germans.

Given the dominance of the Albanian and Yugoslav Partisans by the summer of 1944, however, it is hard to believe that, had Kupi and other Nationalists joined Gani and fought, the outcome of events in Albania and Kosovo would have been very different. Moreover, whatever sympathy may have been felt for the plight of men like Kupi or the Kryezius, the British were never likely to intervene on their behalf. 'Another King gone down the drain!' Churchill wrote to Eden on learning in October of Hoxha's likely political triumph.⁶ And Churchill had long wondered, as he had put it to Eden in May, whether Britain should 'resist' or 'acquiesce in the Communization of the Balkans'.[7] But it was a short-term desire to inconvenience Britain's enemies that had seen MI(R) and Section D told to involve themselves in Albania in 1940. The same desire had then seen SOE officers return to the country in 1943 and continued to guide their efforts despite the fact that, by 1944, Britain was knowingly backing a revolutionary movement whose communist leaders wanted power. Time and again the Chiefs of Staff and the Foreign Office shied away from approving any political intervention for fear of upsetting wider strategy and interests. Hence the refusal to recognise Zog or pronounce on Albania's borders; hence the fact that dismay over Kupi's obvious decline and demise never spurred on the Foreign Office to confront the Partisans' politics.

Perhaps an Allied occupation force sent in at the right moment might have made a difference, as it did when British troops were sent in to Greece. 'I wish we could land two brigades here,' Alan Palmer told Bari in September 1944; 'they would be dead safe and could secure the necessary tenure when the occasion arose. That is, of course, if we want to keep any sort of control here after the war.'[8] Serious plans for such a landing were never laid, however, for the troops were not available and sufficient will was never there. Only where Greece was concerned were the British prepared to divert forces from the final battle against the Germans in order to prevent a communist coup.

Whether more friends would have been won if less effort had been made with Kupi, a man described by one of Sir Jocelyn Percy's gendarmerie inspectors as 'nothing but a highwayman, brave and venal', is another intriguing might-have-been.[9] Certainly McLean's prolonged presence with him was a cause of great friction between the British and the Partisans, and some observers, including Leake and Harry Fultz, had predicted problems. 'We should not be surprised if later we find that these people have no love left for the Allies,' Fultz had warned Washington in February 1944. '[We] cannot hope to promote confidence if we state that we favor and help those who fight [the Germans] and at the same time do things which cause injury to those who fight the Germans. We should not expect to have people believe us if we state that we will not meddle in the internal affairs of a country if at the same time we try to manipulate events to achieve predetermined results.'[10]

Perhaps, had SOE records been accessible at an earlier date, post-war studies might have taken greater account of the Allies' short-term priorities and the reality and implications of Partisan strength in 1944. 'This was clearly a case in which a small but useful military diversion had been earned by limited investment in the guerilla movement,' concludes the Albanian chapter of William Mackenzie's Cabinet Office history of SOE, written with privileged access to SOE files and completed in 1948 but long classified. As for those who were capable of doing and did the bulk of the fighting in 1944, Mackenzie acknowledged that 'action against the Germans was possible only through FNC, who recovered and expanded quickly after the set-backs of the winter'. The Balli Kombëtar, by comparison, was 'hopelessly compromised' while Abas Kupi was shown 'conclusively' to be 'too close to the verge of collaboration to be of any value'.[11]

Within months of the communists coming to power, the culling of 'traitors' was well underway. One early casualty was Lef Nosi, tracked down and arrested in the summer of 1945. The following February, with Anton Harapi, another Regent who had failed to flee the country, he was accused of collaborating with the Axis, found guilty and shot.

Efforts to crush and prevent any anticommunist opposition saw communities and villages on the coast and in the north become particular targets; consequently, among the thousands of victims were plenty of men and women who had worked during the war with the British. Ymer Bardoshi, for example, much praised in Tony Neel's reports for his readiness to resist, was imprisoned for sixteen years. Ram Muja, who had guided John Hibberdine's party down from the north in 1944, was cornered and killed in the mountains west of Dega. Maliq Koshena, headman of Dukati, was marched away in 1945 and sentenced to thirty years; five years later he was shot, or so his family was told: decades later a story came out that he had lingered on in prison for a further twelve years. Xhelil Çela, who had helped both the British and Americans on the coast, found himself in Italy when the war came to an end, but relatives he had left behind were stripped of their land and interned.

Wartime Partisans, many of whom had held senior commands, were not immune from persecution. Those who suffered included Nexhip Vinçani, once commander of the 4th Brigade, a man rated highly by the British. Denounced in the 1950s as an 'enemy of the party' and stripped of his rank, he was accused, in 1982, at the age of sixty-six, of 'agitation and propaganda' and arrested, imprisoned and tortured, then exiled from his family. When a search of his house turned up an old photograph of SOE officers, he was also accused of being a British agent. 'It's difficult to describe,' he wrote to Marcus Lyon in 1993; 'homeless, without family'.[12]

Bedri Spahiu, the first guerrilla leader Billy McLean had met, went on to become state prosecutor at post-war trials of traitors and war criminals; appointed Minister of Education in 1955, party infighting saw him purged shortly afterwards and his internment ended only in 1991. Dali Ndreu, 1st Corps commander in 1944, was shot in 1956. It is thought today that even Mehmet Shehu, commander of the 1st Brigade in 1943, who went on to become Prime Minister in 1954, fell foul of Hoxha eventually, dying in strange circumstances in 1981.

Among those who made it out, Kupi and Said Kryeziu settled in New York, where Kupi died in 1976 and Kryeziu twenty years later. Ihsan Toptani, who had helped care for Arthur Nicholls and escaped Albania in the same boat as Kupi, settled in London, became a British citizen and died in 2001.

After spells on health grounds in Switzerland and Cyprus, Margaret Hasluck moved to Dublin, where she died in 1948. Until the end she stayed in touch with several SOE officers she had known. They, in turn, maintained their affection for her. Billy McLean and Anthony Quayle were among a number who, hearing she was in financial difficulties, made anonymous payments into her bank account.

Of Hasluck's 'boys', those who survived Albania also survived the war. Not all survived for long. Johnny Shaw won an immediate MC in 1945 for SOE work with Burmese tribes against the Japanese, then returned to the Royal Ulster Rifles and was awarded the DSO in Korea in early 1951; weeks later he was dead, killed on the Imjin River. Trotsky Davies, despite the concerns of friends and family that his health was not up to it, was another who stayed in the Army; when he died, still serving, in 1952, it was felt the wounds he had suffered in 1944 had most likely strained his heart. George Seymour received an MC for his work in Albania, rejoined the Royal Scots Fusiliers, took on a series of staff posts and died in Singapore in 1953. Andy Hands, who went on to fight the Japanese, and Ian Merrett, demobilised when his gravedigging was done, neither of whom settled easily into civilian life, also died young.

Billy McLean ended the war as consul in Sianking. He left the Army soon afterwards, was employed for a time by MI6 and tried to enter politics, finally securing a seat in 1954 as Conservative MP for Inverness. Both in and out of parliament, which he left a decade later, he spent much time overseas, travelling and politicking, particularly in the Middle East. He died in 1986.

Julian Amery married Harold Macmillan's daughter in 1950, was elected the same year as Conservative MP for Preston North and went on to hold office in the Macmillan and Heath governments. As a passionate imperialist, secretary of the Suez group and a champion of Ian Smith's white regime in Rhodesia, he was no stranger to being at odds with the majority and, for all his energy and ambition, never reached the Cabinet. Elevated to the House of Lords in 1992, he died four years later.

David Smiley parachuted into Siam in 1945, added a military OBE to his two MCs and remained in the Army after the war mixing regimental service with attaché posts. In the early 1950s he commanded the Blues. From 1958 he spent three years commanding the Sultan of Oman's forces and later worked closely with the Imam of Yemen. After retiring from the Army he farmed quietly in Spain. Today he lives in London.

Garry Duffy, awarded an MC for saving the stranded American nurses, also stayed in the Army, retiring as a major in 1961; he settled in the Wirral and died in 1990. Willie Williamson, after Albania, was dropped by SOE into northern Italy and captured; he survived, became a teacher and retired to Haddington, outside Edinburgh.

Bill Tilman also parachuted into Italy in 1944. Afterwards he was awarded a DSO, swapped mountaineering for sailing and wrote books about his adventures. In 1977 he sailed out from Rio, bound for the Falklands, and was never seen again. Peter Kemp, too, received a DSO at the end of the war, by which time he had been dropped into both Poland and Siam. Peacetime saw him make a living as an author, journalist and life assurance salesman; foreign assignments took him to South America, Africa and Southeast Asia and in 1990 he wrote with foreboding about the state of tension in Kosovo. He died in 1993.

Tony Neel left SOE in 1945 and returned to RAF duty. In the 1970s, after his retirement, he looked for and found Fred Brandt, then living in West Germany. In 1975 the pair met again and Neel discovered, to his horror, Brandt's post-war fate. After being released by the British in 1947 he had ended up somehow in Soviet hands and been imprisoned for eight years in a series of gulags; when he finally returned to

Germany in 1955 he was a broken man, sick with tuberculosis and other diseases. Neel died in 1993, Brandt two years later.

Jerry Field finished the war working at SOE headquarters in Baker Street. His wartime injuries forced him out of the Army in 1952. For a time he ran the Three Tuns pub in Eggleston, County Durham; later he lived in Ibiza. He died in 1983. Austin DeAth, Field's w/t operator, became a teacher and lives in Hampshire.

Anthony Quayle, Field's replacement, became a highly accomplished actor on stage and screen and helped lay the foundations of what became the Royal Shakespeare Company; his film work included roles in *Ice Cold in Alex, The Guns of Navarone* and *Lawrence of Arabia*. In 1977, when he featured on the television show *This Is Your Life*, friends who surprised him included Sandy Glen and Giuseppe Manzitti. He died in 1989, four years after his knighthood.

Glen finished the war with two DSCs, joined Clarksons, the ship-brokers, and became chairman of the Export Council for Europe and later chairman of the British Tourist Authority; knighted in 1967, he died in 2004. Manzitti returned to Genoa and began a successful career in industry. He died in 1999.

Paul Gray, released from Colditz, fought alongside his American liberators in the final days of the war, then returned to Liverpool where he worked on the docks, in the meat markets and eventually for British Telecom; he also worked for the Labour Party and became a semi-professional jazz-band drummer.

Michael Lis, awarded an MC after leaving Albania, lived and worked afterwards in France where he died in 1994. Jim Chesshire returned to Birmingham and rejoined Chesshire Gibson, the family firm; he died in 2000. Bob Melrose returned to Penicuik, then settled in southern England, and died in 2002. Tony Simcox left the Army in 1947, found it difficult to adjust and served subsequently in the RAF Regiment. Later he joined Unigate and ran a general stores in Devon. He died in 1991. John Davis was dropped into Malaya in 1945, then went to Palestine. Later he emigrated to New Zealand and served in the New Zealand Army and Malayan Police. He lives in Christchurch.

In 1945 Alan Palmer took on the role of political adviser with the British military mission to post-occupation Albania. In 1946 he returned to Huntley & Palmer's, becoming chairman of the firm in 1963, chairman of the Cake and Biscuit Alliance in 1967 and chairman of Associated Biscuit Manufacturers in 1969, when he was appointed CBE. For forty years he was president of Reading's Conservative Association. He died in 1990.

Norman Wheeler rejoined the Royal Ulster Rifles in the summer of 1944 and fought through Northwest Europe. A long and distinguished staff career, interrupted by active service in Cyprus in command of 1 RUR, culminated with his appointment as chief of staff at the headquarters of the British Army of the Rhine. Appointed OBE, CBE and CB, he retired as a major general in 1971 and died in 1990, eight days after Palmer.

Victor Smith was awarded an MC for his work in Albania and went back in 1945 with the British military mission. Afterwards he stayed in the Army, serving as a company commander on operations in Cyprus and in various staff and attaché posts. He retired as a colonel with an MBE and died in 1999.

Marcus Lyon was among several SOE officers trained in 1945 to parachute into prisoner-of-war camps in Germany and prevent the guards massacring the inmates; the war ended before he was needed, though he had prepared three times to go. After several months in Germany hunting war criminals, he, too, returned to Albania with the British military mission. Back in London in 1946 he abandoned his pre-war architectural studies for a course at Chelsea School of Art. After some film illustration work and a period painting murals and designing London night-clubs, he married, moved to Crowborough and began teaching, finally becoming director of art and art history at Eastbourne College. He died in 2007.

Jack Dumoulin parachuted into Malaya in 1945, stayed on for some months after the Japanese surrender and was awarded an MBE. He returned to regular medicine in 1946 and specialised in gynaecology. Dumoulin died in 2007. Tony Northrop also finished the war in the Far East, where he parachuted into Borneo in 1945 and received a sword wound to the head while skirmishing with Japanese troops. Leaving the Army in 1949, he went to work for the Colonial Office, then for MI6 and finally for Unilever. He retired to Suffolk and died in 2000.

Others with post-war intelligence careers were John Hibberdine, Philip Oliver and Alan Hare. Hibberdine, who parachuted into Siam with SOE in 1945, died in 1982. Oliver, who had also gone into Siam, died in 1989. Alan Hare left MI6 in 1961, shortly after being appointed head of its political intelligence section, and took up the first of a series of senior posts with the Pearson Group. In the early 1980s he was chairman of the *Financial Times*; after that he became president of Château Latour. He died in 1995.

Reginald Hibbert finished the war fighting in tanks in northern Italy. Afterwards he completed his Oxford studies and had a successful Foreign Office career that culminated in a knighthood and appointment as British ambassador in Paris. Retirement allowed him to publish, in 1991, the first detailed account by a former SOE officer that argued for the rightness of British support for Hoxha's Partisans.[13] For a long time he had put the case privately; he had also been hauled in for questioning when, according to Hibbert, a wartime colleague, Rowland Winn, spread stories of him being a communist. Cleared of the charge, Hibbert felt the tales had their root in heated arguments he and Winn had had on an Albanian mountainside in 1944. Winn, newly arrived, had believed that British support for the Partisans was wrong; Hibbert, with ten months of Albania behind him, had said it made sense. 'I expect I added that had I been an Albanian, I would have been a Partisan,' he recalled in his book. 'I would have been conscious, in saying this, that by September 1944 the word "partisan" was becoming synonymous with communist.'[14]

Hugh Munro parachuted into Malaya with SOE in 1945; he returned to the Inland Revenue in Inverness and settled eventually in Buckie, working as a tax inspector and becoming a regional councillor for the Scottish National Party. Mary Çelo, the Russian he had smuggled out of Albania in a box, came to Britain, remarried and remained a close friend. Dare Newell also parachuted into Malaya, ending the war with an MBE. From 1950 he played a key role in the development of the post-war SAS, commanded a squadron in Malaya and was employed at the Ministry of Defence as selection and training officer. Appointed OBE in 1973, he remained very active in the SAS Association until his death in 1988. Brian Ensor served in Palestine with the Parachute Regiment, then was demobilised, returned to Dublin and began working for Unilever; he died in 1987. Tommy Renfree ended up as South Africa's chief military strategist and died in 1997. Mike Thornton, who had been studying economics before the war, went to work for the Bank of England, rising to become chief of its economic intelligence department. He retired to Cornwall with a CBE and died in 1989.

After a period in Albania in 1945 with the British military mission, Eliot Watrous returned to London and joined the BBC Overseas Service.

Seconded to the Colonial Office in 1951, his first job was to write anti-communist propaganda for broadcast to Malaya; his sons recall 'a staunch conservative and libertarian' whose antipathy even to socialism almost prompted him to emigrate when Harold Wilson became Prime Minister.[15] After retiring from the BBC in 1971 he set up a travel company in Greece. He died in 1984. Jon Naar married a girl in OSS and in 1946 went to live in the United States. After studying at Columbia he wrote for a medical journal, then forged a career in photography and as a writer and lecturer on renewable energy and the environment. Today he lives in New Jersey.

Air Vice-Marshal William Elliot, knighted in 1946, became air ADC to George VI and the young Queen Elizabeth and for three years in Washington chaired the British joint services mission. Retiring as an air chief marshal, he died in 1971. Bill Harcourt was appointed CBE in 1945 and returned to Morgan Grenfell, becoming chairman in 1968. After periods in the United States as economic minister in the British embassy and head of the Treasury delegation, he also became United Kingdom executive director of the International Monetary Fund. He died in 1979. Kit Steel, knighted in 1951, concluded his diplomatic career as British ambassador in Bonn and died in 1973. Philip Broad served later in Trieste and as consul in Istanbul, dying in 1966. David Talbot Rice returned to Edinburgh and resumed his academic career; after his death, in 1972, the university's art gallery was named after him. Eddie Boxshall joined the Foreign Office and, in time, became custodian of SOE's surviving records; he died in 1984.

For more than forty years, such was the communists' grip on Albania that former SOE officers and NCOs wishing to revisit their wartime haunts found doing so impossible. Willie Williamson was one who went close. On holiday one year in Yugoslavia he took a bus to the border and 'we could see these mountains going straight up to heaven and I said, "That's where I spent my war". After so many years it seemed amazing that these were the mountains that I had lived in. You forget at times.'[16] Eventually, on their own or in small groups, some did make it back. Probably the first was John Davis, who returned on an organised tour in 1989 when the country was still communist-run. 'I had been advised by David Smiley not to admit that I had been to Albania during the war, so I kept quiet about it.'[17] When communism collapsed and visiting became easier, more managed to make the trip. Smiley, Julian Amery and Alan Hare returned together in 1991. Reg Hibbert,

Richard Riddell and Jack Dumoulin went in 1992. Smiley made several subsequent visits, as did Hibbert. These trips could be sobering. In 1944, Dumoulin had been assisted by a young Partisan nurse, Drita Kosturi. Only when he met her again half a century later did he discover that she had endured torture and four decades in a labour camp after the communists turned up in her possession a wartime card marked: 'Captain J. G. Dumoulin, RAMC'. Finding her in ailing health, Dumoulin flew her to Britain for treatment.

While the intensity of the Albanian experience forged lifelong friend-ships among SOE personnel, disagreements over the wisdom of wartime policy saw divisions deepen and feuds develop. When Marcus Lyon organised a series of reunions, Peter Kemp and Rowland Winn threat-ened not to come if Reg Hibbert attended. 'They thought he was a communist all of a sudden. It's not true.'[18] Yet a belief that Albania fell to communism by default may have had consequences more unfor-tunate than clubland gossip and inaccuracies in the historical record.

In recent years, the Cold War coup attempt of 1949–53, when MI6 and the CIA embarked on a disastrous covert effort to undermine Hoxha's new regime, has come under closer scrutiny than previously possible. The plan had been to recruit and train Albanian exiles and then send them in secretly to whip up a revolt to bring the commun-ists down. A recent history of MI6 has suggested the operation mirrored the unsuccessful Section D, MI(R) and SOE venture of 1940–41.[19] The comparison is a good one, though not entirely apt. Both were British-inspired, launched with confidence and intended to meet other countries' strategic interests by removing or destabilising Albania's rulers. Both involved similar characters. Julian Amery and Dayrell Oakley-Hill were brought on board the later project, as were Billy McLean, David Smiley, Alan Hare, John Hibberdine, Tony Northrop and Peter Kemp. Abas Kupi and Said Kryeziu were among the exiles to whom the British and Americans looked for support. So were Midhat Frashëri and Abas Ermenjë of the Balli Kombëtar. But the ambitious plans of 1940–41, forged by an under-resourced organisation heedless of wider concerns – a 'relatively unsupported body of amateurs bent on the crudest forms of sabotage' to quote Section D's own War Diary – never received the full go-ahead.[20] The later venture was sanctioned at the highest levels. Yet many of those infiltrated were killed or caught and executed, the regime added to the toll with waves of reprisals and show trials of suspect sympathisers and Hoxha survived with relative ease. He died of natural causes in 1985, still at the head of his country.

One explanation long put forward for its failure is the presence then in MI6 of Kim Philby, who is accused of passing word of the enterprise to Moscow. A fact rarely acknowledged is that proof of Philby's decisive role in the debacle has never been produced, while recent studies have shown that the regime was aware in good time and from a variety of sources about what was being planned. The secrecy and security surrounding the recruitment, intentions and training of the agents were poor, and had been penetrated by Hoxha's own intelligence men, while the basic desire of the British and Americans to get rid of Hoxha was no secret at all long before the operation began. Indeed, although most records of the 1949–53 episode remain classified, given what is known it is hard not to wonder about the thought put into the planning. Although compromised by being well known as wartime entry points, old SOE and OSS dropping grounds and beaches, including Biza, Dega and the dogleg cove at Seaview, were re-used. Hopes were placed again in communities like Dukati but locals still remember the agents who arrived in the night to sound out the village about the chances of future help, and Dukati, no less vulnerable than it had been five years before, could do little. And, despite the disasters that overtook it from the start, the enterprise was left to run, even as survivors scrambled out with stories of fierce security and of locals too scared and weak to act. What came to seem like over-confidence and disregard for agents' lives sowed dissension in the MI6 ranks. As agents left for Albania in their parties of threes and fours, then disappeared, Tony Northrop, running a training camp on Malta, was sure that lives were being thrown away. Once he and his wife rushed to hospital one trainee so depressed by the prospect of his impending mission that he had swallowed his cyanide pill. Had he bitten it he would have been dead; a stomach pump saved his life.

It has also been said in the past that the operation's fate surprised some old SOE hands: who could have predicted that the communists were in such control? Lobbying hard for the decision to move against Hoxha, Julian Amery had claimed consistently, as he did in January 1949 in the London journal *Time and Tide*, that the Albanian people 'are seething with discontent against their Communist masters . . . In the face of a popular revolt the regime would be hard put to defend itself.'[21] Only four years before, however, one SOE officer after another had arrived in Bari after months with the Nationalists to warn that the very basis of Nationalist society negated the likelihood of any significant rising. All testified to the lack of patriotic feeling, the insular and parochial interests and the vulnerability to reprisals of local communities, which bred disunity and an over-riding desire to seek salvation from danger.

To understand that, George Seymour wrote, it was necessary to understand the 'natural independence of mountain chieftains' and the 'great rivalry and mistrust' that could exist between them; and to understand that, he went on, 'it must be appreciated that the northern and central districts of Albania are entirely feudal':

> Villages and clans follow their own chief blindly. His political views are their political views and his enemies their enemies. They will however only follow the chieftain whilst he remains strong enough to retain his position. If he is usurped they will follow the new leader just as blindly. Blood feuds also are rife which prevents this part of the country being welded into a coherent whole.[22]

'The peasants will follow a chief who is successful, or who has powerful support which promises a success,' echoed Richard Riddell and Reg Hibbert. 'At no time would they have followed any chief who made open war on Italians and Germans, and so brought upon his area the destruction and burning which has fallen on South Albania . . . If a chief wished to oppose the invader, he needed the support of a far larger organisation than his own immediate following. Without such support he would have been utterly destroyed.'[23]

'Every chieftain and minor chief is regarded by his supporters as a sage, whose political opinions are sought after and propagated throughout the area, down the social scale,' Roy Bullock reported. 'Through fear of losing their own status after German reprisals . . . the Northern Chiefs, with the exception of Gani Kryeziu, hesitated to commit themselves against the enemy. In fact Muharrem Bajraktar told me quite openly in July that he would not attempt any action when he knew that an adverse conclusion would be foregone, with the consequent drop in morale.'[24]

'In all the parts of Albania I have visited I should say that the area from Scutari to Kukes, North of the road up to the Serbian border, is the most disunited and unsettled,' wrote Tony Neel after more than a year in the field. 'I cannot think of one man who could be called the most influential in these parts, and for that reason the people do not know who to follow. Some are Catholics and some are Musselmen – on religious grounds this makes no difference because very few of either practice their religion, but it just helps to make another split.' Certainly, he felt, although few leaders had anything good to say about each other, 'their dislike and fear of communism' was a unifying factor, but strong guidance and help were essential for action. 'These people are like children and they need a firm hand.'[25]

Alan Hare had had as close a view of both the Partisans and Nationalists as any SOE officer. Hare is particularly interesting since others have presented him since as another who, after the war, relished the idea of overthrowing Hoxha and righting the wrongs of wartime policy. But from the long report he wrote on being evacuated to Bari that October it is apparent that the Nationalists' incapacity for fighting had convinced him that the Partisans had been firmly in the ascendant long before McLean returned to work with Kupi. He was also clear-eyed enough to see that the Partisans were firmly in control and that the influence of the old order had gone. Once the Partisans survived the winter, 'Kupi and his movement were doomed to defeat and extinction whatever action he had taken.' The 'very nature' of Kupi's organisation 'made it incapable of fighting the Germans over a long period due to its inability to stand up to reverses and reprisals, except possibly with enormous monetary and political support from us.'

Hare also argued that Britain needed to face the reality of what had happened and was happening if it wished to have any future influence in the country. Addressing the hot topic of the day of whether Kupi should be evacuated, he felt the 'strongest argument' for doing so and, in fact, for 'a policy of maintaining some relationship with pro-British Nationalist elements even in exile' was that abandoning him would be 'the final blow to British political prestige'. But Hare also recognised that Kupi now represented 'very little politically'. He had been 'successfully painted' by the FNC 'as one of the chief defenders of the old feudal order' and was 'hated by many FNC moderates' both for representing Zog and because, they felt, the movement might not have become so communist-dominated had he not decided to split from it. Indeed, Hare went on, abandonment 'should be interpreted by many as a more realistic attitude by us to the actual situation.' Also, 'the communist elements would no longer be able to couple the old order with Great

Britain in their propaganda, and the non-communistic elements would feel free to collaborate with us without fear of losing their own gains in the revolution'. But whatever action was taken, 'the chances of exerting political influence over Albania by peaceful methods in the next twenty years are slender'. Moreover, Hare concluded, 'one thing is certain, if we persist in identifying ourselves with a system in Albania which is no longer even an issue, and if we do not seek for support elsewhere, any chances of British influence are non-existent for forty years.'[26]

Probably Hoxha's government was indeed hated by many. It would be interesting to know more about Amery's grounds for claiming it an easy target. In 1944 even he had seen how the old order could fight only if convinced of rapid rewards at little cost. Unless the strength and ruthlessness of the regime had diminished considerably since then, which, as events proved, they had not, its grip was unlikely to have been loosened very much by the same vulnerable communities that had proved so incapable of resistance just a few short years before.

ACKNOWLEDGEMENTS

First and foremost I would like to thank the following men and women for sharing with me their memories and private records: the late Nigel Clive; Lynette Croudace; Basil Davidson; John Davis; the late Sir William Deakin; Austin DeAth; Dr Jack Dumoulin; Ted Fry; the late Sir Alexander Glen; the late Professor Nicholas Hammond; the late Sir Reginald Hibbert; Jim Hudson; Peggy Kraay; Nick Kukich; Peter Lee; the late Marcus Lyon; Agnes Mangerich; Bryan McSwiney; Hugh Munro; Jon Naar; the late Tony Northrop; John Orr-Ewing; Margaret Pawley; the late Peter Payne; Laura Pope; Richard Riddell; Bob Rogers; Dr John Ross; Denys Salt; the late Dr Kenneth Sinclair-Loutit; Colonel David Smiley; the late Annette Street; and Willie Williamson.

I would also like to thank the following relatives and friends of SOE personnel: Bodie Andrew, for details of the wartime service of Tony Andrew; Rosie Astley and Jenny and Chris Quayle, for memories and for use of the papers of Sir Anthony Quayle; Major Robin Bruford-Davies, for memories and for use of the papers of Brigadier 'Trotsky' Davies; David and Margaret Bryer, for details of the life and wartime service of Arthur Nicholls; Harry Clement and the late Phyllis Simcox, for memories and for use of the papers of Tony Simcox; Doreen Cowie and Alistair McDonald, for memories of George Cowie; Philip Gray, for memories of Paul Gray; Nigel Hands, for use of the papers of Andy Hands; Felicity Hibberdine-Fairhurst, for memories and for use of the papers of John Hibberdine; Kenneth Martin Leake, for memories and for use of the papers of Philip Leake; Robin Melrose, for use of the memoirs of Robert Melrose; Jill Merrett, for memories of Ian Merrett; Peter, Clive, Rosemary and Joan Neel, Philip Sanders and John, Peter and Elizabeth Pentreath, for memories and records of Tony Neel; David, Robin and the late Ruby Oakley-Hill, for memories and records of Dayrell Oakley-Hill; Laura Renfree, for records of Tommy Renfree; Helena Sully and the late Tryce Womack, for memories and for use of the papers of Sir Jocelyn Percy; Elizabeth Talbot Rice, for details of the wartime service of David Talbot Rice; and David and Richard Watrous, for memories of Eliot Watrous. I wish also to thank the Felkel family for memories of Fred Brandt and to acknowledge the debt I owe to my late grandmother, Joan Anstey, whose memories of my grandfather, Ian Merrett, set me off on this research in the first place. The papers of Tony Andrew, Trotsky Davies, John Hibberdine, Philip Leake and Tony Simcox are now preserved as collections in the Department of Documents at the Imperial War Museum; Trotsky Davies' papers include the surviving copy of Arthur Nicholls' diary. Extracts from Billy McLean's papers are printed by permission of Marina Cobbald. Extracts from *The Oak Tree* are reprinted by permission of Major John Ellis and the Cheshire Military Museum. Extracts from John Eyre's *The God Trip* are reprinted by permission of Peter Owen.

For contacts and additional help and information I would like to thank Geoffrey Ashe, Major Jeff Beadle, Rafal Brzeski, Ann Clayton, Bejtullah Destani, Oliver Gilkes, Bruce Johnston, Hope Kerr, Hugh Martin-Leake, Ned Nicholas and Paddy O'Hegarty. I am grateful also to the late Brigadier Ken Trevor for memories of Julius Faure-Field; to Sandy Leishman at Home Headquarters, Royal Highland Fusiliers, and Major Antony Gordon for details of the regimental service of George Seymour; and to Major R. J. Walker, Terence Nelson and Pamela Agnew of the Royal Ulster Rifles Association.

Thank you, too, to the following for their time and advice: Professor Christopher Andrew, who supervised my MPhil; Professor Rhodri Jeffreys-Jones and Dr David Stafford, who supervised my doctorate, and Dr Jeremy Crang and Professor Richard Aldrich, for their comments on it; Dr Marc Clark; Dr Bernd Fischer; Professor M.R.D. Foot; Professor Anthony Glees; Dr Stephanie Schwandner-Sievers; Jason Tomes; Dr Mark Wheeler; and Dr Tom Winnifrith.

I owe a heavy debt to Sir Alistair Horne and the Warden and Fellows of St Antony's College, Oxford, for electing me to the Alistair Horne Fellowship, which allowed me the time and space to prepare much of this book for publication. Funding from the University of Edinburgh, the Harry S. Truman Library, the Franklin D. Roosevelt Library and the Roosevelt Study Center enabled me to work on archives overseas. A fellowship from the Winston Churchill Memorial Trust allowed me to conduct research in more isolated parts of Albania.

Duncan Stuart, formerly SOE Adviser at the Foreign & Commonwealth Office, and Valerie Collins, his assistant, allowed me generous access to information from SOE files prior to its declassification. John Taylor at the National Archives, College Park, Maryland, was an essential guide to the OSS archive. Dr Thomas Boghardt, now of the Spy Museum, Washington, D.C., helped with research in Germany. For assistance with interpreting and translation I would like to thank Alex Bouwhuys, Sara Hands, Sally Martin, Lala Meredith-Vula and Bledi Toska. John Napolitano shared details of SOE finds among weapons and munitions collected in Albania by the UNDP. Karen Francis gave me valuable contacts and superior maps.

I received wonderful hospitality from countless people in Albania and Kosovo and would like to acknowledge especially the assistance of the following: Avni Hoxha, whose father sheltered the British at Dega in 1943–44; Bilbil Vangjeli, Musa Koshena, Sherif Tava and the Çela family of Dukati and the Dukati valley; Auron Tare, whose kindness and contacts made trips to the south so productive; Vladimir Nika of Nivan; Viktori Tona of Vithkuq; Spiro Gaqi Kola of Saranda; the Kryeziu, Vula and Haxhibeqeri families of Gjakova; the late Fadil Hoxha; and Foto Bici of Sheper, who gave me a bed in Bill Tilman's old HQ after I stumbled into the village one stormy night in 1999.

Thank you to Gillon Aitken, my agent, and Dan Franklin, at Cape, for their faith in me, to Alex Bowler for helping things through to publication and to Jeremy Lewis for his selfless encouragement. Thanks to Dr Emily Mayhew for help with choosing photographs. Finally I would like to thank Lianne for her patience and emotional support and my parents for their patience and financial support.

NOMINAL ROLL, AWARDS, CASUALTIES AND CODE-NAMES

NAME, RANK		IN		OUT/FATE (to Feb 1945)	AWARDS
McLEAN, N.L.D., Lt Col	1	17. 04. 43	1	23. 11. 43	DSO
	2	19. 04. 44	2	28. 10. 44	
SMILEY, D. de C., Maj	1	17. 04. 43	1	23. 11. 43	MC & bar
	2	19. 04. 44	2	25. 10. 44	
DUFFY, G.B., Capt		17. 04. 43		09. 01. 44	MC
WILLIAMSON, W.B., Cpl		17. 04. 43		09. 01. 44	
BELL, H.G., Sgt		11. 06. 43		09. 01. 44	MM
HANDS, A.G., S/Ldr		13. 07. 43		15. 08. 44	DSO
BRANDRICK, W., C/Sgt		13. 07. 43		15. 08. 44	MM
JENKINS, G., L/Sgt		13. 07. 43		25. 10. 44	MM
SMITH, H., S/Sgt		13. 07. 43		15. 08. 44	
NEEL, P.A.B., W/Cdr		17. 07. 43		13. 10. 44	
COOPER, Sgt		17. 07. 43		06. 07. 44	
JONES, C.C., Sgt		17. 07. 43		25. 10. 44	
ROBERTS, S.G., Cpl		17. 07. 43		22. 12. 43 (Died)	MM
TILMAN MC, H.W., Maj		09. 08. 43		22. 05. 44	
DAWSON, J., Sgt	1	09. 08. 43	1	22. 05. 44	
	2	26. 07. 44	2	27. 12. 44	

Name		Date		Date	Award
BUTTERWORTH, S.H.W., Sgt		09. 08. 43		20. 03. 44	
FAURE-FIELD, J.A., Maj	1	09. 08. 43	1	01. 12. 43	
	2	—. 12. 43	2	31. 12. 43	
DEATH, A.W.W., Cpl		09. 08. 43		04. 02. 44	
EDEN, W., Cpl		09. 08. 43		04. 02. 44	
SEYMOUR, Hon. G.V., Maj		09. 08. 43		06. 07. 44	MC
HILL, W.A., Bdr		09. 08. 43		07. 11. 43 (Killed)	BEM
SMITH, J.R., Sgt		09. 08. 43		08. 01. 44 (Captured)	DCM, MM
KEMP, P.M.M., Maj		09. 08. 43		30. 3. 44	
GREGSON-ALLCOTT, R., Sgt		09. 08. 43		06. 07. 44	
DAVIES MC, E.F., Brig		15. 10. 43		08. 01. 44 (Captured)	DSO
CHESSHIRE, J.H.C., Maj		15. 10. 43		08. 01. 44 (Captured)	MC
MELROSE, R., Sgt		15. 10. 43		—. 12. 43 (Captured)	
NICHOLLS, A.F.C., Lt Col		15. 10. 43		11. 02. 44 (Died)	GC
PALMER, C.A.S., Lt Col	1	15. 10. 43	1	06. 07. 44	DSO
	2	14. 07. 44	2	27. 07. 44	
	3	29. 08. 44	3	05. 10. 44	
	4	16. 12. 44	4	21. 12. 44	
	5	24. 12. 44	5	15. 01. 45	
	6	26. 01. 45	6	—	
SMITH, W.V.G., Maj	1	15. 10. 43	1	13. 06. 44	MC
	2	07. 07. 44	2	05. 11. 44	
BUTTON, H.V., Sgt		15. 10. 43		16. 10. 44 (Died)	
HARE, Hon. A.V., Maj		16. 10. 43		26. 10. 44	MC
SMYTH, F.G.W., Capt		16. 10. 43		15. 08. 44	
BULMAN, J.M., Capt		16. 10. 43		15. 08. 44	
LIS, M., Lt		16. 10. 43		06. 07. 44	MC
HUXTABLE, A., Sgt	1	16. 10. 43	1	06. 07. 44	
	2	14. 07. 44	2	17. 12. 44	

CHISHOLM, B.A., S/Sgt		16. 10. 43		06. 07. 44	
TRAYHORN, F., Lt		20. 10. 43		25. 12. 44 (Captured)	
RIDDELL, R.E., Maj		20. 10. 43		08. 10. 44	
SIMCOX, A.C., Capt		20. 10. 43		26. 10. 44	
DAVIS, J.H., Cpl		20. 10. 43		28. 10. 44	
CARELESS, A., Capt		20. 10. 43		20. 10. 43 (Killed)	
ROCKINGHAM, D.W., Cpl		20. 10. 43		20. 10. 43 (Killed)	
SMART, I.A., Capt		30. 11. 43		30. 11. 43 (Killed)	
STEPHENSON, J.C., Capt		30. 11. 43		30. 11. 43 (Killed)	
TOLEY, A.W., Lt		30. 11. 43		30. 11. 43 (Killed)	
KESTERTON, I.D., Sgt		30. 11. 43		30. 11. 43 (Killed)	
MCKENNA, G.H., Gnr		30. 11. 43		30. 11. 43 (Killed)	
LYON, J.M., Capt	1 2	07. 12. 43 14. 07. 44	1 2	13. 06. 44 02. 12. 44	
NORTHROP, E., Capt	1 2	07. 12. 43 26. 07. 44	1 2	13. 06. 44 06. 12. 44	
CHARNLEY, E., C of H		07. 12. 43		22. 05. 44	
CARPENTER, D.P., Cpl	1 2	07. 12. 43 07. 07. 44	2 2	13. 06. 44 06. 02. 45	
WHEELER, T.N.S., Lt Col		15. 12. 43		22. 05. 44	
LAYZELL, G.E., Maj		15. 12. 43		02. 02. 44 (Died)	
DUMOULIN, J.G., Capt	1 2 3	15. 12. 43 02. 08. 44 28. 10. 44	1 2 3	13. 06. 44 17. 10. 44 27. 12. 44	
LOFTUS, W., Sgt	1 2	15. 12. 43 02. 08. 44	1 2	13. 06. 44 27. 12. 44	
CLAYDEN, T.D., Cpl	1	15. 12. 43	1	13. 06. 44	

		2	07. 09. 44	2	04. 02. 45		
PICKERING, J., Cpl			15. 12. 43		22. 05. 44		
MERRETT, V.F.I., Capt			19. 12. 43		25. 10. 44		
GOODIER, R.A., Cpl			19. 12. 43		15. 08. 44		
OTTER, H., Sgt			19. 12. 43		26. 10. 44		
HIBBERDINE, J.G., Capt			19. 12. 43		28. 10. 44		
HIBBERT, R.A., Capt			19. 12. 43		08. 10. 44		
ELVIDGE, G., Sgt			19. 12. 43		08. 10. 44		
CLIFTON, I.H., Cpl			19. 12. 43		15. 08. 44	MM	
GRAY, P.J., Bdr			–. 12. 43		02. 02. 44 (Captured)		
CRANE, H.H.V., Sgt		1	–. 12. 43	1	–. 04. 44		
		2	11. 05. 44	2	24. 05. 44		
QUAYLE, J.A., Maj			31. 12. 43		03. 04. 44		
DAVIES, G.T., Cpl			31. 12. 43		13. 06. 44		
NEWELL, C.L.D., Capt		1	03. 02. 44	1	06. 07. 44		
		2	14. 07. 44	2	29. 07. 44		
		3	07. 09. 44	3	27. 12. 44		
ENSOR, B.R., Capt		1	03. 02. 44	1	15. 09. 44		
		2	30. 09. 44	2	18. 10. 44		
YOUNG, J.A., Lt			03. 02. 44		11. 05. 44		
ASHURST, T., Cpl			03. 02. 44		22. 05. 44		
BOWKETT, S., Cpl		1	03. 02. 44	1	11. 05. 44		
		2	03. 08. 44	2	20. 11. 44		
ROUS, Hon. P.J.M., Capt			14. 02. 44		13. 06. 44		
BULLOCK R.J.R., Capt			31. 03. 44		13. 10. 44		
AMERY, J. Capt			19. 04. 44		28. 10. 44		
SHAW, J.K.H., Maj			04. 05. 44		08. 11. 44		
STILL, N.A., L/Sgt		1	04. 05. 44	1	29. 07. 44		
		2	02. 09. 44	2	–		
CHRISTIE, A.F., Cpl			04. 05. 44		08. 11. 44		
WRIGHT, H.H., Capt		1	04. 05. 44	1	11. 06. 44		
		2	14. 07. 44	2	16. 12. 44		

MERRY, H.W., Lt	1	04. 05. 44	1	13. 06. 44
	2	26. 07. 44	2	20. 12. 44
LEAKE, S.P.M., Maj		10. 05. 44		07. 06. 44
				(Killed)
NICHOLLS, D., CSM	1	16. 05. 44	1	13. 06. 44
	2	02. 09. 44	2	17. 12. 44
BLAKE, A.H., Cpl		16. 05. 44		29. 07. 44
				(Died 30. 07. 44)
COLLINS, W.J., Sgt		16. 05. 44		26. 10. 44
JONES, C.F., Cpl	1	16. 05. 44	1	13. 06. 44
	2	11. 08. 44	2	17. 12. 44
LANE, J.W., Cpl	1	22. 05. 44	1	13. 06. 44
	2	14. 07. 44	2	–
HIBBITT, W.A., Cpl		06. 07. 44		16. 12. 44
CUTCHIE, C.M., Cpl		14. 07. 44		–
COLE, R.A., Cpl		26. 07. 44		20. 12. 44
MUNRO, H.A.C., Lt	1	02. 08. 44	1	30. 09. 44
	2	16. 10. 44	2	04. 02. 45
RENFREE, T.J., Lt		03. 08. 44		20. 12. 44
HARLOW, E.C.G., Capt		12. 08. 44		11. 02. 45
THORNTON MC, M.J., Maj	1	02. 09. 44	1	30. 12. 44
	2	04. 01. 45	2	09. 01. 45
	3	31. 01. 45	3	–
OLIVER, J.P.F., Maj	1	08. 09. 44	1	05. 12. 44
	2	11. 12. 44	2	31. 12. 44
WINN, Hon. R.D.G., Lt		19. 09. 44		16. 12. 44
ANDREW, F.A., Lt		19. 09. 44		06. 02. 45
BOULTON, F. W., Cpl		19. 09. 44		12. 12. 44
FLEURY, P.G., Cpl		30. 09. 44		27. 12. 44
STEVANS, D., Sgt		05. 10. 44		05. 02. 45
WILKINSON, G.C., Lt		16. 10. 44		11. 02. 45
BISHOP, E.N., Capt		22. 10. 44		–
COMBER, F. Cpl		22. 10. 44		22. 01. 45
DURCAN, J.P., Capt		22. 10. 44		06. 02. 45

WHYTE, G.E.A., Lt	22. 10. 44	22. 01. 45
RAYNBIRD, E.P.G., Lt	24. 10. 44	12. 12. 44
CROZIER, T.A., Sgt	24. 10. 44	–
LAWSON, A.J., Lt	24. 10. 44	09. 01. 45
SQUIRES, W., Capt	28. 10. 44	27. 12. 44
HUMPHREY, J.J., Sgt	05. 11. 44	27. 12. 44
BURTON, J.A., Cpl	05. 11. 44	05. 02. 45
ROGERS, C.R., Bdr	28. 11. 44	30. 12. 44
HILL, W.A., Cpl	05. 12. 44	11. 12. 44

To avoid confusion, all code-names have been omitted from this book. Early on, every officer and NCO going into Albania had one. Most were puns or a play on each man's name. McLean was PASTE, Smiley was GRIN, Duffy was PLUM, Neel was BEG, Hands was FOOT, Kemp was TOWN, Field was HAY and so on. By October 1943 the practice of issuing individuals with code-names had proved pointless and been drawn to a close.

All missions had code-names. McLean's first mission was CONCENSUS, complete with spelling mistake. His second mission was known variously as CONCENSUS II and BERNARD. Others included SPINSTER (Hands); SLENDER (Neel, then Seymour, then Simcox); SCULPTOR (Tilman, then Shaw); SAPLING (Field, then Quayle); STEP-MOTHER (Kemp); SCONCE (Seymour); SPILLWAY (Davies); SWIFTER (Palmer, Smith, Wheeler and Lyon); STABLES (Riddell, Simcox and Hibbert); PRIMUS (Smith); COOPERATION (Neel and Hibberdine); VERTEBRAE (Ensor, then Newell, then Munro); FIGURE (Northrop); GUNMAN (Wright); CAMERON (Thornton).

PRONUNCIATION AND
PLACE-NAMES

THE Albanian alphabet has thirty-six letters; English-speakers should note the following approximate pronunciations:

a	as in cart
ç	as in church
ë	as in agenda; almost silent at the end of a word
dh	as in this
gj	as in jab
j	as in yell
ll	as in fall
nj	as in lanyard
q	as in chap
rr	as in horror
th	as in wrath; softer than 'dh'
u	as in moon
x	as in roads
xh	as in jar; thus 'Hoxha' rhymes with 'lodger'
y	as in put
zh	as in treasure

Albanian place-names take both definite and indefinite forms. Here they are treated in line with common usage in English-language works.

NOTES

Prologue

1. Colonel A. B. Lawson to War Office, 16 November 1945, The National Archives (hereafter TNA) WO 170/7365
2. Lieutenant Colonel A. Nicholls, diary entry, 26 December 1943
3. GR&E Pool War Diary, 23 September 1945, TNA WO 170/7365
4. Colonel A. B. Lawson to War Office, 18 March 1946, TNA WO 170/9124
5. Major F. McIntosh, 'Graves Registration and Concentration in Albania: Closing Report', TNA WO 170/9124
6. Ibid.
7. Major F. McIntosh, 'Report on Activities in Albania', 25 December 1945, TNA WO 170/7365
8. Major F. McIntosh, 'Graves Registration and Concentration in Albania: Closing Report', TNA WO 170/9124
9. Major F. McIntosh, 'Report on Activities in Albania', 25 December 1945, TNA WO 170/7365
10. Ibid.
11. Major F. McIntosh, 'Graves Registration and Concentration in Albania: Closing Report', TNA WO 170/9124
12. Ibid.
13. P. Broad to Foreign Office, telegram, 20 February 1946, TNA FO 369/3360; Macpherson to Foreign Office, telegram, 30 March 1946, TNA FO 369/3360
14. Colonel A. B. Lawson to War Office, 18 March 1946, TNA WO 170/9124
15. British Embassy, Paris, to French Government, 25 February 1950, TNA FO 369/4401
16. Major H. Bucknel to Imperial War Graves Commission, 16 May 1950, TNA FO 369/4401
17. In 1992, prompted by Colonel David Smiley, a former SOE officer, the new

Albanian Government investigated and confirmed that the graves had been moved. Digs by Britain's Commonwealth War Graves Commission found nothing but in 1994, among the pines of a Tirana park, close to where the remains of the original were thought to be, a new military cemetery was marked out. A plaque was also put up. 'The men in whose memory these headstones are erected gave their lives in Albania and are buried near this spot,' the simple inscription reads. 'Their glory shall not be blotted out.'

18. For critiques of British policy in wartime Albania and the conduct of SOE's Albanian section headquarters, see, for example: J. Amery, *Sons of the Eagle: A Study in Guerrilla Warfare*; P. Kemp, *No Colours or Crest*; A. Glen, *Footholds against a Whirlwind*; D. Smiley, *Albanian Assignment* and foreword by Patrick Leigh Fermor; D. Smiley, *Irregular Regular*; X. Fielding, *One Man in His Time: The Life of Lieutenant-Colonel N. L. D. 'Billy' McLean*. These issues are still raised periodically in the British press: in 1991, for example, when Amery, Smiley and Alan Hare returned to Albania and newspapers at home carried stories about the visit. See: S. Courtauld, 'Three Honourable Englishmen', *Sunday Telegraph*, 15 September 1991; N. Shakespeare, 'Return to the Land of Zog', *Daily Telegraph*, 5 October 1991; letters, *Daily Telegraph*, 23 October 1991. In 1997 the issues were revived when the catastrophic aftermath of a collapsing pyramid investment scheme thrust Albania on to the front pages. See: M. Glenny, 'Now it's war among the British friends of Albania', *Sunday Times*, 23 March 1997; R. Norton-Taylor, 'Champions go to War', *Guardian*, 10 March 1997; letters, *Independent*, 5 March 1997; letters, *Sunday Times*, 6 April 1997.

Chapter 1. 'Tip and run thuggery'

1. V. Noakes (ed.), *Edward Lear: Selected Letters*, p. 97
2. Ibid., p. 93; E. Lear, *Journals of a Landscape Painter in Albania &c* p. 92
3. Ibid., p. 101
4. V. Noakes (ed.), *Edward Lear: Selected Letters*, p. 93
5. E. Lear, *Journals of a Landscape Painter in Albania, &c*, pp. 234, 243–4
6. Ibid., p. 245
7. M. Blind (ed.), *The Letters of Lord Byron* pp. 29, 35; L. Marchand (ed.), *Byron's Letters and Journals*, Vol. I: *In My Hot Youth (1798–1810)*, pp. 248, 228
8. *The Poetical Works of Lord Byron*, Vol. I, p. 214
9. W. M. Leake, *Travels in Northern Greece*
10. Leake's despatches can be found in TNA FO 78/57 and TNA FO 78/65. I am grateful to Oliver Gilkes for drawing my attention to these.
11. Captain J. J. Best, *Excursions in Albania: Comprising a Description of*

the Wild Boar, Deer, and Woodcock Shooting in that Country; and a Journey from thence to Thessalonica and Constantinople and up the Danube to Pest, p. 3

12. Ibid., pp. 63, 139, 25, 64, 11–13
13. See, for example: J. Baker, *Turkey in Europe*; Sir Charles Eliot, *Turkey in Europe*; E. Durham, *The Burden of the Balkans* and *High Albania*
14. J. Buchan, *Greenmantle*, p.12
15. W. M. Leake, *Travels in Northern Greece*, Vol. I, p. 20
16. J. Buchan, *The Thirty-Nine Steps*, pp. 11–12
17. *Sphere*, 29 April 1933
18. *Daily Telegraph*, 15, 17 October 1928
19. Interview, Saranda, July 2000
20. Captain Bowyer-Smith to Earl of Perth, 13 April 1939, TNA FO 371/23713
21. Sir A. Ryan to E. Ingram, 11 April 1939, TNA FO 371/23713
22. C. Andrew, *Secret Service: The Making of the British Intelligence Community*, p. 420
23. H. Macmillan, *Winds of Change, 1914–1939*, p. 592
24. COS (39) 21st Meeting, 18 September 1939, TNA CAB 79/1
25. COS (39) 96th Meeting, 4 December 1939, TNA CAB 79/1
26. D. Oakley-Hill, *An Englishman in Albania*, p. 123
27. Captain F. T. Davies to P. Broad, 8 April 1940, TNA FO 371/24866
28. D. Oakley-Hill, *An Englishman in Albania*, p. 111
29. General Sir J. Percy to Colonel E. de Renzy Martin, 11 December 1940, TNA HS 5/61
30. Ibid.
31. J. Amery, *Sons of the Eagle*, p. 24
32. Ibid., p. 29
33. J. Amery, 'Possibilities of Action in Albania, based on a conversation with Gani Beg', 4 May 1940, TNA HS 5/60
34. In December 1940 it was 'ascertained indirectly' from an official at the Belgrade Ministry of Foreign Affairs that Gani was receiving 'a subsidy of 10,000 dinars a month' from secret Ministry funds. It was learnt, too, 'that he was regarded by the Yugo Slavs as a candidate for the Albanian crown in preference to Zog who was out of favour on account of his unfriendly attitude towards Yugo Slavia during the latter part of his reign'. Foreign Office to War Office, telegram, 28 January 1941, TNA HS 5/7; SOE War Diary, TNA HS 7/212
35. 'Albania', memorandum, 12 May 1940, TNA HS 5/60
36. Section D War Diary, TNA HS 7/4
37. J. Hanau to G. Taylor, 25 May 1940, TNA HS 5/60
38. 'Albania', memorandum, 27 May 1940, TNA HS 5/60

39. J. Amery, *Sons of the Eagle*, p. 34
40. A. Goodwill to Brigadier E. J. Shearer, 'Political Policy in Albania and Istria', 19 July 1940, TNA HS 5/60
41. Section D War Diary, TNA HS 7/4
42. Major I. Pirie, 'SOE Activities in Greece 1940–42', TNA HS 7/150
43. 'Albania', memorandum, 25 August 1940, TNA HS 5/60
44. SOE War Diary, TNA HS 7/211
45. Section D War Diary, TNA HS 7/4
46. T. E. Lawrence, *Revolt in the Desert*, pp. 434, 327
47. Lieutenant Colonel W. F. Stirling to A. Goodwill, 'Albania', 19 August 1940, TNA HS 5/60
48. Dr H. Dalton to Prime Minister, 10 November 1940 TNA HS 5/90
49. I. Pirie to R. Searight, 'Albania', 27 January 1941, TNA HS 5/63
50. Lieutenant Colonel W. F. Stirling, memorandum, c. August 1940, TNA HS 5/60
51. Ibid.
52. R. Campbell to Mr Hopkinson, telegram, 16 August 1940, TNA HS 5/928
53. P. Broad to Sir Godfrey Thomas, 6 September 1940, TNA HS 5/928
54. D. Oakley-Hill, 'Plan for Revolt in Northern Albania', January 1941, TNA HS 5/63
55. General Sir J. Percy to Lieutenant Colonel E. de Renzy Martin, 11 December 1940, TNA HS 5/61
56. Lieutenant Colonel E. de Renzy Martin, 'Albanian Revolt', 11 January 1941, TNA HS 5/61
57. Idem., 'Albania', c. December 1940, TNA HS 5/61
58. E. Barker, *British Policy in South East Europe in the Second World War*, p. 49
59. W. F. Stirling, *Safety Last*, pp. 199–200
60. T. Masterson and D. Oakley-Hill to SOE London, telegrams, 18 December 1940, TNA HS 5/61
61. Major I. Pirie, 'SOE Activities in Greece 1940–42', TNA HS 7/150
62. R. Searight to A. Goodwill, telegram, 25 December 1940, TNA HS 5/61
63. R. Searight to I. Pirie, telegram, 10 January 1941, TNA HS 5/61
64. Lieutenant Colonel E. de Renzy Martin, 'Albania', c. December 1940, TNA HS 5/61
65. Idem., 'Albanian Revolt', 29 December 1940, TNA HS 5/61
66. Colonel Simic, report, 17 May 1940, TNA HS 5/60
67. T. Masterson and D. Oakley-Hill to SOE London, telegram, 18 December 1940, TNA HS 5/61
68. H. Watts to A. Goodwill, 'Revolt in Albania', 21 December 1940, TNA HS 5/61

69. I. Pirie to T. Masterson and D. Oakley-Hill, 'Albania', 24 January 1941, TNA HS 5/63
70. Ibid.
71. G. Taylor to Sir F. Nelson, 'Report on SO Organisation and Plans in the Balkans', 26 February 1941, TNA HS 5/166
72. J. Amery, *Sons of the Eagle*, p. 43
73. D. Oakley-Hill, *An Englishman in Albania*, pp. 122, 124–5
74. Ibid., pp. 121–2, 131–2

Chapter 2. 'A few volunteers'

1. SOE War Diary, TNA HS 7/227
2. Information from the SOE Adviser to the Foreign & Commonwealth Office (hereafter SOE Adviser)
3. D. Smiley, *Albanian Assignment*, pp. 8–9
4. J. Naar, interview, December 2000
5. J. Pearson to G. Taylor, 3 December 1940, TNA HS 5/63
6. Interview, Elbasan, September 2000
7. Major I. Pirie, 'SOE Activities in Greece 1940–42', TNA HS 7/150.
8. M. Hasluck to Lord Glenconner, 'SOE in Albania', 17 May 1943, TNA HS 5/87
9. Major P. Boughey to Lieutenant Colonel J. Pearson, 'Albania', 24 June 1942, TNA HS 5/102
10. SOE Cairo memorandum, 'Albanian Situation', 20 June 1942, TNA HS 5/86
11. SOE Cairo Albanian desk 'Fortnightly Appreciation', 29 November 1942, TNA HS 5/96
12. N. Davis to Lord Glenconner, 'Albania', 28 April 1943, TNA HS 5/87
13. Major P. Boughey to Lieutenant Colonel J. Pearson, 'Albania', 24 June 1942, TNA HS 5/102
14. M. Hasluck to SOE Cairo, 11 April 1942, TNA HS 5/86
15. Idem., 'The Albanians in Istanbul', 14 April 1942, TNA HS 5/107
16. N. Davis to M. Hasluck, 27 August 1943, TNA HS 5/107
17. SOE War Diary, TNA HS 7/229
18. P. Dixon to Lord Glenconner, 10 June 1942, TNA FO 371/33112
19. E. Barker, *British Policy in South-East Europe*, pp. 174–5
20. A. Eden, 17 December 1942, Hansard, Vol. 385, HC Debates, Fifth Series, Col. 2114
21. D. McAdoo to E. Brennan and P. Adams, 'Proposals of Qemal Butka and others for an Albanian Committee', 13 October 1943, NARA RG 226 Entry 190 Box 178 Folio 1383
22. SOE Cairo memorandum, 'Albanian Situation', 20 June 1942, TNA HS 5/86
23. M. Hasluck to N. Davis, 'Stavro Skendi', 22 July 1943, TNA HS 5/65

24. D. McAdoo to H. Fultz, 28 February 1944, NARA RG 226 Entry 190 Box 567 Folio 306

25. M. Hasluck to SOE Cairo, 'Men for Palestine', 12 May 1942, TNA HS 5/107

26. Ibid., 20 May 1942, TNA HS 5/107

27. Ibid., 12 May 1942, TNA HS 5/107

28. Ibid., 30 May 1942, TNA HS 5/86

29. Idem., 'Palestine Training of 25-landers', 28 July 1942, TNA HS 5/109

30. M. Hasluck to Major P. Leake, 7 May 1943, TNA HS 5/103

31. M. Hasluck to SOE Cairo, 'On the Austro-Hungarian Frontier', 4 April 1942, TNA HS 5/86

32. Idem., 'Leakages', 27 June 1942, with annotation by Lieutenant Colonel J. Pearson, TNA HS 5/107

33. Major P. Boughey annotation to M. Hasluck to Major E. Boxshall, 21 November 1943, TNA HS 5/26

34. Major P. Boughey to Lieutenant Colonel J. Pearson, 'Albania', 24 June 1942, TNA HS 5/102

35. Information from the SOE Adviser

36. Chiefs of Staff Memorandum COS(43)142(0), 'Special Operations Executive Directive for 1943', 20 March 1943, TNA CAB 80/68

37. P.A.B. Neel, interview with C. Neel, 1991

38. H. Munro to author, May 2002

39. Dr J. Dumoulin, interview, February 2000

40. J. Davis to author, June 2000

41. R. Melrose, unpublished memoir

42. Information from Phillip Gray

43. H. Munro, interview, January 2000

44. Dr J. Dumoulin, interview, February 2000

45. M. Lyon, interview, November 1999

46. R. Melrose, unpublished memoir

47. H. Munro, interview, January 2000

48. P. Kemp, *No Colours or Crest*, pp. 78–9

49. M. Lyon, unpublished memoir

50. A. Quayle, *A Time to Speak*, p. 260

51. M. Hasluck, *Albanian Phrase Book* (1944)

52. M. Hasluck, *Këndime Englisht-Shquip or Albanian-English Reader: Sixteen Albanian Folk-Stories Collected and Translated, with Two Grammars and Vocabularies*, p. xi

53. Sir R. Hibbert, interview, February 1998

54. M. Hasluck, *Këndime Englisht-Shqip*, pp. 46–7

55. M. Lyon, unpublished memoir

56. A. Quayle, *A Time to Speak*, p. 288

57. P. Kemp, *No Colours or Crest*, p. 86

58. W.E.D. Allen, *Guerrilla Warfare in Abyssinia*, p. 124
59. D. Smiley, *Albanian Assignment*, p. 14
60. Ibid., p. 8
61. Major N. McLean to Lieutenant Colonel G. Tamplin, 'Plan for the Advance Mission to Albania', 29 March 1943, TNA HS 5/66
62. W. Williamson, interview, March 2000
63. Corporal W. Williamson diary, 16 February 1943
64. Ibid., 11, 13, 15 April 1943
65. M. Hasluck to Lieutenant Colonel G. Tamplin, 1 May 1943, TNA HS 5/103
66. Major N. McLean, 'Diary Notes', McLean papers, IWM
67. W. Williamson, interview, March 2000
68. Major N. McLean, 'Diary Notes', McLean papers, IWM
69. Captain D. Smiley, diary entry, 17 April 1943, TNA HS 5/143
70. Major N. McLean, 'Diary Notes', McLean papers, IWM
71. W. Williamson, interview, March 2000
72. Major N. McLean, 'Diary Notes', McLean papers, IWM

Chapter 3. 'Everything going fine'

1. M. Hasluck to Lieutenant Colonel G. Tamplin, 'Macedonia', 25 May 1943, TNA HS 5/66. It was heard later that Morgan had been captured by Bulgarian troops.
2. CONCENSUS to SOE Cairo, w/t message, 4 May 1943, McLean papers, IWM
3. SOE War Diary, TNA HS 7/269
4. CONCENSUS to SOE Cairo, w/t message, 11 June 1943, McLean papers, IWM
5. Ibid.
6. Major N. McLean, 'Diary Notes', McLean papers, IWM
7. Captain M. Lyon, 'Report on the National Liberation Movement', December 1944, TNA HS 5/7
8. Major N. McLean, report, 1943, McLean papers, IWM
9. Major N. McLean, 'Diary Notes', McLean papers, IWM
10. Major N. McLean, report, 1943, McLean papers, IWM
11. Proclamation, 7 July 1943, McLean papers, IWM
12. CONCENSUS to SOE Cairo, w/t message, 15 July 1943, McLean papers, IWM
13. Major N. McLean, 'Diary Notes', McLean papers, IWM
14. CONCENSUS to SOE Cairo, w/t message, 29 July 1943, McLean papers, IWM
15. CONCENSUS to SOE Cairo, w/t message, 31 July 1943, McLean papers, IWM
16. Major N. McLean, 'Diary Notes', McLean papers, IWM

17. Captain D. Smiley, diary entry, 30 October 1943, TNA HS 5/143
18. Corporal H. Bell, report, 1944, TNA HS 5/124
19. W. Williamson, interview, March 2000
20. Captain D. Smiley diary, 18 July 1943, TNA HS 5/143. Such was the confusion that one young Partisan there that night remained certain, fifty-seven years later, that it was the Halifax that had dropped the bombs. Interview, Vithkuq, September 2000
21. Major J. Shaw, report, 1944, TNA HS 5/140
22. Major A. Hare, report, 1944, TNA HS 5/139
23. Captain J. Hibberdine, diary entry, 19 January 1944
24. Major N. McLean, 'Diary Notes', McLean papers, IWM
25. W. Williamson, interview, March 2000
26. Major A. Hare, report, 1944, TNA HS 5/139
27. Corporal W. Williamson, diary entry, November 1943
28. W. Williamson, interview, March 2000
29. Corporal W. Williamson, diary entry, November 1943
30. Major R. Riddell and Captain R. Hibbert, report, 1944, TNA HS 5/142
31. Major A. Hare, report, 1944, TNA HS 5/139
32. Ibid.
33. Major V. Smith, report, 1944, TNA HS 5/129
34. Major A. Hare, report, 1944, TNA HS 5/139
35. W. Williamson, interview, March 2000
36. Captain D. Smiley diary entry, 4 August 1943, TNA HS 5/143
37. Captain J. Hibberdine, diary entry, 23 February 1944
38. Major G. Seymour, report, 1944, TNA HS 5/123
39. *Journal of the Royal Scots Fusiliers*, vol xxi, January 1954, No. 1
40. B. McSwiney, interview, January 2000
41. L.S. Amery to Lord Selborne, 2 November 1944, TNA HS 8/908
42. A. DeAth, unpublished memoir
43. Major J. Faure-Field, 'Albania', in *The Oak Tree*, Summer 1947, p. 87
44. Major V. Smith, report, 1944, TNA HS 5/129
45. Major G. Seymour, report, 1944, TNA HS 5/123
46. CONCENSUS to SOE Cairo, w/t message, 14 August 1943, McLean papers, IWM
47. W. Williamson, interview, March 2000
48. CONCENSUS to SOE Cairo, w/t message, 3 September 1943, McLean papers, IWM
49. Major P. Kemp, report, 1944, TNA HS 5/144
50. Proceedings of a conference on British and European Resistance, 1939–1945, held at St Antony's College, Oxford, December 1962.
51. Squadron Leader A. Hands to Major N. McLean, 16 August 1943, McLean papers, IWM

52. Major H. W. Tilman, report, 1944, TNA HS 5/128
53. Wing Commander P.A.B. Neel to Major N. McLean, 11 August 1943, McLean papers, IWM
54. Squadron Leader A. Hands to Major N. McLean, 21 August 1943, McLean papers, IWM
55. Wing Commander P.A.B. Neel to Major N. McLean, 11 August 1943, McLean papers, IWM
56. CSDIC Report, 16 July 1944, TNA WO 204/9534
57. Major G. Seymour, report, 1944, TNA HS 5/123
58. Ibid.
59. CSDIC Report, 16 July 1944, TNA WO 204/9534
60. Major H.W. Tilman, report, 1944, TNA HS 5/128. Although sources conflict as to the precise date and location and the number of Italians killed, executions certainly took place. One eyewitness, an Italian doctor attached to the *Perugia*, remembered that the last organised elements of the division, out of food and ammunition, had surrendered to the Germans on 4 October. Nearly a hundred officers were shot and more were killed elsewhere. Doctors and other noncombatants were spared. Locals remember that the Germans took the corpses out to sea and weighed them down with stones, though many bodies washed back to the shore. Chiminello's head, it was rumoured, was put on display in Saranda. Interviews, Saranda and Himara, 2000.
61. Major J. Faure-Field, 'Albania', in *The Oak Tree*, December 1947, pp. 213–15; spring 1948, pp. 17–21
62. Ibid., summer 1948, p. 55
63. Major H.W. Tilman, report, 1944, TNA HS 5/128
64. W. Williamson, interview, March 2000
65. Major G. Seymour, report, 1944, TNA HS 5/123
66. Major P. Kemp report, 1944, TNA HS 5/144
67. CONCENSUS to SOE Cairo, w/t message, 4 September 1943, McLean papers, IWM
68. Lieutenant G. Duffy to Major N. McLean, 24 September 1943, Mclean papers, IWM
69. Ibid., 29 September 1943, McLean papers, IWM
70. Major G. Seymour, report, 1944, TNA HS 5/123
71. N. McLean, 'Diary Notes', McLean papers, IWM

Chapter 4. 'Endurance Vile'

1. Memorandum, 'Albania', 16 July 1943, TNA HS 5/10
2. Lieutenant Colonel J. Pearson to Group Captain J. Fenner, 6 July 1943, TNA HS 5/102

3. MI3b to Joint Planning Staff, memorandum, 'Guerrilla Activity in Albania', 19 August 1943, TNA HS 5/23

4. Memorandum, 'Albania: Operational Policy', c. end August 1943, TNA HS 5/66

5. Lieutenant Colonel B. Sweet-Escott to Major General C. Gubbins, 'Albania: Appreciation', 30 June 1943, TNA HS 5/82

6. 'SOC Directive to Brigadier E. F. Davies', October 1943, TNA HS 5/59

7. Quoted in Brigadier H. P. Currie, 'The Late Brigadier E. F. (Trotsky) Davies DSO MC: An Appreciation,' *Quis Separabit*, Journal of the Royal Ulster Rifles, 1952, p. 64

8. Ibid., pp. 64–5

9. M. Lyon, unpublished memoir

10. M. Lyon to author, March 2001

11. M. Lyon, interview, November 1999

12. M. Lyon, unpublished memoir

13. Lieutenant Colonel A. Nicholls, diary entry, 18 October 1943

14. D. Smiley, diary entries, 20 and 21 October 1943, TNA HS 5/143

15. R. Melrose, unpublished memoir

16. Lieutenant Colonel A. Nicholls, diary entry, 26 October 1943

17. Ibid., 31 October, 1 November 1943

18. Ibid., 31, 27 and 30 October 1943

19. Ibid., 2 November 1943

20. SOE War Diary, TNA HS 7/271

21. Lieutenant Colonel A. Nicholls, diary entries, 2 and 3 November 1943

22. SOE War Diary, TNA HS 7/271

23. Lieutenant Colonel A. Nicholls, diary entry, 3 November 1943

24. Ibid., 6 November 1943

25. Ibid., 8 and 9 November 1943

26. Ibid., 11 November 1943

27. Ibid., 12 and 15 November 1943

28. Major G. Seymour, report, 1944, TNA HS 5/123

29. Lieutenant Colonel A. Nicholls, diary entry, 15 November 1943

30. P. Kemp, *No Colours or Crest*, p. 91

31. Lieutenant Colonel A. Nicholls, diary entries, 14, 16 and 17 November 1943

32. Ibid., 15 and 20 November 1943

33. P. Kemp, *No Colours or Crest*, pp. 176–7

34. Lieutenant Colonel A. Nicholls, diary entries, 23 November to 1 December 1943

35. Ibid., 2 December 1943

36. R. Melrose, unpublished memoir

37. Lieutenant Colonel A. Nicholls, diary entry, 1 December 1943

38. Ibid., 5, 6, 7, 8, 11 and 12 December 1943

39. Ibid., 15 December 1943
40. Ibid., 16 to 19 December 1943
41. R. Melrose, unpublished memoir
42. Lieutenant Colonel A. Nicholls, diary entry, 20 December 1943
43. Ibid., 22 December 1943
44. Ibid., 22 and 23 December 1943
45. Ibid., 24 to 27 December 1943
46. Ibid., 28 December 1943 to 3 January 1944
47. Major J. Chesshire, diary entries, 22 to 25 and 30 December 1943 and 3 January 1944
48. J. Davis to author, September 2000
49. R. Melrose, unpublished memoir
50. Lieutenant Colonel A. Nicholls, diary entries, 4 to 6 January 1944
51. Ibid., 7 January 1944
52. Ibid., 8 January 1944
53. Major A. Hare, 'Report on the Capture of Brig. Davis [sic]', 1944, TNA HS 9/399/7
54. Ibid.
55. Ibid.
56. Lieutenant Colonel A. Nicholls, diary entry, 8 January 1944
57. Ibid., 9 and 10 January 1944
58. Ibid., 10 to 14 January 1944
59. Captain A. Hare, diary entry, 15 January 1944
60. Ibid., 17, 19, 22, 26, 28, 29 January, 1, 5 to 8, 10, 13 to 16, 18 to 20 February 1944
61. Major G. Seymour, report, 'Conduct of the late A/Brigadier A. F. C. Nicholls, Coldstream Guards', 10 December 1944, TNA HS 9/1644
62. Major G. Seymour to SOE Cairo, w/t message, 6 February 1944 quoted in Lieutenant J. Eyre to Major E. Boxshall, 15 February 1944, TNA HS 9/1644
63. I. Toptani, report, 1944, TNA HS 9/1644
64. Major G. Seymour, report, 'Conduct of the late A/Brigadier A. F. C. Nicholls, Coldstream Guards', 10 December 1944, TNA HS 9/1644
65. Lieutenant Colonel Penman, report, 1944, TNA HS 9/1644
66. In late January the Tirana press announced that Davies and other British personnel were prisoners. In February the Berlin press declared the same.
67. Captain J. Hibberdine, diary entry, 22 March 1943
68. Lieutenant J. Taylor, undated note, 'Albania', NARA, RG 226 Entry 154 Box 17 Folio 237

Chapter 5. 'Enthusiasm and romanticism'

1. SOE War Diary, TNA HS 7/271
2. Ibid.
3. CONCENSUS to SOE Cairo, 29 September 1943, McLean papers, IWM
4. Ibid., 18 October 1943, McLean papers, IWM
5. SOE War Diary, TNA HS 7/271
6. Major P. Leake, memorandum, 'Albania: Appreciation', 14 December 1943, TNA HS 5/67
7. Major P. Leake to COS, 15 November 1943, TNA HS 5/66
8. 'Copy of Homebrewed 3 or 17 Dec', 19 December 1943, TNA HS 5/66
9. W. Churchill, *The Second World War*, Vol. V, p. 416
10. See, for example: D. Martin, Introductory Essay in *Patriot or Traitor: The Case of General Mihailovich*, pp. 117–19; D. Martin, *The Web of Disinformation*, ch. 1 passim, pp. 94–110; D. Martin, 'James Klugmann, SOE-Cairo and the Mihailovich Deception', pp. 53–84; M. Lees, *The Rape of Serbia*, ch. 1 passim, pp. 206–7, 230–36; C. Pincher, *Too Secret Too Long*, pp. 397–401; R. Deacon, *The British Connection*, pp. 162–70.
11. The proposed decision to drop Mihailović, Klugmann argued in one paper prepared in December 1943, had been 'taken on its merits'. Listing reasons for withdrawing British missions with the Chetniks, he also claimed that they had carried out 'only five small-scale demolitions' since they had had BLOs attached to them. Captain J. Klugmann to Lieutenant Colonel F. W. Deakin, memorandum, 'Note on Evacuation of British Missions from Mihailovic Areas', 21 December 1943, TNA HS 5/901. Signals from SOE missions with Mihailović confirm that five relatively insignificant bridge demolitions were carried out between September and December 1943. Arguably Klugmann could also have pointed to numerous train derailments and railway line blows by British personnel attached to Mihailović in September, October and November; though sometimes carried out with only minimal Chetnik help, all had been reported to Cairo. He might also have acknowledged reports of independent Chetnik attacks on German and Bulgarian forces in October and November. Most conspicuously, perhaps, Klugmann did not mention the recent demolition of the bridge at Višegrad on 5 October. That omission seems especially odd since, shortly after that attack, SOE officers with the Chetniks were disturbed to hear the BBC attribute it to the Partisans and transmitted strong protests to Cairo urging the BBC to get its facts right. Brigadier C. Armstrong to SOE Cairo, cipher telegram, 18 November 1943, TNA WO 202/140.
12. Untitled transcript, 8 August 1945, TNA KV 2/791
13. Sir D. Petrie to Major General Sir S. Menzies, 29 August 1945, TNA KV 2/791.

14. Quoted in J. Cripps, 'Mihailovic or Tito?', in M. Smith and R. Erskine, *Action this Day*, p. 256

15. Ibid.

16. F. H. Hinsley, *British Intelligence in the Second World War: Its Influence on Strategy and Operations* Vol. II, Part I p. 29

17. M. Hasluck to Major E. Boxshall, 21 November 1943, TNA HS 5/26

18. See, for example, E. Hoxha, *The Anglo-American Threat to Albania*, p. 72

19. M. Hasluck to N. Davis, 7 August 1942, TNA HS 5/86

20. SOE Albanian Section 'Fortnightly Intelligence Summary', 15 December 1943, TNA WO 204/9527

21. M. Hasluck to Major E. Boxshall, memorandum, 'PWE Fortnightly Intelligence Summary', 6 December 1943, TNA HS 5/26

22. Idem., 'Council of Regents', 19 December 1943, TNA HS 5/26

23. Major E. Boxshall to Lieutenant Colonel D. Talbot Rice, undated covering note to M. Hasluck to Major E. Boxshall, memorandum, 'Council of Regents', 19 December 1943, TNA HS 5/26

24. P. Kemp, *No Colours or Crest*, pp. 75–6

25. 'Corpus Christi College: The Pelican Record', Vol. XVII, No. 4, December 1925, p. 64

26. B. Sweet-Escott, *Baker Street Irregular*, p. 83

27. Major H.J. Legg, unpublished memoir, IWM

28. Mrs M. Kraay, interview, June 2001

29. J. Naar to author, September 1999

30. J. Naar, interview, December 2000

31. J. Naar to author, September 1999

32. M. Hasluck to Major General W. Stawell, 8 February 1944, TNA HS 5/67

33. Major P. Leake to Brigadier K. Barker-Benfield, 14 December 1943, TNA HS 5/66

34. 'Allied Military Mission: Albania. Proposed Policy Change', 24 December 1943, TNA HS 5/79

35. SOE London to Force 133, cipher telegram, 24 November 1943, TNA HS 5/66

36. C. Steel to Foreign Office, cipher telegrams, 1 January 1944, TNA HS 5/66

37. GHQ Middle East Directive No. 195, 24 January 1944, TNA HS 5/11

38. Major P. Leake, memorandum, 'Albania: Appreciation', 14 December 1943, TNA HS 5/67

39. Major P. Leake to SOE London, cipher telegram, 1 January 1944, TNA HS 5/12

40. Lieutenant Colonel A. Nicholls, diary entries, 15 and 17 December 1943

41. Ibid., 31 December 1943

42. SOE London, 'Resume of recent proposals regarding policy in Albania', 16 February 1944, TNA HS 5/68

43. M. Hasluck to Major General W. Stawell, 8 February 1944, TNA HS 5/67

44. J. Naar to author, September 2000

45. J. Naar, interview, December 2000

46. Ibid.

47. J. Naar to author, September 1999

48. M. Hasluck to Major E. Boxshall, memorandum, 'Albanian Guerillas', 1 January 1944, TNA HS 5/68

49. Idem., 'LNC and BBC', 15 January 1944, TNA HS 5/68

50. J. Naar, interview, December 2000

51. SOE Albanian Section 'Fortnightly Intelligence Summary', 9 January 1944, TNA HS 5/67

52. Applicant questionnaire, 1943, NARA RG 226 Entry 92A Box 46 Folio 766

53. J. Hudson to author, February 2003

54. H.T. Fultz to Major Koch, memorandum, 'Policies and Recommendations Relative to Albania', 18 January 1944, NARA RG 226 Entry 154 Box 14 Folio 181

55. Major P. Leake to Brigadier W. Stawell, memorandum, 'Status of Mrs Hasluck', 18 January 1944, TNA HS 5/66

56. M. Hasluck to C. Steel, memorandum, 'Conditions in Albania', 8 February 1944, TNA HS 5/67

57. M. Hasluck to Major E. Boxshall, memorandum, 'The Crisis', 9 February 1944 TNA HS 5/68

58. Major E. Boxshall to Captain D. Oakley-Hill, annotation on M. Hasluck to Major E. Boxshall, memorandum, 'The Crisis', 9 February 1944 TNA HS 5/68

59. M. Hasluck to Major E. Boxshall, February 1944, TNA HS 5/68

60. Information from the SOE Adviser

61. Captain D. Smiley, diary entries, 17 and 18 November 1943, TNA HS 5/143

62. Major N. McLean, 'Memorandum on Albania', McLean papers, IWM

63. Major P. Leake, 'Appreciation and Plan for "Underdone"', 29 January 1944, TNA AIR 20/8378

64. Major G. Seymour to SOE Cairo, w/t message, 5 February 1944, quoted in M. Hasluck to C. Steel, 8 February 1944, TNA HS 5/67

65. Major P. Leake to C. Steel, memorandum, 'Abas Kupi's Personal Message', 7 February 1944, TNA HS 5/9

66. Major P. Leake, memorandum, 'Albania: Support of Major Kupi's Legitimacy Movement', 12 February 1944, TNA HS 5/79

67. Major P. Leake, memorandum, 'Albania: Appreciation', 14 December 1943, TNA HS 5/67

68. Major P. Leake to SOE London, cipher telegram, 1 January 1944, TNA HS 5/12
69. Major P. Leake to C. Steel, 8 February 1944, TNA HS 5/66
70. C. Steel to Foreign Office, cipher telegram, 12 February 1944, TNA HS 5/12
71. Major P. Leake to Major E. Boxshall, 13 March 1944, TNA HS 5/68
72. Colonel D. Keswick to Major General C. Gubbins, 14 February 1944, TNA HS 5/11
73. W. Houstoun-Boswall to Major General C. Gubbins, 28 February 1944, TNA HS 5/68
74. Colonel D. Keswick to Major General C. Gubbins, 25 February 1944, TNA HS 5/11
75. Major P. Leake to C. Steel, 17 February 1944, and C. Steel, hand-written annotation, 18 February 1944, TNA HS 5/66
76. D. Howard to Lieutenant Colonel D. Talbot Rice, 3 February 1944, TNA HS 5/11
77. Major G. Seymour, report, 1944, TNA HS 5/123
78. Major G. Seymour, diary entries, 22, 25, 28 February, 1, 5, 7 March 1944
79. Ibid., 8, 11, 12, 13, 17, 22, 24 to 26 March 1944
80. Lieutenant Colonel W. Harcourt, 'Comments on Report by Lt Col McLean DSO, Major Smiley MC and Capt Amery dated Nov 28 1944', c. December 1944, TNA HS 5/126
81. Major G. Seymour, diary entries, 30 March, 1 and 19 April 1944
82. Information from the SOE Adviser
83. Ibid.
84. SOE War Diary, TNA HS 7/268
85. Information from the SOE Adviser
86. J. Amery to N. McLean, 4 June 1948, McLean papers, IWM
87. Major E. Boxshall to D. Howard, 17 May 1944, TNA HS 5/11

Chapter 6. 'A nightmare beyond description'

1. Major G. Seymour, diary entry, 18 April 1944
2. Squadron Leader A. Hands, report, 1944, TNA HS 5/138
3. Wing Commander P.A.B. Neel, report, 1944, TNA HS 5/132
4. Captain J. Hibberdine, diary entry, 19 December 1943
5. Ibid., 19, 20, 25, 21 December 1943
6. R. Hibbert, Albania's National Liberation Struggle, p. 88
7. Captain J. Hibberdine, diary entry, c. 25 December 1943
8. Ibid., 25 December 1943
9. Force 133 Daily Situation Report, 1 January 1944, TNA HS 5/158
10. Major G. Seymour, report, 1944, TNA HS 5/123
11. Wing Commander P.A.B. Neel, report, 1944, TNA HS 5/132

12. CONCENSUS to SOE Cairo, w/t message, 29 July 1943, McLean papers, IWM

13. P. Kemp, *No Colours or Crest*, p. 97

14. CONCENSUS to SOE Cairo, w/t message, 8 August 1943, McLean papers, IWM

15. Major P. Kemp to SOE Cairo, w/t message, 29 September 1943, paraphrased in Major P. Leake to 'G.Ops' and C. Steel, 'Inflation No. 12 of February 4', 5 February 1944, TNA HS 5/79

16. W. Churchill, *The Second World War*, Vol. III, p. 393

17. Major P. Kemp, report, 1944, TNA HS 5/144

18. Minutes of SOC (43) 6th Meeting, 13 October 1943, TNA WO 201/2790

19. SOE Cairo to Brigadier E.F. Davies, w/t message, 21 October 1943, recorded in Major P. Leake to Major General W. Stawell, memorandum, 5 February 1944, TNA HS 5/79. British diplomats were neither blind to the issues at stake nor unsympathetic to Albanian claims, but few now doubted Kosovo's probable post-war fate. In July 1943, Arnold Toynbee's Foreign Research and Press Service, part of the Royal Institute of International Affairs, completed a study of 'The Albano–Yugoslav Frontier' which conceded that the 1941 border created by the Germans 'did approximate justice from the ethnic point of view'. 'The Albano–Yugoslav Frontier', TNA FO 371/37135. In February 1943, however, the FRPS had also passed to the Foreign Office a draft study, 'Albania as an International Problem', which contained the line: 'It is very probable that at the end of the war a reconstructed Yugoslavia will reclaim the territory lost to Albania in 1941.' Draft paper, 'Albania as an International Problem', TNA FO 371/37135. Denis Laskey, Foreign Office desk officer for Albania, highlighted that sentence and minuted: 'In paragraph 11 it is said that Yugoslavia will "very probably" reclaim the territory lost to Albania in 1941. I should have thought that this could be regarded as virtually certain.' D. Laskey, minute, 9 April 1943, TNA FO 371/37135. Douglas Howard, Head of the Southern Department, agreed and incorporated Laskey's minute in his formal comments on the draft. D. Howard to B. Wall, 9 June 1943, TNA FO 371/37135

20. Major P. Kemp, report, 1944, TNA HS 5/144

21. Captain J. Hibberdine, diary entry, 1 January 1944

22. Ibid., 14 January 1944

23. C-in-C Middle East to War Office, 'Balkan sitrep', 19 January 1944, TNA HS 5/82

24. Captain J. Hibberdine, diary entry, 23 December 1943

25. Major P. Kemp, report, 1944, TNA HS 5/144

26. Captain J. Hibberdine, diary entries, 5 and 16 January 1944

27. Ibid., 7 and 2 January 1944

28. Major P. Kemp, report, 1944, TNA HS 5/144

29. Ibid.
30. Ibid.
31. Captain J. Hibberdine, diary entries, 22 and 24 January 1944
32. Squadron Leader A. Hands, report, 1944, TNA HS 5/138
33. Major A. Hunter to SOE Cairo, w/t message, 17 January 1944, TNA WO 202/143
34. Major P. Leake to SOE Yugoslav Section, Cairo, 18 January 1944, TNA HS 5/79
35. Captain J. Hibberdine, diary entry, 27 January 1944
36. F. Hoxha, interview, November 2000
37. Captain J. Hibberdine, diary entry, 9 January 1944; S. J. Sales to Major Edward Boxshall, 'Copy of signal from SPINSTER', 8 February 1944, HS 5/67
38. Major P. Leake, memorandum, 'Kosovo Region', 21 January 1944, TNA HS 5/66
39. Minutes of SOC (W) (44) 10th Meeting, 22 January 1944, TNA WO 201/2860
40. Captain J. Hibberdine, diary entries, 24 and 27 January 1944
41. Major P. Leake, memorandum, 'Liaison with the Kosovo–Metohija (Kosmet) Partisans', 5 February 1944, TNA HS 5/79
42. Idem., 'Kosovo Region', 21 January 1944, TNA HS 5/66
43. Idem., 'Liaison with the Kosovo–Metohija (Kosmet) Partisans', 5 February 1944, TNA HS 5/79
44. Major P. Kemp, report, 1944, TNA HS 5/144
45. Squadron Leader A. Hands, report, 1944, TNA HS 5/138
46. Idem., via Corsair, 1944, Hands papers
47. Captain J. Hibberdine, diary entries, 2, 3, 6, 7, 9 and 10 February 1944
48. Wing Commander P. A. B. Neel, report, 1944, TNA HS 5/132
49. Captain J. Hibberdine, diary entry, 19 February 1944
50. Ibid., 23 February 1944
51. Ibid., 6 to 9 March 1944
52. Ibid., 14 and 15 March 1944
53. Major G. Seymour, diary entries, 13 and 18 April 1944
54. R. Riddell to author, February 2000
55. Major R. Riddell and Captain R. Hibbert, report, 1944, TNA HS 5/142

Chapter 7. 'This God-forsaken, savage country'

1. Major J. Field, report, 1943, TNA HS 5/124
2. Ibid.
3. A. DeAth, unpublished memoir
4. Major J. Field, report, 1943, TNA HS 5/124

5. Captain D. Smiley, diary entry, 10 November 1943 TNA HS 5/143

6. Major D. McAdoo to H.T. Fultz, undated note, NARA RG 226 Entry 190 Box 178 Folio 1383

7. Idem., 29 December 1943, NARA RG 226 Entry 190 Box 178 Folio 1383

8. Information Form, c. May 1944, NARA RG 226 Entry 190 Box 178 Folio 1383

9. E. Brennan to Chief, SI, 7 June 1944, NARA RG 226 Entry 92A Box 18 Folio 266

10. Lieutenant Colonel P. West, undated note, NARA RG 226 A3304 Roll 94

11. D. McAdoo to E. Brennan, 17 July 1943, NARA RG 226 Entry 92A Box 18 Folio 266

12. Lieutenant Colonel A. Nicholls, diary entry, 23 November 1943

13. R. Melrose, unpublished memoir

14. H. T. Fultz to Lieutenant Commander T. McBaine, 18 December 1943, NARA RG 226 Entry 190 Box 179 Folio 1384

15. Major D. McAdoo to H. T. Fultz, 3 February 1944, NARA RG 226 Entry 190 Box 178 Folio 1383

16. F. D. Roosevelt to A. J. D. Biddle, Jr 3 May 1943, Office File 576, Franklin D. Roosevelt Library

17. Memorandum for the President, 27 May 1944, Office File 576, Franklin D. Roosevelt Library

18. Major D. McAdoo to H. T. Fultz, 5 December 1943, NARA RG 226 Entry 190 Box 178 Folio 1383

19. Idem., 16 December 1943, NARA RG 226 Entry 190 Box 178 Folio 1383

20. Major D. McAdoo to Lieutenant Commander T. McBaine, 18 February 1944, NARA RG 226 Entry 210 Box 217 Folio 7

21. Sergeant N. Kukich to H. T. Fultz, 27 January 1944, NARA RG 226 Entry 190 Box 178 Folio 1383

22. Major D. McAdoo, 'Preliminary Survey of Albanian Situation', c. mid-December 1943, NARA RG 226 Entry 190 Box 178 Folio 1383

23. Major D. McAdoo to H. T. Fultz, 17 December 1944, NARA RG 226 Entry 190 Box 178 Folio 1383

24. H. T. Fultz to Major D. McAdoo, 19 December 1944, NARA RG 226 Entry 190 Box 178 Folio 1383

25. Major D. McAdoo annotation on H. T. Fultz to Major D. McAdoo, 19 December 1944, NARA RG 226 Entry 190 Box 178 Folio 1383

26. H. T. Fultz to P. Adams, 24 February 1944, NARA RG 226 Entry 154 Box 14 Folio 181

27. H. T. Fultz to 1st Lieutenant J. Hudson, 9 April 1944, NARA RG 226 Entry 154 Box 16 Folio 235

28. H. T. Fultz to P. Adams, 24 February 1944, NARA RG 226 Entry 154 Box 14 Folio 181

29. Sir A. Glen, interview, January 2000
30. Information from the SOE Adviser
31. Major P. Leake, 'Albania: Appreciation', 14 December 1943, TNA HS 5/67
32. Major A. Quayle, SAPLING report, 28 January 1944, TNA HS 5/141
33. Sir A. Glen, interview, January 2000
34. Major D. McAdoo to H. T. Fultz, c. 18 January 1944, NARA RG 226 Entry 190 Box 178 Folio 1383
35. Idem., 28 January 1944, NARA RG 226 Entry 190 Box 178 Entry 1383
36. Major A. Quayle, SAPLING report, 28 January 1944, TNA HS 5/141
37. Ibid.
38. Ibid.
39. Ibid.
40. Ibid.
41. Major D. McAdoo to H. T. Fultz, 28 January 1944, NARA RG 226 Entry 190 Box 178 Folio 1383
42. Major A. Quayle, SAPLING report, 28 January 1944, TNA HS 5/141
43. Major D. McAdoo to H. T. Fultz, undated note, NARA RG 226 Entry 190 Box 178 Folio 1383
44. Idem., 3 February 1944, NARA RG 226 Entry 190 Box 178 Folio 1383
45. Major D. McAdoo annotation on H.T. Fultz to Major D. McAdoo, 19 December 1943, NARA RG 226 Entry 190 Box 178 Folio 1383
46. Major D. McAdoo to H. T. Fultz, 25 January 1944, NARA RG 226 Entry 190 Box 178 Folio 1383
47. D. McAdoo annotation on H. T. Fultz to Major D. McAdoo, 15 December 1943, NARA RG 226 Entry 190 Box 178 Folio 1383
48. Major D. McAdoo to H. T. Fultz, 29 January 1944, NARA RG 226 Entry 190 Box 178 Folio 1383
49. Gunnery Sergeant N. Kukich to H. T. Fultz, 1–10 March 1944, NARA RG 226 Entry 154 Box 7 Folio 108
50. Major A. Quayle, diary entry, 29 January 1944, Quayle papers
51. Major D. McAdoo to H. T. Fultz, 3 February 1944, NARA RG 226 Entry 190 Box 178 Folio 1383
52. Major A. Quayle, 'Diary and Notes 3 Feb: 3 April 1944', Quayle papers
53. Major D. McAdoo to H. T. Fultz, 3 February 1944, NARA RG 226 Entry 190 Box 178 Folio 1383
54. Major A. Quayle, SAPLING report, 28 January 1944, TNA HS 5/141
55. Ibid.
56. Major General N. Wheeler in *The Blackthorn*, Journal of the Royal Irish Rangers, 1987; Sir R. Hibbert to author, September 1999
57. Information from the SOE Adviser
58. Major A. Quayle, 'Diary and Notes 3 Feb: 3 April 1944', Quayle papers
59. Ibid.

60. Ibid.
61. P. Gray to A. Quayle, April 1946, Quayle papers
62. Major A. Quayle, 'Diary and Notes 3 Feb: 3 April 1944', Quayle papers
63. C. Steel to D. Howard, cipher telegram, 26 February 1944, TNA HS 5/12
64. Major A. Quayle, 'Diary and Notes 3 Feb: 3 April 1944', Quayle papers
65. Tirana to Berlin, 6 April 1944, TNA HW 19/244
66. Idem., 17 August 1944, TNA HW 19/247
67. Major A. Quayle, 'Diary and Notes 3 Feb: 3 April 1944', Quayle papers
68. Major A. Quayle, diary entries, 30, 31 March, 1, 2 and 4 April 1944, Quayle papers
69. Ibid., 13 April 1944, Quayle papers
70. Lieutenant G. Manzitti to Major A. Quayle, 2 May 1944, Quayle papers
71. Ibid.
72. Lieutenant T. Stefan to H.T. Fultz, 5 May 1944, NARA RG 226 Entry 154 Box 17 Folio 238
73. 1st Lieutenant J. Hudson, 'Report on activities of BILL from 14 March to 24 May 1944', 5 June 1944, NARA RG 226 Entry 210 Box 217 Folio 7
74. Lieutenant G. Manzitti to Major A. Quayle, 2 May 1944, Quayle papers
75. Ibid.
76. 1st Lieutenant J. Hudson, 'Report on activities of BILL from 14 March to 24 May 1944', 5 June 1944, NARA RG 226 Entry 210 Box 217 Folio 7
77. Ibid.
78. H.T. Fultz to R. Joyce, 20 May 1944, NARA RG 226 Entry 180 Box 178 Folio 1380
79. Major A. Quayle, diary entry, 24 May 1944, Quayle papers
80. H. Meto to H.T. Fultz, 27 August 1944, NARA RG 226 Entry 154 Box 17 Folio 237
81. H.T. Fultz to 1st Lieutenant T. Stefan, 9 June 1944, NARA RG 226 Entry 154 Box 17 Folio 238

Chapter 8. 'Second Front started. Huns all around'

1. Mrs M. Kraay, interview, June 2001
2. P. Kemp, No Colours or Crest, p. 241
3. Dr J. Dumoulin, interview, February 2000
4. M. Lyon, unpublished memoir
5. Dr J. Dumoulin, interview, February 2000
6. M. Lyon, unpublished memoir
7. Ibid.
8. J. Naar, interview, December 2000
9. Corporal W. Williamson, diary entry, 29 December 1943
10. Lieutenant G. Duffy, report, 1944, TNA HS 5/130

11. W. Williamson, interview, March 2000
12. 'History of the Allied Military Mission, Albania 1942–1945', TNA HS 7/70
13. Major V. Smith, report, 1944, TNA HS 5/129
14. Captain J. Dumoulin, diary entries, 3 and 4 January 1944
15. Ibid., 11 January 1944
16. Lieutenant Colonel N. Wheeler, report, 1944, TNA HS 5/127
17. Captain J. Dumoulin, report, 1944, TNA HS 5/127
18. Captain M. Lyon, diary entries, 12–15 January 1944
19. Major H. W. Tilman, report, 1944, TNA HS 5/128
20. M. Lyon, unpublished memoir
21. Major H. W. Tilman, report, 1944, TNA HS 5/128
22. M. Lyon, unpublished memoir
23. Lieutenant Colonel N. Wheeler, report, 1944, TNA HS 5/127
24. M. Lyon, unpublished memoir
25. Captain J. Dumoulin, 'With the Partisans in Albania', 18 April 1945, TNA HS 5/114
26. 1st Lieutenant T. Stefan to H. T. Fultz, 12 June 1944, NARA RG Entry 154 Box 17 Folio 237
27. C. Molony, *History of the Second World War: The Mediterranean and Middle East*, Vol. VI, p. 391; R. Hibbert, *Albania's National Liberation Struggle*, p. 113
28. W. Mackenzie, *The Secret History of SOE*, p. 439
29. CONCENSUS to SOE Cairo, w/t message, 20 June 1943, McLean papers, IWM
30. Captain M. Lyon, report, 21 June 1944, NARA RG 226 Entry 21 Box 350 Report No. L40188
31. M. Lyon, unpublished memoir
32. Lieutenant Colonel N. Wheeler, report 1944, TNA HS 5/127
33. Major H. W. Tilman, report, 1944, TNA HS 5/128
34. Ibid.
35. 1st Lieutenant T. Stefan to H. T. Fultz, c. late April 1944, NARA RG Entry 154 Box 17 Folio 238
36. Report by Captain B. Ensor, 1944, TNA HS 5/136
37. Lieutenant Colonel N. Wheeler, report, 1944, TNA HS 5/127
38. Major H. W. Tilman, report, 1944, TNA HS 5/128
39. Information from the SOE Adviser
40. M. Lyon, 'Lt Colonel Alan Palmer CBE DSO', draft obituary for the Special Forces Club newsletter
41. Major V. Smith, report, 1944, TNA HS 5/129
42. SOE Bari to SOE London, 1 May 1944, TNA HS 5/68
43. H. Macmillan to P. Broad, cipher telegram, 9 May 1944, TNA HS 5/77
44. P. Broad to H. Macmillan, cipher telegram, 12 May 1944, TNA HS 5/77

45. Major V. Smith, report, 1944, TNA HS 5/129

46. Major J. Shaw, report, 1944, TNA HS 5/140

47. Major P. Leake to Major E. Boxshall, 9 May 1944, TNA HS 5/68

48. Major E. Watrous to Major P. Leake, 22 May 1944, TNA HS 5/39

49. Major V. Smith, report, 1944, TNA HS 5/129

50. Major P. Leake to SOE Bari, w/t message, 15 May 1944, TNA HS 5/68

51. Idem., 20 May 1944, TNA HS 5/68

52. SOE Albanian Section, Bari, to SOE London, cipher telegram, 4 July 1944, TNA HS 5/11

53. Report by Major J. Shaw, 1944, TNA HS 5/140

54. Lieutenant Colonel A. Palmer to Major E. Watrous, c. 15 June 1944, TNA HS 5/39

55. Major P. Leake to SOE Bari, w/t messages, 14 and 15 May 1944, TNA HS 5/68

56. Major V. Smith, report, 1944, TNA HS 5/129

57. Ibid.

58. Ibid.

59. Major J. Shaw, report, 1944, TNA HS 5/140

60. H. Lanz, 'Partisan Warfare in the Mountains (Based upon Experiences in Greece and Southern Albania)', 1952, NARA RG 338 MS P055a

61. Captain J. Dumoulin, diary entries, 3 and 4 June 1944

62. M. Lyon, unpublished memoir

63. 1st Lieutenant T. Stefan to H. T. Fultz, 12 June 1944, NARA RG 226 Box 17 Entry 237

64. Corporal A. Metro and Corporal A. Tolie to H. T. Fultz, c. 13 June 1944, NARA RG 226 Entry 154 Box 17 Folio 238

65. Captain J. Dumoulin, diary entry, 6 June 1944

66. Major V. Smith, report, 1944, TNA HS 5/129

67. 1st Lieutenant T. Stefan to H. T. Fultz, 12 June 1944, NARA RG 226 Box 17 Entry 237

68. Major V. Smith, report, 1944, TNA HS 5/129

69. M. Lyon, unpublished memoir

70. Major V. Smith, report, 1944, TNA HS 5/129

71. M. Lyon, unpublished memoir

72. Captain J. Dumoulin, diary entry, 10 June 1944

73. Major V. Smith, report, 1944, TNA HS 5/129

74. Captain J. Dumoulin, diary entry, 11 June 1944

75. M. Lyon, unpublished memoir

76. Major V. Smith, report, 1944, TNA HS 5/129

77. Lieutenant Colonel A. Palmer to Major E. Watrous, c. 12 June 1944, TNA HS 5/39

78. 1st Lieutenant T. Stefan to H. T. Fultz, 12 June 1944, NARA RG 226 Entry 154 Box 17 Folio 237

79. Captain J. Dumoulin, diary entry, 13 June 1944

80. Ibid., 26 June 1944

81. Major J. Shaw, report, 1944, TNA HS 5/140

82. Captain J. Dumoulin, diary entry, 29 June 1944

83. Captain B. Ensor, report, 1944, TNA HS 5/136

84. 1st Lieutenant T. Stefan, 3 July 1944, RG 226 Entry 154 Box 17 Folio 237

Chapter 9. 'Colleagues in conspiracy'

1. J. Amery, *Sons of the Eagle*, p. 298

2. Ibid., pp. 298, 336, 334, 298

3. A. Glen, *Footholds Against a Whirlwind*, p.157. See also Patrick Leigh Fermor's foreword to Smiley's *Albanian Assignment* and obituary of Billy McLean in *Spectator*, 29 November 1986.

4. M.R.D. Foot, *SOE: An Outline History of the Special Operations Executive*, pp. 146, 240–41

5. Mrs M. Kraay, interview, June 2001

6. B. Sweet-Escott to Mrs J. Martin Leake, 20 June 1944. I am indebted to Kenneth Martin Leake for permission to use correspondence received by the Martin Leake family after his brother's death.

7. Major General W. Stawell to Mrs J. Martin Leake, 8 June 1944

8. Lieutenant Colonel A. Palmer to Major E. Watrous, c. 12 June 1944, TNA HS 5/39

9. CONCENSUS II to SOE Bari, w/t message, 18 June 1944, McLean papers, IWM

10. Major E. Boxshall to SOE Bari, 12 July 1944, TNA HS 5/10

11. Major E. Watrous to Major E. Boxshall, 26 June 1944, enclosing CONCENSUS II to SOE Bari, w/t messages, 18 and 19 June 1944, TNA HS 5/82

12. Captain G. Cowie to Major E. Boxshall, 1 July 1944, enclosing CONCENSUS II to SOE Bari, w/t messages, 5, 10, 21 and 24 June, TNA HS 5/69

13. Major E. Boxshall to SOE Bari, 12 July 1944, TNA HS 5/10

14. D. Smiley, *Albanian Assignment*, p. 152; D. Smiley, *Irregular Regular*, pp. 107, 111; see also X. Fielding, *One Man in His Time*, p. 51

15. Major D. Smiley, diary entry, 29 October 1944, McLean papers, IWM

16. CONCENSUS II to SOE Bari, w/t message, 23 May 1944, McLean papers, IWM

17. SOE Bari to SOE London, cipher telegram, 26 May 1944; Major E. Boxshall to D. Howard, 28 May 1944, TNA HS 5/11; P. Broad to Algiers and London, cipher telegram, 26 May 1944, TNA HS 5/11

18. A. Dew to SOE London, 26 June 1944, TNA HS 5/11
19. CONCENSUS II to SOE Bari, w/t message, 25 October 1944, TNA HS 5/72; P. Broad to AFHQ, cipher telegram, 27 October 1944, TNA HS 5/71
20. Foreign Secretary to Foreign Office, cipher telegram, 31 October 1944, TNA HS 5/77
21. Major G. Seymour, report, 1944, TNA HS 5/123
22. Lieutenant Colonel D. Talbot Rice to Colonel D. Keswick, 5 January 1945, TNA HS 5/123
23. Information from the SOE Adviser
24. Captain E. Watrous to C. Steel, 4 March 1944, TNA HS 5/66
25. Major E. Watrous to Lieutenant Colonel P. Leake, 22 May 1944, TNA HS 5/39
26. Major E. Watrous to Major E. Boxshall, 7 June 1944, TNA HS 5/68
27. Major E. Watrous to Mr Broad and Lieutenant Colonel W. Harcourt, 1 June 1944, TNA HS 5/11; Major E. Watrous to Lieutenant Colonel A. Palmer, 8 June 1944, TNA HS 5/39
28. Major E. Watrous to Major E. Boxshall, 26 June 1944, TNA HS 5/82
29. CONCENSUS II and Lieutenant Colonel A. Palmer to SOE Bari, w/t messages, late June 1944, quoted in copy of SOE Bari to SOE London, cipher telegram, 4 July 1944, TNA HS 5/11
30. M. Lyon to author, February, April 1998
31. J. Naar, interview, December 2000
32. Major E. Boxshall to Force 266, 9 June 1944, TNA HS 5/68
33. Sir R. Hibbert to author, May 2001
34. SOE Bari to CONCENSUS II, w/t messages, 21 September and 2 October 1944, McLean papers, IWM
35. Sir R. Hibbert to author, May 2001
36. J. Naar to author, September 2000
37. Idem., September 1999
38. Ibid.
39. P. Broad to Algiers, 30 June 1944; D. Laskey, minute, c. 14 July 1944, TNA FO 371/43551
40. Colonel D. Keswick to General C. Gubbins, 8 July 1944, TNA HS 5/11
41. General C. Gubbins to All Directors, Regional and Country Section Heads, 12 July 1944, TNA HS 5/35
42. History of the Balkan Air Force, TNA AIR 23/1508
43. Ibid.
44. Information from the SOE Adviser
45. Lieutenant Colonel W. Harcourt to Lieutenant Colonel D. Talbot Rice, 19 September 1944, TNA HS 5/71
46. H. T. Fultz to P. Adams, 'Arrival of Sgt Milios and Cpl Thanas. General Situation', 12 June 1944, NARA Entry 190 Box 321 Folio 473

47. 'HQ SOM Intelligence Appreciation No. 5: The Importance of the Albanian Partisans', 22 June 1944, TNA HS 5/90

48. For more on Zeppelin, the major Allied deception plan to contain German forces in Italy and the Balkans, to which Wilson was trying to contribute, see T. Holt, *The Deceivers: Allied Military Deception in the Second World War* pp. 597–605

49. General Wilson to Chiefs of Staff, cipher telegram, 16 June 1944, TNA HS 5/11

50. Major P. Leake to Major E. Boxshall, 9 May 1944, TNA HS 5/68

51. Major G. Seymour, report, 1944, TNA HS 5/123

52. CONCENSUS II to SOE Bari, w/t message, 23 May 1944, McLean papers, IWM

53. Idem., w/t message, 24 June 1944, McLean papers, IWM

54. Lieutenant Colonel W. Harcourt, 'Appreciation on Special Operations in Albania', 20 June 1944, TNA HS 5/77

55. Idem., 'Comments on Report by Lt Col McLean DSO, Major Smiley MC, and Captain Amery', c. early December 1944, TNA HS 5/126

56. Chiefs of Staff to AFHQ, cipher telegram, 8 June 1944, TNA HS 5/11

57. General Wilson to Chiefs of Staff, cipher telegram, 16 June 1944, TNA HS 5/11

58. Lieutenant Colonel W. Harcourt, 'Appreciation on Special Operations in Albania', 20 June 1944, TNA HS 5/77

59. P. Broad to H. Macmillan, cipher telegram, 10 June 1944, TNA HS 5/77

60. H. Macmillan to P. Broad, cipher telegram, 14 June 1944, TNA HS 5/77

61. Foreign Office to H. Macmillan, cipher telegram, 4 July 1944, TNA HS 5/77

62. D. Smiley, *Albanian Assignment*, pp. 133–4

63. Lieutenant Colonel W. Harcourt, 'Comments on Report by Lt Col McLean DSO, Major Smiley MC, and Captain Amery', c. early December 1944, TNA HS 5/126

64. Air Commodore A. Boyle to Colonel D. Keswick, 24 July 1944, TNA HS 5/11

65. Tirana to Berlin, 24 and 26 May 1944, TNA HW 19/244

66. 'Erlaeuterungen zur Bandenkarte v. Albanien', 14 April 1944, BA-MA, RH 19 XI 10b, folios 64–66

67. 'Report No. 2514', 13 July 1944, TNA HS 5/113; note marked 'TOPSEC U', dated 22 July 1944, TNA HS 5/11

68. Major J. Shaw, report, 1944, TNA HS 5/140

69. Lieutenant Colonel A. Palmer to SOE Bari, w/t message, 16 July 1944, TNA HS 5/69

70. Major R. Riddell to SOE Bari, w/t message, 16 July 1944, TNA HS 5/69

71. Lieutenant Colonel W. Harcourt, 'Comments on Report by Lt Col Mclean

DSO, Major Smiley MC, and Captain Amery', c. early December 1944, TNA HS 5/126

72. Balkan Air Force Policy Committee Meeting, minutes, 14 September 1944, TNA HS 5/72

73. P. Broad to H. Macmillan, cipher telegram, 14 September 1944, TNA HS 5/77

74. CONCENSUS II to SOE Bari, w/t message, 10 September 1944, McLean papers. For Amery's claim that the Tajiks killed about a hundred, see R. Miller, *Behind The Lines*, p. 178

75. Idem., 15 September 1944, McLean papers

76. P. Broad to Algiers and London, cipher telegram, 18 July 1944, TNA PREM 3/41

77. Prime Minister to Foreign Office, 19 July 1944, TNA PREM 3/41

78. Foreign Secretary to Prime Minister, 23 July 1944, TNA PREM 3/41

79. A. Dew and Sir Orme Sargent, minutes, 13 August 1944, TNA FO 371/43551

80. Foreign Secretary, minute, 8 September 1944, TNA FO 371/43553

81. P. Broad to H. Macmillan, cipher telegram, 28 October 1944, TNA HS 5/77

82. P. Broad to Lieutenant Colonel W. Harcourt, 27 October 1944, TNA HS 5/80; Lieutenant Colonel W. Harcourt to Lieutenant Staniszewski, 27 October 1944, TNA HS 5/72

83. Colonel D. Keswick to Major General C. Gubbins, 20 December 1944, TNA HS 5/75

84. Major General C. Gubbins to Lord Selborne, 23 December 1944, TNA HS 5/75

85. Foreign Secretary to Foreign Office, London, cipher telegram, 31 October 1944, TNA HS 5/77. The Foreign Secretary's support for McLean and Amery can be overstated. 'I hear that Billy McLean and Julian Amery will be home shortly,' Alan Palmer wrote to him in December, 'so you will no doubt be getting a blast of more right-wing sentiments soon.' Lieutenant Colonel A. Palmer to Foreign Secretary, 3 December 1944, TNA FO 371/43556. '[D]on't fear that I shall be corrupted by other visitors,' Eden replied; 'unhappily I had to put them off.' Foreign Secretary to Lieutenant Colonel A. Palmer, 25 December 1944, TNA FO 371/43556. Palmer and Eden were on first-name terms, their wives being close friends.

86. Lieutenant R. Bullock, 'Report on Sgt Button', 20 October 1944, TNA HS 9/249/4

87. Lieutenant Commander A. de Cosson, 'Report on Operation Elbert', 16 October 1944, TNA HS 9/249/4

88. P. Kemp, *No Colours or Crest*, pp. 242–3. Kemp had arrived in Surabaja for a briefing at General Robert Mansergh's divisional headquarters in

February 1946, en route to handle the Japanese surrender in Bali. P. Kemp, *Alms for Oblivion*, p. 83

89. D. Smiley, *Albanian Assignment*, p. 152; D. Smiley, *Irregular Regular*, p. 107

90. X. Fielding, *One Man in His Time*, p. 52; M. R. D. Foot, *SOE*, p. 146

91. J. Eyre, *The God Trip: The Story of a Mid-century Man*, pp. 7–9

92. Ibid., pp. 17–18, 23, 44, 23–6

93. I am grateful to the staff of the Maddermarket Theatre for these details.

94. R. Riddell to author, May 2000

95. B. McSwiney, interview, January 2000

96. Information from the SOE Adviser

97. J. Naar, interview, December 2000

98. J. Naar to author, September 1999

99. J. Naar, interview, January 2000

100. J. Naar to author, September 2000

101. Information from the SOE Adviser

102. J. Naar to author, September 1999

103. Major E. Watrous, 'Recommendations on policy to be adopted towards Major Abas Kupi and the Movement of Legality', 14 August 1944, TNA HS 5/2

104. Untitled document, c. early August 1944, TNA WO 204/9428

105. See, for example, Lieutenant J. Eyre, 'Kosovë', sent to PWE London under covering note, 5 March 1944, and Miss E. Barker to Lieutenant J. Eyre, 25 March 1944, enclosing comments and corrections by Captain V. Robinson, TNA WO 204/9428

106. Captain J. Eyre, 'Albanian Background: June 1944', sent under note, P. Broad to the Foreign Office in London, 18 July 1944; minute by D. Laskey, 25 July 1944, TNA FO 371/43551

107. J. Eyre, *The God Trip*, pp. 24–5

108. Information from the SOE Adviser

109. S. van der Wal, P. Drooglever and M. Schouten, *Officiële Bescheiden betreffende de Nederlands-Indonesische Betrekkingen 1945–1950* (NIB 1), Vol. 3. pp. 137,141. In a long contemporary report reproduced in *The Admiral's Baby*, a memoir of his time assisting in the political administration of Java, Laurens van der Post referred briefly to one British unit operating in Java in 1945–6 called the Far Eastern Publicity Detachment (FEPD). The FEPD, according to the report, had formerly operated in Burma as a psychological warfare unit and, in Batavia, today's Djakarta, took charge of the radio station, printed newspapers and generally coordinated and supervised press and propaganda matters. Van der Post even recorded handing control of the radio station to a young British major. L. van der Post, *The Admiral's Baby*, p. 251

110. D. Bardens, *Mysterious Worlds: A Personal Investigation of the Weird, the Uncanny and the Unexplained*, pp. 170–181

Chapter 10: 'Why should we attack them now?'

1. See, for example, M.R.D. Foot, *Resistance: An Analysis of European Resistance to Nazism 1940–1945*, p.185
2. Tirana to Berlin, 12 August 1944, TNA HW 19/246
3. Tirana to Berlin, 16 and 17 September 1944, TNA HW 19/246
4. 1st Lieutenant N. Kukich to H.T. Fultz, 19 August 1944, NARA RG 226 Entry 154 Box 17 Folio 239
5. Captain M. Lyon, report, 1944, TNA HS 5/7
6. Captain T. Stefan to H.T. Fultz, w/t message, 19 September 1944, NARA RG 226 Entry 136 Box 34 Folio 366
7. Idem., 17 September 1944, NARA RG 226 Entry 154 Box 7 Folio 115
8. Captain M. Lyon to SOE Bari, 25 August 1944, NARA RG 226 Entry 125 Box 54 Folio 641
9. CONCENSUS II to SOE Bari, w/t message, 14 September 1944, McLean papers, IWM
10. SOE Bari to CONCENSUS II, w/t message, 16 September 1944, McLean papers, IWM
11. Idem., w/t message, 12 July 1944, McLean papers, IWM
12. Wing Commander P.A.B. Neel, report, 1944, TNA HS 5/132
13. E. Hoxha, *The Anglo-American Threat to Albania: Memoirs of the National Liberation War*, p.294. See also E. Hoxha, 'Speech delivered at the 1st Congress of the Communist Party of Albania', 8 November 1948, quoted in *Selected Works*, Vol. II, p.75
14. Wing Commander P.A.B. Neel, report, 15 December 1944, TNA HS 5/98
15. Ibid.
16. Ibid.
17. Ibid.
18. Lieutenant Colonel N. McLean, diary entry, 28 May 1944, McLean papers, IWM
19. Captain J. Gwyer to Major E. Watrous, 9 August 1944, TNA HS 5/71
20. J. Naar to author, October 1999
21. Captain J. Gwyer to Major E. Watrous, 1 September 1944, TNA HS 5/98
22. T. Neel, interview with C. Neel, 1991
23. Memorandum, 'Brandt', 30 November 1944, TNA KV 2/752
24. See, for example, H. Spaeter, *Die Brandenburger: eine deutsche Kommandotruppe*, pp.391–401; E. Lefevre, *La Division Brandenbourg*, pp.244–256; F. Kurowski, *Deutsche Kommandotrupps 1939–1945, Band 2: Die "Brandenburger" im weltweiten Einsatz*, pp.228–237

25. Information provided by Deutsche Dienststelle für die Benachrichtigung der nächsten Angehörigen von Gefallenen der ehemaligen Wehrmacht.
26. SILO interim report on F.H. Brandt, December 1944, TNA HS 5/98
27. SILO report, 28 November 1944, TNA HS 5/98
28. Captain J. Eyre, pencil note, 3 November 1944, TNA HS 5/98
29. SILO interim report on F.H. Brandt, December 1944, TNA HS 5/98
30. MI5 interim report on Fred Hermann Brandt, January 1945, TNA KV 2/752
31. SILO interim report on F.H. Brandt, December 1944, TNA HS 5/98
32. Major V. Smith to SOE Bari, w/t message, 28 August 1944, quoted in SOE Bari to CONCENSUS II, w/t message, 10 September 1944, McLean papers, IWM
33. Major P. Kemp, report, 1944, TNA HS 5/144
34. CONCENSUS II to SOE Bari, w/t message, 12 June 1944, McLean papers, IWM
35. Ibid., quoted in Major E. Boxshall to A. Smyth, 16 November 1944, TNA HS 5/73
36. Major A. Simcox, report, 1944, TSA HS 5/135
37. Major A. Simcox to Major R. Riddell, 22 June 1944, McLean papers, IWM
38. Major A. Simcox, report, 1944, TNA HS 5/135
39. Major A. Simcox to Wing Commander P.A.B. Neel, 8 July 1944, Simcox papers
40. Major A. Simcox, report, 1944, TNA HS 5/135
41. SOE weekly review, 10–16 July 1944, NARA RG 226, A 3304, Roll 94
42. 'Erlaeuterungen zur Bandenkarte v. Albanien', 14 April 1944, BA MA, RH 19 XI 10b, folio 64
43. Brigadier D.E.P. Hodgson, 'Gani Bey Kryeziu', memorandum, 20 May 1945, TNA HS 5/73
44. Tirana to Berlin, 29 June 1944, TNA HW 19/246
45. CONCENSUS II to SOE Bari, w/t message, 16 September 1944, McLean papers, IWM
46. Major A. Simcox, report, 1944, TNA HS 5/135
47. P. Broad to H. Macmillan, 22 October 1944, TNA HS 5/70
48. Ibid., cipher telegram, 15 April 1945, TNA HS 5/73
49. Sir Ralph Stevenson to Foreign Office, cipher telegrams, 25 April, 5 May and 2 June 1945, TNA HS 5/73
50. Ibid., cipher telegram, 23 July 1945, TNA HS 5/73
51. Foreign Office to Belgrade, cipher telegram, 27 July 1945, TNA HS 5/73
52. Major E. Boxshall to D. Laskey, 22 October 1945, enclosing personal telegram, Said Kryeziu to Major S.E. Watrous, 19 October 1945, TNA HS 5/73; F. W. Deakin to Foreign Office, cipher telegrams, 26 October and 2 November 1945, TNA HS 5/73

53. Major A. Simcox, 'Gani Bey Kryeziu', report, TNA HS 5/73; Major E. Boxshall to A. Smyth, 16 November 1945, TNA HS 5/73; F. W. Deakin to General Velebit, 12 December 1945, TNA HS 5/73

54. British Embassy, Belgrade, to Foreign Office, 31 May 1946, TNA FO 371/58472

55. Yugoslav Foreign Minister to British Embassy, Belgrade, 21 February 1948, TNA FO 371/72110

56. U. Butka, *Ringjalle*, p.113

57. Major A. Simcox, report, 1944, TNA HS 5/135

58. Lieutenant Colonel D. Talbot Rice to Colonel D. Keswick, 1 December 1944, TNA HS 5/75

59. M. Lyon, unpublished memoir

60. Major J. Shaw, report, 1944, TNA HS 5/140

61. Major R. Riddell and Captain R. Hibbert, report, 1944, TNA HS 5/142

62. Captain B. Ensor, report, 1944, TNA HS 5/136

63. Brigadier G.M.O. Davy, 'LFA report on Operation HEALING II', 7 August 1944, TNA WO 204/8430

64. Appendix to Balkan Air Force Weekly Summary, 'The Spilje Raid – 29 July 1944', August 1944, TNA WO 218/64

65. Captain B. Ensor, report, 1944, TNA HS 5/136

66. 'Report on Operation MERCERISED', 21 November 1944, TNA WO 204/8430

67. Lieutenant Colonel A. Palmer to Major E. Watrous, 19–24 September 1944, TNA HS 5/39

68. M. Lyon to author, March 1998

69. Lieutenant Colonel W. Harcourt to D. Talbot Rice, 20 October 1944, TNA HS 5/71

70. General C. Gubbins to Major General W. Stawell, 2 October 1944, TNA HS 3/199

71. M. Lyon, unpublished memoir

72. Captain E. Northrop, report, 1944, TNA HS 5/133

73. Major P. Oliver, report, 1944, TNA HS 5/134

74. Ibid.

75. OSS report, 'German Methods During Battle of Tirana', sent under Major G. Cowie to Major E. Boxshall, 2 January 1945, TNA HS 5/17

76. 'History of the Allied Military Mission, Albania 1942–1945', TNA HS 7/70

77. Appendix C, Operation Report No. 136, 14 December 1944, TNA WO 204/8460

78. 'German Methods During Battle of Tirana', OSS report sent under Major G. Cowie to Major E. Boxshall, 2 January 1945, TNA HS 5/17

79. Major M. Thornton to SOE Bari, w/t message, 22 November 1944, AIR 20/8410

80. Ibid.
81. Captain M. Lyon to Major E. Watrous, 19 November 1944, TNA HS 5/39
82. M. Lyon, unpublished memoir
83. Rosenberg to Bari, via Captain T. Stefan to H.T. Fultz, w/t messages, 1 December 1944, NARA RG 226 Entry 139 Box 40 Folio 297
84. M. Lyon, unpublished memoir
85. Captain T. Stefan to H.T. Fultz, w/t message, 29 November 1944, NARA RG 226 Entry 139 Box 40 Folio 301
86. SI summary, 'Albania', December 1944, NARA RG 226 Entry 190 Box 177 Folio 1368
87. 'Notes on Conversations with Capts. Durcan and Andrew', 10 February 1945, TNA WO 204/11417
88. Captain J. Durcan to SOE Bari, w/t message, 11 January 1945, TNA AIR 20/8410
89. Master Sergeant S. Peters to Dr W. Langer, 10 February 1945, NARA RG 226 Entry 154 Box 8 Folio 118
90. Captain T. Stefan to H.T. Fultz, 11 February 1945, NARA RG 226 Entry 154 Box 16 Folio 230
91. Lieutenant T. Renfree, report, 1944, TNA HS 5/125
92. Lieutenant G. Wilkinson, report, 1945, TNA WO 204/11417
93. Major M. Thornton to SOE Bari, w/t message, 22 November 1944, TNA AIR 20/8410
94. Captain T. Stefan to H.T. Fultz, early November 1944, NARA RG 226 Entry 154 Box 8 Folio 119
95. H. Munro to author, 2001

Epilogue

1. 'History of the Allied Military Mission, Albania 1942–1945', TNA HS 7/70
2. Proceedings of a Conference on British and European resistance, 1939–1945, held at St Antony's College, Oxford, December 1962.
3. 'History of the Allied Military Mission, Albania 1942–1945', TNA HS 7/70
4. B. Fischer, Albania at War, p.268
5. Major E. Watrous to Major E. Boxshall, 19 June 1944, TNA HS 5/69
6. Prime Minister to Foreign Secretary, 11 October 1944, TNA PREM 3/41
7. Idem., 4 May 1944, TNA FO 371/43636
8. Lieutenant Colonel A. Palmer to Major E. Watrous, 19–24 September 1944, TNA HS 5/39
9. Colonel E. de Renzy Martin, report, 'Albanian Revolt', 29 December 1940, TNA HS 5/61

10. H.T. Fultz to P. Adams, 24 February 1944, NARA RG 226 Entry 154 Box 14 Folio 181

11. W. Mackenzie, History of the Special Operations Executive, TNA CAB 103/566. Mackenzie's study has now been published as W. Mackenzie, *The Secret History of SOE: The Special Operations Executive 1940-45.*

12. N. Vinçani to M. Lyon, 15 April 1993

13. R. Hibbert, *Albania's National Liberation Struggle.* Hibbert, who made good use of wartime Foreign and War Office files released in the 1970s, has not been alone in challenging in print the claims that Albania had fallen to communism by default and by double-dealing on the part of SOE staff officers. From work on similar files, the historians Elisabeth Barker and David Stafford also suggested that the key decisions favouring the Albanian Partisans had been taken above the heads of SOE and to meet short-term strategic requirements. E. Barker, *British Policy in South East Europe in the Second World War,* p.181; D. Stafford, *Britain and European Resistance 1940-1945: A Survey of the Special Operations Executive,* pp. 170-2. As for explaining the communists' success, Bernd Fischer, a German historian based in the United States, has shown convincingly, in an incisive recent study of Albania's wartime history, how important was the simple fact that only the Partisans had the capacity, passion and ruthlessness necessary to wage sustained resistance. B. Fischer, *Albania at War.*

14. R. Hibbert, *Albania's National Liberation Struggle,* p.242

15. R. Watrous to author, July 2001

16. W. Williamson, interview, March 2000

17. J. Davis to author, May 2000

18. M. Lyon, interview, November 1999

19. S. Dorril, *MI6: Fifty Years of Special Operations,* p. 363

20. Section D War Diary, TNA HS 7/4

21. J. Amery, 'The Case for Retaliation', *Time and Tide,* 22 January 1949

22. Major G. Seymour, report, 1944, TNA HS 5/123

23. Major R. Riddell and Captain R. Hibbert, report, 1944, TNA HS 5/142

24. Lieutenant R. Bullock, report, 1944, TNA HS 5/131

25. Wing Commander P.A.B. Neel, report, 1944, TNA HS 5/132

26. Major A. Hare, report, 1944, TNA HS 5/139

SOURCES AND BIBLIOGRAPHY

ARCHIVES

Balliol College, Oxford
Bickham Sweet-Escott papers

British Library of Political and Economic Science, London
Hugh Dalton papers

Bundesarchiv-Militärarchiv (BA-MA), Freiburg, Germany
Heeresgruppenkommandos (Army Group Command)
  Heeresgruppe F/Oberbefehlshaber Südost (Army Group F/Commander in
  Chief South East) (RH 19 XI)
Waffen SS
  21 Waffen-Gebirgs-Division der SS Skanderbeg (21st Waffen SS 'Skanderbeg'
  Mountain Division) (RS 3–21)

Franklin D. Roosevelt Library, Hyde Park, New York
Roosevelt Office Files

Harry S. Truman Library, Independence, Missouri
Truman Office Files

Imperial War Museum (IWM), London
Major General T. B. L. Churchill papers
Sub Lieutenant J. W. Cloke papers
Brigadier G. M. O. Davy papers
Major H. J. Legg papers

Major General D. L. Lloyd Owen papers
Major I. G. Macpherson papers
Lieutenant Colonel N. L. D. McLean papers
Major W. S. Moss papers
Mrs A. Street papers

Institute of Netherlands History, The Hague, Netherlands
Archives on relations between the Netherlands and Indonesia 1945–63

Liddell Hart Centre for Military Archives, King's College, London
Count Julian Dobrski papers
Air Vice Marshal Sir William Elliot papers
Major Patrick Evans papers

National Archives (NARA), College Park, Maryland
Foreign Military Studies (RG 338)
Office of Strategic Services records (RG 226)
State Department records (RG 59)
William J. Donovan records (Microfilm series 1642)

Roosevelt Study Center, Middelburg, Netherlands
Adolf Berle papers (microform copies)
Cordell Hull papers (microform copies)
Henry Morgenthau papers (microform copies)
Henry Stimson papers (microform copies)

Royal Geographical Society, London
H. W. Tilman papers

St Antony's College, Oxford
Lord Killearn papers
Proceedings of a conference on British and European Resistance, 1939–1945, held at St Antony's College, Oxford, 10–16 December 1962

Taylor Institute, Oxford
Margaret Hasluck papers

The National Archives (TNA), London
Air Ministry
    Air Historical Branch: Unregistered Papers (AIR 20)
    Royal Air Force Overseas Commands: Reports and Correspondence (AIR 23)

Cabinet Office
  Chiefs of Staff Committee: Minutes (CAB 79)
  Chiefs of Staff Committee: Memoranda (CAB 80)
Foreign Office
  Consular Department: General Correspondence (FO 369)
  Political Departments: General Correspondence (FO 371)
Government Code & Cypher School
  ISOS Section and ISK Section: Decrypts of German Secret Service (Abwehr
  and Sicherheitsdienst) Messages (HW 19)
Prime Minister's Office
  Operational Correspondence and Papers (PREM 3)
Security Service
  Personal Files (KV 2)
Special Operations Executive
  Africa and Middle East Group: Registered Files (HS 3)
  Balkans: Registered Files (HS 5)
  Histories and War Diaries: Registered Files (HS 7)
  Headquarters: Records (HS 8)
  Personnel Files (HS 9)
War Office
  Central Mediterranean Forces: War Diaries (WO 170)
  Middle East Forces: Military Headquarters Papers (WO 201)
  British Military Missions: Military Headquarters Papers (WO 202)
  Allied Forces, Mediterranean Theatre: Military Headquarters Papers (WO 204)
  Special Services: War Diaries (WO 218)

UNPUBLISHED PAPERS IN PRIVATE HANDS

Gefreiter F. W. Brandt; Brigadier E. F. Davies; Corporal A. W. W. DeAth; Major
J. G. Dumoulin; Squadron Leader A. G. Hands; Major A. V. Hare; Major J. G.
Hibberdine; Captain J. W. Hudson; Lieutenant N. R. Kukich; Major S. P. M.
Leake; Lieutenant M. Lis; Major J. M. Lyon; Sergeant R. Melrose; Major H. A.
C. Munro; Wing Commander P. A. B. Neel; Major L. J. Naar; Lieutenant Colonel
A. F. C. Nicholls; Captain D. R. Oakley-Hill; Major General Sir Jocelyn Percy;
Lieutenant T. J. Renfree; Major R. E. Riddell; Major J. A. Quayle; Major G. V.
Seymour; Major A. C. Simcox; Colonel D. de C. Smiley; Lieutenant Commander
H. A. Thompson; Corporal W. B. Williamson

INTERVIEWS AND CORRESPONDENCE

Nigel Clive (MI6 officer in Greece, 1944–5); Mrs Lynette Croudace (FANY
staff at SOE Headquarters in Cairo and Bari, 1943–4); Basil Davidson (Section
D and SOE officer in the Balkans, 1940–1 and 1943–5, and on Yugoslav

Section staff at SOE Headquarters in Cairo, 1942–3); John Davis (SOE w/t operator in Albania, 1943–4); Austin DeAth (SOE w/t operator in Albania, 1943–4); Sir William Deakin (SOE officer on Yugoslav Section staff at SOE Headquarters in Cairo and Bari, 1942–4, and in Yugoslavia, 1944); Dr Jack Dumoulin (SOE officer in Albania, 1943–4); Ted Fry (SOE w/t operator in Italy, 1944–5); Sir Alexander Glen (Section D and SOE officer in the Balkans, 1940–1 and 1943–5, including Albania, 1943–4); Sir Reginald Hibbert (SOE officer in Albania, 1943–4); Patrick Howarth (SOE officer on staff at SOE Headquarters in Cairo, 1943–4); Fadil Hoxha (Partisan commander, 1942–5); James Hudson (OSS officer in Albania, 1944); Mrs Peggy Kraay (civilian staff at SOE Headquarters in Cairo and Bari, 1943–4); Nick Kukich (OSS officer in Albania, 1943–4); Peter Lee (SOE security officer in Bari, 1943–4); Marcus Lyon (SOE officer in Albania, 1943–5); Mrs Agnes Jensen Mangerich (US nurse in Albania, 1943–4); Bryan McSwiney (SOE officer on SOE Albanian Section staff at SOE Headquarters in Cairo and Bari, 1944); Hugh Munro (SOE officer on Albanian Section staff at SOE Headquarters in Cairo and Bari, 1943–4, and in Albania, 1944–5); Jon Naar (SOE officer on Albanian Section staff at SOE Headquarters in Cairo and Bari, 1943–5); Tony Neel (SOE officer in Albania, 1943–4; interview recorded by son); Tony Northrop (SOE officer in Albania, 1943–4); Mrs Ruby Oakley-Hill (civilian staff at SOE Headquarters in London, 1944–5; widow of Major Dayrell Oakley-Hill); John Orr-Ewing (SOE officer in Italy, 1944–5); Mrs Margaret Pawley (FANY staff at SOE Headquarters in Cairo and Bari, 1943–5); Peter Payne (MI6 officer in Albania, 1944); Mrs Laura Pope (civilian staff at SOE Headquarters in Cairo, 1942–4); Richard Riddell (SOE officer in Albania, 1943–4); Bob Rogers (SOE w/t operator in Albania, 1944); Dr John Ross (SOE officer in Italy, 1944–5); Denys Salt (British Army officer and intelligence officer on staff of Allied Military Liaison (Albania) mission, 1944–5); Dr Kenneth Sinclair-Loutit (British Army officer in Cairo, 1943–4, and Yugoslavia, 1944–5); Colonel David Smiley (SOE officer in Albania, 1943–4); Mrs Annette Street (civilian staff at SOE Headquarters in Cairo and Bari, 1942–4); Willie Williamson (SOE w/t operator in Albania, 1943–4); Christopher Woods (SOE officer in Italy, 1944–5, and FEPD officer in Java, 1945–6)

PUBLISHED DOCUMENTS

Documents on British Foreign Policy, 1919–39. London: HMSO, 1946.

The Greek White Book: Diplomatic Documents Relating to Italy's Aggression against Greece. Washington: Agence D'Athènes, 1943.

Foreign Relations of the United States: Diplomatic Papers 1943. 6 volumes. Washington DC: U.S. Government Printing Office, 1963–5.

Foreign Relations of the United States: Diplomatic Papers 1944. 5 volumes. Washington DC: U.S. Government Printing Office, 1965–7.

NEWSPAPERS, PERIODICALS, REGIMENTAL JOURNALS

The Blackthorn (Journal of the Royal Irish Rangers), *Daily Telegraph*, *Drita* (Newsletter/Magazine of the Anglo-Albanian Association), *The Fighting Forces*, *Guardian*, *Independent*, *Journal of the Royal Scots Fusiliers*, *Listener*, *New York Times*, *The Oak Tree* (Journal of the Cheshire Regiment), *Picture Post*, *Quis Separabit* (Journal of the Royal Ulster Rifles), *Spectator*, *Sunday Telegraph*, *Time and Tide*, *Sunday Times*, *The Times*

BOOKS

Albania. Naval Intelligence Division, 1945.

Aldrich, R. *The Hidden Hand: Britain, America and Cold War Secret Intelligence.* London: John Murray, 2001.

Allen, W. E. D. *Guerrilla Warfare in Abyssinia.* London: Penguin, 1943.

Amery, J. *Sons of the Eagle: A Study in Guerrilla War.* London: Macmillan, 1948.

——. *Approach March: A Venture into Autobiography.* London: Hutchinson, 1973.

Anderson, J. R. L. *A Biography of H. W. Tilman.* London: Victor Gollancz, 1980.

Andrew, C. *Secret Service: The Making of the British Intelligence Community.* London: Heinemann, 1985.

Andrew, C., and Mitrokhin, V., *The Sword and the Shield: The Mitrokhin Archive and the Secret History of the KGB.* New York: Basic Books 1999.

Atherton, L. *SOE: Operations in the Middle East. An Introductory Guide to the Newly Released Records of the Special Operations Executive in the Public Record Office.* London: PRO Publications, 1997.

——. *SOE: Operations in the Balkans. An Introductory Guide to the Newly Released Records of the Special Operations Executive in the Public Record Office.* London: PRO Publications, 1997.

Auty, P., and Clogg, R. (eds). *British Policy towards Wartime Resistance in Yugoslavia and Greece.* London: London University Press/Methuen, 1975.

Baerentzen, L. (ed.). *British Reports on Greece 1943–44.* Copenhagen: Museum Tusculanum Press, 1982.

Baker, J. *Turkey in Europe.* London: Cassell, Petter & Galpin, 1877.

Bardens, D. *Mysterious Worlds: A Personal Investigation of the Weird, the Uncanny and the Unexplained.* London: W. H. Allen, 1970.

Barker, E. *British Policy in South-East Europe in the Second World War*. London: Macmillan, 1976.

———. *Churchill and Eden at War*. London: Macmillan, 1978.

Barnes, J., and Nicholson, D. *The Empire at Bay: The Leo Amery Diaries 1929–1945*. London: Hutchinson, 1988.

Beck, A. *Bis Stalingrad, Albanien and Jugoslawien*. Ulm: Helmuth Abt, 1983.

Beevor, A. *Crete: The Battle and the Resistance*. London: Penguin, 1992.

Beevor, J. *SOE: Recollections and Reflections, 1940–1945*. London: The Bodley Head, 1981.

Beloff, N. *Tito's Flawed Legacy: Yugoslavia and the West, 1939–84*. London: Victor Gollancz 1985.

Bennett, G. (ed.). *The End of the War in Europe, 1945*. London: HMSO, 1996.

Bennett, R. *Ultra and Mediterranean Strategy, 1941–1945*. London: Hamish Hamilton 1989.

———. *Behind the Battle: Intelligence in the War with Germany 1939–1945*. London: Pimlico 1999.

Best, J. J. *Excursions in Albania; Comprising a Description of the Wild Boar, Deer, and Woodcock Shooting in that Country; and a Journey from thence to Thessalonica and Constantinople and up the Danube to Pest*. London: William H. Allen and Co., 1842.

Bethell, N. *The Great Betrayal: The Untold Story of Kim Philby's Biggest Coup*. London: Hodder & Stoughton, 1984.

———. *The Great Betrayal: The Untold Story of Kim Philby's Final Act of Treachery*. London: Coronet revised edition, 1986.

———. *Spies and Other Secrets*. London: Viking, 1994.

Blair, C. N. M. *Guerilla Warfare*. War Office Publication, 1957.

Bland, W., and Price, I. *A Tangled Web: A History of Anglo-American Relations with Albania 1912–1955*. London: The Albanian Society, 1986.

Blind, M. (ed.). *The Letters of Lord Byron*. London: Walter Scott, 1887.

Boyle, A. *The Climate of Treason: Five who Spied for Russia*. London: Hutchinson, 1979.

Buchan, J. *Greenmantle*. London: Hodder & Stoughton, 1918.

———. *The Thirty-Nine Steps*. London: William Blackwood and Sons, 1915.

Butka, U. *Ringjalle*. Tirana: Phoenix, Ariz., 2000.

Butler, J. R .M. *History of the Second World War: Grand Strategy*. Volume II: *September 1939 to June 1941*. London: HMSO, 1957.

Burr, M. *Slouch Hat*. London: George Allen & Unwin, 1935.

Byron, Lord. *The Poetical Works of Lord Byron*. Volume I. London: John Murray, 1879.

Çapo, A. *Dukati ynë*. Tirana: Dudaj Group, 1998.

Carter, M. *Anthony Blunt: His Lives*. London: Macmillan, 2001.

Charters, A., and Tugwell, M. (eds). *Deception Operations Studies in the East–West Context*. London: Brasseys, 1990.

Churchill, T. B. L. *Commando Crusade*. William Kimber: London, 1987.

Churchill, W. S. *The Second World War*. Volume III: *The Grand Alliance*. London: Cassell, 1950.

——. *The Second World War*. Volume V: *Closing the Ring*. London: Cassell, 1952.

Clayton, A. *Martin Leake Double VC*. London: Leo Cooper, 1994.

Clive, N. *A Greek Experience 1943–1948*. London: Michael Russell, 1985

Cooper, A. *Cairo in the War*. London: Hamish Hamilton, 1989.

Costa, N. *Albania: A European Enigma*. Boulder, Colo.: East European Monographs and Columbia University Press, 1995.

Corvo, M. *The O.S.S. in Italy 1942–45: A Personal Memoir*. New York: Praeger. 1990.

Courtney, G. B. *The SBS in World War Two*. London: Robert Hale, 1985.

Craig, F. W. S. (ed.). *British Parliamentary Election Results 1950–1973*. London: Parliamentary Research Services, 1983.

Cruickshank, C. *Deception in World War II*. Oxford: OUP, 1979

——. *The Fourth Arm: Psychological Warfare 1938–45*. Oxford: OUP, 1981.

——. *SOE in the Far East*. Oxford: OUP, 1983.

Dalton, H. *The Fateful Years: Memoirs 1931–1945*. London: Frederick Muller, 1957.

Danchev, A., and Todman, D. (eds). *War Diaries 1939–1945: Field Marshal Lord Alanbrooke*. London: Weidenfeld & Nicolson, 2001.

Davidson, B. *Special Operations Europe: Scenes from the Anti-Nazi War*. London: Victor Gollancz, 1980.

Davies, E. F. *Illyrian Venture: The Story of the British Military Mission to Enemy-occupied Albania 1943–44*. London: The Bodley Head, 1952.

Deacon, R. *The British Connection: Russia's Manipulation of British Individuals and Institutions*. London: Hamish Hamilton, 1979.

Deakin, F. W. *The Embattled Mountain*. Oxford: OUP, 1971.

Deakin, F. W., Barker, E., and Chadwick, J. *British Policy and Military Strategy in Central, Eastern and Southern Europe in 1944*. London: St Martin's Press, 1988.

Dimbleby, R. *The Frontiers are Green*. London: Hodder & Stoughton, 1943.

Dixon, A., and Heilbrunn, O. *Communist Guerrilla Warfare*. London: Allen & Unwin, 1954.

Dorril, S. *MI6: Fifty Years of Special Operations*. London: Fourth Estate, 2000.

Durham, E. *The Burden of the Balkans*. London: Edward Arnold, 1905.

——. *High Albania*. London: Edward Arnold, 1909.

Ehrman, J. *History of the Second World War: Grand Strategy*. Volume V: *August 1943 to September 1944*. London: HMSO, 1956.

——. *History of the Second World War: Grand Strategy*. Volume VI: *October 1944 to August 1945*. London: HMSO, 1956.

Eliot, C. *Turkey in Europe*. London: Edward Arnold, 1900.

Eyre, J. *The God Trip: The Story of a Mid-century Man*. London: Peter Owen, 1976.

Faber, D. *Speaking for England: Leo, Julian and John Amery: The Tragedy of a Political Family*. London: Free Press, 2005.

Felix, C. *A Short Course in the Secret War*. New York: Dutton, 1963.

Field, G. *Three Seconds to Die*. London: P. R. Macmillan, 1958.

Fielding, X. *One Man in His Time: The Life of Lieutenant-Colonel NLD ('Billy') McLean*. London: Macmillan, 1990.

Fischer, B. *King Zog and the Struggle for Stability in Albania*. Boulder, Colo.: East European Monographs and Columbia University Press, 1984.

——. *Albania at War 1939–1945*. Indiana: Purdue University Press, 1999.

Fitzherbert, M. *The Man Who Was Greenmantle: A Biography of Aubrey Herbert*. London: John Murray, 1983.

Foot, M. R. D. *SOE in France*. London: HMSO, 1966.

——. *Resistance: An Analysis of European Resistance to Nazism 1940–45*. London: Methuen, 1976.

——. *SOE: An Outline History of the Special Operations Executive, 1940–46*. London: BBC Books, 1984.

Foot, M. R. D., and Langley, J. M. *MI9: Escape and Evasion 1939–1945*. London: The Bodley Head, 1979.

Ford, Jr, K. *OSS and the Yugoslav Resistance 1943–1945*. Texas: A&M University Press, 1992.

Francis, K. *Explorations in Albania, 1930–39*. London: British School at Athens, 2005.

Fultz Kontos, J. *Red Cross, Black Eagle: A Biography of Albania's American School*. Boulder, Colo.: East European Monographs, 1981.

Gardiner, L. *The Eagle Spreads His Claws: A History of the Corfu Channel Dispute and of Albania's Relations with the West 1945–1965*. London: Blackwood, 1966.

Garnett, D. *The Secret History of PWE 1939–45: The Political Warfare Executive 1939–1945*. London: St Ermins, 2002.

Gilbert, M. *Winston S. Churchill: Road to Victory 1941–1945*. Boston: Houghton Mifflin, 1986.

Gjecovi, X. *Lufta Naçionalclirimtarë ne Shqiperi 1939–1944*. Tirana: Arbri, 1999.

Glees, A. *The Secrets of the Service: British Intelligence and Communist Subversion 1939–51*. London: Jonathan Cape, 1987.

Glen, A. *Footholds Against a Whirlwind*. London: Hutchinson, 1975.

Glenny, M. *The Balkans, 1904–1999: Nationalism, War and the Great Powers*. London: Granta, 1999.

Grose, P. *Operation Rollback: America's Secret War behind the Iron Curtain.* New York: Houghton & Mifflin, 2000.

Halliday, J. *The Artful Albanian: The Memoirs of Enver Hoxha.* London: Chatto Press, 1986.

Hamilton-Hill, D. *SOE Assignment.* London: William Kimber, 1973.

Hammond, N. *The Allied Military Mission in West Macedonia.* Thessaloniki: Institute for Balkan Studies, 1993.

——. *Venture into Greece: With the Guerrillas 1943–44.* London: William Kimber, 1983.

Hasluck, M. *Këdime Englisht-Shqip or Albanian–English Reader: Sixteen Albanian Folk-Stories Collected and Translated, with Two Grammars and Vocabularies.* Cambridge: CUP, 1932.

——. *Albanian Phrase Book.* 1944.

——. *The Unwritten Law in Albania.* Cambridge: CUP, 1954.

Hawes, S., and White, R. (eds). *Resistance in Europe: 1939–45.* London: Allen Lane, 1975.

Hersh, B. *The Old Boys: The American Elite and the Origins of the CIA.* New York: Charles Scribner's Sons, 1992.

Heuser, B. *Western Containment Policies in the Cold War: The Yugoslav Case, 1948–54.* London: Routledge, 1989.

Hibbert, R. *Albania's National Liberation Struggle: The Bitter Victory.* London: Pinter, 1991.

Hinsley, F. H. *British Intelligence in the Second World War: Its Influence on Strategy and Operations.* Volume 1. London: HMSO, 1979.

Hinsley, F. H. et al. *British Intelligence in the Second World War: Its Influence on Strategy and Operations.* Volume III, Part 1. London: HMSO, 1984.

——. *British Intelligence in the Second World War: Its Influence on Strategy and Operations.* Volume III, Part II. London: HMSO, 1988.

Hoare, O. (ed). *Camp 020: MI5 and the Nazi Spies.* London: Public Record office, 2000.

Holt, T. *The Deceivers: Allied Military Deception in the Second World War.* New York: Scribner, 2004.

Horne, A. *Macmillan, 1894–1956.* Vol I. London: Macmillan, 1988.

Howard, M. *The Mediterranean Strategy in the Second World War.* London: Weidenfeld & Nicolson, 1968.

——. *Strategic Deception in the Second World War.* London: Pimlico, 1990.

Howarth, P. (ed.). *Special Operations.* London: Routledge & Kegan Paul, 1955.

——. *Undercover: The Men and Women of the Special Operations Executive.* London: Routledge & Kegan Paul, 1980.

Hoxha, E. *Selected Works.* 6 Volumes. Tirana: 8 Nëntori, 1974–87.

——. *The Titoites.* Tirana: 8 Nëntori, 1982.

———. *The Anglo-American Threat to Albania: Memoirs of the National Liberation War*. Tirana: 8 Nëntori, 1982.

Hudson, J. *Beyond OSS*. Baltimore: Publish America, 2004.

Jackson, R. *The Secret Squadrons: Special Duty Units of the RAF and USAAF in the Second World War*. London: Robson Books, 1983.

Jackson, W. *History of the Second World War: The Mediterranean and Middle East*. Volume VI: *Victory in the Mediterranean*, Part II: *June to October 1944*. London: HMSO, 1987

———. *History of the Second World War: The Mediterranean and Middle East*. Volume VI: *Victory in the Mediterranean*, Part III: *November 1944 to May 1945*. London: HMSO, 1988.

Jakub, J. *Spies and Saboteurs: Anglo-American Collaboration and Rivalry in Human Intelligence Collection and Special Operations, 1940–45*. London: Macmillan, 1999.

Jebb, G. *The Memoirs of Lord Gladwyn*. London: Weidenfeld & Nicolson, 1972.

Jeffreys-Jones, R. *American Espionage: From Secret Service to CIA*. New York: Free Press, 1977.

Judah, T. *Kosovo: War and Revenge*. London: Yale University Press, 2000.

Kadare, I. *The General of the Dead Army* – with an introduction by David Smiley. London: Quartet, 1986.

Kasneci, L. *Steeled in the Heat of Battle: A Brief Survey of the National Liberation War of the Albanian People, 1941–1945*. Tirana: Naim Frashëri, 1966.

Kemp, P. *No Colours or Crest*. London: Cassell, 1958.

———. *Alms for Oblivion*. London: Cassell, 1961.

———. *The Thorns of Memory*. London: Sinclair-Stevenson, 1990.

Knightley, P. *The Master Spy: The Story of Kim Philby*. New York: Alfred A. Knopf, 1988.

Kurowski, F. *Deutsche Kommandotrupps 1939–1945, Band 2: Die 'Brandenburger' im weltweiten Einsatz*. Stuttgart: Motorbuch Verlag, 2003.

Lawrence, T. E. *Revolt in the Desert*. London: Jonathan Cape, 1927.

———. *The Seven Pillars of Wisdom*. London: Jonathan Cape, 1935.

Leake, W. M. *Travels in Northern Greece*. London, J. Rodwell, 1835.

Lear, E. *Journals of a Landscape Painter in Albania, &c*. London: Richard Bentley, 1851.

Lefèvre, E. *La Division Brandenbourg*. Paris: Presses de la Cité, 1984.

Lees, M. *Special Operations Executed*. London: William Kimber, 1986.

———. *The Rape of Serbia: The British Role in Tito's Grab for Power, 1943–1944*. New York: Harcourt, Brace, Jovanovich, 1990.

Lindsay, F. *Beacons in the Night: With the OSS and Tito's Partisans in Wartime Yugoslavia*. Stanford, Calif.: Stanford University Press, 1993.

Lloyd Owen, D. *Providence Their Guide: A Personal Account of the Long Range Desert Group 1940–45*. London: Harrap, 1980.

Logoreci, A. *The Albanians: Europe's Forgotten Survivors*. London: Victor Gollancz, 1977.

Macintosh, C. *From Cloak to Dagger: An SOE agent in Italy 1943–45*. London: William Kimber, 1982.

Mackenzie, C. *First Athenian Memories*. London: Cassell, 1931.

Mackenzie, W. J. M. *The Secret History of SOE: The Special Operations Executive 1940–45*. London: St Ermin's Press, 2000.

Maclean, F. *Eastern Approaches*. London: Jonathan Cape, 1949.

——. *Disputed Barricade: The Life and Times of Josip Broz Tito*. London: Jonathan Cape, 1957.

Macmillan, H. *Winds of Change, 1914–1939*. London: Macmillan, 1966.

——. *The Blast of War 1939–1945*. London: Harper & Row, 1968.

——. *War Diaries: Politics and War in the Mediterranean, July 1943 – May 1945*. London: St Martin's Press, 1984.

Madge, T. *The Last Hero: Bill Tilman*. London: Hodder & Stoughton, 1995.

Malcolm, N. *Kosovo: A Short History*. London: Macmillan, 1998.

Mangerich, A. *Albanian Escape: The True Story of US Army Nurses Behind Enemy Lines*. Kentucky: University of Kentucky Press, 1999.

Manzitti, G. *Tempo di Ricordare*. Genova: De Ferrari, 1999

Marchand, L. (ed.). *Byron's Letters and Journals*, Volume I: *In My Hot Youth (1798–1810)*. London: John Murray, 1973.

Marmallaku, R. *Albania and the Albanians*. London: Hurst & Co., 1975.

Martin, D. Introductory Essay in *Patriot or Traitor: The Case of General Mihailovich: Proceedings and Report of the Commission of Inquiry of the Committee for a Fair Trial of Draja Mihailovich*. Stanford: Hoover Institution Press 1979.

——. *The Web of Disinformation: Churchill's Yugoslavia Blunder*. New York: Harcourt, Brace, Jovanovich, 1990.

McConville, M. *A Small War in the Balkans: British Involvement in Wartime Yugoslavia*. London: Macmillan, 1986.

McLynn, F. *Fitzroy Maclean*. London: John Murray, 1990.

Merrick, K. *Flights of the Forgotten*. London: Arms and Armour, 1989.

Messenger, C. *The Commandos 1940–1946*. London: William Kimber, 1985.

Michel, H. *The Shadow War: Resistance in Europe 1939–1945*. London: André Deutsch, 1972.

Miller, R. *Behind the Lines: The Oral History of Special Operations in World War II*. New York: New American Library, 2004.

Molony, C. *History of the Second World War: The Mediterranean and Middle East*. Volume V: *The Campaign in Sicily 1943. The Campaign in Italy 3 September 1943 to 31 March 1944*. London: HMSO, 1973.

——. *History of the Second World War: The Mediterranean and Middle East.* Volume VI: *Victory in the Mediterranean,* Part I: *1 April to 4 June 1944.* London: HMSO, 1984.

Mountfield, D. *The Partisans.* London: Hamlyn, 1979.

Muggeridge, M. (ed.). *Ciano's Diary, 1939–1943.* London: Heinemann, 1947.

Myers, E. *Greek Entanglement.* London: Rupert Hart-Davis, 1955.

Noakes, V. *Edward Lear: Selected Letters.* Oxford: Clarendon Press, 1988.

Oakley-Hill, D. *An Englishman in Albania Memoirs of a British Officer 1929–1955.* London: Centre for Albanian Studies, 2002.

Pawley, M. *In Obedience to Instructions: FANY with the SOE in the Mediterranean.* Barnsley: Leo Cooper, 1999.

Pearson, O. *Albania and King Zog.* London: I. B. Tauris, 2005.

——. *Albania in Occupation and War.* London: I. B. Tauris, 2005.

——. *Albania as Dictatorship and Democracy.* London: I. B. Tauris, 2006.

Philby, K. *My Silent War.* London: MacGibbon & Kee, 1968.

Pimlott, B. *Hugh Dalton.* London: Jonathan Cape, 1985.

——. (ed). *The Second World War Diary of Hugh Dalton.* London: Jonathan Cape, 1986.

Pincher, C. *Too Secret Too Long: The Great Betrayal of Britain's Crucial Secrets and the Cover-up.* London: Sidgwick & Jackson, 1984.

——. *Traitors: The Labyrinths of Treason.* Sidgwick & Jackson, 1987.

Playfair, I. S. O. *History of the Second World War: The Mediterranean and Middle East.* Volume I: *The Early Success Against Italy (to May 1941).* London: HMSO, 1954.

Puto, A. *From the Annals of British Diplomacy: The Anti-Albanian Plans of Great Britain during the Second World War according to Foreign Office Documents of 1939–1944.* Tirana: 8 Nëntori Press, 1981.

Quayle, A. *Eight Hours from England.* London: Heinemann, 1945.

——. *A Time to Speak.* London: Barrie & Jenkins, 1990.

Rhodes James, R. *Winston Churchill: His Complete Speeches 1797–1963,* Volume VII: *1943–1949.* London: Chelsea House, 1974.

Richards, B. *Secret Flotillas.* Volume II: *Clandestine Sea Operations in the Mediterranean, North Africa and the Adriatic 1940–1944.* London: Frank Cass, 2004.

Roosevelt, K. (ed.). *The Overseas Targets: War Report of the OSS,* Volume II. New York: Walker & Co., 1976.

Ryan, A. *Last of the Dragomans.* London: Geoffrey Bles, 1951.

Schreiber, G., Stegemann, B., and Vogel, D. *Germany in the Second World War.* Volume III: *The Mediterranean, South-east Europe, and North Africa 1939–1941.* Oxford: Clarendon Press, 1995.

Schwandner-Sievers, S., and Fischer, B. (eds). *Albanian Identities: Myth, Narrative and Politics.* New York: Hurst & Co., 2002.

Seton-Watson, H. *The East European Revolution*. London: Methuen, 1950.

Shehu, M. *On the Experience of the National Liberation War and the Development of Our National Army*. Tirana: 8 Nëntori Press, 1978.

Simpson, C. *Blowback: U.S. Recruitment of Nazis and its Effects on the Cold War*. New York: Weidenfeld & Nicolson, 1988.

Sinani, H. *Tragjasi Përmes Historisë (Deri më 1939)*. Vlora: 2003.

Skendi, S. *Albania under the Communists*. London: Atlantic Press, 1957.

Smiley, D. *Albanian Assignment*. London: Chatto & Windus, 1984.

——. *Irregular Regular*. London: Michael Russell, 1994.

Smith, Bradley F. *The Shadow Warriors: OSS and the Origins of the CIA*. New York: Basic Books, 1983.

Smith, R. H. *OSS: The Secret History of America's First Central Intelligence Agency*. Berkeley: University of California Press, 1972.

Spaeter, H. *Die Brandenburger: eine deutsche Kommandotruppe*. Munich: Walter Angerer, 1978.

Stafford, D. *Britain and European Resistance 1940–1945: A Survey of the Special Operations Executive, with Documents*. London: Macmillan, 1983.

Stirling, W. F. *Safety Last*. London: Hollis and Carter, 1953.

Sulzberger, C. L. *A Long Row of Candles: Memoirs and Diaries, 1934–1954*. New York: Macmillan, 1969.

Sweet-Escott, B. *Greece: A Political and Economic Survey*. London: Royal Institute of International Affairs, 1954.

——. *Baker Street Irregular*. London: Methuen, 1965.

Swire, J. Albania. *The Rise of a Kingdom*. London: Williams & Norgate, 1929.

——. *King Zog's Albania*. London: Robert Hale, 1937.

Tava, S. *Historia e Dukatit*. Vlora: 2002.

Thompson, J. *The Imperial War Museum Book of War Behind Enemy Lines*. London: Sidgwick & Jackson, 1998.

Tilman, H. W. *When Men and Mountains Meet*. Cambridge: CUP, 1946.

Tinkner, H. (ed.). *Burma: The Struggle for Independence 1944–1948*. Volume I: *From Military Occupation to Civil Government 1 January 1944 to 31 August 1946*. London: HMSO, 1983.

Tomes, J. *King Zog: Self-Made Monarch of Albania*. Stroud: Sutton, 2003.

Trew, S. *Britain, Mihailovic and the Chetniks, 1941–42*. London: Macmillan, 1998.

Van der Post, L. *The Admiral's Baby*. London: John Murray, 1996.

Van der Wal, S., Drooglever, P., and Schouten, M. *Officiële Bescheiden betreffende de Nederlands-Indonesische Betrekkingen 1945–1950* (NIB 1). Den Haag, 1970–1996, Volume 3.

Vickers, M. *The Albanians: A Modern History*. London: I. B. Tauris, 1995.

——. *Between Serb and Albanian: A History of Kosovo*. London: Hurst & Co., 1998.

Vickers, M. and Pettifer, J. *Albania: From Anarchy to a Balkan Identity.* London: Hurst & Co, 1997.

West, N. *MI5: British Security Service Operations, 1909–1945.* London: The Bodley Head, 1981.

——. *Secret War: The Story of SOE, Britain's Wartime Sabotage Organisation.* London: Hodder & Stoughton, 1992.

Wheeler, M. *Britain and the War for Yugoslavia 1940–1943.* Boulder, Colo.: East European Monographs, 1980.

Wilkinson, P. *Foreign Fields: The Story of an SOE Operative.* London: I. B. Tauris, 1997.

Wilkinson, P. and Bright Astley, J. *Gubbins and SOE.* London: Leo Cooper, 1993.

Williams, H. *Parachutes, Patriots and Partisans: The Special Operations Executive and Yugoslavia, 1941–1945.* London: Hurst & Co., 2003.

Wilson, H. M. *Eight Years Overseas.* London: Hutchinson, 1950.

Winks, R. W. *Cloak and Gown: Scholars in the Secret War 1939–1961.* New York: Morrow, 1987.

Winnifrith, T. *Badlands-Borderlands: A History of Northern Epirus/Southern Albania.* London: Duckworth, 2002.

Woodburn Kirby, S. *History of the Second World War: The War Against Japan,* Volume V: *The Surrender of Japan.* London: HMSO, 1969.

Woodhouse, C. *Apple of Discord: A Survey of Greek Politics in their International Setting.* London: Hutchinson, 1948.

Woodhouse, H. *The British School at Athens: The First Hundred Years.* London: BSA, 1986.

Woodward, L. *History of the Second World War: British Foreign Policy in the Second World War.* 5 Volumes. London: HMSO, 1971–7.

Yugoslavia. Naval Intelligence Division, 1944.

ARTICLES

Amery, J. 'Billy McLean: 1918–1986'. *Central Asian Survey* 6/2, 1987.

——. 'The Case for Retaliation', *Time and Tide*, 22 January 1949.

Bailey, R. 'Communist in SOE: Explaining James Klugmann's Recruitment and Retention'. *Intelligence and National Security* 20/1, 2005. Also in N. Wylie (ed.) *The Politics and Strategy of Clandestine War: Special Operations Executive, 1940–46.* London: Routledge, 2006.

——. 'Margaret Hasluck and the Special Operations Executive' in D. Shankland (ed.) *Anthropology, Archaeology and Heritage in the Balkans and Anatolia: The Life and Times of F. W. Hasluck (1878–1920).* Istanbul: Isis, 2004.

——. 'Operation 'Healing': The Raid on Spiljë, July 1944' in K. Francis (ed.) *Further Investigations of Luigi Cardini's caves at Himara in South-western Albania: Report for the Institute for Aegean Prehistory, Philadelphia.* Norwich: UEA, 2002.

——. 'OSS–SOE relations, Albania 1943–44'. *Intelligence and National Security* 15/2, 2000. Also in R. Jeffreys-Jones and D. Stafford (eds) *ABC: American-British-Canadian Intelligence Relations.* London: Frank Cass, 2000.

——. 'Smoke without fire? Albania, SOE and the Communist "Conspiracy Theory"' in S. Schwandner-Sievers and B. Fischer (eds) *Albanian Identities: Myth, Narrative and Politics.* New York: Hurst & Co., 2002.

——. 'SOE in Albania: The Conspiracy Theory Reassessed' in M. Seaman (ed.) *The Special Operations Executive: A New Instrument of War.* London: Routledge, 2005.

Brewer, R. 'Albania: New Aspects, Old Documents'. *East European Quarterly* 26/1, March 1992.

Clark, M. 'Margaret Masson Hasluck' in J. B. Allcock and A. Young (eds) *Black Lambs and Grey Falcons: Women Travellers in the Balkans.* Oxford: Berghahn Books, revised edition 2000.

Cripps, J. 'Mihailovic or Tito?' in R. Erskine and M. Smith (eds) *Action This Day.* London: Bantam 2001.

Dawkins, R. 'Margaret Masson Hasluck'. *Folklore* 60/2, June 1949.

Dravis, M. 'Storming Fortress Albania: American Covert Operations in Microcosm, 1949–54. *Intelligence and National Security* 7/4, 1992.

Dumoulin, Major J. 'With the Partisans in Albania'. *British Medical Journal*, 19 January 1946.

Faure-Field, Major J. A. 'Albania'. *The Oak Tree.* Journal of the Cheshire Regiment, 1947–48.

Fischer, B. 'Abas Kupi and British Intelligence in Albania, 1943–4' in J. Morison (ed.) *Eastern Europe and the West: Selected Papers from the 4th World*

Congress for Soviet and East European Studies, Harrogate, 1990. London: Macmillan, 1992.

——. 'Resistance in Albania during the Second World War: Partisans, Nationalists and the SOE'. *East European Quarterly* 25/1, March 1991.

——. 'Albania and the Italian Invasion of Greece, October 1940' in *Greece and the War in the Balkans, 1940–1941*. Thessaloniki: Institute for Balkan Studies, 1992.

Foot, M. R. D. 'Was SOE Any Good?' *Journal of Contemporary History* 16, 1981.

Hammond, N. 'Memories of a British Officer Serving in Special Operations Executive in Greece, 1941' in *Balkan Studies* 23, 1982.

Harrison, E. D. R. 'British Subversion in French East Africa, 1941–42: SOE's Todd Mission.' *English Historical Review* 114/456, April 1999.

Hibbert, R. Reviews of D. Smiley, *Albanian Assignment* and N. Bethell, *The Great Betrayal*. *International Affairs* 61/2, Spring 1985.

——. 'The War in Albania and the Conspiracy Theory'. *Albania Life* 57, Spring 1995.

Kondis, B. 'A British Attempt to Organize a Revolt in Northern Albania during the Greek–Italian War' in *Greece and the War in the Balkans, 1940–41*. Thessaloniki: Institute for Balkan Studies, 1992.

Maclagan, M. Preface to D. Talbot Rice, *Byzantine Art and its Influences: Collected Studies*. London: Variorum Reprints, 1973.

Martin, D. 'James Klugmann, SOE-Cairo, and the Mihailovich Deception' in A. Charters and M. Tugwell (eds) *Deception Operations Studies in the East–West Context*. London: Brasseys, 1990.

Martin, S. 'The Gendarme Mission in Albania, 1925–38: A Move on the English Chess Board?' *Contemporary European History* 7/2, 1998.

Oakley-Hill, D. R. 'The Albanian Gendarmerie, 1925–1938, and its British Officers'. *Albania*. National Democratic Committee for a Free Albania, 1962.

Wheeler, M. 'The SOE Phenomenon'. *Journal of Contemporary History* 16, 1981.

INDEX

www.vintage-books.co.uk